Research Methodologies in Translation Studies

Gabriela Saldanha and Sharon O'Brien

Routledge
Taylor & Francis Group

LONDON AND NEW YORK

First published 2013 by St Jerome Publishing

Published 2014 by Routledge
2 Park Square, Milton Park, Abingdon, Oxon OX14 4RN
711 Third Avenue, New York, NY, 10017, USA

Routledge is an imprint of the Taylor & Francis Group, an informa business

British Library Cataloguing in Publication Data
A catalogue record of this book is available from the British Library

Library of Congress Cataloging-in-Publication Data
Saldanha, Gabriela, author.
   Research methodologies in translation studies / Gabriela Saldanha and Sharon O'Brien.
     pages cm
   Includes bibliographical references and index.
   ISBN 978-1-909485-00-6 (pbk : alk. paper)
1. Translating and interpreting--Research--Methodology. I. O'Brien, Sharon, 1969- author. II. Title.
   P306.S244 2013
   418'.02--dc23

2013030989

ISBN: 978-1-909485-00-6 (pbk)

Delta Typesetters, Cairo, Egypt

For Fionn, Rebeca, Rián, Martina

Research Methodologies in Translation Studies

As an interdisciplinary area of research, translation studies attracts students and scholars with a wide range of backgrounds, who then need to face the challenge of accounting for a complex object of enquiry that does not adapt itself well to traditional methods in other fields of investigation. This book addresses the needs of such scholars – whether they are students doing research at postgraduate level or more experienced researchers who want to familiarize themselves with methods outside their current field of expertise. The book promotes a discerning and critical approach to scholarly investigation by providing the reader not only with the know-how but also with new insights into how new questions can be fruitfully explored through the coherent integration of different methods of research. Understanding core principles of reliability, validity and ethics is essential for any researcher no matter what methodology they adopt, and a whole chapter is therefore devoted to these issues.

While necessarily partial, the survey presented here focuses on methodologies that have been more frequently applied and therefore more thoroughly tested. It is divided into four different chapters, according to whether the research focuses on the translation product, the process of translation, the participants involved or the context in which translation takes place. An introductory chapter discusses issues of reliability, credibility, validity and ethics. The impact of our research depends not only on its quality but also on successful dissemination, and the final chapter therefore deals with what is also generally the final stage of the research process: producing a research report.

Gabriela Saldanha is a Lecturer in Translation Studies at the Department of English Language and Applied Linguistics, University of Birmingham, UK, where she convenes both the distance and campus-based MA programmes in Translation Studies. Her research has focused on gender-related stylistic features in translation and on translator style, using corpus linguistics as a methodology. Her teaching focuses on translation theory, research methods and translation technology. She is co-editor of the second, revised edition of the *Routledge Encyclopedia of Translation Studies* (2009). She is co-editor of *Translation Studies Abstracts* and is on the editorial board of *InTRAlinea*.

Sharon O'Brien is a Senior Lecturer in Translation Studies at the School of Applied Language and Intercultural Studies, Dublin City University, Ireland, where she teaches postgraduate and undergraduate courses in Translation Studies. Her research has focused on translation technology, especially the post-editing of machine translation output, translation processes, and controlled authoring using keyboard logging, screen recording and eye tracking. Her teaching focuses on translation technology, software localization, translation theory and research methods. She is co-editor of St. Jerome's *Translation Practices Explained* series and a track editor for the journal *Translation Spaces*.

Contents

Acknowledgements   xiii

Chapter 1. Introduction

1.1	Motivation and Intended audience	1
1.2	Scope and limitations	2
1.3	Research model, structure and content of the book	5

Chapter 2. Principles and ethics in research

2.1	Introduction	10
2.2	Ontology and epistemology	10
2.3	Research terminology	12
2.4	Types of research	14
2.5	Research questions and hypotheses	16
2.6	The literature review	19
2.7	Data	20
2.8	Qualitative, quantitative and mixed-methods approaches	22
2.9	Research operationalization	23
	2.9.1 Measurable variables	25
2.10	Research quality	27
	2.10.1 Validity	27
	2.10.2 Reliability	35
	2.10.3 Generalizability	36
	2.10.4 Qualitative methods, credibility and warrantability	38
2.11	Research ethics	41
	2.11.1 Ethics in context	42
	2.11.2 Ethics approval	43
	2.11.3 Informed consent	43
	2.11.4 Deception	45
	2.11.5 Power relations	45
	2.11.6 Protection from harm	46
	2.11.7 Internet-mediated research	47
	2.11.8 Plagiarism	48
2.12	Summary	49

Chapter 3. Product-oriented research

3.1	Introduction	50
3.2	A descriptive/explanatory approach to the analysis of language	50

	3.2.1 Critical discourse analysis	51
	3.2.2 Corpus linguistics	55
	3.2.3 Strength and weaknesses of critical discourse analysis and corpus linguistics	57
3.3	Designing studies in critical discourse analysis and corpus linguistics	61
	3.3.1 Corpus-driven, corpus-based, argument-centred and problem-based designs	61
	3.3.2 Selecting and delimiting texts as units of investigation	64
	3.3.3 The need for comparative data	66
	3.3.4 Corpus typology	67
3.4	Building corpora	70
	3.4.1 Corpus design criteria	71
	3.4.2 Annotation and alignment	76
3.5	Analyzing texts and corpora	80
	3.5.1 The linguistic toolkit	80
	3.5.2 Fairclough's relational approach to critical discourse analysis	83
	3.5.3 The tools of corpus analysis	85
	3.5.4 Addressing issues of quality in critical discourse analysis and corpus linguistics	92
3.6	Research on translation quality assessment – Introduction	95
	3.6.1 Strengths and weaknesses	96
	3.6.2 Design	97
	3.6.3 Which QA model(s)?	100
	3.6.4 Data collection	105
	3.6.5 Analysis	107
3.7	Summary	108

Chapter 4. Process-oriented research

4.1	Introduction	109
	4.1.1 Common topics	111
4.2	General translation process research issues	113
	4.2.1 Design	113
	4.2.2 Data elicitation	118
	4.2.3 Analysis	119
4.3	Introspection	122
	4.3.1 Design	124
	4.3.2 Data elicitation	126
	4.3.3 Transcription	128
	4.3.4 Analysis	130
4.4	Keystroke logging	132
	4.4.1 Design	133
	4.4.2 Data elicitation	134
	4.4.3 Analysis	135

4.5   Eye tracking   136
       4.5.1 Design   138
       4.5.2 Data elicitation   141
       4.5.3 Analysis   142
             4.5.3.1 Analysis of temporal data   143
             4.5.3.2 Analysis of attentional data   143
             4.5.3.3 Analysis of data pertaining to cognitive effort   144
             4.5.3.4 Analysis of linked data   145
4.6   Complementary methods   145
       4.6.1 Contextual inquiry   145
       4.6.2 Personality profiling   146
       4.6.3 Physiological measurements   148
4.7   Summary   148

Chapter 5. Participant-oriented research

5.1   Introduction   150
5.2   Questionnaires   151
       5.2.1 Overview   151
       5.2.2 Strengths and weaknesses   152
5.3   Designing questionnaire surveys   153
       5.3.1 Operationalization   153
       5.3.2 Number and phrasing of questions   154
       5.3.3. Open and closed questions   157
       5.3.4 Likert scales   157
       5.3.5 Pilot testing   158
       5.3.6 Reliability and validity   159
       5.3.7 Ethical considerations   161
5.4   Data collection using questionnaires   163
       5.4.1 Sampling   164
       5.4.2 Response rate   165
       5.4.3 Internet-mediated collection methods   166
5.5   Interviews and focus groups   168
       5.5.1 Overview   168
       5.5.2 Strengths and weaknesses   169
5.6   Designing interviews and focus groups   171
       5.6.1 Types of interviews and focus groups   172
       5.6.2 Designing interview and focus group schedules   174
       5.6.3 Language issues   177
       5.6.4 Piloting   178
       5.6.5 Ethical considerations   179
5.7   Eliciting data using interviews and focus groups   180
       5.7.1 Sampling and recruiting participants   180
       5.7.2 Interviewing and moderating: Basic principles and
              key challenges   184

5.7.3 Face-to-face, telephone and Internet-mediated interviews
and focus groups 186
5.8 Analyzing qualitative data 188
5.9 Analyzing quantitative data 194
5.10 Data analysis in mixed methods research 201
5.11 Summary 204

Chapter 6: Context-oriented research: case studies

6.1 Introduction 205
6.2 Definition of case study 207
6.3 When to use case studies 209
6.4 Case study design 211
6.4.1. Types of case studies 211
6.4.2 Delimiting case studies 215
6.5 Collecting data 217
6.5.1 Written sources 218
6.5.2 Verbal reports 220
6.5.3 Observation 221
6.5.4 Physical artefacts 224
6.5.5 Quantitative data 224
6.5.6 Using a database to manage data 224
6.5.7 Ethical considerations 225
6.6 Analyzing case-study data 227
6.6.1 General principles 227
6.6.2 Practical suggestions 230
6.6.3 Computer-aided qualitative analysis 231
6.7 Summary 232

Chapter 7: Conclusion: The research report

7.1 Introduction 234
7.2 Structuring the report 234
7.3 Framing the report: introduction, literature review and
conclusion 236
7.4 Reporting methods 237
7.5 Reporting qualitative data 240
7.6 Reporting quantitative data 241
7.7 Reporting linguistic data 242
7.8 Summary 242

References 244

Index 270

List of Figures

Figure 2.1   Example of Research Terminology Applied to TS   14
Figure 2.2   A theoretical model expressing relationship between
              time pressure (X axis) and translation quality (nominal scale
              on the Y axis)   26

Figure 3.1   Design of a bidirectional parallel corpus   68
Figure 3.2   Sample header file from the Translational English Corpus   77
Figure 3.3   Example of tagged text taken from the British National
              Corpus   78
Figure 3.4   Example of a parallel concordance obtained with
              Paraconc   79
Figure 3.5   Fairclough's relational model (adapted from Fairclough
              2003:36)   84
Figure 3.6   A concordance of the node 'source' obtained using the
              BYU_BNC interface for the British National Corpus   90
Figure 3.7   A sketch engine profile of the word 'source'   91

Figure 4.1   Example of TAP transcription from the TransComp project
              (http://gams.uni-graz.at/fedora/get/o:tc-095-201/bdef:
              TEI/get), post-phase_2, participant: Professional AEF)
              Source Text A1   129
Figure 4.2   Example of Translog linear data   132
Figure 4.3   Example of fixations during a reading task from a study by
              Doherty and O'Brien (2012)   137

Figure 5.1   Example of bell curve in normal distribution   197

List of Tables

Table 2.1   Threats to validity identified by Frey *et al.* (1999)   30

Table 5.1   Examples of coding of semi-structured interview data   191
Table 5.2   Example of quartile data: from processing times
              measurement in Guerberof (2008:38)   198

Acknowledgements

Many people assisted us in the writing of this book and we are enormously grateful for that assistance, no matter how small or large the contribution. We would especially like to thank Jenny Williams for providing us with insightful and helpful feedback on a draft of this book. We drew on the expertise of many others for advice and feedback on specific chapters and we express our sincere gratitude to them: Fabio Alves, Andrew Chesterman, Claire Hewson, Dorothy Kenny, Kaisa Koskinen, Ian Mason, Rebecca Tipton. Any errors are, of course, of our own making. Finally, we are hugely grateful to our families for their patience and support.

Chapter 1. Introduction

1.1 Motivation and Intended audience

Recent years have witnessed an increase in the number of translation training programmes across the world, with a resulting explosion in the number of masters and doctoral students and, as reported in Mason (2009a), a concomitant move towards explicit forms of research training in translation studies. The book entitled *The Map: A Beginner's Guide to Doing Research in Translation Studies*, co-authored by Jenny Williams and Andrew Chesterman and published in 2002, was given a very warm welcome by the translation studies community and is still highly regarded by established and novice researchers alike. Clearly there was, and still is, a thirst for a book that was specifically focused on research within the domain of translation studies. Since the publication of *The Map*, there have been some methodological developments in the field with, for example, the application of methods such as keystroke logging, eye tracking, Internet-mediated research, as well as an increased focus on sociological and ethnographic approaches to research and on research ethics. We feel it is now time to build on the excellent foundation set by Williams and Chesterman. *The Map* establishes the foundations of translation studies research and is particularly useful for those who are starting to think about doing research in this area, and who need to decide between different areas of research, theoretical models, types of research, and so on. The focus of this book is on specific methodologies. We describe in detail when and how to apply different methodologies and we provide examples from translation studies research. There are, already, many excellent publications that describe how these methodogies are applied in related domains such as applied linguistics, social science, psychology and cultural studies. These books are, of course, valuable to the translation researcher. However, it is our experience that even in related disciplines the books fail to answer all our questions about doing research in translation. Often the examples feel distant or even irrelevant, thus failing to inspire translation studies researchers. We are convinced that discussing methodologies within the translation studies context and offering examples of current best practice has a value above and beyond standard, generic textbooks.

The Map is a beginner's guide, as stated in the title, and is mostly directed at PhD students. This book will also hopefully be useful to PhD, Masters and Undergraduate students. Research students are expected to develop core research skills, such as understanding what counts as creativity, originality, and the exercise of academic judgement. We have kept these needs in mind during the writing process. However, we feel that a need exists beyond this readership too. As discussed below, translation studies is interdisciplinary by nature. While the professionalization of translation and the recognition of translation as an academic discipline have resulted in translation-specific educational pathways all the way from the undergraduate to the doctoral level, the field of translation studies continues to attract researchers from many different backgrounds who may not be familiar with the wide range of methodological practices in the field. By bringing together in one publication methodologies originating in different disciplines and discussing how they can be fruitfully combined for the study of translation we aim to contribute to the cross-fertilization of the different research practices that inform translation studies.

1.2   Scope and limitations

Guba and Lincoln (2005:191) argue that "[m]ethodology is inevitably interwoven with and emerges from the nature of particular disciplines". Linguistics and literary criticism were for a long time the main source of theories and methods in translation research, which was based on comparative text analysis carried out with varying levels of linguistic or literary insight. Much of the research on literary translation is still embedded within a comparative literature framework and linguistic approaches are still widely used, although rarely with the same narrow focus they initially adopted. During the 1980s, translation scholars began to draw more heavily on methodologies borrowed from other disciplines, including psychology, communication theory, anthropology, philosophy and cultural studies (Baker 1998:278). More recently, the importation of theories and models from social theory has again widened the range of methodologies applied within translation studies. In 1998, Baker suggested that:

> Although some scholars see translation studies as interdisciplinary by nature (Snell-Hornby 1988), this does not mean that the discipline is not developing or cannot develop a coherent research methodology of its own. Indeed, the various methodologies and theoretical frameworks borrowed from different disciplines are increasingly being adapted and reassessed to meet the specific needs of translation scholars. (Baker 1998:279)

The picture emerging from the current book is not of a single coherent methodology that could be described as specific to translation studies. However, there is indeed evidence of adaptation and reassessment, which is perhaps most clear in the dynamism with which different theoretical frameworks and methodologies are being combined for the purpose of addressing translation studies' concerns, since none of the methodological apparatuses of related disciplines can, on their own, fully account for translation phenomena (see, for example, the 2013 special issue of *Target* on interdisciplinarity in translation process research).

   In their overview of the main paradigms in contemporary qualitative research, Guba and Lincoln (2005:191) note that "[i]ndeed, the various paradigms are beginning to 'interbreed' such that two theorists previously thought to be in irreconcilable conflict may now appear, under a different theoretical rubric, to be informing one another's arguments". We believe that translation studies has now successfully moved beyond the paradigm conflicts of the 1990s (Baker

1998) and has succeeded not only in celebrating and accepting a diversity of approaches but in 'interbreeding' for the benefit of a more comprehensive and nuanced account of the object of study.

In terms of this particular book, while we have made an effort to reflect the interdisciplinarity of translation studies and have tried our best to represent the different epistemological and ontological positions within the discipline, our account is necessarily partial, reflecting our own academic backgrounds and experiences. We have aimed to remain aware, insofar as our in-built biases allow us, that our way of seeing and thinking about research methods may not necessarily be in agreement with the way others see or think about them. In what follows we justify our choices and acknowledge their limitations regarding the contents of the book and the views they reflect.

Translation studies is interdisciplinary not only because it borrows from a wide range of disciplines but also because it covers a wide range of practices. While we have made an attempt to reflect this diversity in the examples we have selected for discussion, there are areas of translation research that are not adequately covered by the methodologies described here, such as interpreting and translation history.

In her reflections on the periods of fragmentation experienced by translation studies while fighting to establish itself as an academic discipline in its own right, Baker (1998:279) mentions the fact that theoretical models in translation studies have tended to ignore interpreting and produced research that is of no relevance to those interested in that field. While our impression is that there has been progress in this regard, our experience is mainly within translation studies and we may not be the best people to judge. We see interpreting studies at the forefront of many of the methodological advances in the discipline in recent years, and this view is reflected here in recurrent examples from interpreting studies, particularly in the discussion of critical discourse analysis, interviews and focus groups. However, we also acknowledge that the nature of interpreting as spoken interaction presents certain challenges in terms of research methodology which we are not in a position to discuss in detail.

The same could be said about translation history. The methodology described in Chapter 6, case studies, has often been used in historical translation research and two of the examples used in that chapter deal with historical phenomena. However, the specificities of researching the past are not the focus of the chapter. It is worth noting that translation history is the one area of translation studies research where there is a book-length publication devoted to questions of methodology (Pym 1998).

One topic that has dominated the literature in translation studies in the past few years is the question of centre and periphery, dominant and subservient, Western and non-Western perspectives, and we feel it is important to reflect on these matters in relation to our approach. A question we have often asked ourselves while writing this book is: how 'universal' are the research methods described here? Susam-Sarajeva (2002) helpfully rules out the use of the terms 'Western/non-Western'. She argues that "[b]eing 'non-Western' has apparently become the only common denominator behind otherwise vastly different languages and cultures" (*ibid.*:193). Equally, "the same dichotomy renders 'the West' more homogeneous than it actually is" (*ibid.*). She argues instead for the terms 'centre' and 'periphery' but acknowledges that these are also problematic. Susam-Sarajeva highlights the danger that those operating in 'the periphery' will regard their own concepts and ways of thinking as inferior; they will be "'educated away' from their own culture and society" (*ibid.*:199). This, she says, is inevitable, because for research to be considered 'useful', 'publishable' and 'quotable' it must refer to the established (central) frameworks. In order to be rated highly as a researcher, one needs to publish in specific journals, most of which use English as the language of publication and prioritize their own research agendas, with their concomitant limitations in terms of research models and methodologies. One of the authors of this book originates from South America and left behind a country and a language to pursue an academic career. The other originates from and lives in a former colony on the periphery of Europe. Therefore, these issues are close to our hearts as individuals. Nevertheless, there is no denying that our academic perspective is 'central' in Susam-Sarajeva's terms, even if this is by (de)fault rather than choice, since it reflects the environment in which we have been immersed during our academic careers and the one in which we operate more comfortably. We can think of many good reasons for academics to start operating outside their comfort zones, but we take the view that a book on research methodologies is not the best place to do that. However, in the writing of this book we do not intend to present specific frameworks as the *only* relevant ones and we hope that they are relevant as one way to do things no matter where the research is being conducted or where the researcher or the researched come from.

Our expertise is limited mainly to empirical research, which not only has implications for the scope of the book, focusing on empirical methods and methodologies, but probably also permeates the content in a more pervasive and subtle manner in terms of our assumptions as to what constitutes good academic practice, with its emphasis on evidence, hypotheses and operationalization. Despite acknowledging our limited focus, we have chosen not to call the book 'empirical research methodologies' because we do not believe in a clear-cut distinction between conceptual and empirical research. Good empirical research needs to be based on conceptual research and conceptual research, to be useful, needs to be supplemented by evidence. Evidence and theory are crucial to all researchers: "[y]ou need the 'facts' – imperfect though they may be; and you need to be able to understand or explain them (theory)" (Gillham 2000:12). Although we generally talk about theories as the basis on which we build our empirical studies, we should not forget that theory is also what researchers create, the way they account for the data, particularly in inductive approaches to research (see Chapter 2). In other words, research can be seen as theory building as well as theory testing; as providing answers (for example, in hypothesis-testing research) as well as framing questions (in hypothesis-generating research).

A further clarification to be made in relation to our understanding of empirical research is that we do not believe that empirical research is necessarily descriptive or incompatible with critical-interpretive approaches. There has been a tendency in translation studies to equate empiricism with descriptivism and the latter with a-historical and uncritical methods that aim to produce generalizations about patterns of translational behaviour with predictive power (Crisafulli 2002). While there is a need for non-prescriptive research that establishes what translators normally do and why, as opposed to telling translators what to do, we also agree with Crisafulli that this does not mean that description must, or can, be non-evaluative: "value judgements influence the selection of data as well as the descriptive categories of analysis and the explanatory theories into which these are organized" (2002:32).

When describing a phenomenon we inevitably foreground certain relationships at the expense of others and thus prioritize certain explanations over others. For example, in a corpus-based study of explicitation, the design of the corpus (whether it is comparable or parallel, whether it includes translations from more than one language or from more than one translator) will necessarily limit the otherwise extremely wide range of factors that could be seen as having an impact on the frequency of instances of explicitation to be found in the corpus. A self-reflective approach to research should acknowledge this inherent bias while at the same time highlighting the benefits of exploring certain variables in depth at the expense of excluding others. It should also look for potentially contradictory evidence as well as seek to back up any results with relevant data from other sources. We consider methodological triangulation to be the backbone of solid, high quality research and so it is implicitly suggested throughout each chapter.

1.3 Research model, structure and content of the book

Empirical research involves gathering observations (in naturalistic or experimental settings) about the world of our experience. Generally, the choice of what aspect to observe will impose certain restrictions in terms of the methods we use. Therefore, we have chosen to divide the chapters of this book according to the focus of our observations: the texts that are the **product** of translation (Chapter 3), the translation **process** (Chapter 4), the **participants** involved in that process (Chapter 5) and the **context** in which translations are produced and received (Chapter 6). It is important to stress, however, that (1) whether a piece of research is process-, product-, participant- or context-oriented is not determined by the methodology itself or even the source of data but by the ultimate aims of the researcher, and (2) when investigating any of these aspects of translation it is impossible to exclude from view all the others; there is inevitable overlap.

We are aware that, in adopting this division of translation phenomena, we are offering the outline of yet another model of translation studies research, rather than drawing on those already proposed by, for example, Marco (2009) or Chesterman (2000). Our model of translation research is by no means flawless or complete; it reflects the perspectives from which translation has been viewed rather than those from which we could possibly view it. In what follows we explain how this model compares to Chesterman's and Marco's.

Chesterman distinguishes three types of models: **comparative models**, which aim to discover language-pair translation rules, language-system contrasts, or translation product universals (also known as features of translation); **process models**, which represent change (from state A to state B) over a time interval (although the process is not necessarily linear) and allow us to understand decision-making in translation and cognitive factors influencing this process; and **causal models**, which aim to explain why translations are the way they are by reference to three dimensions of causation: the translator's cognition (translator's knowledge, attitude, identity, skills), the translation event (translator's brief, payment, deadlines) and the socio-cultural factors (ideology, censorship, cultural traditions, audience). Chesterman (2000:21) argues that the causal model is "the richest and most powerful" because it contains the other two models – linguistic and cognitive factors are taken as causal conditions, and effects at the linguistic and cognitive levels are recorded – and it encourages explanatory and predictive hypotheses. On a superficial level, we could say that the product-oriented methodologies described in Chapter 3 correspond to Chesterman's comparative model; the process-oriented methodologies described in Chapter 4 to the cognitive one; the context-oriented methodologies described in Chapter 6 to the causal one; and participant-oriented methodologies might be mapped either onto a cognitive or causal model according to the precise focus of the research. However, as explained above, an underlying assumption of our approach is that there cannot be purely descriptive (comparative or procedural) research, because any (good) research necessarily takes into account possible explanations, and descriptions are never neutral. Therefore, another way of mapping our model onto Chesterman's three types would be to classify it in its entirety as a causal model that recognizes three different dimensions of causality (linguistic, cognitive and contextual).

A rather complex issue that is necessarily brought to the fore by this mapping of models and which cannot be addressed in much detail here is the potentially different ways of understanding causality in the two approaches (Chesterman's, as outlined in his 2000 publication, and ours). Our understanding is very broad: we simply suggest that empirical research needs to address questions of 'why' at some point in the research process. Sometimes explanations remain at the level of speculation but the research should at least point out potential avenues for further research which could explain the results, and these suggestions need to be grounded in the evidence and in the state of the art in the field. Koskinen (2010) suggests that Chesterman (2000) first adopts a Hempellian understanding of causality, according to which "[c]ausality is ... a (probable) relation between particular premises and observable phenomena" (Koskinen 2010:166), and then repositions himself in a later article (Chesterman 2008a) where he supports an *'agency theory* of causation' (Koskinen 2010:179, emphasis in original). Compared to his earlier approach, Chesterman (2008a) favours a less limited understanding of causes and follows a teleological model based on the notion of intentionally making something happen. An agency theory of causation offers a wider range of avenues for research; apart from probabilistic norms and laws, it considers goals, intentions, motivations, and the ethics of action (Koskinen 2010:179).

Koskinen suggests an alternative way of studying causality which is particularly useful for case studies and which – instead of attempting to establish correlations or causal laws – focuses on causal mechanisms, i.e. on explaining "*how* a particular factor can instigate a change in another factor" (2010:181, emphasis in original). She describes this approach as a "a more down-to-earth attempt to identify a plausible account of the sequence of events, conditions or processes linking the explanans and the explanandum" (*ibid.*:182). In her own work, Koskinen adopts a *nexus model*, which "is based on placing the object of study ... at the centre of our attention and then trying to establish the kinds of relations it enters into and how these relations interact with it and each other" (*ibid.*:180). Chesterman (private communication) believes this model should be incorporated into the typology described in Chesterman (2000). The nexus model is particularly suited to case studies, a research methodology that allows us to focus on causal mechanisms rather than causal effects (see Chapter 6). We revisit the difference between mechanisms and effects in Chapter 2, Section 2.10.3.

Marco (2009) proposes four (non-exhaustive) models of research in TS: (1) textual-descriptivist, (2) cognitive, (3) culturalist and (4) sociological. Marco's classification also overlaps to some extent with the one proposed in this book; our product-oriented methods are also text-oriented, our process-oriented methods have a strong focus on cognitive processes, participant-oriented research tends to be sociological in nature and there is also overlap between cultural and contextual research. The key difference between Marco's models and ours is that his establish a closer link between research methods and theoretical approaches or schools of thought. We prefer to encourage a looser connection between methods and schools of thought so as to offer flexibility in terms of what researchers take and discard from each methodology and from each school, and encourage creativity in terms of combining methods and theories.

While the book discusses both methods and methodologies, we decided to highlight the latter in the title as the more encompassing term and because most of the chapters discuss methodologies rather than methods (see Chapter 2, Section 2.3 for a definition of these terms). Every piece of research begins with theoretical assumptions, for example, about what science is and how knowledge is constructed. Our choice of methodology depends on those assumptions as well as on our research question and/or hypothesis. The success of our methodology in addressing the research question(s) depends on how well the methods suit the research question(s) and the aim of the research. These are questions of validity and reliability which are at the basis of empirical research. Understanding such core principles is essential for any researcher no matter what methodology they adopt, and these are therefore discussed before we actually delve into methodologies *per se*, in **Chapter 2**. This chapter lays the foundations for high quality research independently of the research methodology adopted and the aspect of translation we focus on. It also discusses general ethical issues, which are then followed up in other chapters as appropriate according to the specific characteristics of the methodology.

Chapter 3 discusses how critical discourse analysis and corpus linguistics can be used to examine translated texts (including transcripts of interpreted-mediated events). As explained in that chapter, critical discourse analysis is not actually a methodology but a school of thought that follows a series of principles in its understanding of language and its approach to language research. Here, we focus on the text-oriented methodology developed by Fairclough (2003, 2010) and how it has been adopted and applied in translation studies. While some linguists would argue that corpus linguistics is a research paradigm in its own right (Laviosa 2002), within the context of the present book it is presented as a methodology that can be used to pursue a wide range of research aims. Corpus linguistics and critical discourse analysis are presented as both alternative and complementary methodologies; in other words, they can be used on their own or combined. Therefore, while we take care to clearly distinguish the principles underlying each methodology, their strengths and weaknesses, and to discuss their distinctive tools and procedures, much of the discussion in that chapter concerning general principles of linguistic research applies to both methodologies.

No book on research methodologies in translation studies would be complete without considering the complex nature of research involving translation quality. Such research tends to be primarily product-oriented (though alternative approaches are, of course, possible), and thus Chapter 3 also includes a discussion of research involving translation quality assessment.

Chapter 4 introduces process-oriented research. We outline what the main objects of inquiry have been to date in translation process research and discuss general issues of research design, data elicitation and analysis, before focusing specifically on four methods: verbal reports, keystroke logging, screen recording and eye tracking. **Chapter 5** focuses on the 'participants' (also called 'agents') involved in the process of translations, such as translators, trainers, students, commissioners and agents. This chapter discusses both quantitative and qualitative approaches to participant-oriented research and is divided into two main parts: the first discusses questionnaires and the analysis of quantitative data derived from them, and the second discusses interviews and focus groups and the analysis of qualitative data.

The focus in **Chapter 6** is on external – political, economic, social and ideological – factors affecting individual translators, the circumstances in which translations take place and how translations impact the receiving culture. The object of enquiry is much broader than in previous chapters and a wide range of methodologies could be used in the investigation of the very different contextual factors that can potentially be accounted for. We have chosen to focus on the case study for two reasons: first, because of its flexibility in terms of drawing from a wide range of sources of data, and second, because the label 'case study' is often used in translation studies research without consideration of the particular characteristics and requirements of case study as a methodology (Susam-Sarajeva 2009).

While each of the chapters focuses on different research objects and methodologies, we have attempted – as far as possible – to adopt a similar structure in each of them so as to cover consistently what we see as key aspects of any methodology: research design, data collection and/or elicitation, and analysis. In empirical social research a distinction is made between "elicitation and evaluation methods: between ways of collecting data and procedures that have been developed for the analysis of observed data" (Titscher *et al.* 2000:6). All chapters make a distinction between these two stages, but it is important to note that in some cases these are not two necessarily subsequent stages in a linear progression. This is particularly the case when doing qualitative research that follows an iterative process as opposed to a linear one.

While many researchers use elicitation and collection as two interchangeable terms, we distinguish between the two where appropriate. Collection suggests the recording of data that already exist whereas elicitation evokes a more active generation of data which are then collected or recorded. Elicitation also suggests that a stimulus is involved, such as a text that needs to be translated according to specific instructions, and it is therefore particularly appropriate for the discussion in Chapter 4 on process-oriented methods.

In our final chapter (**Chapter 7**) we deal with what is also generally the final stage of the research process: producing a research report. Research can be reported in a variety of formats, from conference presentations to PhD theses. Here we focus on written reports. Since many of the issues around reporting research span all our chapters and all methodologies, we discuss them at both a general as well as specific levels in this chapter.

Chapter 2. Principles and ethics in research

2.1 Introduction

The aim of this chapter is to highlight issues that should be of concern to all researchers and to place these in the context of translation studies research by offering examples from that domain. We commence with a discussion on ontology and epistemology, terminology and types of research. This discussion is necessarily brief: our aim is to introduce the core terms and concepts here, and we recommend that researchers turn to general works on research methodologies for fuller discussions of the issues that arise. We then turn our attention to research questions, hypotheses and types of data before considering different methodological approaches (quantitative, qualitative and mixed). The last section focuses on questions pertaining to research quality and ethics.

2.2 Ontology and epistemology

There are many books on research methodologies in the humanities and social sciences which cover important philosophical questions such as *How do we know what we know?* or *What is the truth?* Here we will summarize the main philosophical questions, present the most important concepts and terms, and explain their importance for research in translation studies.

It is far too easy to delve into a research project without first questioning one's own view of the world, and, especially, of knowledge acquisition and 'truth'. Having an appreciation for different ways of seeing the world will not only help with the decision regarding what research approach to take, but will also help us as researchers to question our own underlying assumptions, thereby hopefully strengthening our research.

One of the core terms that should be understood prior to engaging in research is **ontology**. In social research, one way of defining ontology is as "the way the social world is seen to be and what can be assumed about the nature and reality of the social phenomena that make up the social world" (Matthews and Ross 2010:23). A key related term is **epistemology**, which is "the theory of knowledge and how we know things" (*ibid*.). Here, we follow Matthews and Ross in distinguishing, in very broad terms, three different ways of seeing the social world – **objectivism**, **constructivism** and **realism** – and three epistemological positions linked to these ontological categories: **positivism**, **interpretivism** and **realism**. These categories are somewhat convenient simplifications; in fact, there are many more than three ontological and epistemological positions, and there are also several versions of each of the positions we present here. However, analyzing these three approaches should be enough to give us an idea of the range of perspectives that can be adopted and their implications. Further reading on these questions is therefore recommended. Guba and Lincoln (2005:193) provide a helpful table that identifies five different paradigms (positivism, postpositivism, critical theory, constructivism, and participatory/cooperative) and basic beliefs associated with them concerning, for example, ontology, epistemology, methodology, ethics, inquirer posture and quality criteria. This may be a good starting point for considering the position researchers think they might be most comfortable with as this will probably influence the approach taken in research.

According to Matthews and Ross (2010:24-25), objectivism "asserts that the social phenomena that make up our social world have an existence of their own [...], apart from and independent of the social actors (humans) who are involved". This position derives from the approach adopted by natural scientists when they investigate phenomena in nature and assume that the researchers' relationship to the phenomena they study is one of objective observation. Constructivism, on the other hand, asserts that social phenomena "are only real in the sense that they are constructed ideas which are continually being reviewed by those involved in them [the social actors]" (*ibid*.:25). In other words, the meanings of any social phenomenon are not inherent but are ascribed to it by social actors (*ibid*.:28). Realism presents an intermediate position between objectivism and constructivism: it accepts that social phenomena can have a reality that is separate from the social actors involved in it but also recognizes that there is another dimension that relates to what we know about the social world as social beings. This dimension includes "structures and mechanisms that trigger or affect the social reality that can be observed" (*ibid*.:26).

As mentioned above, each of the ontological positions described is linked to an epistemological position, that is, it entails some beliefs as to what counts as knowledge and how knowledge can be obtained. The ontological position of objectivism assumes a positivist epistemology, which asserts that social phenomena can be objectively researched, data about the social world can be collected and measured, and the resulting observations must remain independent of the researchers' subjective understandings; that is to say, the researcher remains independent and has no impact on the data. Positivism is often linked with quantitative approaches to research and to **empiricism**, i.e. the collection of observable evidence (see Chapter 1). However, in postpositivist research, empiricism and objectivism are treated as distinct positions; just because research is 'empirical' in nature does not mean that it is 'objective' (Tymoczko 2007:146). In postpositivism it is held that observation and measurement are fallible, and the participation and influence of the researcher are acknowledged. As Crisafulli (2002:33) puts it,

> empirical facts do not exist independently of the scholar's viewpoint; indeed, it is the scholar who creates the empirical facts of the analysis by making observable (raw) data relevant to his/her perspective.

Interpretivism is linked to the ontological position of constructivism; it prioritizes people's subjective understandings and interpretations of social phenomena and is often linked with qualitative approaches to research, where the researchers attempt to explore the social world from the point of view of the actors and reflect on their own subjective interpretations. Realism is both an ontological and epistemological position. As an epistemological approach it claims that certain social phenomena exist outside the human mind and can be objectively investigated using approaches similar to those in the natural sciences. In this respect, realism agrees with positivism. However, it also recognizes the existence of invisible but powerful structures and mechanisms that cannot be directly observable but whose effects are apparent, and these effects can provide evidence of the underlying structures and mechanisms (Matthews and Ross 2010:29); Realist approaches to research might typically adopt both quantitative and qualitative tools and methods.

We will not prescribe a specific ontological or epistemological framework here. In fact, the approaches outlined are not necessarily mutually exclusive, and we consider the way in which one standpoint or the other has divided researchers in the past to be unhelpful. As Guba and Lincoln state, "there is no single 'truth' … all truths are but partial truths" (2005:212). However, as researchers bring a number of beliefs, prior knowledge and experience to research, it is helpful to reflect on these prior to commencing research.

2.3   Research terminology

Along with the terms used above, many other terms are used in research in a way that assumes general agreement about the meaning assigned to those terms. However, even seasoned researchers can use research terminology inconsistently, and this can lead to much confusion and frustration on the part of the reader and, especially, the novice researcher. Terms such as *model, framework, theory, typology, concept, method* and *methodology* often go unexplained or are used synonymously, resulting in a lack of comprehension. Here we provide some definitions for common terms, drawing mainly on Silverman (2006:13), with the exception of the definitions for 'framework' and 'typology', which are taken from Matthews and Ross (2010:34 & 112 respectively). Not everyone will agree with these definitions, which represent but one way of defining the concepts. What is important for each researcher is to carefully consider their use of research terminology, to justify the definitions used for their given purpose and to use terms consistently, while being aware and drawing attention to the fact that others might use the terms in a different way.

A **model** is a representation of the 'reality' of your research topic or domain. In Chapter 1 we compared the model of translation studies research suggested by this book with the models proposed by Chesterman (2000) and Marco (2009). Note, however, that it is frequently the case that models are not made explicit in research projects and that sometimes there can be a disconnect between the assumed model and the object of investigation (Tymoczko 2007). A **framework** is the set of ideas and approaches that can be used to view and gather knowledge about a particular domain. As described in Chapter 3, Halliday's systemic functional grammar is often used as an analytical framework in corpus-based translation and critical discourse analysis research. A **concept** is an idea deriving from a model or a framework. A **theory** organizes sets of concepts to define and explain some phenomenon or, in Chesterman's words, a theory is "an instrument of understanding" (2007:1). A **typology** is a typical model of the way items tend to be found in relation to each other. For example, one might try to construct a typology of translation strategies used in specific circumstances. A **methodology** is a general approach to studying a phenomenon whereas a **method** is a specific research technique. In Sealy's words, "methodology is the science of method" (2010:61). Saukko differentiates between the two concepts in the following way (2003:8; our emphasis):

> whereas methods refer to practical 'tools' to make sense of empirical reality, methodology refers to the wider package of both tools and **a philosophical and political commitment** that come with a particular research approach.

The relation between a theory and a method is expressed by Chesterman in the following way: "methods are the ways in which one actually uses, develops, applies and tests a theory in order to reach the understanding it offers" (2007:1). Methods and **tools** are also frequently confused. Perhaps the best way to demonstrate how these terms might be applied to a domain within translation studies would be to take the example of translation process research. In this example, our model might be a particular model of cognitive processing, i.e. a representation of the phenomenon whereby the brain perceives signals, processes them and converts them into meaning and instructions. Our framework might be cognitive load, i.e. a set of ideas about brain processing capacity during a specific task, where we expect that there is a limit to the amount of information (signals) that can be processed by the human brain at any moment in time. Concepts within that framework might include the translation process, i.e. an activity the brain engages in when a human is translating from one language to another, short-term memory, long-term memory, limitations on the capacity of the brain, to name just a few. Our theory might be the MiniMax theory (otherwise known as the 'principle of least effort' (Krings 1986a, Séguinot 1989, Lörscher 1991), which posits that humans (translators in this case) opt for a strategy whereby they employ the highest level of cognitive processing possible and do not proceed to a deeper level of processing, which entails a greater cognitive load, unless the first level proves to be unsuccessful or unsatisfactory. Our methodology for studying this might be empirical (we will gather evidence from translators at work) and might combine both qualitative and quantitative methods such as think-aloud protocol and keystroke logging. We may wish to propose a typology of the translation strategies used to achieve the principle of least effort. Finally, the tools we might use are a voice recording device, screen recording software and a keystroke logging tool. We summarize this example in Figure 2.1.

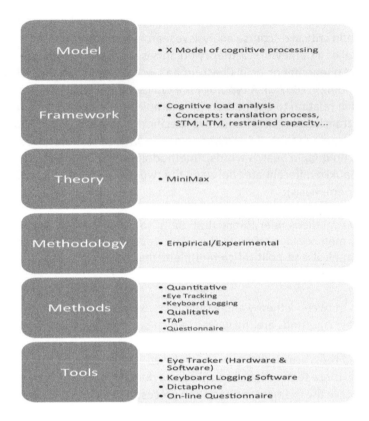

Figure 2.1 Example of Research Terminology Applied to TS

Laying out one's research domain in these terms is not always an easy task, and we expect that there will be some who do not agree with our categorization in Figure 2.1, but the exercise is worthwhile because it forces the researcher not only to think about the research terminology but also about the concepts one is subscribing to, how to communicate these to the wider research community, and, ultimately, what the researcher's view of the world is.

2.4   Types of research

There are many questions to be answered before conducting research, such as what is the research question, which method or methods are most appropriate, what kind of data will be collected, how will the data be analysed and so on. We have argued that it is worthwhile thinking about one's epistemological framework before diving into such details. Likewise, we argue that it is important to consider what type of research we are engaging in. An initial question pertaining to type of research is what logical system it subscribes to, i.e. whether it is being conducted from an inductive or a deductive positioning. **Induction** involves the development of theories and hypotheses from the data collected (it moves from particular instances to general statements), whereas **deduction** involves the testing of existing theories or hypotheses through data (it moves from general statements to specific instances). A third position, **abduction**, is also possible. This position was first mentioned by C.S. Pierce in 1878; it proposes to isolate the most convincing reasons (hypotheses) from a research result and to research these hypotheses further. Johnson and Onwuegbuzie (2004:17) helpfully characterize the three as discovery of patterns (induction), testing of hypotheses (deduction) and seeking understanding by uncovering and relying on "the best of a set of explanations for understanding one's results".

In addition to the question of logical positioning, there is the question of the nature of the research. As explained in Chapter 1, this book focuses on empirical research. Williams and Chesterman (2002:58) explain that **empirical research** "seeks new data, new information derived from the observation of data and from experimental work; it seeks evidence which supports or disconfirms hypotheses, or generates new ones". This type of research is generally seen in opposition to **conceptual research**, which "aims to define and clarify concepts, to interpret or reinterpret new ideas, to relate concepts into larger systems, to introduce new concepts or metaphors or frameworks that allow a better understanding of the object of research" (*ibid.*). However, as discussed in Chapter 1, the distinction is not always clear cut and these two types of research are not mutually exclusive (see the discussion of argument-centred research designs in Chapter 3). Empirical researchers can engage in either **basic** or **applied research**. Although the distinction between these two types is not clearcut either, basic research is generally understood to mean fundamental research, the primary aim of which is to acquire new knowledge. Applied research is generally understood to mean research on practical problems, research that has an application in life. Research may also be characterized as **experimental**, in which case the researcher seeks to establish cause and effect relations (if X happens, then what is the effect on Y?). Such research might be carried out in a controlled environment, although this is not always practical in humanities and social science research, and is often comparative; it compares two groups and their properties of behaviour when certain variables are manipulated. It may be designed in such a way that there is an **'experimental group'** (also known as a 'treatment group') and a **'control group'**. Members of the former group are exposed to some sort of 'treatment', or manipulation, while the latter are not. Note that the groups are not necessarily populated by humans, but can also be composed of texts, for example. The creation of control groups in translation studies research is not without challenges, however. Comparable groups of translators or translations may simply not exist. To compensate for this, Tymoczko (2002:21) suggests the use of other translations of the translated text that is under investigation or even other passages from the translated text that 'are neutral with respect to the issues being investigated', or the use of a corpus of parallel texts (see the discussion on obtaining comparable textual data in Chapter 3, Section 3.3.2). Experimental research in translation studies is discussed in more detail in Chapter 4.

Basic or applied research does not necessarily have to be experimental, though, and might also be **explorative**. An example of explorative research is **phenomenology**, where rather than asking what is the effect on Y if X happens, or what X is, the lived experience or appearance of a particular phenomenon is explored. Phenomenology is an interpretive, subjective approach to research, which is interested in gaining insights from personal experiences. For further discussion on phenomenology see, for example, O'Leary (2010) and Lewis and Staehler (2010).

Research can also be **evaluative**, attempting to establish the value of a particular initiative once it has been implemented (**summative evaluation**) and the intended or unintended effects of the initiative, or it might evaluate the delivery of an initiative (**formative** or **process evaluation**).

The goal of research can extend beyond that of evaluation or looking for relationships between X and Y; it can also lead to change, and this is where the term **action research** is applied. Action research tackles "real-world problems in participatory and collaborative ways in order to produce action and knowledge in an integrated fashion through a cyclical process" (O'Leary 2010:146). Action research is collaborative: it seeks to empower the stakeholders and moves away from the concepts of the 'researcher' and the 'researched'. See Chapter 5, Section 5.7.1, for an example of action research in interpreting.

Research might also be **ethnographic**, when it explores cultural groups "in a bid to understand, describe, and interpret a way of life from the point of view of its participants" (*ibid.*:116). One example is Koskinen's (2008) study of the Finnish translation unit at the European Commission. The ethnographic approach is discussed in detail in Chapter 6. For a more detailed discussion of ethnographic research methods, see, for example, Madden (2010).

2.5   Research questions and hypotheses

Before we as researchers select methodologies, we must first identify at least a tentative research question, and possibly several sub-questions, which are often refined as the research develops. The sub-questions allow the researcher to unpack the main research question into more specific, highly focused questions.

Williams and Chesterman (2002) have identified many research domains in translation studies. The research question may very well 'belong' to one of these research domains but it may also straddle more than one domain, or explore new domains. As translation studies expands its horizons, we can expect research questions to touch on many more and varied topics than it has done to date.

There are different types of research questions (Matthews and Ross 2010:57). A question might be explorative, in which case it seeks to find out what knowledge exists about a particular phenomenon. If we return to our previous example of translation processes and the theory of a MiniMax strategy, an explorative research question might be *What evidence is there to show that the MiniMax strategy is employed by translators?* A descriptive research question seeks to elicit data through which a phenomenon can be described in detail, e.g. *What micro-strategies do translators employ when they apply the MiniMax macro-strategy?* An explanatory research question is a 'why' question. In our example, this might be formulated as *Why do translators employ the MiniMax strategy while translating?* The fourth type of question is an evaluative question which seeks to understand the value of a phenomenon, e.g. *What is the impact on translation quality when translators employ the MiniMax strategy?*

We stated in Chapter 1 that we do not believe in a clear-cut distinction between descriptive and explanatory research, and it is important to stress here again that research questions do not always fit neatly into one of the four categories above. A researcher may have an explorative question, which is then followed by a descriptive or an evaluative sub-question, for example. Questions might also have a hierarchy of sorts, with one being a primary research question, followed by one or several secondary research questions. Indeed, some primary research questions cannot be 'operationalized' until they are broken down into more specific sub-questions (Sunderland 2009); see below for a discussion of operationalization.

Researchers will select questions based on their interest in the topic, but the question should also be one that is of interest to the community at large. Unfortunately, questions worthy of future research are not always made explicit in research publications, but it is still possible to extract questions by identifying what has not been said by authors. This requires a critical reading of research publications, where the reader considers what questions might arise from the argument being put forward and whether or not they are addressed by the author(s).

It is generally accepted that research questions evolve over time. This is a normal development in the research cycle: as we become more familiar with the domain we are better able to critique our own research question and to refine it; to do so is to be recommended. This refinement frequently involves reducing the scope of the research question, or making it more specific, or introducing some sub-questions which will allow us to investigate the general question in more detail. Some research methods almost demand that questions evolve over a period of time, by the very nature of the method itself. For example, ethnographic research in general or case studies in particular might demand multiple cycles where research questions evolve as the research takes shape (see Chapter 6). Also, the use of abduction, as mentioned above, can contribute to the evolution of research questions and hypotheses.

It might seem overly simplistic to say that a research question should be formulated as a question, but not doing so is a common mistake, especially among novice researchers. When novice researchers are asked about their research *questions* they often describe their *topic* instead, confusing the two and failing to formulate a question (Sunderland 2009). Williams and Chesterman (2002:57) reinforce the importance of the question type by recommending the selection of the research model based on the type of question asked. Olohan and Baker (2009:152) make an important point regarding the wording of research questions for doctoral studies: "Almost every word used in a research question sets up specific expectations, some of which a student may not be able or willing to fulfill", but this issue might also be relevant beyond Master's or doctoral research. Sunderland (2009) echoes this point and adds that the researcher needs to understand, and explain, exactly what each word in the question means.

According to Matthews and Ross, **hypotheses** are specific types of research questions that are not phrased as questions but as statements about relationships; they define a hypothesis as "[a] *testable assertion* about a relationship or relationships between *two* or more concepts" (2010:58, emphasis in original). A research question, then, can sometimes be rephrased as a hypothesis. If we take the descriptive research question mentioned above (*What micro-strategies do translators employ when they apply the MiniMax macro-strategy?*), we might express the following hypothesis in relation to this question: *When translators employ the MiniMax strategy, they make use of micro-strategies that are different from those they use when they are not employing the MiniMax strategy* (but see comments about the null hypothesis below). In other words, the researcher is asserting that there is a relationship between the use of the MiniMax strategy and the type of micro-strategies employed. Note that the hypothesis is not just an expression of the research question in the form of a statement. We have had to refine it somewhat in order to express it as a hypothesis, and it probably still needs further refinement. It can be illuminating to ask oneself what one's hypotheses are, once the research question(s) has/have been formulated. In doing so, we are asking what we *expect to find* and the research project should aim to find evidence which either supports our hypotheses or contradicts them. Note that even if our hypothesis is not supported (or fully supported), this is still a valuable research outcome.

Not all research questions can be expressed in terms of a hypothesis. In fact, those who disagree with the positivist approach to research would claim that hypotheses are reductionist devices which constrain social research (O'Leary 2010:55). Olohan and Baker (2009), in their discussion of research training for doctoral students in translation studies, comment that they favour open research questions over hypotheses for several reasons, including, for example, that an open research question provides broader scope for interrogating data from several perspectives; they encourage students to keep an open mind about the data and potential findings. Hypotheses are commonly (though not exclusively) used in situations where data can be gathered to measure each concept and where statistical tests can be executed to establish if there is a relationship between concepts.

The relationships expressed in a hypothesis can be **causal** or **associative** (Matthews and Ross 2010:59). Causal relationships assert that a change in one concept (X) causes a change in the other (Y). Associative relationships recognize the influence of one concept on another. In the latter case, there might be a third factor, Z, an **intervening variable** (cf. Silverman 2006:289), which influences Y.

Chesterman (2007) recognizes four types of hypotheses: descriptive, explanatory, predictive and interpretive. The first three can be grouped together as **empirical hypotheses**, whereas the interpretive kind has a different status. According to Chesterman, a **descriptive hypothesis** is formulated along the lines of 'All Xs have features F, or belong to class Y'; an **explanatory hypothesis** states that 'X is caused or made possible by Y'; and a **predictive hypothesis** is formulated as 'In conditions ABC, X will (tend to) occur'. The interpretive hypothesis asks whether something (X) can be usefully interpreted as Y, or better understood if we 'see it' as something else. Chesterman (2001a) notes that classifications and categories (e.g. types of equivalence) are interpretive hypotheses in themselves. **Interpretive hypotheses** pertain to conceptual (as opposed to empirical) research and are "conjectures about what something means" (Chesterman 2008b:49); they are "what we use when we try to understand meaningful yet obscure phenomena" (Chesterman 2008b:56). An example of an interpretive hypothesis would be 'translation is best conceptualized as a type of artistic performance rather than as a reproduction'. As Chesterman notes (2000:23), interpretive hypotheses are rarely presented explicitly as such, to be tested like any other hypotheses.

In research that adopts a mainly quantitative approach, it is traditionally assumed that no relationship exists between two variables, and statistical tests are based on this assumption (Rasinger 2008:176). The hypothesis mentioned above would therefore be phrased as: When translators employ the MiniMax strategy, they make use of the same micro-strategies they use when they are not employing the MiniMax strategy. In other words, there is no relationship between the MiniMax strategy and the type of micro-strategies used in translation. This is called the null hypothesis and is given the notation H_0. We are usually interested in disproving the null hypothesis, in demonstrating that its opposite, or the alternative hypothesis (H_1) is true. We discuss the falsification of hypotheses in more detail in Section 2.10.4.

2.6   The literature review

It was mentioned above that one way of identifying interesting research questions is by performing a thorough literature review. The literature review gives researchers an opportunity to explain their motivation and potential contribution. According to Fink (2005:3), the literature review is "a systematic, explicit, and reproducible method for identifying, evaluating, and synthesizing the existing body of completed and recorded work produced by researchers, scholars, and practitioners".

Let us examine each of these qualifiers in turn: Systematic means that it is not random, i.e. that all key sources of published research on the topic have been identified, read and evaluated. Explicit implies that there is clarity regarding what works, authors, time period, domain, languages, regions, etc. have been included and, of equal importance, what has been excluded and why. Reproducible demands that everything is documented clearly, with appropriate referencing, so that any other researcher could track down the sources used and confirm the summary of the included works.

The literature review identifies all relevant work and synthesizes core concepts and findings. Care is needed in the synthesizing task as this does not simply involve repeating verbatim what other researchers have said, but rather summarizing the main themes, ideas, questions/hypotheses and conclusions. There are two significant challenges when synthesizing: avoiding plagiarism and deciding how to structure one's work. Plagiarism will be discussed below in Section 2.11.8.

A number of questions could be asked when considering how to structure the literature review: do you work author by author, era by era, language by language, etc., or do you amalgamate into common themes and topics? Opinions will vary on this, but generally speaking a literature review that is structured along thematic lines might be more effective and accessible than one structured chronologically and/or according to author.

Arguably one of the most important features of a literature review is that it evaluates critically. For a novice researcher, who is perhaps new to doing research and to the topic itself, this is one of the most challenging aspects of the literature review. Assuming a position of modesty, the novice researcher might think that they are not in a position to criticize an author who has published one or several papers or books. However, it is the job of the researcher to critically explore previous research. We should aim to identify both strengths and weaknesses in earlier work, concepts that have not been fully investigated or researched at all, concepts that have been researched particularly well or that have been over-researched, weaknesses in assumptions, methods, research questions, and so on. There is an important comparative aspect to this commentary too: we should aim to highlight contradictory findings as well as findings which support those of previous research, and we should aim to identify differences in assumptions, theories and definitions and how these can lead to different conclusions.

The literature review is an important vehicle through which researchers can identify and describe the most relevant theoretical framework(s) for their own research. Tymoczko (2007) directs attention to the interrelationship between data and theory, emphasizing that in postpositivist approaches to research the recognition of the interdependence between data and theory is essential. In the analysis of data, researchers have an opportunity to explore this interrelationship and to make explicit links to the theoretical framework(s) they have identified as being important.

2.7   Data

To find answers to research questions, we need to collect appropriate data for analysis. Data can be spoken or written, non-verbal, structured in different ways, produced by individuals or groups, be factual or representing opinions, and it can include the researcher's own reflections (Matthews and Ross 2010:181).

Methods for data collection and analysis will be discussed in more detail in relation to the different methodologies presented in Chapters 3 to 6. For the moment, we need to differentiate between **primary** and **secondary data**. Primary data are collected by the researcher him or herself while the term secondary data refers to collections of data, e.g. interview transcriptions, questionnaire responses, translations etc., that have been collected by other researchers and made available to the research community for analysis. Corpora could be considered in this category, so an example of secondary data for translation research would be the Translational English Corpus, a computerised collection of contemporary translational English text held at the Centre for Translation and Intercultural Studies at the University of Manchester.[1] A researcher interested in analyzing some aspect of translated English could use this resource as secondary data while also creating their own corpus. Primary and secondary data might be structured in different ways. When comparing primary and secondary data, it is important to take into account that the circumstances under which data were collected, and the number and nature of the people who generated the data and the time of data collection or elicitation might vary and this may affect the comparability of the two data sets.

The type of data collected is also important because it will determine whether we use qualitative and/or quantitative approaches in our research. Quantitative approaches will generate **structured** data which can be represented numerically and analyzed statistically, whereas the qualitative approach will generate **semi-** or **unstructured** data. In questionnaire surveys, for example, structured data are generated by asking the same questions to all research participants and limiting the ways in which they can provide answers (through tick boxes in question-naires, for example). Qualitative interviews, on the other hand, generally result in semi- or unstructured data because the questions asked vary to some degree, the respondents are given some or a lot of freedom when answering and not all questions are necessarily answered. See also the discussion of quantitative and qualitative approaches to textual analysis in Chapter 3.

For data that can be quantified, it is also important to take into account what kind of measurements we can apply. Rasinger (2008:25-26) distinguishes four different levels of measurement. The first level pertains to **categorical scale data** (also termed **nominal data**), where data can fall into only one category, such as 'pregnant'/'not pregnant'. The second level is **ordinal scale data**, where a concept can be ranked, but where it is not possible to measure differences between each label. The example given by Rasinger here is for ranking of university lectures on a dullness scale, where it is impossible to say that 'very dull' is twice as dull as 'dull'. The next level is **interval scale data**, where again categories can be labelled, but the difference between them is fixed. A typical example mentioned by Rasinger is the grading system used to evaluate student work. The final level is **ratio scale data** where, like interval data, there is a fixed value between points, but unlike interval data, ratio data have an absolute zero point.

---

[1] http://www.llc.manchester.ac.uk/ctis/research/english-corpus/ [Last accessed 2 December 2012].

At what point do we have sufficient data? This is a frequently asked question which is difficult to answer because it depends on so many variables (the methodology, the research questions, hypotheses, time allocation, among others). Chapters 3 to 6 discuss data collection and address some of the relevant issues in more detail, including the length of text and corpora for analysis and the concept of saturation in participant-oriented and case-study research. In social science and humanities research in general, and translation research in particular, the trend is for researchers to work on their own. Examples of large teams of people analyzing data sets are few.[2] Consequently, it is not always possible to analyze very large data sets. Also, the nature of the data collected in translation research – for example, written or spoken linguistic data, behavioural data, narratives – compared with the natural sciences, means that automatic analysis is challenging and not always desirable. This, in turn, tends to restrict the amount of data analyzed. While some automation is possible in translation research (see, for example, later chapters on corpus analysis and translation process research), most of the analysis is manual.

Before researchers decide whether they have collected 'enough' data to address their research questions, they will first have to consider issues of validity and credibility, which are addressed below. It is sometimes helpful to carry out a small-scale **pilot study** prior to the main data collection phase. This will allow the researcher to test selected methods of analysis and will give a feeling for how much data might need to be collected to establish some level of credibility. Pilot studies are discussed in more detail, where relevant, in relation to each of the methodological approaches presented in Chapters 3 to 6. Another approach to establish whether data are sufficient is to add layers of data over time, until one sees a stabilization in the variability of results.

2.8   Qualitative, quantitative and mixed-methods approaches

The approach to take to one's research should be determined by the research question(s) and how best it/they might be addressed. The **quantitative approach** is associated with the positivist epistemological position we mentioned earlier while a **qualitative approach** is generally associated with the interpretivist position. According to O'Leary (2010:113), the qualitative tradition

> calls on inductive as well as deductive logic, appreciates subjectivities, accepts multiple perspectives and realities, recognizes the power of research on both participants and researchers, and does not necessarily shy away from political agendas.

Each approach has specific methodologies associated with it. A qualitative ap-

---

[2] One current example is the PACTE translation competence research group at the Universitat Autònoma de Barcelona, in Spain: http://grupsderecerca.uab.cat/pacte/es [Last accessed 2 December 2012].

proach in translation research can include critical discourse analysis, interviews, focus groups, questionnaires (see Chapters 3, 5 and 6) while the quantitative approach might be associated with corpus analysis, eye tracking, keystroke logging (see Chapters 3 and 4). It is important to point out that some methods can produce data that can be analyzed both qualitatively and quantitatively (e.g. survey data, think-aloud protocols and corpus analysis). A **mixed-methods** approach is the term used when several methods are used to collect or analyze data. This is often understood to mean using *both* qualitative and quantitative approaches. The two types of data can be collected simultaneously. Alternatively, the researcher might opt for an initial qualitative phase followed by a quantitative phase, or vice versa. The first sequence has the advantage of allowing the researcher to explore data qualitatively and to follow this exploration up with a more focused quantitative analysis of the topic or sub-topic, while the alternative of commencing with a quantitative phase has the potential advantage of exposing some trends that can then be further probed via qualitative data. Chapter 5 discusses mixed methods in participant-oriented research in more detail and illustrates different ways of 'quantitizing' and 'qualitizing' data, that is, deriving quantitative data from qualitative data and vice-versa.

Guba and Lincoln (2005:201) raise an important concern regarding the commensurability of competing paradigms (e.g. positivism and interpretivism), stating that commensurability can be an issue "when researchers want to 'pick and mix' among the axioms of positivist and interpretivist models, because the axioms are contradictory and mutually exclusive". As we mentioned above, in the end, the research question will dictate what the most appropriate approach is, but it is worth taking potential contradictions into account when adopting a mixed-methods approach. As Creswell and Plano Clark (2007) point out, mixed methods research is not just a way of combining qualitative and quantitative approaches, but also "a research design with philosophical assumptions" (*ibid.*:5). The central premise is that "the use of quantitative and qualitative approaches in combination provides a better understanding of research problems than either approach alone" (*ibid.*). An argument along similar lines is made in Chapter 3 in relation to the combination of corpus linguistics and critical discourse analysis.

When two methods are used to collect and analyze data on the same research question, this is called **triangulation**, which means cross-checking the results one set of data provides with results from another set of data. This is a practice we would generally endorse, and we point to opportunities for triangulation of results where appropriate in the chapters that follow.

2.9 Research operationalization

An important question to ask about the data to be collected and analyzed pertains to the **unit of data**. Data can pertain to either the macro or micro level (Matthews and Ross 2010:114). **Macro-level data** are collected, for example, from organizations, countries, systems and social entities, while **micro-level data** are at the level of the individual, word, or text. In the case of translation research, macro-level data might pertain to professional translator associations, country-specific laws regarding language and translation, to translation practices within organizations, or to literary polysystems, to mention just a few examples. Micro-level data might pertain to the use of specific strategies in a translated text, individual translation strategies, or the length of time taken to translate a text. Tymoczko (2002) aligns macro-level research with the cultural approach to research in translation and micro-level research with the linguistic approach. In her attempt to connect the two approaches, rather than allowing them to be seen as competing and exclusive of one another, she encourages a convergence which makes use of both macro-level and micro-level analysis, with data from one type of analysis complementing and, hopefully, confirming the other.

Yet another important concept is the **unit of analysis**. This is not the same as the unit of data. For example, the unit of data might be at the micro-level of 'text' and, while a researcher might analyze text in general, it is quite likely that the unit of analysis (or measurement) will be further broken down into measurable concepts such as lexical items, sentences, clauses, phrases, collocations and so on. On the macro level, the unit of data might be 'legislation pertaining to language and translation in country X', but the unit of analysis in this context might be specific laws or legal clauses.[3]

The unit of analysis is linked with the important concept of operational definitions or **operationalization**. Strictly speaking, operationalization refers to the operations involved in measuring the dependent variable. Operationalization does not pertain only to quantitative approaches to research but is equally important for qualitative approaches, where the operational definition can be thought of as an explicit and precise definition that isolates the core components of the variable under investigation. Let us go back to the example of the theory of a MiniMax strategy we used earlier which, as a reminder, posits that translators opt for the minimum amount of cognitive effort possible before proceeding to deeper levels of processing. An important question from the outset is *how can I operationalize the MiniMax theory*, i.e. how can I turn this somewhat abstract theory into a measurable entity? An example of how this might be achieved comes from Lörscher (1991), who equates evidence for a MiniMax strategy with a dominance of sign-oriented translation, which he defines as a transfer of the source language form into a target language form, without recourse to the sense of the text segments involved. Sign-oriented translation could be operationalized both via the translated product (where there is evidence of form substitution without recourse to sense) and via the utterances of translators produced in think-aloud protocols either during or after the translation process (for example, where a translator might say during the course of a translation: '*Entwicklung*, yes that's *development* in English..., that'll do'). Operationalization becomes even more challenging with more abstract concepts, such as *culture* or the *status*

---

[3] For a discussion of the problem of identifying a unit of analysis in an emerging field like translation studies, see Tymoczko (2007:153). We discuss the unit of analysis with specific reference to translation process research in Chapter 4.

of the translator. A good example is provided by Koskinen's operationalization of 'culture' in the context of an ethnographic study of institutional translation (2008:40-43). Koskinen chooses a definition of organizational culture proposed by Martin (2002, in Koskinen *ibid.*:41) that is useful for her purposes because it describes aspects of culture, both material and ideational, that are manifested and observable, such as stories people tell, relations among people, official policies and formal arrangement (to name just a few). This definition is then related to Scott's (2001, *ibid.*) systemic view of the three pillars of institutions: regulative systems, normative systems and cultural cognitive systems. Finally, Koskinen identifies methods that will allow her to explore the manifestations of culture described in the definition and belonging to those three pillars from an ethnographic perspective.

Two crucial questions ought to be asked when operationalizing a concept: (1) what influence does the researcher's beliefs and ideology have on the proposed operationalization of the concept, and (2) whether or not the tools selected can actually measure the concept the researcher wishes to measure? Take, as one example, the concept of 'source text difficulty', i.e. how complex the source text is and how this might impact on the translation process and/or product. There are numerous ways in which the concept 'source text difficulty' might be and has been measured in translation research, such as subjectively using native speakers as evaluators, using traditional readability indices, or using rhetorical structure theory (Taboada and Mann 2006). The ability of any of these methods to measure the construct or the degree to which they can do this is open to question.

Operational definitions will dictate the approach for gathering data and the type of analysis that can be performed on the data. Previously, we mentioned using secondary data. There is a possibility that the operational definition used when collecting secondary data differs from the researcher's own operational definition and, therefore, the implications of using secondary data that were collated under a different operational definition should be considered. At the very least, differences in operationalization ought to be acknowledged.

2.9.1   *Measurable variables*

A variable "is simply something that *varies* ... in some way that we seek to measure" (Langridge and Hagger-Johnson 2009:40, original emphasis). This concept is used primarily in quantitative approaches to research. The **dependent variable** is the core concept we are trying to assess in our research question. We expect it to change when it is exposed to varying treatment. The **independent variables**, on the other hand, are things that we manipulate in order to see what the effect is on our dependent variable.

Let us consider, for example, the research question: *What is the effect on translation quality when time pressure is increased?* The null hypothesis might be expressed as: *There is no change in translation quality when time pressure is increased.* (In fact, as we stated earlier, we expect that the opposite – alternative – hypothesis is true.) Let us assume for a moment that we have found acceptable ways of operationalizing *translation quality* and *time pressure*. Then, we might expect the results shown in Figure 2.2.

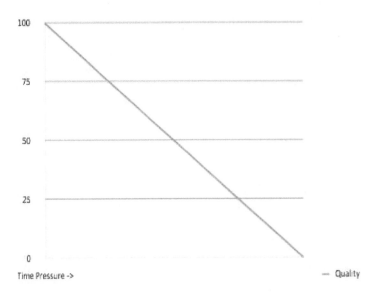

Figure 2.2 A theoretical model expressing the relationship between time pressure (X axis) and translation quality (nominal scale on the Y axis)

In other words, as time pressure increases we expect translation quality to decrease. Of course, we would be naïve to expect such a straight linear correlation between time pressure and quality, but this figure illustrates our alternative hypothesis and our *expected* relationship between the dependent variable (quality) and the independent variable (time pressure).

One of the challenges is how to successfully isolate dependent and independent variables so that they are not influenced by other ('**confounding**') variables. In the example above, it would not be unreasonable to expect that the complexity of the text for translation might also have an impact on quality, especially under conditions where there is significant time pressure applied. So, text complexity might be another independent variable, as might degree of experience of the translator (can more experienced translators cope better with time pressure than less experienced ones?), or degree of specialization (hypothesis: translators specialized in a specific domain will produce higher quality texts even under time pressure than those not specialized in the domain), to name just two examples. We can design a research project to investigate the effect of multiple independent variables on one dependent variable or, indeed, even on multiple dependent variables.

Dependent and independent variables are typically associated with quantitative approaches to research, but qualitative approaches do not exclude them. A qualitative approach to a research question may also be able to identify dependent and independent variables.

When items are complex and harder to measure than other items, they are typically called 'research constructs' rather than variables: "Constructs are unobservable variables, and therefore variables that have to be measured indirectly" (Langdridge and Hagger-Johnson 2009:40). Complex ideas such as 'status', 'acceptability', or 'equivalence' may be best explored as constructs in translation research. However, see Ji (2012) for examples of how the relationships between (1) texts and source texts, (2) target texts and the target language linguistic and cultural system, and (3) translation style and the historical development of the target language system, can be mapped in terms of dependent and independent variables. In relation to the second type of relationship, Ji suggests that the independent variables can be the ideological stances of the translator, and the dependent variables the particular translation strategies developed for their work (*ibid.*:56).

On the topic of variables in translation research, another useful distinction is proposed by Chesterman (2001a), who identifies two main variable types: **profile variables**, which refer to aspects of the form of a translation such as stylistic or syntactic features, and **context variables**, which refer to aspects of the translation context and its consequences, such as text type or skopos, to name just two.

2.10 Research quality

> Short of reliable methods and valid conclusions, research descends into a bedlam where the only battles that are won are by those who shout the loudest.
>
> (Silverman 2006:310)

The issues discussed so far in this chapter are important to ensure that research is planned in such a way that it meets high quality standards: considering our epistemological viewpoint prior to commencing the project; identifying the model, concepts, frameworks etc. with which we are working; giving due consideration to the formulation and scope of our research question and hypotheses; carrying out a literature review according to recommended practices; thinking about the approaches we wish to take and the nature of the data we wish to collect; and identifying independent and dependent variables in advance where appropriate. However, undertaking a research project also includes undertaking to make some contribution to the knowledge that already exists about a topic, and to ensure that a contribution is made, the research should meet certain quality criteria: validity, reliability and generalizability, each of which is discussed below in some detail (Section 2.10). Since some of these criteria have been criticized as not being applicable to qualitative research and an interpretivist stance, we also devote another section to alternative ways of measuring research quality (Section 2.10.4).

2.10.1 *Validity*

Validity is a multi-faceted, and somewhat contested, topic and hence significant space is given to its discussion here. The central question around validity, according to Guba and Lincoln (2005:205) is whether one's findings are "sufficiently authentic (isomorphic to some reality, trustworthy, related to the way others construct their social worlds) that I may trust myself in acting on their implications". The very possibility of *validation* in translation studies research is contested. Tymoczko (2007:155) points out that the expansion of the concept of 'translation' and the subsequent inclusion of a broader range of scholars has led to disagreement over the possibility of validation. However, she insists on the importance of addressing the question of validation to strengthen research methods in this field and suggests that it is important to acknowledge the limitations around claims of validity and replicability and to face these methodological problems head on (*ibid.*:159).[4] Here, rather than attempting to argue the possibility, or impossibility, of validation in translation research, we feel it will be more fruitful to highlight the challenges and potential solutions for achieving validity in qualitative and quantitative approaches to research so that researchers can make up their own minds as to what understanding of validity they subscribe to.

At the most basic level, the validity of our results will depend on the extent to which the data we collate and analyze can contribute to answering our research question. For example, let us imagine we are interested in researching translation students' attitudes towards the teaching methods they have been exposed to in a particular university programme. We may decide to use a questionnaire to collect data. The inclusion of a question about student attitudes towards the particular university's infrastructure (facilities, services, buildings, etc.) will not help us answer our research question, and the validity of the data accumulated through responses to that question is therefore questionable (notwithstanding the fact that the responses might give us some interesting secondary data).

The definition of **validity** by Guba and Lincoln quoted above, according to which validity is the degree to which results match as closely as possible the real state of the world, assumes a positivistic research perspective. A less rigid (and postpositivistic) understanding of validity "concerns the extent to which justifiable *inferences* can be made on the basis of the evidence gathered" (Le Grange and Beets 2005:115, drawing on Messick 1989; our emphasis). The reference to inferences implies that, especially when using qualitative approaches to research, one cannot claim absolute validity. In the past, this resulted in some tension between the quantitative and qualitative schools of thought. As a result, qualitative researchers have proposed a new set of validity measurements which seek to ensure research quality, such as credibility and warrantability, discussed below.

It is worth remembering here the different ontological and epistemological perspectives described above. If we adopt a constructivist view of the social world, then measuring validity does not make sense, because we do not believe that there is an objective reality out there, independent of our notions about it, that needs to be captured by our methods. Theorists in cultural studies (Saukko 2003:18) and discourse analysis (Wood and Kroger 2000) reject the positivistic

---

[4] For more on this topic see Tymoczko (2007, Chapter 4) and Tymoczko (2002).

understanding of scientific validity because they consider that asserting validity means nothing less than asserting truth. If valid results are those that match as closely as possible the real state of the world, then this is something that might be achieved within the realm of a natural, relatively stable world, but not in the realm of a dynamic, constantly changing social world:

> Propositions describing atoms and electrons have a long half-life, and the physical theorist can regard the processes in his world as steady. Rarely is a social or behavioural phenomenon isolated enough to have this steady-state property. Hence the explanations we live by will perhaps always remain partial, and distant from real events... and rather short lived. (Cronbach 1975:122-23, in Lincoln and Guba 1979/2000:32)

And even in the natural sciences, as Wood and Kroger (2000:166) point out, measures for selecting among competing versions of the world (e.g. measures of statistical significance such as $p < .05$) are often arbitrary and therefore disputable.

If we believe that reality is constructed, then we need to accept that there are multiple realities and that different theories, methods and modes of writing open up partial and necessarily political views on reality. This view has been criticized because of its relativism, which may appear to claim that any view is as valid as any other. However, Wood and Kroger (2000:166) argue that adopting this stance does not mean that there are no criteria for selecting among different versions, or that any version is as true as another; nor does it mean that relativists must remain politically neutral. According to Wood and Kroger, there are two sets of criteria to choose among versions: scientific and moral. They propose the notion of warrantability, which in terms of scientific criteria requires demonstrating that the analyses are sound, principled and well grounded on evidence, and thus credible and convincing (see discussion below). Moral criteria require researchers to consider how they are constructing versions of reality (through self-reflection and open acknowledgement of our personal and ideological background) and what the consequences of such constructions might be (see discussion of ethics below).

In the discussion of validity that follows we focus first on concepts such as reliability and sampling methods which are generally applicable to quantitative research, followed by credibility and warrantability as alternative parameters for research quality assessment in qualitative research (Section 2.10.4). The reader should note, however, that much of the discussion of validity in quantitative approaches is also relevant for qualitative approaches and vice versa. A clean dividing line is neither possible nor desirable.

Threats to validity have been allocated to three categories by Frey *et al* (1999): internal threats, external threats and threats regarding measurement (See Table 2.1 below). Internal threats to validity can come from the researcher him- or herself, from how the research is conducted, or from the research participants (if there are any). Two possible threats to internal validity can be posed by researchers. The first is the **researcher personal attribute effect**. It has been suggested that different researcher characteristics (e.g. race, gender) can influence participants' responses (*ibid.*). This is likely to occur under two conditions: when the research task is ambiguous, such that participants look to the researcher for information on how to perform; and when the research task is related to the personal characteristics of the researcher (e.g. colour, creed). While the latter can obviously occur in participant-based research, it can also occur in text-based research as researchers bring ideologies and expectations with them to the research process, sometimes without either realizing or acknowledging this fact. Indeed, no researcher is free from theory or ideology, and many commentators therefore do not see this as a 'threat' to validity but as an inevitable consequence of the nature of social research which has to be acknowledged and dealt with through **self-reflexivity** (e.g. Saukko 2003). We will discuss this concept in more detail in Section 2.10.4.

Internal threats	Threats posed by the researcher	Researcher personal attribute effect
		Researcher unintentional expectancy effect
	Threats posed by how the research is conducted	Procedures (validity and reliability)
		History
		Sensitization
		Data analysis
	Threats posed by research participants	The Hawthorne effect
		Statistical regression
		Mortality
		Maturation
		Intersubject bias
External threats	Related to ecological validity	
	Related to replication	
Threats regarding measurement	Sampling methods	
	Sample size	

Table 2.1 Threats to validity identified by Frey et al. (1999)

The second effect is known as the **researcher unintentional expectancy effect**. This occurs when researchers influence subjects' responses by unwittingly revealing the type of results they desire. This revelation can occur through the formulation of leading questions – for example, *Do you think this translation is* *bad?* See Chapter 5, Sections 5.3.2 and 5.7.3 for a more detailed discussion of the phrasing of questions to avoid such effects.

To control for both of these effects, the researcher can remove him or herself from the study and employ research assistants who are blind to the objectives of the research (of course this is rather unrealistic in humanities or social science research that is not always well funded). In experimental settings, an alternative, and more viable suggestion for participant-oriented research is to follow standard procedures so that everyone is exposed to the same research environment. A pre-task protocol can be written in advance and followed by the researcher so that all participants are given exactly the same task instructions. This level of control is, however, neither possible nor desirable in all types of research (cf. the discussion below about face and catalytic validity in qualitative research).

The second threat to internal validity identified by Frey *et al* is that which is posed by how the research is conducted. The factors contributing to this effect include the general validity and reliability of the procedures used, history, sensitization and data analysis. Reliability is discussed below in Section 2.10.2; the various types of validity are broken down for individual discussion in this section. The second factor, history, refers to all changes in the environment that are external to the study and which may influence the results. This is particularly important for longitudinal research. Of course, the researcher may be interested in analyzing the effects that such changes can bring to their research topic, but there may also be cases where changes due to time lapses are undesirable for the researcher, and such changes should be taken into account when research is conducted longitudinally. Case study research where the 'case' extends over long periods of time would be an example here – see Chapter 6.

When analyzing data, the analyst may be influenced by an initial measurement or procedure when carrying out a subsequent measure or procedure; this is known as **'sensitization'**. Krings, for example, reports that the evaluators in his study became more 'lenient' towards poor quality machine translation output as they progressed through the texts (Krings 2001:263). Sensitization can be avoided by implementing careful procedures for data analysis and evaluation. In addition, multiple evaluators or transcribers who are trained in the same way can be employed, and measures of inter-rater agreement (such as the Cohen/Fleiss Kappa score) can be implemented.[5]

Frey *et al* identify a number of threats to internal validity due to research participants: the Hawthorne effect, statistical regression, mortality, maturation, and intersubject bias. The **Hawthorne effect** occurs when people alter (usually improve) their normal behaviour because they are aware that they are being studied. In research which involves human participants, the threat of a change in behaviour is a very real one. One way to control for this is not to let people know that they are being studied. However, this raises serious ethical concerns, which are discussed in more detail below under 'Research Ethics'. Other ways to control for the Hawthorne effect are to ensure that the participant group is large

---

[5] See Fleiss *et al* (2003) and Chapter 4, Section 4.3.4.

enough to control for modified behaviour and to reimburse participants (this assumes that they will take the research task seriously, but it does not necessarily prevent them from altering their behaviour). Additionally, a post-task debriefing can prove to be very useful as sometimes participants will reveal alterations to 'normal' behaviour and the researcher can then consider removing their data from the analysis. To do so can be very disappointing for a researcher given the time and effort required to collect data and the scarcity of appropriate research participants in some cases. However, not to do so decreases the reliability of the research outcomes.

Statistical regression to the mean refers to the phenomenon where the second measurement of a non-random sample is closer to the mean for the population than the first measure (or vice versa). Although the word regression is used, implying a reduction of sorts, the change can be positive or negative. Regression to the mean is a frequently observed statistical tendency but it can lead to unfounded claims about causal relationships, which threaten the validity of research results. To further explain, it is probable that a non-random sample of students who have lower than average scores in a translation test would actually have scores closer to the mean on completion of a second test. This is the statistical phenomenon known as regression to the mean. It would be misguided for the researcher to link this change in scores with a causal effect arising from changes in the teaching method, for example. Regression to the mean is most likely to occur when the sample is non-random and the two variables being tested are not well correlated. These issues should be considered by the researcher in order to avoid making invalid claims about the sample and the effect of the treatment that sample has undergone.

Mortality refers not only to the loss of participants from the beginning to the end of a research cycle, but also to the loss or destruction of documents or data. The researcher obviously has no control over the first scenario, but has significant control over the second one! At the risk of stating the very obvious, a regular backing-up of data is necessary and a data security plan is to be recommended, for small and large projects alike.

Maturation refers to internal changes that occur within people (as opposed to the environment) over the course of time. The researcher cannot prevent this, but should at least be aware of it and consider its implications for the study being conducted. We discuss this further under the rubric of *desirable* changes in research participants ('emancipatory research') below. See also Chapter 5, Section 5.9, where the issue of intra-coder reliability is mentioned in relation to the analysis of qualitative data.

Intersubject bias occurs when those being studied influence each other. This is a risk when, for example, a group of people are brought to the same location at the same time to perform a task. To control for this, and when group interaction is not an integral part of the data collection method (as in the case of focus groups, see Chapter 5), research sessions can be conducted on an individual basis. If this is not feasible, alternative measures are possible, such as producing a briefing document specifically asking participants not to discuss the study with other participants or, if breaks are necessary during the task, staggering them so that participants are not tempted to discuss the research procedure with one another.

External threats can be related to ecological validity or replication. We discuss replication in Section 2.10.2. **Ecological validity** centres around the need to conduct research so that it reflects real-life situations. Frey *et al* put it as follows:

> Studying communication behaviour in natural settings increases the generalizability of research because communication processes may be thought of as streams of behavior, and like all streams, their course is shaped by the terrain through which they flow. If we ignore the banks and study only the stream or divert the stream into an artificial container and study it there, our knowledge of that stream is inevitably limited. (1999:136)

Ecological validity is most pressing when we claim to study people (e.g. professional translators or interpreters) or processes (e.g. the process of professional conference interpreting). If we want to study the process of conference interpreting as performed by professionals, conducting an experiment in a classroom with student interpreters would have very low ecological validity. Designing and executing studies that have high ecological validity can be challenging. For example, research on some aspect of conference interpreting would ideally need to be carried out in the interpreting booths at a conference to maximize ecological validity. Nonetheless, it is worthwhile to strive for ecological validity because this will add to the quality and credibility of the research. What should be avoided are claims regarding professionals or their behaviour when the study has not been carried out in an ecologically valid way.

Measurement validity refers to the techniques we use to acquire our research data and to the appropriateness of the scales we use to measure that data. It is obviously impossible to include all translators or all translated texts in a research project, and we are forced instead to select a sample of participants or texts for inclusion. To make sure that the selected sample enables the researcher to answer the research question, consideration must be given to the sampling technique. There are many ways of collecting samples in research, some of which are more reliable than others. **Random sampling** (also called **probability** sampling) is considered the 'gold standard' of sampling and refers to the ideal scenario where every member of the population being studied has an equal chance of being selected as a participant in the research project. This would be done by assigning a number to every member of the population and then using a random number generator (a device used to generate a sequence of random numbers) to select the participants for the study. Imagine, for a moment, that the 'population' we wish to study is a body of text, i.e. we want to compare airline marketing material written by native speakers of German with airline marketing material that has been translated into German. We are interested in investigating differences in linguistic features between the native-speaker produced text and the translated text. In theory, our population would be every airline marketing text that has been written by a native-speaker of German or translated into German at any point in time. Although compiling such a corpus would probably be impossible, let us assume for the purpose of illustration that we have managed to do this. We would then assign a number to each text and, because we cannot analyze every text, we would use a random number generator to select the texts to be included in our sample.

Systematic sampling is seen as a substitute for random sampling. It involves drawing a sample at fixed intervals from a list. So, from the example above, we might decide to select every tenth text in our population. **Stratified sampling** may be random or systematic, but also ensures that specific groups (or strata) within the population are represented. Using the example of airline marketing texts in German, some of these texts might appear on the World Wide Web, others in magazines, others in newspapers, etc. A stratified sample would ensure that texts from each group are included in the sample.

Cluster sampling is the term used when the natural sampling unit is a group or cluster of individual units. The sample might first involve members of the group and then individual members will be focused on during the research. **Stage sampling** involves taking a random sample from a large population or group, followed by a smaller sample from the same population or group, and is a good approach for very large studies. **Purposive sampling** involves selecting a sample based on pre-defined critical parameters. This technique is commonly used in corpus-based studies (see Chapter 3, Section 3.3.1) and in interview-based studies (see Chapter 5, Section 5.8.1). Selection of 'cases' in case study research could also be viewed as an example of this type of sampling (see Chapter 6, Section 6.4).

By far the most common types of sampling in humanities and social science research (often due to lack of resources), however, are the less rigorous **convenience** and **snowball sampling** methods. Convenience sampling is carried out by recruiting the research participants or selecting the texts (or other types of input to the research) that are most easily accessible. For example, convenience sampling might entail taking samples of text from Internet sites. The limitations of only using text published in one medium are obvious and, hopefully, the implications for validity are also obvious. Snowball sampling is also a convenience sampling method, but involves the recruitment of a group of participants who in turn recruit other participants.

In translation research, where recruitment of translators as research participants is quite popular, convenience sampling is common. Frequently, master's students or final year undergraduate students participate in studies where claims are then made about the products, processes, attitudes or behaviours of 'professional translators'. Some studies even use 'bilinguals' or 'language students' and purport to produce findings about 'translation'. This is the worst example of convenience sampling. While there is nothing wrong with doing research on bilinguals' ability to 'translate', for example, studies which do this should not make claims about professional translation behaviour because, quite simply, the sample would not conform to the general understanding of what a 'professional translator' is. This leads to a very important point: the **population** under investigation – whether animate (e.g. translators) or inanimate (e.g. text) – should be properly defined prior to sampling (see Chapter 3, Section 3.3.1 for a discussion of how populations can be defined in product-oriented research). Even a term such as 'professional translator' is very broad, and any study making claims about such a population would increase its credibility significantly by first operationalizing what is meant by a 'professional translator' (see Section 2.9). Obtaining an ideal sample is very difficult, if not impossible, but the goal of the researcher is to reduce bias and increase validity by using the most appropriate sampling methods under the circumstances.

The sampling method is not our only concern, though. The size of the sample is also an important consideration. Achieving a sufficiently large sample to justify claims is difficult in translation studies for numerous reasons. For example, there might simply not be enough of the required type of texts, comparable contexts, or equally qualified people to include in the research design. Or, even if a sufficient number exist, the researcher may not have the funding or the time required to include a large sample. Nonetheless, a lack of time or funding cannot be used as an excuse in every case. Small sample sizes can impose significant limitations on the generalizability of findings (see below) and researchers ought to take this into account when designing research projects in the first instance. We will revisit the topic of sampling throughout the various sections on data collection/elicitation in forthcoming chapters.

2.10.2 Reliability

Reliability refers to the extent to which other researchers (or the researcher herself) could generate the same results, or come to the same conclusion, if investigating the same question, using the same data and methods at a different time. This is also called **reproducibility** or **replicability**. However, as Matthews and Ross point out, "no sane social science researcher would expect exactly the same results, but [they] should be similar for similar groups of people" (2010:11). Even in quantitative approaches to research, replication is not easy (see, for example, Alves *et al's* (2011) attempt at replication of a translation process/eye tracking study). To increase reliability, the researcher should be able to convincingly demonstrate that the data collection and analysis methods used are dependable (for example, that the same method was used for all research participants) and that the methods are transparent and, consequently, the results are credible. By not discussing data collection and analysis methods in a transparent way, the researcher prevents other researchers from replicating or auditing the results, and so they cannot be tested and credibility is undermined. Note that transparency does not only refer to methods used, but also to 'theoretical transparency', i.e. making one's theoretical standpoint (and terminology) clear (Silverman 2006:282).

2.10.3   *Generalizability*

Research projects are necessarily limited in scope, yet they seek to investigate a greater social reality. In many (though not all) cases, the researcher will want to extrapolate from his or her findings, which are limited to a particular scenario, corpus of texts, group of people etc., to make claims about the larger population. Such extrapolation is called **generalization**. Reports on research findings can be considerably weakened by not taking into account the generalizability of results or by assuming generalizabilty, without carefully considering the validity of such an assumption. The extent to which generalizability can be claimed generally hinges on the sampling method selected and the size of the sample (discussed above). Let us assume that the results from our survey of student attitudes, mentioned above, lead to the conclusion that the cohort of students were generally unhappy about the particular teaching approach taken. Can the researcher reasonably claim that the same will be true for all translation students who are exposed to this teaching approach? This is highly unlikely, and so the researcher would have to acknowledge that the results are *not* generalizable to the global population of translation students. It is important to point out, however, that a lack of generalizability does not necessarily invalidate a research project, as we argue below.

Broadly speaking, we can distinguish three instances in which research that is not generalizable can, nevertheless, make contributions to knowledge beyond the particular: (1) in exploring questions of *how* and *why*, (2) for hypothesis generating (as opposed to hypothesis testing), and (3) for testing the viability of a theoretical framework. These three scenarios are described below.

The usefulness of exploring questions of *how* and *why* is related to the difference between **causal mechanisms** and **causal effects** (see Gerring 2007:43-44 and Koskinen 2010). Empirical research into causes tends to have two goals: (1) to establish whether X has a certain effect, Y, and the magnitude of such an effect; and (2) to establish how such effect is brought about, that is to say, the causal *mechanism*. The causal effect depends on whether Y is always the result of X. The larger the number of instances that show that X leads to Y, the more certain we can be of the magnitude of the impact, so we need to look at several instances of the same phenomenon. A good example of hypotheses predicting causal effects in translation studies are Toury's laws, such as the law of growing standardization and the law of interference (Toury 1995).

It is common in research into large populations that correlations between inputs (X) and outputs (Y) are demonstrated without clarifying the reasons for those correlations. This is where the detailed and rich perspective offered by qualitative research comes in useful; a case study, for example, allows the researcher to 'see' X and Y interact. In other words, it can show *how* the interaction takes place, sometimes by establishing chains of causation. It can also explore **agency**, i.e. "the *willingness* and *ability* to act" (Koskinen and Kinnunen 2010:6) in ways that are not necessarily predictable by the structures within which humans operate. For example, by looking at the production of translations in several literary systems under conditions of state censorship it may be possible to determine that censorship generally results in an overall more restricted field of literary production. However, only by having a look at a particular case in enough detail is it possible to establish which of the direct and indirect mechanisms of censorship are effective and to what extent, since they do not work in a completely predictive manner, as the work of Sturge (2004) demonstrates (see Chapter 6).

Questions of how and why are also worth answering when the situation itself is intrinsically interesting. The question of why the First World War occurred still fascinates historians and yet it is unlikely that an answer will help us understand why other wars are triggered, since the constellation of factors is unlikely to be repeated again. To bring this example closer to home, Baumgarten's (2009) analysis of Hitler's *Mein Kampf* and its English translations is intrinsically interesting as an extreme case of politically sensitive texts.

In other cases, exploring questions of how and why in relation to one particular situation can help us formulate hypotheses that may be useful in investigating other situations, which brings us to the second goal of small-scale qualitative research listed above: **generating hypotheses**. In qualitative research, the complex nature of the data as well as the lack of repeated patterns allows for the generation of a large number of hypotheses. Therefore, qualitative research can be used to stimulate the imagination towards acquiring new insights into general problems and suggesting theoretical solutions.

In this case the researcher may discuss the **transferability** of the findings, referring to the lessons learned which might provide rich learning experiences for those working in similar contexts (O'Leary 2010:43). When would a working hypothesis developed in Context A be applicable in Context B? The degree of transferability is a direct function of the similarity between the two contexts, what Lincoln and Guba call 'fittingness' (1979/2000:40). To make the judgement of transferability we need to know both contexts well.

It is also useful to examine elements unique to a particular case in that they enrich our repertoire of possible scenarios in relation to our object of study. In discussing case studies, Stake (1978/2000:22) argues that they are useful in providing

> full and thorough knowledge of the particular, recognizing it also in new and foreign contexts. That knowledge is a form of generalization too, not scientific induction but *naturalistic generalization*, arrived at by recognizing the similarities of objects and issues in and out of context and by sensing the natural covariations of happenings. (emphasis in original)

These generalizations are called naturalistic because they develop naturally within a person as a product of their experience. In a scientific context, they seldom take the form of predictions but lead regularly to expectation.

The third scenario where small-scale qualitative research can contribute to general knowledge is when it is used to test the viability of a recently proposed model, or to test the limits of more established ones. Hanna (2006), for example, uses Arabic translations of Shakespeare's great tragedies in order to see whether it is possible to apply the sociological model developed by Bourdieu to the field of drama translation. Yin calls this use of our knowledge *analytical generalization*:

> a previously developed theory is used as a template with which to com-
> pare the empirical results of a case study. If two or more cases are shown
> to support the same theory, replication can be claimed. The empirical
> results may be considered more potent if two or more cases support
> the same theory but do not support an equally plausible, *rival* theory.
> (2009:38-39)

In brief, it is important to consider how our research contributes to knowledge be-yond the particular. Reports on research findings can be considerably weakened by not taking into account either the generalizability or transferability of results or by assuming generalizabilty, without considering the validity of such an assumption.

2.10.4 *Qualitative methods, credibility and warrantability*

The importance of validity, reliability and generalizability is sometimes down-played by qualitative researchers but some feel that this also plays into the hands of quantitative critics (Silverman 2006) and risks lowering the standing of qualitative research. Without discussion of such issues, qualitative researchers can steer close to what is called 'anecdotalism' (*ibid.*:279). Qualitative research-ers have responded to such criticisms by reconceptualizing concepts such as 'validity', especially for qualitative research. Two such reconceptualizations are discussed here. First, we discuss credibility as understood by Lather (1986) and Silverman (2006), and then we discuss the notion of warrantability proposed by Wood and Kroger (2000).

Lather (1986) writes about reconceptualizing validity in 'openly ideological research' (some of her examples include research conducted in the domains of feminism and neo-Marxism). She is concerned with empirical research which advances emancipatory theory-building and empowers the researched.[6] In order to better establish data credibility in qualitative research, Lather (*ibid.*:78) offers a number of suggestions:

> At minimum, I argue that we must build the following into our research
> designs:
>
> – triangulation of *methods*, *data sources*, and *theories*
> – reflexive subjectivity (some documentation of how the researcher's as-
>   sumptions have been affected by the logic of the data)
> – face validity (established by recycling categories, emerging analysis,

---

[6] For a discussion of developing an empowering approach to research in sign language inter-preting, for example, see Turner and Harrington (2000:257), who express the view that their research should be 'on, for and with' all stakeholders.

and conclusions back through at least a subsample of participants)
- catalytic validity (some documentation that the research process has led to insight and, ideally, activism on the part of the respondents)

Note that Lather's concept of triangulation goes beyond the one we provided earlier, which was limited to triangulating results from different data sources. **Face validity** involves the concept of 'member checks', i.e. taking tentative results back to the researched community and refining them in light of the community's reaction, a practice which, Lather argues, needs to be more integral to the research process. See Monacelli (2000) for an example of research in interpreting that seeks to include the researched in an effort to corroborate findings and to establish catalytic validity by changing interpreters' behaviour. **Catalytic validity** is the one concept that is considerably different from more conventional notions of validity; it involves acknowledging the reality-changing impact of the research itself and channelling that impact back towards the researched in the hope of increasing self-understanding and self-determination. Note, though, that the notion of deliberately seeking to influence and change the 'researched' is in direct opposition to the more traditional recommendation of preventing threats to validity via researcher attributes (see section 2.10.1).

Silverman (2006), however, is not convinced of the value of either triangulation or face validity (which he calls **'respondent validation'**). Triangulation via different methods, he argues, can increase rigour, but due to the different situated character of the methods applied, this will not necessarily add up to a truer picture of the researched topic (*ibid.:*292). Face validity is problematic because participants are not always available or interested in validating results and also because the discourse produced by researchers can also be inaccessible to the researched. In his view, the more appropriate methods for validation of qualitative research include:

- a comparative case (finding other cases through which one can test provisional hypotheses, or starting with a small set of data, generating hypotheses and then confirming or falsifying hypotheses by gradually increasing the data set);
- deviant-case analysis (actively seeking out and addressing deviant cases – see below for more discussion);
- comprehensive data treatment (where all data are incorporated into the analysis and data are examined repeatedly);
- using appropriate tabulations (i.e. using simple counting techniques, which can generate hypotheses to be tested in a more detailed and qualitative way). Silverman makes the important point here that qualitative research does not have to be synonymous with innumeracy, a point we also stress in Chapter 5.

Despite the slight differences in suggestions for dealing with validity, Silverman and Lather agree on two core ideas. The first is the importance of **falsifiability**,

Karl Popper's notion that a theory or hypothesis can only be scientifically valid if it is falsifiable. To be falsifiable means that it is possible to *demonstrate* that a theory or hypothesis is false, if that were to be the case. One of the common examples used to illustrate the notion is the statement 'All swans are white'. This statement is falsifiable if just one black (or other coloured!) swan is shown to exist. Since black swans do exist in Australia, this demonstrates the importance of clearly delimiting the scope of a hypothesis. In the context of qualitative research credibility, we are expected to falsify, or refute, our theories and hypotheses and not just to verify them (Silverman 2007:280). Importantly, however, it has been pointed out that strict falsification may not be realistic (even for the hard sciences) and that interpretive hypotheses (see Section 2.5) are not falsifiable (see Chesterman 2008b for a more detailed discussion). Chalmers (1999) discusses the concept of falsification in depth and refers to 'sophisticated falsificationism' as opposed to 'naïve falsificationism'. The latter simply asks if a theory is falsifiable, whereas the more sophisticated approach is comparative and asks '[i]s this newly proposed theory a viable replacement for the one it challenges' (*ibid.*:74).

The second idea around which Silverman and Lather agree is the importance of engaging in, and demonstrating, self-reflexivity in research. Silverman offers two concrete suggestions for how to do this: one involves the use of a research diary or log and the second is to engage in reflexivity through team discussion (if a research team exists). The latter is perhaps a little problematic for translation studies researchers who come from a humanities background, where research teams are not so common, but discussions with colleagues or fellow research students, for example, might be a good substitute. If the research context permits, a move away from the standard model of a lone researcher towards research teams might prove to be advantageous to translation researchers.

As mentioned above, Wood and Kroger (2000), in the context of discourse analysis, propose warrantability as a way of evaluating research quality. **Warrantability** is co-constructed, between the researcher, the readers who evaluate the researcher, and even the participants who have access to the research and can, on occasions, be invited to comment on the results. An analysis is warrantable to the extent that it is both trustworthy and sound (*ibid.*:167). Below we summarize the requirements established by Wood and Kroger (2000) to achieve warrantability:

- Orderliness and documentation;
- Accountability: the study should be carried out and reported in such a way that an external auditor can examine and assess the processes;
- Demonstration: we should show how the argument is constructed, step by step, on the basis of the evidence, as opposed to telling about the argument and pointing to excerpts as illustrations;
- Patterns: the existence of patterns needs to be demonstrated by showing how the pattern fulfils a certain function that variations to the pattern could not, and by accounting for exceptions, in other words by

demonstrating that the analysis is exhaustive;
- Coherence: claims need to be demonstrated by discussing potential alternatives and counter claims and showing that the relationships established are logical despite the possibility of alternative readings;
- Plausibility: claims should make sense in relation to other knowledge, both implicit and explicit;
- Fruitfulness: our work should have implications for future work, to make sense of new situations and generate novel explanations.

2.11 Research ethics

The topic of 'ethics', as it pertains to the act and profession of translation, has enjoyed increasing attention over the last number of years. Indeed, Goodwin (2010:19) even argues that if we believe that the beginning of ethics is "the encounter with the Other" then "translation must represent an extraordinarily fertile ground for the development of thinking about ethics" (*ibid.*). Our aim here, however, is not to discuss how ethics pertain to the act of translating, the translator or the profession. This discussion has already commenced (cf., for example, Pym 2001, Chesterman 2001b, Inghilleri 2009a, Goodwin 2010, Baker 2011, especially Chapter 8, Pym 2012) and will no doubt be developed further (cf. Baker and Maier 2011). Although the issues may overlap, we will restrict our discussion here to ethical concerns in translation research.

Translation research involves research into human behaviour and society, as well as into language and text. It may involve, as its core focus, the translator, the interpreter, the author, the commissioner, the student, the publisher, the recipient, the culture, the politics, power and ideology of those cultures and so on. When we consider the broad nature of the discipline, it quickly becomes clear that people, as well as language and text, ideology and power are potential research topics and researchers ought to consider what impact their research will have. No matter what the core data source is, ethical issues should be given careful consideration. Many of the books or chapters dedicated to research ethics in the social sciences discuss the topic from the point of view of the human participant, and here we also discuss the inclusion of human participants in translation research. However, those who conduct translation research on language, style, corpora, texts, etc. are equally obliged to consider the impact of their choices and findings from an ethical viewpoint. When we talk about 'research participants' below, we are not only referring to those who participate directly in research projects (for example, by being interviewed or answering surveys) but also to the larger set of participants who are necessarily involved in the research by virtue of the choice of text to be analyzed, for example. Researchers themselves can also be seen as 'participants' in the research.

Tymoczko states that "[i]n any field researchers have an obligation to interrogate the ethical bias of their work; neither the natural sciences nor translation studies is exempt" (2007:143). All research is influenced by the values and ideology of the researcher, which drive topic selection and focus. Researchers ought to be aware of their own bias and should explicitly interrogate their own motivations. In her chapter on translation, interpreting and ethics, Baker (2011) argues for going beyond ethical concerns that are embedded in one moment or episode to 'virtue ethics' which span all domains of life. The translator and interpreter is encouraged to ask not only 'what should I do in these circumstances?' but also 'what kind of person should I be?', 'what kind of translator should I be'? Baker's discussion centres around translation and interpreting practices in general and does not focus on research. However, we might add here that the translation researcher could ask 'what kind of researcher should I be?'. Baker emphasizes that there is no easy answer to such questions and that no 'code of conduct' will provide all the answers to specific ethical dilemmas.[7]

The primary guiding principle for ethical research is to treat participants with respect. Of course this is a little vague since individuals and cultures have different expectations regarding respect. For that reason, more specific guidelines and illustrative examples are given below. First we consider the notion of ethics-in-context, that is to say, the need to take the context of the research into account and to consider the researcher's own bias, ideology and power. Then we discuss some of the more traditional concepts in research ethics, such as institutional approval, informed consent, non-deception and protection from harm. A special section is dedicated to how research ethics might apply in the context of Internet-mediated research and, finally, we discuss plagiarism.

2.11.1   Ethics in context

In this section we outline some arguments provided by scholars in favour of a stance that requires the researcher to consider the context in which the research is to take place. Silverman (2007) lists two crucial questions that researchers should ask themselves prior to conducting research: (1) Why am I researching this topic? and (2) Is my research going to help those I research? The first question forces researchers to interrogate their motivations; is the proposed research being undertaken primarily to enhance a career or reputation, or is it primarily seeking to benefit society or perhaps it aims to do both? The second question pertains to the impact on those who are researched, either directly or indirectly, and touches on the notion of 'emancipatory research' we mentioned above in Section 2.10.4 (Lather 1986). Does the research seek to help those who are being researched or is it simply using them as 'research fodder' (Silverman 2007:315)? Will it contribute, even partially, towards the solution of a problem, an imbalance, an unfairness? At the very least, does it protect those who are being researched and ensure that they are not worse off as a result of the research?

Matthews and Ross (2010:82) stress that researchers do not pay enough attention to cultural diversity, and this is particularly problematic for culture-specific notions of privacy and informed consent. In her discussion of ethical dilemmas

---

[7] For a more detailed discussion of different ethical stances, including relativism, universalism, utilitarianism, Kantian ethics, and their implications see Baker (2011), Chapter 8.

encountered while conducting research in vulnerable communities in South India, Riessman (2005) stresses that a researcher cannot assume ethical universalism, i.e. that institutional (read: Western) notions of ethics, informed consent and protection carry over to other cultures. Thus, Riessman argues for an ethics-in-context. She describes a situation where, when doing field work on infertile women in South India, a participant and her family mistakenly believed that the researcher would diagnose the problem and refer the participant to a hospital (*ibid.*). This demonstrates not only how the concept of informed consent does not carry over to all cultures (the participant read and signed the form, which had been translated into her own language and had been presented to her orally by a research assistant from her own culture), but also the level of power that is sometimes (mistakenly) attributed to the researcher by participants. Riessman (2005) provides another example where some of her participants were very reluctant to sign informed consent forms because the act of signing an official-looking document raised fear among potential participants, due to the negative associations they drew between official documents and repression.

2.11.2 Ethics approval

Different countries and institutions will have varying requirements regarding ethical approval for research, and the prospective researcher should therefore inform him or herself about these prior to commencing research. Thinking about ethical questions during or after the research is risky because it can be difficult to resolve ethical dilemmas retrospectively, sometimes with very serious consequences. Therefore, potential ethical issues should be given consideration during the research design phase. In most institutional settings, approval is often sought from a research ethics committee. Having to apply to a committee for ethics approval can add to the timescale of a research project and this needs to be borne in mind by the researcher.

2.11.3 Informed consent

Informed consent is one of the core principles in ethically-designed research. It is the responsibility of the researcher to ensure that participants fully understand what they are consenting to participate in. Usually, this involves presenting the participant with a form outlining information, in plain language, on the nature of the research and requesting them to sign and date the form. An informed consent form normally contains a few sentences describing the research and its main objectives. It states who is conducting the research and, in the case of a student, will also give the name and full contact details of the academic supervisor as well as information on the approving body (e.g. the university ethics committee). Any potential risks to the participant are then outlined and this is followed by the expected benefits to the participant. A statement is then provided to the effect that participation is voluntary and that the participant can withdraw at any point in the study, without any repercussions whatsoever. The participants may be asked to tick boxes confirming that they have read the statement, understand the information provided, have been given an opportunity to ask questions, are aware that they will be audio- or video-recorded, etc.

An important part of the form is the section which details how the data will be managed: whether it will be **anonymized**, how this will be guaranteed, where the data will be stored and how it will be protected, who will have access to it and how long will it be kept on record. The data management requirements depend on country-specific legislation concerning data protection. Researchers should familiarize themselves with the requirements of the country in which the research is being conducted. The use of video recording (and possibly also audio recording) clearly raises special issues regarding the anonymization of data; researchers need to be aware of these and to discuss the implications of recordings for anonymization with each participant. Note also that official requirements and cultural expectations may differ; for some cultures not being named as a participant might be insulting, since being named is a sign of honour and respect (Silverman 2007:320). The original form should be kept on file by the researcher, and it is good practice to give the participant a copy of the signed form.

Simply seeking and recording informed consent is, however, not always sufficient. Indeed, some commentators on ethics and research, especially those who conduct ethnographic research among vulnerable populations, bemoan the fact that ethical approval is reduced to a once-off rubber-stamping by an institutional committee and argue in favour of consent as an ongoing negotiation with the participants (Riessman 2005). Ongoing negotiation ties in, to some extent, with the notion of face and catalytic validity, discussed above.

An ethical researcher should consider the capacity of the participants to understand the research proposal and the potential effects on them. For research involving children and adolescents, it is normally the case that informed consent is given by proxy through legal guardians, the assumption being that such guardians can judge what impact participation in the research might have on the minor. Can the researcher be sure that the guardian has made the correct judgement on behalf of a minor? Even when the proposed participant is not a minor and is thought to be *compos mentis*, the researcher needs to consider whether or not the participant can fully understand the objectives of the research and the possible impacts. Silverman (2007) suggests that participants are not always in a position to even imagine potential impacts before participating in research. When being interviewed, for example, participants do not know what answer they will provide in response to questions, especially when they are unaware of what questions will be posed in advance of an interview. In focus groups (cf. Chapter 5), a participant cannot anticipate the contributions of other participants and how she or he might react to them. Therefore, it is sometimes necessary to seek informed consent from participants on more than one occasion, as data emerge and are being analyzed.

2.11.4 Deception

In the past, some level of deception regarding the focus of a research project was acceptable, but more recently this has come to be seen as unacceptable if the participant is likely to object or show discomfort once he or she has been debriefed (Langdridge and Hagger-Johnson 2009:502). By deception we mean that the participants are informed that the research is about one topic, when in fact it is about a different, or related topic. Deception is a tempting way of ensuring that participants do not alter their behaviour once they know what aspect is being studied. Langdridge and Hagger-Johnson emphasize that a distinction can be drawn between providing deliberately false information and withholding some details of the study, the latter being considered more acceptable but only if it can be justified on strong scientific grounds. They also recommend that if deception is used the participant must be debriefed prior to exiting the research location; this debriefing must be interactive (not just a leaflet to read on the way home) and the participant should be given ample opportunity to ask questions about the real research objectives.

Related to deception is the practice of using observational techniques without informed consent. Again, this practice does not generally meet with approval. The guiding principle here is that if no consent has been given, observation can only be carried out in situations where people might normally expect to be observed. As with individual expectations regarding respect, individual expectations of when it is appropriate to be observed will vary. If you are walking down the main street of a town, is it ethical for somebody else to observe your behaviour for research purposes without first seeking your consent? To give a more domain-specific example, would it be ethical to observe, analyze and report on court interpreters' behaviour in a public court without getting consent from those interpreters? Again the guiding principle of treating others with the respect you would like to receive yourself is relevant, but different levels of tolerance should also be taken into consideration.

2.11.5 Power relations

As mentioned above, participation in a research study should be voluntary and withdrawal without question should be guaranteed. However, as with all aspects of life, power relations can interfere with these aspirations. It is important for the researcher to be aware of such power relations and the impact they might have on participants. For example, if you are a lecturer and are seeking to recruit participants from among your own student body, a power relation already exists; students might feel that you would see them in a better light if they 'volunteer' for your study (even if you state that the study is completely separate from their courses). Age can come into play here too, as in the case of senior researchers and junior participants (or vice versa). Cultural differences can also play a role, especially if the participant comes from a culture where there is a high power distance value and the researcher comes from a low power-distance culture (cf. Hofstede *et al* 2010).

A less obvious ethical issue arises from the (accidental) exclusion of groups from a study. Exclusion may occur within categories such as ethnic group, race, gender, age etc. and may be caused by a lack of 'visibility' of specific groups in the population being studied. Exclusion might also occur due to the sampling method employed (see above for more discussion on sampling) or to the methods selected. For example, investigating translators' attitudes to online termbases by using only online data collection methods could exclude those who deliberately avoid technology, but opinions of the latter group might nonetheless be illuminating. The language used in the research design might also contribute to an exclusion effect since those who do not speak the language, or who are less competent in its use, will either select not to participate or will automatically be excluded. Researchers who are also translation scholars are generally highly sensitized to issues of language, meaning and mediation and, therefore, consideration of these issues will most likely come about by default.

2.11.6   *Protection from harm*

Protection from harm is another guiding principle for ethically-designed research. Again, when considering translation research the first reaction to this concept might be that it is irrelevant. After all, we are not dealing with experimental drugs! However, there are scenarios in translation research where the principle of doing no physical or psychological harm to your participant is relevant. Take the example of assessing the quality of translation produced by individual translators in a translation agency. If the participants themselves have access to the results that pertain to them, how might this affect them? What if their employer also gained access to the results and used them to demote or dismiss the employee?

Generally speaking (and this is only common sense), research should only be undertaken in locations where no physical harm can come to the participant. Additionally, researchers ought to consider the potential psychological impact their research could have on the participant. What should a researcher do if the participant discloses some personal and troubling information about, for example, harassment or bullying at work, during an interview? It is unlikely that translation researchers would have the training necessary to deal with such disclosures, but can the researcher ignore the disclosure and carry on as if nothing had been said? Such occurrences are (hopefully) rare, but they are nonetheless possible, so it is useful for researchers to give some thought to protecting participants (and themselves) from harm and to dealing with difficult situations, should they arise. One cannot anticipate every risk that might arise, but some suggestions for dealing with such difficult situations is for the researcher to have a list of helplines for dealing with specific traumas and to follow up with the participant shortly after the research event to confirm that they are alright. These measures might seem inadequate for dealing with serious trauma revealed by participants, but having some measures in place is preferable to having none at all.

Protection from harm applies equally to the researcher, and Riessman (2005) comments on how this requirement is mostly ignored. The researcher has an equal right to a physically safe environment in which to conduct research. What is perhaps less easy to guarantee is the emotional and mental protection of the researcher. Being exposed to a traumatic experience revealed by a participant can result in a negative emotional impact on the researcher, especially if the revelation is unexpected and the researcher is unprepared for it. The emotional strain caused by interpreting in difficult circumstances, for example in the courts or in mental health settings, has been documented to some extent (e.g. Doherty *et al* 2010; Napier et al 2006) and conducting research in such contexts can also have an impact on the researcher. However, emotional and mental stress is not restricted to participant-related research; the textual material the researcher reads may also present similar difficulties.

2.11.7 *Internet-mediated research*

Internet-mediated research is "research conducted on the Internet"; it refers to all stages of research but the term is more frequently used in connection with specific online data collection methods (Langdridge and Hagger Johnson 2009:137). Internet-mediated research is on the increase, and the ethical dilemmas posed by this type of research are perhaps even more complex than more traditional approaches. The two main questions that arise are (1) are participants aware that they are being studied? and (2) are they identifiable? (*ibid.*). Four different categories of participant are outlined by Langdridge and Hagger Johnson (*ibid.*), each of which presents different levels of ethical dilemma. Participants may be:

- Recruited and Identifiable
- Unaware and Identifiable
- Recruited and Anonymous
- Unaware and Anonymous

The category of 'Unaware and Identifiable' is obviously the most problematic from an ethical viewpoint. Is it justifiable to use data posted by people in public online discussions without their knowledge? Just because they have written something in a 'public' forum, does that give you permission to use it for other purposes? And what is 'public' anyway? If you have to become a member and sign in to an online forum, is that still public? If you quote a person's words directly in your research, so that they can be located via a search engine and identified, is that ethically sound? These are some of the difficult questions raised by Langdridge and Hagger Johnson (*ibid.*). The category of 'Recruited and Anonymous' is, according to them, the most ethically straightforward because such participants are aware that their behaviour is being studied and, in theory, their anonymity is protected. This last point, however, requires clarification since it is impossible to guarantee absolute confidentially of any data that have been transferred electronically, and it is recommended that, along with the information that is usually provided in consent forms, a statement be given to this effect (*ibid.*). Also on the topic of online informed consent forms, the adequacy of one 'I Consent' or 'I Agree' button is questionable. How can we be certain that the participant has actually read the information? While it is impossible to know this for certain, one recommendation is to break the consent down into specific and separate statements and to 'force' participants to agree to each one in turn (by not allowing them to continue to the next online page, for instance). For example,

- I have read the general description and understand the objectives of this study: Yes/No
- I understand that the data will be anonymized and stored securely for a duration of three years from commencement of the study: Yes/No
- I understand that I can withdraw from this study at any time and without any repercussions: Yes/No
- and so on...

We will return to the concept of Internet-mediated research in Chapter 5 in the context of participant-oriented research.

2.11.8 Plagiarism

We cannot discuss the concept of ethical research without discussing techniques for avoiding plagiarism, which is probably one of the most common ethical problems in research, especially among novice researchers. Plagiarism is the use of somebody else's work as if it were your own. However, it is much more than taking a published author's words (or pictures) and using them in your own work without giving an appropriate reference. Plagiarism also includes the use of the ideas of other people (such as a fellow colleague or student) and even the re-use of one's own work, without acknowledgement.

Plagiarism can be avoided by adhering to strict referencing procedures and acknowledging other people's contributions where appropriate. All notes taken while reading literature ought to be recorded fully, including author, title, publisher and page number so that if the work in question is later unavailable, the information required for a full reference is still available to the researcher. It is sometimes tempting to cut corners when reading literature by, for example, not noting exact page numbers or whether the note is a direct word-for-word copy or a paraphrase. However, this can result in 'accidental' plagiarism at a later stage or can require back-tracking, so it is frequently not worth the time saved initially. Electronic referencing systems exist which can help with the online recording of bibliographic details, but one does not necessarily have to use such a system; details can be recorded in a word processor or spreadsheet or simply on paper. No matter which 'system' is used, the important point is that full information should be recorded when taking notes and that information should be provided when writing up reports.

Coming to an understanding of what level of source referencing is required, appropriate and, indeed, ethical can take time for a novice researcher. One recommendation for learning what is appropriate is to read peer-reviewed journal articles in the domain. This will give the researcher a flavour of how referencing should be done. Getting the balance right between under-referencing and over-referencing is difficult, but comes with time. If in doubt, the reference should always be given, as accusations (and proof) of plagiarism can have very serious consequences. It should also be kept in mind that different cultures understand and treat plagiarism in different ways. Researchers should ensure that they are familiar with the rules and guidelines regarding referencing in the institution and country in which they are carrying out the research.

To conclude on ethics, we should also note that ethical citing involves much more than avoiding plagiarism. There are many ways in which a researcher might behave unethically with regard to citing, by, for example, citing papers that have not actually been read first-hand, citing only references that are favourable to the researcher's own position, omitting to cite references that contradict the researcher's findings, or citing results without commenting on the replicability or credibility of the research by which such results were achieved.

2.12   Summary

The aim of this chapter was to introduce and explore some of the core principles of doing research. Where possible, we provided examples from translation studies in order to clarify concepts. Throughout the chapter we have tried to emphasize the importance of reflecting on one's approach to research, commencing with an examination of our own epistemological position, moving on to discussions about formulation and operationalization of research questions and appropriate methods for investigating them. We ended with a discussion of research ethics, which should ideally underpin all research activity. We will build on many of the concepts introduced here in the following chapters; however, as it was not practical to discuss all the concepts and ideas in full here, further reading of the works mentioned throughout is also encouraged.

Chapter 3. Product-oriented research

3.1 Introduction

This chapter discusses methodological approaches to researching the textual product that is the outcome of the translation or interpreting process.[1] As we pointed out in the introduction, whether a piece of research is process-, product- or context-oriented is not determined by the methodology itself or even the source of data, but the ultimate aims of the researcher. Broadly speaking, research on translated texts can be carried out with a descriptive/explanatory or an evaluative purpose in mind. These two types of research have generally relied on rather different methodological approaches, even when they occasionally share the use of the same resources, as in the case of corpora. Therefore, we discuss them in different sections. Sections 3.2 to 3.5 discuss the use of critical discourse analysis (CDA) and corpus linguistics (CL) for descriptive/ explanatory research. The evaluation of the translated product is then dealt with in Section 3.6, where the focus is on translation quality assessment and the challenges of conducting research that involves assessment of the quality of the translated product.

It has been suggested that by observing the products of translation it is possible to make inferences about the process as well (Bell 1991). This is the assumption underlying the work of Bowker and Bennison (2003) and Alves and Vale (2011), and is in line with a more general movement towards the integration of process- and product-oriented research (Alves *et al* 2010, see Chapter 4). The analysis of texts in their context of production and reception offers evidence of translators' decision making, which allows some insight into the translation process. This is particularly true of discourse analytical approaches where the focus is not only on texts as products but on the "process of meaning negotiation", which involves using language to engage our extralinguistic reality (Widdowson 2004:8). Halverson (2009:95) suggests that there is a problem of validity in using corpora to make inferences about the cognitive process of translation, because corpora do not provide immediate evidence of underlying cognitive structures. As pointed out in Chapter 4, Section 4.2, no research method can give *direct* access to cognitive processes, and this is a problem shared by all the disciplines interested in cognitive processes, such as cognitive psychology and psycholinguistics.

3.2 A descriptive/explanatory approach to the analysis of language

This section introduces the use of CDA and CL in translation studies. It is important to note that while the examples used throughout this chapter are of research on

---

[1] The terms 'translated text' and 'translations' are used here to refer to both translator- and interpreter-mediated texts.

translated and interpreted texts, CDA and CL can be adopted to investigate texts other than translations, such as translators' prefaces, transcribed interviews, reviews of translations, and so on. A corpus of paratexts could be used as part of a case study focusing on the context of translation, or we could use CDA to examine data obtained in a participant-oriented study based on interviews.

While texts can be a source of data in a variety of research projects, linguistic evidence is used differently in each of them. Baxter (2010) draws a useful distinction between analyzing text as a means to an end and analyzing it as an end in itself. Language – in the form of interviews, focus group discussions or questionnaires, for example – is one of the many sources of evidence used by researchers in a wide range of disciplines, such as sociology, psychology, education, cultural studies and media studies, to mention just a few. As Baxter explains, non-linguists often view "discourse as data" (i.e. as a means to an end) under the assumption that it provides "a transparent medium to external reality, or as a direct index of subjects' feelings and meanings" (*ibid.*:118). From the perspective of CDA, on the other hand, language is never seen as a neutral conduit of information about the real world it encodes: any account of experience is a form of interpretation. Wood and Kroger (2000:8) make a similar distinction between 'talk as resource' and 'talk as topic':

> The emphasis on discourse as action and as constitutive of phenomena entails a shift from the usual focus of interest in the phenomena to which the discourse refers to a focus on the discourse itself. .... [A] shift from using features of talk to explain behaviour (talk as resource) to a focus on the features of talk as the behaviour to be explained (talk as topic).

The view of language as a transparent way of encoding reality is typical of the realist ontology described in Chapter 2. Different critical discourse-analytic approaches adopt different ontological and epistemological perspectives. Overall, however, they are generally closer to the constructivist and interpretivist end of the scale. We will go into more detail about the positions adopted by discourse analysts later on. First we need to define 'discourse'.

3.2.1 Critical discourse analysis

In this section we focus on methodological aspects of CDA and, in particular, on Fairclough's (2003, 2010) approach to CDA. CDA is not in itself a methodology but an umbrella term used to refer to a series of theories and practices that share certain principles (see below) in terms of their approach to language study, a 'school' in Wodak and Meyer's words (2009:5). In fact, discourse analysis (DA) – the broader approach to the study of discourse of which CDA is a variety – is used within a range of disciplines outside linguistics. In this section we highlight the main principles of CDA and what distinguishes it from discourse analysis in general. We do this by focusing, in turn, on the terms 'discourse', 'critical' and 'analysis'. In linguistics, in its most basic and traditional sense, 'discourse' refers to language 'above the sentence'. This means that words, clauses, phrases, or sentences are never considered in isolation, unless they constitute texts in themselves. DA (including CDA) differs from other branches of linguistics in that it focuses on whole texts. Text is understood very broadly as "every type of communicative utterance" (Titscher *et al* 2000:20), and can include anything from a one-word warning sign, a shopping list, a newspaper article, to the transcript of a conversation or a television programme, to give just a few examples. Note that the inclusion of events such as a television programme within the category of text makes text a semiotic rather than a linguistic category, since television programmes involve not only language but also visual images and sound effects.[2] Returning to primarily language data, some theorists require stretches of language to meet certain criteria before they can be called texts. In their seminal book, De Beaugrande and Dressler (1981), for example, argued that texts had to meet what they call the seven standards of textuality: cohesion, coherence, intentionality, acceptability, informativity, situationality and intertextuality.

Widdowson (2004:8) distinguishes text and discourse as follows: "Discourse is the pragmatic process of meaning negotiation. Text is its product". This understanding of discourse as 'language in use' distinguishes DA from other branches of linguistics that rely on intuitive, introspective linguistic judgements based on invented, isolated sentences, or the kind of decontextualized statements used in measurement scales in questionnaires and surveys. The assumption in DA is that language needs to be studied using naturally occurring texts and taking into account the context of production and reception.

The relationship between language and context can be observed from the two vantage points of text and context. We can examine how the context has influenced the choices made in a given text: Wadensjö (1999), for example, compares two interpreter-mediated events involving the same participants and the same case, one conducted by telephone and the other on-site, in order to investigate how social interaction is influenced by those two distinct settings. Alternatively, taking the text as a point of departure, we can use DA or CDA to find out what the text tells us about the context. Pöllabauer (2004) analyzes asylum interviews in order to identify specific factors influencing the speakers' behaviour, focusing on role conflicts, discrepant role expectations, asymmetrical power constellations and the validity of existing (traditional) norm systems.

Critical discourse analysis goes a step further than DA in its understanding of discourse as language in context. CDA sees discourse as social practice, "as an element of social life which is closely interconnected with other elements" (Fairclough 2003:3) and as "historically produced and interpreted" (Wodak 2001:3). This relational aspect of discourse means that the object of CDA is not the discourse *per se* but the "dialectical *relations between* discourse and other objects, elements or moments, as well as analysis of the 'internal relations' of discourse" (Fairclough 2010:4, emphasis in original). In other words, while text analysis is

---

[2] Semiosis includes all forms of meaning making, visual images, body languages, verbal languages (Fairclough 2003:3).

an essential part of CDA, the focus is not only on the relationship between text and context, but also between text and what Fairclough, following Foucault, calls the 'order of discourse', i.e. "the relatively durable social structuring of language which is itself one element of the relatively durable structuring and networking of social practices" (2003:3).

This brings us to a third and wider sense in which the term 'discourse' is used within post-structuralist and critical theory to mean "social and ideological practices which can govern the way in which people think, speak, interact, write and behave" (Baxter 2010:120). This understanding of discourse revolves around the idea that there is more than one way of constructing an object, event, person, etc., and these different ways of constructing reality are reflected in the different discourses used to represent them (discourse in this sense becomes a countable noun).

We mentioned above that critical discourse analysts adopt different ontological and epistemological perspectives but to some degree all reject an objectivist and positivistic stance. Baxter, for example, adopts a post-structuralist perspective, which assumes that different analysts will produce different accounts of the same event and therefore need "to be constantly self-reflective about the constitutive power of their linguistic data" (*ibid.*:119). Fairclough, on the other hand, adopts a critical realist approach, which entails "a recognition that the natural and social worlds differ in that the latter but not the former depends upon human action for its existence and is 'socially constructed'" (2010:4). While the social constructive effects of discourse are a central concern for Fairclough, he makes a distinction between 'construal' and 'construction', and this distinction is at the basis of the 'critical' element in 'critical discourse analysis':

> the world is discursively constructed (or represented) in many various ways, but which construals are to have socially constructive effects depends upon a range of conditions which include for instance power relations but also properties of whatever parts or aspects of the world are being constructed. We cannot transform the world in any old way we happen to construe it; the world is such that some transformations are possible and others are not. So CDA is a 'moderate' or 'contingent' form of social constructivism. (Fairclough 2010:4-5)

The 'critical' aspect of CDA refers not only to the critical epistemological perspective mentioned above (whether in its poststructuralist or critical realist variation) but also to a committed agenda to reveal how discourses produce and reproduce unequal power relations within society. This is another crucial element that distinguishes CDA from DA. The former "aims to investigate critically social inequality as it is expressed, signalled, constituted, legitimized and so on by language use (or in discourse)" (Wodak 2001:2). In particular, it attempts to show how the binaries that underpin language and culture tend to render one side as normal and the other as invisible and un-natural, thus creating social inequalities. Wodak sums up the ways in which discourse analysis can be critical as follows: "'critical' is to be understood as having distance to the data, embedding the data in the social, taking a political stance explicitly, and a focus on self-refection as scholars doing research" (Wodak 2001:9).[3]

We have outlined above the principles of CDA as a theoretical approach to language by describing the specific meaning of the terms 'discourse' as adopted within DA and CDA and by discussing the meaning of the term 'critical' in relation to CDA. We also need to say something about the nature of the 'analysis' in DA and CDA. Again, we find that there is some shared ground. Wood and Kroger (2000:95) describe the goal of DA as follows:

> to explain what is being done in the discourse and how this is accom- plished, that is, how the discourse is structured or organized to perform various functions and achieve various effects or consequences. It re- quires the systematic identification and interpretation of patterns in the discourse, that is, of systematic variability or similarity in content and structure, and the formation and checking of claims (conventionally, hypotheses) about functions and effects through a search for evidence in the discourse.

The purpose of any communication will determine its structure. DA (including CDA) involves finding out how texts are used to perform certain functions. This is done by identifying patterns (i.e. systematic variability or similarity), and propos- ing and checking claims through a search for further evidence. The identification of patterns is often facilitated by resorting to a set of analytical concepts (Wood and Kroger 2000:99). The analytical concepts can suggest what to look for and may belong to a wide variety of levels; they may relate to content (e.g. use of key words, or words within one semantic field), linguistic features (e.g. intensi- fiers), structure (e.g. turn taking in conversation) or discursive functions (e.g. constructing a motive). CDA has relied extensively on a set of analytical concepts derived from Halliday's systemic functional grammar as well as on pragmatics. Munday (2007:197) borrows the term 'linguistic toolkit' from critical linguistics to refer to these concepts, and we do the same here. In Section 3.4.1 we provide examples of some of those analytical concepts and how they have been used in translation studies.

Wodak goes as far as claiming that "an understanding of the basic claims of Halliday's grammar and his approach to linguistic analysis is essential for a proper understanding of CDA" (2001:8). Such a claim is, in our view, debatable. A linguistic toolkit is indeed extremely useful because it enables an analysis that goes beyond the surface of texts, by unveiling patterns that are not immediately obvious when considering exclusively surface forms. When the analysis lacks

---

[3] One criticism of CDA that is not discussed here because it is not particularly relevant to methodological issues is that there is nothing new in this critical perspective, which is part of a broad historical tradition of thought (Stubbs 1997:9) that has been revived within a new critical paradigm observable in a range of fields (Blommaert and Bulcaen 2000:456). CDA is also criticized for failing to acknowledge this tradition (Stubbs 1997) and, despite its insistence on interdisciplinarity, failing to engage with insights from other fields of socio-theoretical enquiry (Blommaert and Bulcaen 2000:456).

a linguistic framework, it risks restating the discourse, paraphrasing the literal meaning of texts, which can lead to uninteresting claims or claims that are not supported by evidence. However, an in-depth knowledge of systemic-functional grammar or pragmatics is not a prerequisite for carrying out CDA. Analysis can rely on a close and critical reading of texts without the need for mapping linguistic functions. Maltby (2010), for example, presents an insightful analysis of how documents describing interpreting policy use notions such as 'neutrality' and 'impartiality'. He shows how the resulting representation of the role of interpreters is ideologically shaped by the institutional objectives, and does so successfully without resorting to a linguistic framework.

While DA and CDA share some basic tenets in terms of their approach to textual analysis, as is to be expected, the critical stance and the particular understanding of the term 'discourse' within CDA have implications for the way in which the analysis is conducted. First, the politically committed agenda of CDA results in a narrower scope in terms of the object of investigation, which focuses on social problems. Secondly, the understanding of discourse as social and ideological practices means that CDA goes beyond DA in terms of attempting to account for the links between a text and the social structure in which it is embedded, requiring the analyst to consider how discourses reflect and constitute different ways of seeing the world. While DA can be socially conscious – as in Wadensjo's (1999) analysis of interpreted discourse mentioned above – CDA goes a step further and "aims at revealing structures of power and unmasking ideologies" (Wodak and Meyer 2009:8). In fact, CDA not only investigates social problems but also aims to have an effect on social practice: "It aims to produce and convey critical knowledge that enables human beings to emancipate themselves from forms of domination through self-reflection" (*ibid.*:7). In other words: it aims "not just to interpret the world but to change the world" (Stubbs 1997/2002:203).

In translation studies, the work of Hatim and Mason (1990, 1997) laid the foundations for the use of CDA. Since then, CDA has been used extensively to explore issues of ideology in the translation of a wide variety of written genres, such as parliamentary speeches (Calzada Pérez 2007), news (Kang 2007; Kuo and Nakamura 2005) and fiction (Munday 2008). It has also been used in interpreting research (Mason 2005, 2006, 2009c; Wadensjö 1998, 2000).

We mentioned above that texts, from the perspective of CDA, are not linguistic but semiotic units. Attention to semiotic devices other than the linguistic ones (see Kress and van Leeuwen 1996, 2001) is another distinguishing feature of current work within CDA which has also been reflected in translation studies in a range of work that focuses on multimodal aspects of translation in areas such as advertising (Millán-Varela 2004; Munday 2004), audiovisual media (Taylor 2003, Valdeón 2005), and simultaneous interpreting (Zagar Galvão and Galhano Rodrigues 2010).

3.2.2 Corpus linguistics

A corpus is "a large collection of authentic texts that have been gathered in electronic form according to a specific set of criteria" (Bowker and Pearson 2002:9).

Corpora have been put to many different uses in fields as varied as natural language processing, CDA and applied linguistics, and could therefore be considered simply as a resource in linguistics. However, within neo-Firthian traditions of text analysis that see linguistics as a social science and language as a means of social interaction, CL is considered a research paradigm in its own right (Tognini-Bonnelli 2001; Laviosa, 2002), on the basis that doing research using corpora generally entails some basic assumptions as to what the object of enquiry is and how it should be studied. Many of these assumptions are shared with CDA: the requirement to use whole texts as a unit of investigation, the emphasis on meaning as inextricably linked to the function of texts and their cultural and historical context, and the focus on naturally-occurring language (Saldanha 2009a, 2009b). On the basis of these shared principles, CDA and CL can be seen as compatible methodologies which can either complement each other, for example as a means to triangulate results, or be combined in one methodology, i.e. using corpora to do CDA (see Conrad 2002; Partington 2004; Baker 2006; Baker *et al* 2008; Mautner 2009). This is how CL and CDA are viewed in this chapter; it should be noted, however, that discourse analysts have tended to use qualitative techniques and analyze texts manually, and some scholars (see, for example, Wood and Kroger 2000:27) see the use of CL, with its reliance on frequency counts and categories, as being incompatible with the interpretivist epistemology of CDA. While this criticism is worth bearing in mind, we feel that the use of CL presents certain advantages as compared to the manual analysis of texts which are particularly useful for CDA, as we explain in Section 3.2.3.

The initial focus of CL was to describe language performance as opposed to language competence by providing quantitative information on the distribution of linguistic features in particular genres or for different functions. In other words, CL was used to answer variations of one over-arching question: "How do people *really* use language?" (Kennedy 1998:88). In translation studies, this focus is evident in the first wave of studies that used corpora and aimed to describe how translations differed from non-translated texts; these were largely limited to the study of recurrent features of translations. Research along these lines has been particularly fruitful (see overviews in Laviosa 2002, 2011 and Olohan 2004; and the edited collection by Mauranen and Kujamäki 2004).

More recently, CL has been applied to research questions that respond to discursive reflections of social issues rather than originating from concerns with linguistic structure *per se* (Mautner 2009:33). This has resulted in CL being used for a much broader array of research purposes in translation studies, such as studies focusing on ideology (Baumgarten 2009, Munday 2008), style (Saldanha 2011a, 2011b, 2011c; Winters 2007, 2009; Ji 2012; Ji and Oakes 2012), translation technology (Flanagan and Kenny 2007); and in applied translation research (Zanettin *et al* 2003).

It is this new concern with the social embedding of texts that brought CL closer to DA. Conrad (2002:76) identifies four approaches within CL that are especially applicable to DA. The first approach involves studies of language features and investigates the associations triggered by the use of such features. An example from translation studies is Valdeón (2007), who uses CDA to examine the implications of the English terms 'separatist' and 'terrorist' and their Spanish counterparts, 'separatista' and 'terrorista', in a corpus of media texts.

The second approach involves examining the realizations of a particular function of language. Corpus tools can help us keep track of the different variables, at different levels, that influence the realization of such function in different texts, such as formality of register, genre, writer/speaker's gender, to mention just a few. An example is provided by Munday (2012), who looks at the evaluative function of language, i.e. how a translator's subjective stance manifests itself linguistically in a text.

The third use of corpora which is particularly applicable for discourse analytical purposes is that of characterizing a variety of language. An example of this use of corpora in translation studies can be found in Bernardini *et al* (2010), who look at the most salient differences between institutional English on the websites of British/Irish vs. Italian universities so as to provide resources for Italian authors and translators working in this area.

The fourth approach involves mapping the occurrence of language features across a text, for example, to see how they contribute to rhetorical organization, or tracking the terms that writers use to refer to themselves and their audience. Mason and Şerban (2003), for example, investigate the use of deixis in a corpus of translations from Romanian literature into English. Their study shows how systematic shifts as well as single occurrences result in a distancing effect (proximals tend to become distals), with the result that "readers are presented with a translation which elicits less involvement on their part than the original text did in its context" (*ibid.*:269).

3.2.3 Strength and weaknesses of critical discourse analysis and corpus linguistics

One of the key differences between CL and DA is their individual potential to provide answers that can be generalized beyond the texts under study. In CDA, texts are chosen because of their intrinsic significance or because they are considered to be typical of a certain discourse. The claim that a text is 'significant' or 'typical' needs to be carefully justified but, ultimately, it is always subjective. Subjectivity, not only in the selection but also in the interpretation of texts, underlies three perceived problems in CDA: the risk of a circular argument, the impossibility of replicating the results, and the assumption of privileged knowledge on the part of the researcher (Mason 2006:107).[4]

The criticism of non-replicability is made in relation to most qualitative research and is, to some extent, a concession that needs to be made in the interests

---

[4] Mason (2006) also lists a fourth criticism of CDA, which is not related to subjectivity, namely, the absence of any consideration of cognitive factors. Approaches from cognitive sciences have now been incorporated, however, as part of the agenda for development in CDA (Wodak and Meyer 2009).

of offering a rich and nuanced view of the data. As argued in Chapter 2, lack of exact replicability does not necessarily invalidate the research, provided our methods are dependable and the methodology transparent. The real problem in CDA is the frequent lack of explicitness in terms of methods of data collection and text analysis. This is a criticism that, as pointed out by Stubbs (1997/2002:204) is made within CDA itself (see also Wodak and Meyer 2009:27).

A circular argument can be produced when texts and units of analysis are selected because they exemplify preconceived ideas – for example, when the analyst wants to demonstrate that source text features are ideologically manipulated in translation and searches for a suitable text containing linguistic evidence of such manipulation, which is then presented as evidence in support of the same point on the basis of which the texts were selected. As Mason (2006) notes, this pitfall can be avoided by not pre-selecting texts to prove a particular point and by providing a comprehensive account of the data (see Section 3.4.1).

The risk of circularity is particularly serious in CDA because the ideological traces left in a text in the process of production are ambiguous; they are not self-evident and cannot be read off the text in a mechanical way, which raises the question of what source of interpretative authority CDA claims (Stubbs 1997/2002) and thus leads to the third criticism mentioned above: the assumption of privileged knowledge. All texts reflect the interests of their producers, and any interpretation is shaped by the predispositions of the interpreter (de Beaugrande and Dressler 1981:199-206), which means that the reading arrived at in CDA is as political as any other. Widdowson (2001:5) argues that "[t]he assumption of critical linguists seems to be that their reading has the authority to override others – it alone is capable of revealing ideological bias which is insinuated into the minds of uninformed readers without them being aware". We cannot speak for the readers unless we have evidence of their response, and CDA generally does not include this sort of evidence (Mason 2006:108).[5] The same can be said about text producers' intentions (Widdowson 1998/2004:367). As argued by Stubbs (1997/2002:207-208), if CDA is to establish a convincing relationship between language and cognition, then it must present data and theory pertinent to both; it needs to supplement linguistic evidence with "non-linguistic evidence of a pattern of beliefs and behaviour" (*ibid.*:208). Stubbs goes on to argue for the incorporation of ethnographic data about actual text production and for the study of text dissemination and audience reception (*ibid.*:209). Likewise, Blommaert and Bulcaen (2000) call for a more dynamic concept of context in CDA and, in particular, for more attention to ethnography as a resource for contextualizing and a theory for interpreting data. We will return to the issue of reader response in our discussion of translation quality assessment in Section 3.6.

The risk of projecting interpretations onto data and of inferring too much about the context on the basis of textual analysis is by no means exclusive to CDA. In fact, it is part and parcel of any linguistic analysis, including corpus analysis

---

[5] In this regard, the distinction made by Widdowson (2001) between externalized and experienced language data is particularly interesting. Widdowson argues that CL's and CDA's account of externalized language does not really capture the reality of experienced language.

and quality assessment. Scholars in translation studies have often highlighted the perils of attributing motivation to text producers when we do not have access to their thought processes (Mason 2000:17; Tymoczko 2002:19). Mason (2009b) has also made a plea for more investigation of reader response in translation studies and presents encouraging results from an initial exploration. As suggested by Stubbs (1997/2002) and Blommaert and Bulcaen (2000), triangulating results with those obtained using other research methods is required in order to address this particular weakness. This is a strategy used by Maltby (2010) in the study of interpreting policy documents, where the results of textual analysis of policy documents by the charity Asylum Aid are combined with interview data with the Casework Manager. Likewise, in her study of translator style (Saldanha 2005, 2011a, 2011b, 2011c), the results of a corpus analysis are supplemented by information obtained from interviews with the translators involved, academic papers written by the translators, and reviews of the translation, which allows for a rich contextualization of the results and for a less speculative consideration of motivation.

We have argued here that the problems of circularity, partiality and privileged knowledge are neither exclusive to CDA nor inherent to it, and can be addressed by being explicit about our methods and criteria for text selection and by triangulating results with data obtained using other methods (see also the discussion of warrantability in Chapter 2 and Section 3.4.1). Another important requirement is to adopt a self-reflective stance, acknowledging our own positions and biases. Still, some would argue that this assumes a possibly unrealistic level of self-awareness on the part of researchers; bias can be exerted at different levels, including subconscious levels which are not easy to acknowledge (Baker 2006:10-12).

What differentiates corpora from other collections of texts is that they are collected in such a way as to attempt, to the extent that this is possible, to ensure that they are representative of a certain language variety (see Section 3.4.1 below for a more detailed discussion of representativeness in corpus design). The advantage of accessing large quantities of texts is that they enable us to explore discourses that are shared within a community rather than those that are personal to the author of a text or to a small group of language users.

Both Stubbs (1997/2002) and Baker (2006) present CL as solving some of the weaknesses of CDA. According to Baker (2006), the use of corpora enables researchers to address some of the concerns relating to subjectivity because corpora place a number of restrictions on our cognitive biases, even though subjectivity can never be completely removed. Stubbs highlights the tendency of CDA to rely on fragmentary evidence about phenomena that are essentially quantitative (such as the claim that some text types are becoming more colloquial and heterogeneous) (1997/2002:206) and the inability of isolated texts to demonstrate how our ways of seeing the world are influenced cumulatively by repeated phrasings in texts (*ibid.*:208). Corpora enable us to study what Baker calls the "incremental" effect of discourse: by collecting repeated examples of a discourse construction in naturally occurring language, we can start to see a cumulative effect and appreciate how evaluative meanings are shared within a discourse community (Baker 2006:13). Corpora also enable us to find counter-examples and compare texts over different time periods, thus offering insights into the resistant and dynamic nature of discourses. Last, but not least, corpora can be used to triangulate results obtained manually using CDA methods.

A considerable proportion, if not most, of the translation studies literature that uses CL as a methodology focuses on (potentially universal) features of translation – the ultimate aim being to describe how translated language differs from non-translated language – and tends to be based on quantitative analysis, which can range from studies reporting frequencies and percentages (the most common), to studies that involve statistical analysis (Laviosa 1998a, 1998b; de Sutter *et al* 2012) and studies using machine learning techniques (Baroni and Bernardini 2006).

There are different views on the usefulness and reliability of significance tests in CL. Many linguists highlight the need to demonstrate that any differences or similarities revealed are not due to chance, especially since sampling procedures cannot always guarantee representativeness. However, statistical tests based on probabilities cannot always be reliably used to measure linguistic data. The most powerful tests used in the social sciences (parametric tests) assume that the data are normally distributed, which is often not true of linguistic data (Oakes 1998:11; McEnery and Wilson 1996:70). Besides, as explained in Chapter 2, statistical tests are based on the null hypothesis and assume that the association between two variables is random but language is never random, because we speak and write with a purpose, so the null hypothesis is never true (Kilgarriff 2005:264). Fortunately, according to Kilgarriff, this generally does not present a problem, because language corpora generally have very large quantities of data, and "[w]here the data is not sparse, the difference between arbitrary and motivated connections is evident in greatly differing relative frequencies" (*ibid.*:272). Because of the multilingual nature of translation research, which makes the compilation of large corpora a greater challenge than for monolingual research, we may not always be so fortunate as Kilgarriff suggests, but it is nevertheless true that statistical tests often do not show anything that cannot be revealed by simply comparing raw frequencies (Stubbs 1995; Danielsson 2003).

Still, as Gries (2006) argues, raw frequencies and percentages do have their disadvantages; for example, they do not allow us to identify the direction of an observed effect (is 3% more or less than you would expect on the basis of chance?). According to Gries, these problems, as well as the pitfalls of null-hypothesis significance testing, can be overcome by doing 'rigorous statistical testing', which involves providing effect sizes (the estimated strength of a relationship) and considering confidence intervals (the reliability of an estimate) as opposed to the significance testing that has been traditionally done (2006:200). Generally speaking, we can observe a trend towards the increasing use of statistics in translation studies using CL, which is partly the result of translation scholars embracing new techniques of analysis and partly the result of statistically-minded linguists starting to pay more attention to translated texts, as the volume entitled *Quantitative Methods in Corpus-Based Translation Studies,* edited by Oakes and Ji (2012), demonstrates.

Another limitation of corpora is that even if they can show that there is an association between two variables, they cannot explain why that is the case.

Halverson (2009) describes studies using comparable and parallel corpora as adopting a cross-sectional research design, where quantitative and quantifiable data are provided in connection with two or more variables, collected at one point in time, to discover patterns of association. She points out that this design is criticized as having a problem of internal validity, because it is not possible to establish the direction of causality: we can show correlation but not causation (see discussion of causality in Chapter 2, Section 2.10.3).

We saw above that CL can come to the rescue of CDA when it comes to restricting bias and generalizing results. When it comes to finding explanations, it is DA that comes to the rescue of CL by providing a qualitative dimension. According to McEnery and Wilson (1996:62-63), quantitative analysis of corpus data "enables one to separate the wheat from the chaff" but "the picture that emerges ... is necessarily less rich than that obtained from qualitative analyses". The aim of qualitative analysis is a complete detailed description; since it is not necessary to make the data fit into a finite number of categories, it enables very fine distinctions to be drawn (*ibid.*:62).Therefore, a combination of quantitative and qualitative approaches is often desirable if fuller descriptions are to be offered, and particularly if we want to suggest potential explanations for the phenomena observed by interpreting the results in relation to the context of situation and culture.

In sum, a combination of CL and DA offers a more powerful means of establishing a connection between everyday routine and cultural transmission than either of those methodologies on their own. In-depth qualitative analysis can form the basis for hypotheses that are tested afterwards through corpus analysis, or the mechanisms behind general patterns discovered using CL can be explained by detailed studies of certain texts, taking into account the context of production and reception. Nevertheless, it is important to bear in mind that the use of corpora for DA has its limitations: the corpus analysis tools currently available are best suited for the investigation of features below sentence level, and they present the analyst with fragments of language which are removed from the environment in which they were designed to be displayed. Mason (2001:7) warns against generalizing from concordance-based analyses that consider isolated sentences and ignore "the rhetorical purposes which give rise to them". In addition, as we will see below, using a corpus does not guarantee generalizability in any case (Conrad 2002).

3.3 Designing studies in critical discourse analysis and corpus linguistics

3.3.1 *Corpus-driven, corpus-based, argument-centred and problem-based designs*

The distinction between inductive and deductive approaches to research described in Chapter 2 has been much discussed in the context of CL, where it is generally framed in terms of **corpus-driven** and **corpus-based** approaches. According to

Tognini-Bonelli (2001:17), the main difference resides in that the corpus-based approach starts with a pre-existing theory which is validated using corpus data, while the corpus-driven approach

> builds up the theory step by step in the presence of the evidence, the observation of certain patterns leads to a hypothesis, which in turns leads to the generalisation in terms of rules of usage and finally finds unification in a theoretical statement.

Tognini-Bonelli advocates using a corpus-driven approach on the grounds that studies that are too strictly embedded in specific linguistic theories forego the potential to challenge pre-formulated theories and descriptions. However, as Tognini-Bonelli herself acknowledges, there is no such thing as pure induction (2001:85). Intuition often plays a part in developing research questions, which are often based on casual observations about language, and in the interpretations of corpus findings, which often involve intuitive impressions about the impact of particular language choices (Conrad 2002:78).

Another problem of starting with a clear hypothesis and trying to find evidence for or against it in any type of text-linguistic research is that an analysis of specific linguistic features necessarily shows a partial view of the data and, given the great diversity of linguistic features and functions in a text, we run the risk of looking too narrowly into those areas where confirmatory evidence is likely to be found and, consequently, of focusing on those results that confirm the hypothesis and ignoring those that contradict it. However, as argued in Saldanha (2004), there are no grounds to assume that corpus-based research will not be committed to the integrity of the data as a whole or will not aim to be comprehensive with respect to corpus-evidence, as Tognini-Bonelli (2001:84) seems to suggest. Saldanha (2004) shows that the use of pre-existing hypotheses is not a problem in itself, as long as the exceptions to the norm are also accounted for and as long as we are prepared to revise our theories in the light of the data when this is required (see discussion of sophisticated falsification in Chapter 2). The problem, as in CDA, results from evidence being used selectively (see Section 3.2.3) and can be resolved by means of a comprehensive account of the data.

A deductive approach has been common where corpora have been used to test hypotheses about distinctive features of translated language, such as normalization, simplification, explicitation, or the 'unique items hypothesis' (for an overview see Laviosa 2002, 2011; Mauranen and Kujamäki 2004). Studies of translator style, on the other hand, have taken a data-driven approach, where corpora are explored with an open mind as to what possible features may be found to be typical and distinctive in the work of one translator (Saldanha 2011a, 2011b, 2011c; Winters 2007, 2009).

Wodak and Meyer (2009:19-20) distinguish between CDA approaches which proceed deductively, by using "closed" theoretical frameworks and illustrating them with examples that fit their claims, and approaches that proceed inductively by selecting problems that are then explored through in-depth case studies and ample data collection. Wodak and Meyer clarify that the approaches they describe are never strictly inductive or deductive – these adjectives simply describe "priorities in choosing entry points and themes" – and add that "of course, all approaches moreover proceed abductively, i.e. oscillate between theory and data analysis in retroductive ways" (*ibid.*:19). Later on, Wodak and Meyer (2009:22, 28) describe most CDA research as proceeding hermeneutically. The hermeneutic circle – which does indeed follow an abductive (rather than a deductive or inductive) logic (see Chapter 2) – describes a process whereby understanding is generated through an analysis that moves continuously to and fro between the more abstract level of concepts and the more concrete level of data. The assumption is that the meaning of one part can only be understood in the context of the whole, but that this in turn is only accessible from its component parts (Wodak and Meyer 2009:22). The circle is ever expanding and does not accept a final interpretation. While this may be true of the kind of CDA research conducted following Fairclough's (2002, 2003) model, ultimately we need to remember that the interdisciplinary character of CDA means that a range of methods are legitimate within this approach, from interpretivist and hermeneutic to deductive and quantitative methods.

Since the diversity and interdisciplinarity of methodological approaches to CDA prevent us from offering one set of specific guidelines for designing research projects, we will describe two different models for illustrative purposes: Fairclough's **problem-based approach** (2002), and what we call an argument-centred approach which is described here with reference to a study by Mason (2009c).

Fairclough's analytical framework starts by identifying a social problem with a semiotic aspect, for example, a linguistic aspect, such as the use of transitivity to attribute or hide agency. As an example of a problem he chooses the widespread notion that global capitalism has no alternative, it is represented in political discourses as a fact of life that is unquestionable; as a result, any feasible alternative ways of organizing economic relations are simply excluded from the political agenda. He then chooses a political text (a government policy document) to show how this representation is achieved and reinforced using subtle linguistic means. The text does not necessarily state that global capitalism is the only option, but economic processes are presented without responsible social agents and in a timeless, ahistorical present. Fairclough then compares it to another political text which presents a competing representation of the same phenomenon, and reveals the linguistic resources used in this other text.

This problem-based approach to CDA is practical and useful, although it needs to be applied with a great deal of critical awareness, since as Fairclough recognizes, "[w]hat is problematic and calls for change is an inherently contested and controversial matter, and CDA is inevitably caught up in social controversy and debate in choosing to focus on certain features of social life as 'problems'" (2002:125). CDA has been criticized for claiming to address social problems, since the impact it can have on those problems is limited. Widdowson (2001), for example, points out that research is mainly disseminated within academic circles and the process of publication takes so long that by the time it is published it has purely historical interest.

CDA has often been used in research that aims to put forward a theoretical argument on the basis of carefully selected evidence, generally drawn from a variety of texts. This design, which we will call here argument-centred, mixes elements from conceptual research and empirical research (see Chapter 1 and Williams and Chesterman 2002). The researcher often starts by proposing a new argument (or hypothesis) and then proceeds to support it with examples. While the research is deductive in the sense that it moves from the general to the par- ticular, the aim is not to *test* hypotheses but rather to propose new avenues for research, for example, new ways of looking at data that the researcher believes have stronger explanatory power than previous ones. It is different from purely conceptual research in that it is grounded in empirical evidence. Argument- centred research is exploratory in nature; the examples, while aiming to support the theoretical argument, are not intended to prove that the argument presented is the only valid way of looking at the phenomenon under investigation. Rather, it seeks to lay the groundwork for further empirical studies that would, using comparable datasets, either falsify or support the emerging hypothesis.

Mason (2009c), for example, argues that the concept of the interpreter's 'role' as applied in dialogue interpreting presents some disadvantages, because it im- plies a "fixed stance" and "pre-determined patterns of behaviour" (*ibid.*:53). He proposes using the notion of 'positioning' (adopted from Davies and Harré 1990) instead, so as to better reflect the constantly evolving and negotiated nature of interaction among participants in interpreter-mediated encounters. Mason supports his argument by analyzing primary sources, a series of immigration interviews taken from a documentary on illegal immigration, as well as examples taken from existing literature on interpreting. The analysis demonstrates how conversation moves can be seen as reflecting the different positionings adopted by interpreters and accepted or rejected by other participants.

3.3.2   *Selecting and delimiting texts as units of investigation*

So far in this section we have looked at different research designs adopted in CL and CDA in very broad terms, focusing on the type of logic guiding the research process. In more practical terms, the researcher needs to define a unit of inves- tigation, which will involve selecting text(s) and corpora. We explained above that CDA is relational, so the researcher will also need to specify the particular relationships between text and context to be explored. Unless we are already using existing corpora, the selection of texts for corpus analysis is a rather com- plex process; this will be described in more detail in Section 3.4. Here we will focus on the selection and delimitation of texts within CDA and on the selection of comparative data (texts and corpora).

We discussed above the problems involved in the necessarily subjective se- lection of texts within CDA. However subjective, the selection of texts needs to be justifiable. Texts in CDA are generally selected on the basis of their intrinsic significance, that is, because of particularities that make them stand out from other texts, or because they are seen as typical of the discourse we are trying to describe. Both significance and typicality are a matter of argument. For a researcher interested in the ideological management involved in the production of translations of politically sensitive texts, as is the case of Baumgarten (2009), the choice of Hitler's *Mein Kampf* and its English translations is appropriate because the text stands out as a particularly sensitive one. For a researcher interested in literary translation and in how French discourses of homosexuality adapted and absorbed American gay discourses in the 1970s (Harvey 2003), the choice to study the French translation of Holleran's *Dancer from the Dance*, a novel that "continues to be judged as one of the most representative – and most distinguished in literary terms – of the new trend of American gay novels from the late 1970s" (*ibid.*:111), is also evidently suitable. Despite obvious cases such as these, neither significance nor typicality should be taken for granted: we should always be explicit about our motivations for selecting a text so that our choices are open to scrutiny. Significance is and will remain a relative and historical concept, which will change depending on the point of view and circumstances under which it is considered.

The problem of delimiting texts as units of investigation is one that also needs some consideration. Understanding texts as semiotic units means that the analysis may not be restricted to linguistic aspects but may also include non-verbal symbols. In fact, delimiting what is and what is not verbal is not straightforward: Is prosody (stress, intonation) non-verbal? There are non-verbal elements that interact with the texts and thereby contribute to meaning making. Posture and eye movement are key elements of the grammar of Sign Language, and are meaning making mechanisms in all languages. Mason (2009c) considers gaze alongside other (verbal) strategies used by interpreters to negotiate positioning in interpreter-mediated encounters. Pauses, hesitations, etc. can also be taken into account; see Yagi (1999) for a description of a computer-aided discourse analysis of interpreted output focusing on 'time-structure' (speech bursts and pauses). Features such as typography and layout can play a similar role to that of prosody and nonverbal aspects of spoken language (see, for example, Saldanha 2011b, Brotherstone 2009). In some genres, like advertising and comics, it is impossible to analyze verbal and non-verbal elements independently from each other. In others, the analysis of non-verbal elements may provide useful insights but may not be essential, but in all cases it is important to be aware of the influence that these elements may exert.

Another aspect of texts that makes it difficult to delimit them as discourse units is intertextuality: "there can be no objective beginning and no clear end, since every discourse is bound up with many others and can only be understood on the basis of others" (Titscher *et al* 2000:26). This means that no analysis can achieve a complete interpretation of the meaning of a text; every analysis needs to be restricted to certain aspects, which are selected by the investigator on the basis of the research question(s).

Because the analysis is relational, connecting text with context, we also need to decide on what contextual factors are to be taken into account. The first thing to highlight is that context in CDA is never limited to the surrounding text (known as co-text in CL). Discourse is situated, it reflects and impacts on the physical environment in which texts are displayed or produced, and particular care thus needs to be taken to gather information on the process of production and reception of the texts under study. One of the main difficulties researchers encounter when attempting to account for contextual factors is how to select from among a wide range of potentially relevant aspects: descriptions are inevitably selective and may unjustifiably prioritize one contextual aspect to the detriment of others (Wood and Kroger 2000:69). For example, when the behaviour of two translators differs, could it be a matter of age or experience? Or of formal training versus learning on the job (which was more common a few years ago)? People belong to different social categories, any one of which might be relevant to discourse production; this means that we need to be careful not to make unwarranted assumptions about those categories.

It is difficult to determine, at the beginning of a research project, which contextual features may turn out to be relevant to our findings, and this is why it is important to gather as much information as possible. As a minimum, researchers need to take into account: the circumstances under which the discourse was produced (e.g. who commissioned a translation, for what purpose; the physical settings in an interpreting scenario); bio-social information about primary agents such as translators, interpreters (e.g. gender and professional background), basic information about other agents (e.g. status of officials in community interpreting or of editors in the translation process); and circumstances of reception (where the texts have been used, in the context of what other texts, information on reviews, circulation, sales figures). We re-emphasize these points in Section 3.6 on translation quality assessment, a domain of research in which these factors are sometimes ignored.

3.3.3   The need for comparative data

As Stubbs (1997/2002:209) points out in relation to CDA, "since the essential claim concerns differences caused by different language use, it follows that studies of language use and cognition must be comparative". Comparison is crucial at the level of both linguistic features and texts. Varieties of language use are defined by clusters of co-occurring features (Stubbs 1997/2002:213), and local features therefore have to be seen in relation to other features. Likewise, texts have to be considered against the background of other texts and, where possible, against the background of large corpora which can function as indicative of textual norms in the specific text type under consideration. In translation studies, source texts are commonly used as a point of reference for comparative purposes. Where possible, a second or third translation of the same text offers the best 'control sample', although the fact that different translations can be produced under very different circumstances can be a potential source of confounding variables (see Chapter 2). Tymoczko discusses the difficulty of using control groups in translation research and argues that, in some cases, even a different set of passages within the source text from those one is researching can act as the control group: "one can pick passages that are neutral with respect to the issues being investigated" (2002:21). According to Tymoczko, for the sort of non-quantified research that is common in translation studies, "it is sufficient to use a sort of virtual control group: to draw comparisons with parallel situations that are already established in translation studies scholarship" (2002:21). Tymoczko's suggestions may or may not be sufficient for CDA in translation research, depending on the individual case and the skill with which the particular researcher deals with them. Ultimately, the suitability of control texts will also depend on the research question(s).

In quantitative corpus research, even on a small scale, comparison is crucial. Statements of frequency ('x is frequent in A') are meaningless unless we provide a relative norm of comparison ('x is more frequent in A than in B'). For example, as argued in Saldanha (2011a), if we want to describe the style of a translator, it is not enough to say that translator A uses a particular stylistic feature (say, foreign words) a certain number of times; we need to compare this frequency, at the very least, to the use of foreign words by another translator in comparable circumstances and, if possible, to the use of foreign words in a more general corpus of translations from and into the same languages. Thus, one of the key decisions to be made when undertaking corpus analysis is the type of corpus to be used, because different types of corpora allow for comparison along very different dimensions.

3.3.4 *Corpus typology*

The most commonly used types of corpora in translation studies are comparable and parallel corpora. It should be noted, however, that in this area the terminology is not consistent (translation corpora is another term often used to refer to parallel corpora, for example) and new modes of multilingual text production blur the lines between categories that are at the basis of any classification of translational corpora. Zanettin (2012), for example, discusses Wikipedia corpora as an example of 'comparable-cum-parallel' corpora.

As mentioned above, corpora have been widely used in order to identify features or regularities of translated language – such as simplification, explicitation, translation of unique items, standardization – for which purpose monolingual comparable corpora are particularly useful. Monolingual **comparable corpora** consist of two sets of texts in the same language, one containing original text and the other translations. The aim is to find patterns that are distinctive of translated texts as opposed to texts produced in a non-translational environment. The best-known corpus of this kind is the Translational English Corpus (TEC), held at the Centre for Translation and Intercultural Studies at the University of Manchester, and often used in combination with a subcorpus of the British National Corpus (BNC). Needless to say, one of the key features of this kind of corpus is the comparability of the two components, which should be similar in as many respects as possible, so as to avoid the interference of other variables that could potentially influence the results (see the discussion of dependent and independent variables in Chapter 2). Laviosa (1997) discusses parameters of comparability in great detail. The Translational English Corpus has been used mainly in investigations of simplification (Laviosa-Braithwaite 1997; Laviosa 1997, 1998a, 1998b) and explicitation (Olohan and Baker 2000; Olohan 2001, 2002, 2003). More detailed overviews of research using comparable corpora can be found in Laviosa (2002), Olohan (2004) and Zanettin (2012).

The other type of corpus widely used in translation studies is generally known as a **parallel corpus**. Parallel corpora are typically made up of source texts in language A and their translations in language B. Sometimes they also include source texts in language B with their translations in language A, in which case they are called bi-directional. Figure 3.1 shows the 4 different components of a bidirectional parallel corpus; the arrows represent possible comparisons.

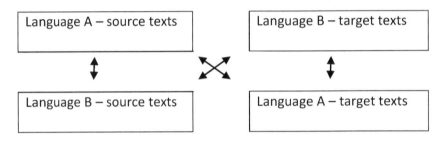

Figure 3.1 Design of a bidirectional parallel corpus

Examples of bilingual parallel corpora include COMPARA (Frankenberg-Garcia and Santos 2003), made up of English and Portuguese texts, and the English Norwegian Parallel Corpus (Johansson *et al*, online). Both are also bidirectional. Most parallel corpora are bilingual but they can also include translations into several languages of the same source texts, as in the case of the MULTEXT-East "1984" corpus, which contains the novel *1984* by George Orwell in the English original, and its translations into Bulgarian, Czech, Estonian, Hungarian, Romanian, and Slovene.[6]

Although we said that the typical parallel corpus contains source texts and translations, strictly speaking, a direct translational relationship does not have to exist between the texts. When using multilingual parallel corpora, each text pair may consist of a source text and its translation or two texts which are translations in two different languages of a text produced in a third language, for example, the Romanian and Slovene translations of the English text *1984* in the MULTEXT-East "1984" corpus.

Parallel corpora have also been used to investigate features of translated language, but given the restrictions in terms of language combinations, the focus has been on 'norms' rather than 'universals', in Toury's (1995) terminology. Kenny's (2001) investigation of normalization in translation from German into

---

[6] http://nl.ijs.si/me/CD/docs/1984.html [Last accessed 25 June 2012].

English is a good example. Another area of research where parallel corpora have been widely used is the investigation of stylistic issues in translation (Munday 2008; Saldanha 2011a, 2011b, 2011c; Winters 2007, 2009; Ji 2102; Ji and Oakes 2012). More detailed overviews of research using parallel corpora can be found in Laviosa (2002), Olohan (2004) and Zanettin (2012).

Despite the fact that both comparable and parallel corpora on their own can provide very valuable insights into translation, there is an increasing recognition that a combination of both types of corpus offers a better resource to test the potential effects of both source texts and language- and genre-specific patterns (Olohan 2004; Kenny 2005; Bernardini 2011). Bidirectional parallel corpora offer the possibility of combining source texts and their translations, as well as both translated and non-translated texts in the same language, with the limitation that they tend to cover only one language pair, which means we cannot really look for features that are specific to translated texts independently of the language of the source text.

Another important tool in filtering the effects of different variables in corpus research is the use of larger monolingual corpora as **reference** or **control corpora**, that is to say, as a point of reference for 'normal' usage in a certain context. The greater the size and the range of the corpus which acts as a reference, the more valid our statements of relative frequency in the specialized corpus. For example, in order to assess the degree of creativity of lexical forms used by translators working from German into English, Kenny (2001) takes into account whether those forms are present or not in an English language corpus (the British National Corpus).

A very interesting design in terms of comparable corpora is that of the European Comparable and Parallel Corpora, which consist of parliamentary speeches in English and Spanish, including: original European Parliament speeches in English and their translations into Spanish, original European Parliament speeches in Spanish and their translations into English, original Spanish speeches from the Spanish Parliament (Congreso de los Diputados), and English speeches from the British House of Commons and the The Irish Dáil Éireann. The advantage of this design is that, apart from providing comparable corpora within which to contextualize the results from the parallel corpus, it also allows researchers to compare political discourses in the context of an international institution with those produced 'at home' (Calzada and Luz 2006).

The corpora described above usually contain published translations by professional translators. However, any of the configurations described above are possible for **learner translation corpora**, which are mostly used in applied translation studies to examine the development of translation competence as well as for research into translation teaching and learning (Zanettin 2012:28-30). One such corpus is the Learner Translation Corpus (LTC) created under the MeLLANGE project.[7] The LTC is a multilingual annotated corpus containing source texts of four different text types (legal, technical, administrative and journalistic) in eleven

---

[7] http://corpus.leeds.ac.uk/mellange/ltc.html [Last accessed 25 June 2012].

European languages and their translations into and from those languages. Learner corpora can be used to identify specific areas of difficulty in different translation scenarios, as well as how learners' output varies according to a number of variables, such as direction of translation, level of proficiency, type of translation problem and teaching method. One of the main challenges presented by learner corpora is that many factors can influence a learner's output, which makes it difficult to design a corpus where all the variables can be controlled. For examples of research carried out using learner corpora see, among others, Bernardini and Zanettin (2000), Zanettin *et al* (2003) and Beeby *et al* (2009).

Although the vast majority of translation research using CL has been conducted on written texts, there is increasing interest in multimodal corpora and important advances have been made lately in relation to the creation and exploration of such corpora. New researchers should bear in mind, however, that multimodal corpora are particularly difficult to build and are used in rather different ways from written corpora (Zanettin 2012:31). Describing multimodal corpora lies outside the scope of this book, but see Setton (2011) for an overview of research in interpreting studies using CL, Leeson (2008) for a description of the Signs of Ireland corpus, which is a corpus of Irish Sign Language, and Valentini and Linardi (2009) on the Forlì Corpus of Screen Translation.

This section has looked at issues of design in studies of translation using CL and CDA. First we discussed issues concerning the type of logic guiding the research project, i.e. whether an inductive, deductive or abductive logic is followed. We described two commonly used research designs in CDA: problem- and argument-centred approaches. We considered important questions in selecting and delimiting texts as units of investigation, such as what counts as significant and typical and what counts as verbal and non-verbal communication. We also discussed the need for comparative data in the form of other texts which can act as points of reference for our analysis. Finally, we looked at how different types of corpora provide different parameters of comparison. In the next section, we offer an overview of the main issues in corpus design.

3.4 Building corpora

Building a corpus, particularly a translational corpus, is a laborious, time-consuming task and one that has not received much support from academic funding bodies. As a result, researchers do not have a great deal of choice in terms of already existing resources (see Zanettin 2012 for information on corpora available at the time of writing).

Because translational corpora are not widely available, many researchers resort to building their own. Here we provide a very brief discussion of the principles and stages in designing and building a corpus, not so much to guide researchers who may take it upon themselves to construct one – they are advised to consult other more detailed guides (Bowker and Pearson 2002, Wynne 2005, Zanettin 2012 are all good starting points) – but because being aware of issues in corpus design can make us more discerning users of these resources.

3.4.1 Corpus design criteria

A corpus is generally built on the assumption that it will be "used as a representative sample of a particular language or subset of that language" (Bowker and
Pearson 2002:9). Using texts as the units in a **population** seems to be the most
common approach to sampling in CL. According to Biber (1993:243), defining
the target population involves deciding what texts are included and excluded
(setting the boundaries of the population), the categories of texts and how these
are defined (organizing the population). Kenny (2001:114) defines her target
population as consisting of German novels published in the 1980s and 1990s
and available in English translation. In order to establish which texts belong to
the target population (range), texts can be categorized according to **external** or
internal criteria. External criteria are situationally defined, they relate the text to
the context and mode of production. The determining factors are, for example,
register, date of publication, author, and so on. Internal criteria are linguistically
defined, based on counts of linguistic features. External distinctions tend to take
precedence because the identification of salient linguistic features requires a
pre-existing representative corpus of texts for analysis (Biber 1993:245) and, in
practice, texts are often selected on external criteria only. According to Atkins
et al (1992:5) this can be problematic:

> A corpus selected entirely on internal criteria would yield no information
> about the relation between language and its context of situation. A corpus
> selected entirely on external criteria would be liable to miss significant
> variation among texts since its categories are not motivated by textual
> (but by contextual) factors.

However, it is possible that we are interested in a particular population of
texts because they fulfill certain external criteria, and if there is little variation
among them then that is an interesting aspect of our population rather than a
problem.

After we have defined our population, we need to find an appropriate sampling frame. A **sampling frame** is an "operational definition of the population, an
itemized listing of population members from which a representative sample can
be chosen" (Biber 1993:244). For written published texts, the most commonly
used frame is a comprehensive bibliographical index. However, finding such an
index for translations can be problematic because, as Kenny (2001:114) notes,
the usual sources of information can be inconsistent in their treatment of translation, for example, by not marking books as translations. If a comprehensive
analysis is not possible, we need to find an appropriate sampling method; this
involves deciding on the number of texts per text type, samples per text, and
words per sample. Every possible attempt has to be made to ensure that the
corpus includes the full range of variability in that population and that there is
a certain balance among the different values in the range. Range and balance
will depend on a thorough definition of the target population and the sampling
methods chosen (Biber 1993:243).

In order to avoid covert or overt bias, texts can be selected using random sampling techniques (see Chapter 2). Biber (1993:244) argues that stratified sampling should be used on the basis that "stratified samples are almost always more representative than non-stratified samples (and they are never less representative)". However, McEnery and Wilson (1996:65) point out that

> strata, like corpus annotation, are an act of interpretation on the part of the corpus builder because they are founded on particular ways of dividing up language into entities such as genres which it may be argued are not naturally inherent within it.

Purposive sampling (see Chapter 2) is another common technique in corpus building. For an example of purposive sampling for building a parallel corpus see Hareide and Hofland (2012). In purposive sampling, there is a tendency to control aspects of production, such as authorship, date of publication, etc. rather than aspects of reception, such as who reads the texts in question or how widely disseminated they are. As a result, the BNC – to give just one example – appears to be dominated by texts published by a small group of metropolitan publishers from Southern England, and the tabloid format is under-represented in the newspaper category because this category is not based on publication/ circulation figures (Ahmad 2008). On the other hand, defining the population in terms of language reception would inevitably assign "tremendous weight to a tiny proportion of the writers and speakers whose language output is received by a very wide audience through the media" (Atkins *et al* 1992:5).

To achieve balance among text types, the size of each subcorpus "must be proportional to the relative frequency of occurrence of these texts in the textual categories represented by it" (Zanettin 2012:45-46). This is rather difficult to achieve simply because the frequency of occurrence of any text or type of language is difficult to calculate. And even then, other constraints – such as how easy it is to obtain the texts – play a part in the selection process. The BNC, for example, was designed to represent a wide cross-section of current British English, but spoken English is significantly under-represented as it constitutes only a tenth of the corpus.

Obtaining a balanced corpus is particularly difficult when dealing with translational corpora, either in the form of comparable or parallel corpora, and in particular if both types are to be combined in the form of a bidirectional parallel corpus. Because translation flows from and into any two languages tend to be unequal, representativeness and comparability are often conflicting goals, as Zanettin (2012:48) explains:

> ... even assuming that a corpus of translated fiction may be representative of fiction translated into that language, a parallel corpus containing its source texts for a given language will not be representative of fiction in that language, since source language texts were not in fact selected to be representative of source language fiction.

Zanettin gives the example of fiction translated from English into Italian and vice versa. The flow of translation into Italian is much more substantial than in the other direction and is dominated by translations from best-selling authors, popular romance and detective stories, published by a few big Italian publishers. In the Italian into English direction, translations are of high-brow fiction published by small specialized publishers. Therefore, if the subcorpora of translated texts are to be representative of translations in those two directions, they will not be comparable, and the non-translational subcorpora will be neither representative nor comparable (Zanettin 2012:50-51).

In translation studies, purpose-built corpora have not generally applied random or stratified sampling techniques; rather, a more pragmatic approach has been favoured, in line with the demands imposed by undertaking to build a corpus for a specific piece of research, which is in itself a considerable challenge. Researchers are generally careful to describe in detail their attempts to obtain a balanced representation of the population, taking as many factors into account as possible (authors, publishers, time-span, translator, translator's gender, translator's experience, etc.). See, for example, Dayrell's (2007) description of the compilation of a comparable translational corpus of Brazilian Portuguese, Hareide and Hofland's (2012) description of how the Norwegian-Spanish parallel corpus was compiled, or Kenny's (2001) detailed description of the compilation of the German-English Parallel Corpus of Literary Texts (GECOLT). Despite researchers' efforts, however, several factors remain outside their control, particularly in the case of researchers working on their own. Kenny (2001:115) notes, for example, that while her aim was to include as many different authors, translators and publishers as possible,

> it soon transpired that copyright holders introduced an element of self-selection into the corpus. It proved impossible, for example, to get permission to use works by best-selling authors such as Doris Dörrie, Günter Grass, and Patrick Süskind, and certain publishers seem to apply a blanket policy of refusing permission for material published by them to be used in electronic form. Other copyright holders simply did not reply to (repeated) requests for permissions, thereby forcing the exclusion from the corpus of certain authors.

The issue of representativeness in corpus design is also related to size. Bowker and Pearson only indicate that a corpus should be 'large'. As a common-sense criterion, Bowker and Pearson suggest "a greater number of texts than you would be able to easily collect and read in printed form" (2002:10). Giving more precise indications of size is problematic because whether a corpus is 'large' will depend on what it tries to represent. If we are interested in genres where the language is particularly restricted, say weather forecasts or personal ads, then we may need fewer texts. If we are interested in genres where there is wide variation among text types, say fiction or journalistic texts, then we may need more texts. The size will also depend on the linguistic features that we want to focus on. Biber

(1993) suggests that a million words would be enough for grammatical studies; for lexicography, however, much larger corpora would be needed. If we do know in advance the variables we want to measure in a corpus, it is possible to calculate the sample size required. Oakes (2012) demonstrates how this can be done, using an example where the aim is to establish the length (in number of words) of the sample required to estimate the mean number of words per line in the poems of Sylvia Plath.

In translation studies, purpose-built corpora have ranged from a few hundred thousand words to 2 million or more. For a study on lexical creativity, including author-specific forms which are, by definition, rare, Kenny (2001) uses a parallel corpus of fourteen novels, amounting to approximately 2 million words. For a study of translator style, Ji and Oakes (2012) use a corpus of 15,420 words consisting of two translations of the first chapter of Xueqin's *Dream of the Red Chamber*. Interestingly, studies using sophisticated statistical techniques often rely on comparatively small corpora (see also Oakes 2012, Ji 2012, Ke 2012), presumably on the basis that the results are nonetheless more reliable because of the use of statistics to determine significance.

Another decision to be made when designing corpora is whether to use full texts or text extracts. The advantage of the latter is that they allow better coverage of a language. Since occurrences of new types (different words) decrease throughout the course of a text, the frequency of new types is consistently higher in cross-text samples than in single-text samples. In addition, having extracts of equal length facilitates statistical comparisons between texts. When text extracts are used instead of full texts, stratified sampling can be applied using typical structural divisions such as chapters, sections and paragraphs.

The problem with using text extracts is that it constitutes a violation of the principle of integrity of the data, and that it is unsafe to assume that any part of a text is representative of the whole (Sinclair 2005). Few linguistic features of a text are evenly distributed throughout the text. Frequency counts for common linguistic features are relatively stable across small samples (1,000 to 5,000 words), while frequency counts for rare features are less stable and require longer text samples to be reliably represented (Biber 1993:249). For studies of discourse, where matters of cohesion or the characteristics of introductory, developmental and concluding sections of texts need to be considered, whole texts are generally preferred, although care needs to be taken that long texts do not exert an undue influence on the results of queries.

As we hope to have made clear in the discussion above, apart from theoretical considerations, when designing a corpus it is important to bear in mind the restrictions imposed by text availability and time. Building a corpus is a time-consuming process, especially when the texts are not already available in electronic format and therefore require scanning. The optical character recognition software that comes with scanners converts the images reproduced by the scanner into editable texts, but the data will require manual editing and proof-reading. Annotating and aligning texts also require a considerable time investment (a description of these processes is offered below).

Nowadays, wherever possible researchers rely on electronic documents.

However, electronic texts generally cannot be used in the format in which they are found and will still need pre-processing, for example by converting PDF documents into plain text files or by stripping web pages of their HTML code and of unwanted text such as menus, titles and links to other pages. The World Wide Web is the largest and most accessible repository of textual data; it is widely used as a source of texts to build corpora. Still, constructing a web-based corpus through manual queries and downloads is extremely time-consuming (partly because of the huge number of texts available). The Wacky! Project[8] has developed a set of tools (including BootCaT)[9] to allow linguists to 'crawl' a section of the web to build corpora and provides access to some fairly large already-built corpora in several languages (Baroni *et al* 2008; Baroni and Bernardini 2004). However, quick access to electronic texts comes at a price; it is not possible, for example, to distinguish between translated and non-translated texts, or texts written by native or non-native speakers.

Some argue that the World Wide Web can be used as a corpus in its own right for linguistic research (Kilgarriff and Grefenstette 2003). Its size and coverage make it an almost exhaustive, rather than representative, 'corpus' of electronic written communication (Zanettin 2012:56). Searches carried out using commercial search engines, such as Google, are of limited usefulness, both in terms of the format in which they provide results and of the range of documents retrieved. However, alternative solutions have been devised (see WebCorp,[10] WebAsCorpus,[11] KWICFinder[12]) to restrict the scope of the searches and present them in a format that is more appropriate for linguistic analysis, for example, by presenting concordances as single lines with the search word aligned in the middle, rather than as links.

Another important practical issue in corpus research is copyright. Making or holding electronic copies of substantial parts of a publication generally requires the consent of the copyright holder. The process of identifying who the copyright holder is, contacting them and negotiating permissions can itself take up valuable time (Kenny 2001; Luz and Baker 2000). Even the use of electronic texts brings up thorny issues of copyright permission, particularly if access to the texts or part of them is to be given over the Internet. The research teams who created COMPARA and TEC requested permission from copyright holders.[13] Davies, the creator of the Corpus of Contemporary American English (COCA), did not. Davies argues that because end users are only able to access snippets of the text at any one time and would have difficulty recreating even a paragraph from the original texts, the availability of COCA on the Internet falls under the category

---

[8] http://wacky.sslmit.unibo.it/doku.php?id=start [Last accessed 26 July 2012].
[9] http://bootcat.sslmit.unibo.it/ [Last accessed 26 July 2012].
[10] http://www.webcorp.org.uk/live/ [Last accessed 26 March 2012].
[11] http://webascorpus.org/ [Last accessed 26 March 2012].
[12] http://www.kwicfinder.com/KWiCFinder.html [Last accessed 26 March 2012].
[13] See section on 'Building COMPARA' at http://193.136.2.104/COMPARA/construcao_compara.php [Last accessed 23 March 2012], and see Luz and Baker (2000:online).

of fair use under American Law.[14] In any case, copyright laws and practices vary considerably from country to country, and no general rules can therefore be established. For the construction of the Norwegian-Spanish parallel corpus Hareide and Hofland (2012) obtained written consent from authors and publishing houses for the Norwegian texts. Few Spanish publishing houses replied to their consent requests, but they received reassurance from Spanish Copyright agency CEDRO stating that consent was not necessary for use in investigation as long as bibliographical information was provided (*ibid.*:84).

We have discussed above the most important issues to consider in selecting criteria for building a corpus. Circumstances will often lead us to make choices that are less than ideal, and in any case, representativeness cannot be taken for granted. For this reason, to ensure the reliability and replicability of results it is particularly important to describe carefully how the sample was selected, to publish a detailed list of what is included in the sample or corpus, and to document and report our decisions so that people reading the research will know what we did, how we did it and how we reached our conclusions (Paltridge 2006:217).

3.4.2   Annotation and alignment

Annotation or mark-up is the process of adding information about the texts to the texts themselves. This information is generally known as metadata, data about data (Burnard 2005). Annotation is generally done using XML (eXtensible Mark-up Language). Texts can be annotated at different levels. Here we distinguish between documentary, structural and linguistic annotation. **Documentary annotation** is essential for purposes of transparency and replicability and consists of bibliographical details (author, source, date of publication, etc.) and information about the text processing carried out (whether the text was available electronically or scanned, whether it was proof-read, etc.). This sort of extra-textual information is usually included in the form of a **header**, that is, a separate file associated with the text but stored separately (see Figure 3.2). Bibliographical information can help users select relevant subcorpora (for example, all translations from a particular language or by a particular translator) and is crucial for the interpretation and contextualization of results. See Baker (2000) for an example of how extra-textual information can be used to suggest explanations for patterns found in corpora.

Structural annotation identifies paragraph breaks, subdivisions, headings, footnotes, and so on. It can be useful to select parts of the corpus for investigation or to establish whether certain linguistic features tend to appear in certain parts of the texts (e.g. in footnotes or in the first chapters). The Text Encoding Initiative (TEI)[15] provides a set of guidelines for encoding documentary and

---

[14] See section on 'Copyright issues' at http://corpus.byu.edu/coca/ [Last accessed 23 March 2012].
[15] See http://www.tei-c.org/ [Last accessed 16 May 2012].

structural information which are intended as a standard for the representation of electronic texts to be used in research and teaching.

There are several levels of **linguistic annotation** that can be added to texts. Leech (2005) distinguishes between: phonetic, prosodic, syntactic, semantic, pragmatic, discourse, stylistic and lexical annotation. This process is usually called 'tagging' because it involves inserting tags associated with the linguistic features described by the tags. Part-of-Speech (POS) tagging is the most common and is usually carried out automatically by computer programs called 'taggers' on the basis of statistical information (likelihood that a given part-of-speech will occur in a given context) or rules of grammar written into the tagger. See Figure 3.3 for an example of a tagged text taken from the British National Corpus.

```
TITLE
Filename: fn000009.txt
Subcorpus: Fiction
Collection: Memoirs of Leticia Valle
TRANSLATOR
Name: Carol Maier
Gender: female
Nationality: American
Employment: Lecturer
TRANSLATION
Mode: written
Extent: 55179
Publisher: University of Nebraska Press
Place: USA
Date: 1994
Copyright: University of Nebraska Press
Comments: Title in European Women Writers Series
TRANSLATION PROCESS
Direction: into mother tongue
Mode: written from written source text
Type: full
AUTHOR
Name: Rosa Chacel
Gender: female
Nationality: Spanish
SOURCE TEXT
Language: Spanish
Mode: written
Status: original
Place: Spain
Date: 1945
```

Figure 3.2. Sample header file from the Translational English Corpus

Extract from John McGahern's Amongst Women as included in the the British
National Corpus:

```
<p>
<s n=0001><w CJS>As <w PNP>he <w VVD>weakened<c PUN>, <w
NP0>Moran <w VVD>became <w AJ0>afraid <w PRF>of <w DPS>his <w
NN2>daughters<c PUN>.
<s n=0002><w DT0>This <w AV0>once <w AJ0>powerful <w NN1>man <w
VBD>was <w AV0>so <w VVD-VVN>implanted <w PRP>in <w DPS>their
<w NN2>lives <w CJT>that <w PNP>they <w VHD>had <w AV0>never <w
AV0>really <w VVN>left <w AJ0>Great <w NN1-NP0>Meadow<c PUN>, <w
PRP>in spite of <w NN2>jobs <w CJC>and <w NN2>marriages <w CJC>and
<w NN2>children <w CJC>and <w NN2>houses <w PRF>of <w DPS>their
<w DT0>own <w PRP>in <w NP0>Dublin <w CJC>and <w NP0>London<c
PUN>.
```

Figure 3.3. Example of tagged text taken from the British National Corpus

Teich (2003) uses a POS-tagged parallel bidirectional (German/English) corpus
of scientific writing to find evidence of interference and normalization in translated texts. Having established certain typological differences between scientific
German and English, POS-based queries are used for retrieving information on
word classes, use of passives, predicative and attributive adjectives, premodi-
fication and postmodification. This allows Teich to test hypotheses such as the
following: if the German translations are normalized, the number of postmodification instances will be lower than in German original texts.

Automatic taggers can achieve 98% accuracy rates in languages such as English
(Leech 2005:27). Syntactic information can also be inserted using automatic pars-
ers, although accuracy rates are only 70% to 80% at best (Meyer 2002:91). The
use of semantic and discourse tagging is also becoming more common, but it is
still done mainly manually. Semino and Short (2004), for example, have created
a written corpus that is manually annotated with speech, writing and thought
presentation categories.

Specialized corpora can also be annotated to serve particular research aims.
Parts of the Learner Translation Corpus, for example, are annotated for translation errors according to a hierarchical scheme of error-typology (see also Section
3.6), which provides for a range of either content-related or language-related
errors (Zanettin 2012:29).

Linguistic annotation is generally seen as an enrichment of plain texts, although some scholars favour the use of 'raw' (unannotated) texts. Tognini-Bonelli
(2001:73-74), for example, points out that in a tagged or parsed corpus, the
categories of analysis are not derived from the data but imposed by the linguist
on the basis of pre-existing theories. As discussed earlier (see Section 3.2.1), this
means that a restriction is already imposed on the findings, because anything
that may challenge pre-existing assumptions will not be revealed. This needs to
be assessed against the greater flexibility and precision obtained by restricting

or widening our searches using part-of-speech information. Zanettin (2012:97) points out that while it makes sense for a lexicographer to start from 'raw' data and distil the meaning of words from their associated contexts, it makes sense for a translation student to learn from data which are already filtered and analyzed. In any case, even when texts are annotated, it is important that annotation can be turned off or disregarded in searches, if appropriate.

When the corpus is a parallel corpus, its usability is greatly enhanced by aligning the source and target texts. The **alignment** process consists of associating source text units with the corresponding target text units, which allows them to be retrieved together using a parallel concordancer. Figure 3.4 shows a parallel concordance for the word 'dijo' in a corpus of seven Spanish narrative texts and their translation into English, obtained using the parallel concordancer Paraconc. Several computational techniques have been developed to align parallel corpora automatically or semi-automatically at paragraph, sentence and word level (for an overview of research done in this area see Oakes and McEnery 2000). A common aligning technique (used by Paraconc, for example) is based on the premise that long sentences in one language are more likely to be translations of long sentences in the other, while short sentences in one language are more likely to be translations of short sentences in the other. This technique has the advantage of not making any assumptions about the lexical content of the sentences and therefore can be used with any language pair, although it obviously works better for some language pairs than others. The main problem with programs based on sentence length is that once they have accidentally misaligned a pair of sentences, they tend to be unable to correct themselves and get back on track before the end of the paragraph (Simard *et al* 2000:41), which means that manual alignment at paragraph level is often a prerequisite.

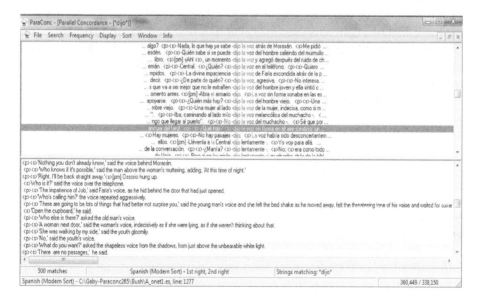

Figure 3.4. Example of a parallel concordance obtained with Paraconc

Sometimes, anchor points are used to help the alignment. These are points in the texts, often determined beforehand, which are highly likely to be translations of each other. Anchor points used to align the Canadian Hansard, for example, were session numbers, names of speakers, time stamps, question numbers and indications of the language in which the original speech was given. Anchor points can also be word pairs obtained from a bilingual primary lexicon. This technique is employed by Translation Corpus Align, the application used to align the English Norwegian Parallel Corpus.

Some texts are better suited to automatic alignment than others; technical texts, for example, are easier to align than literary texts, where it is common to find one sentence translated by two, or vice-versa. In most texts, however, and inevitably in long texts such as whole novels, the alignment has to be corrected manually.

To conclude the discussion of corpus building, it is worth remembering that even purpose-built corpora may well be a permanent asset, and as such should have three key attributes identified by Zanettin (2012:78): stability, flexibility and accessibility. Stability means that corpora should not depend on specific people or software, because the final users may be different from the people who created the corpus. This means that adequate documentation has to be made available. Flexibility is important so that new users can adapt corpora to their purposes; we mentioned above, for example, that it should be possible to remove any tags or add others. Accessibility means that it should be possible to make corpora available to other researchers for cross-validation of results.

3.5   Analyzing texts and corpora

Both CDA and CL rely on linguistic analysis. In this section we introduce some of the basic linguistic concepts used in CDA and CL research. We then describe and illustrate Fairclough's relational approach to text analysis within a CDA framework, before showing how corpus analysis tools can facilitate the search for textual patterns. It is important to bear in mind that CDA and CL are often combined, and the principles discussed in Section 3.5.2 can therefore also be applied to the analysis of texts using corpus tools and the tools discussed in Section 3.5.3 can be applied to text analysis following the model described in Section 3.5.2.

3.5.1   The linguistic toolkit

We mentioned above that although there is no single method in CDA, there is a tendency to rely on categories derived from systemic functional grammar and pragmatics. In this section, we introduce briefly some of these analytical concepts and provide examples of how they have been used in translation studies. This introduction is purely illustrative; for a more detailed discussion of these and other analytical concepts commonly adopted in CDA as applied to the study of translation see Hatim and Mason (1990, 1997).

A key term in CDA is **register**, which refers to the set of choices and configurations that a speaker draws upon in certain conditions. The choices a speaker makes are influenced by the **context of situation**, which has three dimensions: **field** refers to the topic or focus of the activity, **tenor** concerns relations of familiarity, power and solidarity among participants, and **mode** of communication concerns, among other things, whether texts are written or spoken, or whether language is used for action or reflection.

Systemic functional grammar also recognizes a higher level of context, the **context of culture**, which refers to the broader socio-cultural environment in which communication takes place, where ideology, institutions and social conventions all play a part. A related concept is that of **genre**, which describes the institutionalized (conventional, shared) ways in which people within a culture use language to achieve a certain purpose. Genres include forms as disparate as poetry, book reviews, cooking recipes, sermons, academic lectures, etc. Translators adapt their translations according to target language conventions for the particular genre they are dealing with, and when they do not do so, the texts strike target readers as 'odd'. Hatim's (2007) analysis of the translation of historical writing from Arabic into English shows how the conventions of 'hortatory' language (using quotes with a focus on persuasiveness) in academic writing, while appropriate for the Arabic context, can come across as inadequate and misleading (if not risible) in English, where there is a tradition of analytic exposition.

Speakers have at their disposal a range of language varieties and choose between them at different times. Halliday's systemic functional theory of language explains linguistic choices by reference to three main functions that language plays in our lives:

— Language conveys and organizes the cognitive realities of experience through the **ideational function**. Linguistic choices involve patterns of transitivity (nominalization, passivization) and domain-specific lexis, among others.
— Speakers express comments, attitudes and evaluations, and set up a particular relationship with the listener/reader through the **interpersonal function**. Linguistic choices involve, for example, modality markers, use of pronouns, and so on.
— Texts are created by establishing links within the text and between the text and the situation through the **textual function**. Relevant linguistic choices include, for example, word order, repetition and intertextual references.

Discourse has a multifunctional nature, which means that multiple functions can be realized in the same linguistic feature. The repetition of personal pronouns, for example, can be used to imply solidarity with the reader (interpersonal function) and to increase cohesion (textual function).

Munday has argued that greater attention needs to be paid to the interpersonal function in translations because this function is crucial for the writer-reader relationship and, consequently, for investigating instances of translator intervention. He explores the choices made by translators at the interpersonal level, focusing on evaluative language, choice of pronouns and naming devices (2009,

2010) in a range of genres, including political speeches, news, government documents, tourist texts and literary texts. In the English translation of a speech by Venezuelan president Hugo Chávez to the United Nations General Assembly in New York, for example, Munday notes that the strong naming strategy adopted in the source text, which refers to the US president as 'señor dictador imperialista' (Mr imperialist dictator), combining negative vocabulary with the ironically polite 'señor', is softened in the translation to read 'dear world dictator'. Munday concludes that a translator may intervene at critical points that may not coincide with those suggested by models of evaluation based on monolingual English work. These critical points include, for example, instances where 'invoked' (less explicit) attitudinal markers are used, or where the source text is more ambiguous.

Calzada (2007, 2003) carried out an extensive study of the ideational function and the system of **transitivity** in translation. Transitivity involves the representation of processes (realized in the verbal group in English), participants (realized in nominal groups in English) and circumstances (usually realized in prepositional phrases or adverbial groups). A detailed contrastive analysis of speeches delivered in the European Parliament in English and Spanish reveals a number of shifts at the level of transitivity. Calzada (2003, 2007) shows how speakers use a range of linguistic strategies to effect ideological dissimulation of critical standpoint, so as to conform to the norms of the European Parliament debates as a conciliatory genre, where divergence is voiced in a polite and dispassionate manner. The translations, however, do not always conform to such norms and show the speaker as disagreeing more openly, for example, by bringing material processes and agency to the fore.

Pragmatics is the discipline that studies how language users produce and understand meaning by relating the language to the context. CDA makes use of concepts from pragmatics to explain how language both presents and constructs certain world views, as well as how, through the use of language, we represent certain identity positions about ourselves and others. A recognized problem for CDA and CL is that we derive meaning as much from what is not said as from what is said. CL only presents us with what is said. It is sometimes possible to consider what is left unsaid when looking at texts in their context of production (see example from Pöllabauer in Section 3.5.4 below), but filling in unexpressed meanings is a risky interpretive leap to make.

A key concept borrowed from pragmatics and often used in discourse analytical studies of interpreting is the notion of **face**. According to Brown and Levinson's (1987) politeness theory, language users have a public self-image that consists of a negative face (the claim to freedom of action and freedom from imposition) and a positive face (a positive self-image, the desire to be appreciated and approved of). Pöllabauer (2004) notes that in asylum-seeking interviews, officers generally address the asylum seeker in the third person singular ('When did he ...') and the interpreters generally opt for a direct form of address ('When did you...'). However, in cases in which the officer's face is in danger through remarks made by the asylum seeker or the asylum seeker's face is in danger through the officer's question, the interpreters transform the deictic structure and clearly mark the authorship of the questions/statements, thus transferring responsibility for discriminatory discourse to the respective speakers (*ibid.*:163).

3.5.2   *Fairclough's relational approach to critical discourse analysis*

Offering guidelines for doing text analysis within a CDA framework is rather difficult since, ultimately, "there is no CDA way of gathering data" (Wodak and Meyer 2009:27). This does not mean, however, that data can be collected and analyzed in a random manner. In fact, this is one more reason for being explicit about methods, since readers cannot rely on the assumption that standard procedures have been followed.

As is common in qualitative methods, there is no clear distinction between data collection and analysis: "after the first collection exercise, it is a matter of carrying out the first analyses, finding indicators for particular concepts, expanding concepts into categories and, on the basis of these results, collecting further data (*theoretical sampling*)" (Wodak and Meyer 2009:27-28, emphasis in original). Wodak and Meyer (*ibid.*) describe different sets of steps followed during the analysis process according to different CDA approaches. Here, for illustrative purposes, we describe the procedure followed in Fairclough's relational approach to text analysis (Fairclough 2003, Titscher *et al* 2000:153), and offer examples taken from a study by Mason (2005). It is important to note, however, that Mason does not *explicitly* follow the procedure described by Fairclough. His study is chosen to illustrate the process because the different levels of analysis identified by Fairclough are particularly clear in this study. However, Mason has in fact expressed reservations about the ways in which CDA has been applied (Mason 2006, 2009b), and as a result, tends to offer more tentative claims than the ones we see in Fairclough's own work. A particularly interesting aspect of how Mason applies CDA is that claims are based on possible interpretations by discourse participants rather than on the analyst's own interpretation.

Fairclough distinguishes between the external and internal relations of texts (see Figure 3.5). **External relations** are those between texts and their social context, consisting of social events, social practices and social structures. Events, practices and structures represent different levels of abstraction within this social world. A text (for example, a lecture) is itself a social event that happens in the context of a certain social practice (teaching at university level) in a certain social structure (the English language). **Internal relations** can be semantic, grammatical, lexical or phonological. There is also an intermediate level, mediating between the text and its social context, which Fairclough calls the **discourse level**, where interdiscursive relations are formed. These are relations between different genres, discourses and styles. **Genres**, in this model, are understood as ways of (inter)acting discoursally in the world (for example, interviewing is a genre) (Fairclough 2003:26). A **discourse**, in this restricted meaning (as part of the discourse level), is understood as a way of representing the same area of the world from a particular perspective (e.g. the discourse of capitalism). **Style** is a way of constituting social identities through discourse, for example, by identifying oneself as a man or as a student. The interdiscursive character of a text (the particular mix of genres, discourse and styles) is realized in semantic, grammatical, lexical and (in spoken texts) phonological features of the text. This means that particular semantic relations or grammatical categories, for example, are seen as primarily (but not exclusively) associated with certain genres, discourses or styles.

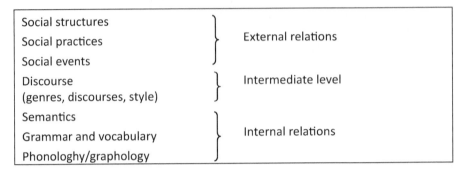

Figure 3.5. Fairclough's relational model (adapted from Fairclough 2003:36)

Fairclough's method is based on three components: description, interpretation and explanation (Titscher *et al* 2000:153). The first component concerns the analysis of discourse-as-text (Fairclough 1992) and consists of describing choices and patterns of vocabulary, grammar, cohesion, text structure, etc. (internal relations). The next component concerns the analysis of discourse-as-discursive-practice (*ibid.*): Internal relations are interpreted in terms of the genres, discourses and styles represented within the text, for example, in terms of the identities adopted by the participants. The explanation involves looking at external relations (discourse-as-social-practice). Given the critical stance of CDA, relations of power and issues of ideology are of central interest. The type of questions asked at the explanation stage are, for example: how are social actors represented (activated/passivated, personal/impersonal) (Fairclough 2003:193)? What value assumptions are made? What is the orientation to difference in the text (an openness to and acceptance of difference? an accentuation of difference?) (*ibid.*:192).

Mason (2005) investigates the construction and perception of identity among participants in dialogue interpreting encounters. He uses a range of analytic concepts derived from linguistics (e.g. 'discoursal shifts', see below), pragmatics (e.g. 'footing' and 'positioning') and conversation analysis ('preferred responses'), as well as more precise terms used in a particular sociolinguistic theory known as audience design. Linguistic choices (internal relations) such as use of pronouns, close or preferred-response questions, and register are interpreted in terms of how they are used by the participants to portray a certain identity, i.e. to present themselves as members of one or more groups to which they could belong at any one time. The different choices are then explained in terms of power relations among the participants. Drawing on data presented in studies by Bolden (2000) and Meyer (2001), Mason discusses cases where the interpreter translates a particular lexical choice using terms from a different register. In one case, an everyday expression used by a patient ('life circumstances' in Russian) is translated into English by the medical term 'stress'; in another case, the German term for 'bile', used by a doctor, is translated into the Portuguese colloquial equivalent ('the rabbit's poison'). These shifts are described as discoursal because they reflect ways of seeing and ways of identifying with certain social groups or institutions. The interpreters' choices are significant because they are ways in which the interpreter positions other participants. The concept of positioning refers to the process whereby individuals are "located in conversation as observably and subjectively coherent participants in jointly produced story lines, informed by particular discourses" (Davies and Harré 1990:48, in Mason 2005:36). The way in which interpreters position other participants in the communication event has "consequences for the ongoing negotiation of identity" between those participants (Mason 2005:41). For example, the patient may assume the use of a colloquial term is the doctor's choice and may perceive it as a move to reduce the distance between them. Mason argues that these and other examples discussed in the paper show how issues of identity and power are closely interrelated and, in particular, how the playing of power relations within exchanges such as interpreter-mediated doctor-patient conversations or asylum-seeking interviews is closely involved with the negotiation of identity.

3.5.3   *The tools of corpus analysis*

Baker *et al* (2008:295) suggest a series of stages (listed below) that could be undertaken in order to carry out corpus-assisted CDA:

(1) Context-based analysis of topic via history/politics/culture/etymology. Identify existing topoi/discourses/strategies via wider reading, reference to other studies using critical discourse analysis;
(2) Establish research questions/corpus building procedures;
(3) Corpus analysis of frequencies, clusters, keywords, dispersion, etc. – identify potential sites of interest in the corpus along with possible discourses/topoi/strategies, relate to those existing in the literature;
(4) Qualitative or CDA analysis of a smaller, representative set of data (e.g. concordances of certain lexical items or of a particular text or set of texts within the corpus) – identify discourses/topoi/strategies;
(5) Formulation of new hypotheses or research questions;
(6) Further corpus analysis based on new hypotheses, identify further discourses/topoi/strategies, etc.;
(7) Analysis of intertextuallty or interdiscursivity[16] based on findings from corpus analysis;

---

[16] "Interdiscursivity indicates that discourses are linked to each other in various ways. If we define discourse as primarily topic-related, i.e., a discourse on X, then a discourse on un/employment often refers, for example, to topics or subtopics of other discourses, such as gender or racism: arguments on systematically lower salaries for women or migrants might be included in discourses on employment" (Baker *at al* 2008:299).

(8) New hypotheses;
(9) Further corpus analysis, identify additional discourses/topoi/strate-
     gies, etc.

In line with an abductive logic, these stages take the form of an iterative process,
where steps are repeated and the results of each step are used as the starting
point for the next step. An initial textual analysis results in the identification of
certain patterns of language use. A preliminary interpretation of these patterns
suggests other textual aspects to be explored in the text, and we start the process again. The premise is that text both reflects and constructs context and, as
a result, "one utterance can be analyzed for itself and be treated as context for
others" (Wood and Kroger 2000:96). Wood and Kroger (*ibid.*:97) argue that this
process helps to ensure reliability and validity, in that the interpretation is not
checked via agreement (i.e. against the coding of another researcher, see Chapter
5, Section 5.9 for a discussion of code checking), but rather it is checked by using
it in further analysis. The aim is to then integrate the observations gathered in
each stage into a coherent principle. The stages described by Baker *et al* (2008)
constitute just one model that could be followed to carry out CDA using corpora,
though other research designs are also possible.

   There are a number of software tools that can be used to interrogate corpora
in a variety of ways and display the results in a matter of seconds. This does not
mean, however, that you will have the answers to your research question(s) in a
matter of seconds too. Interpreting corpus data requires skill and patience. The
key is to ask the right questions.

   For small corpora, corpus analysis software of the type generally known as
'concordancers' is widely available and relatively user-friendly. See Wiechmann
and Fuhs (2006) for a review of some of these tools, but note that most of
them are designed to be used with monolingual corpora. Examples of currently
available standalone monolingual concordancers include Wordsmith Tools and
AntConc, and a popular multilingual concordancer is Paraconc. The three are
quite user-friendly and AntConc can be downloaded for free. Two popular web-
based programs are Sketch Engine[17] and Wmatrix.[18]

   When using concordancers, the different operations related to text retrieval
and display are integrated into the user interface and all you have to do is select
the files that you want analyzed, which are usually on the same computer on
which the software is installed. These concordancers would be too slow if they
had to handle very large corpora; therefore, for large projects, a number of corpus
management tools are used to access data that reside on a remote server. This
is known as a client-server architecture, where the client is the computer that is
used for formulating the queries and displaying the results.

   Applications for the management of annotated corpus resources which are
freely available for research purposes include XAIRA, the MODNLP-tec suite and

---

[17] http://www.sketchengine.co.uk/ [Last accessed 26 July 2012].
[18] ucrel.lancs.ac.uk/wmatrix/ [Last accessed 26 July 2012].

the Corpus Workbench (CBW). These tools not only allow for the interrogation of larger corpora but also for more complex analyses than standalone concordancers. Here we will limit ourselves to describing the type of basic analysis that can be carried out using standalone corpus tools. For more information and further references about other resources, see Zanettin (2012).

Most analyses are based on **word indexes**, i.e. information about the frequency of word forms (types) and their location in the text. This information can be displayed in the form of **frequency lists** for individual words or word clusters. Basic indexes present some problems in that they do not take homographs or spelling variants into account. Thus, 'chair' will be one type whether it refers to a piece of furniture or a person, while 'favor' and 'favour' will be counted as two types. **POS tagging** and **lemmatization** can solve this to some extent. Lemmatization consists in grouping different forms of a word together so that, for instance, 'am' and 'were' are labelled as forms of the lemma 'be'. Unless the word indexes are lemmatized, inflected words from the same lemma will also be counted as different types.

Despite being rather rudimentary, simple frequency lists can provide very useful information. The heads of frequency lists, i.e. the part of a frequency list that contains the most frequent types, have been used by Laviosa to measure simplification in translated texts, based on the assumption that the percentage of the most frequent words is a measure of richness of vocabulary closely related to lexical density (Laviosa-Braithwaite 1997:536). Kenny (2001), on the other hand, uses the 'tail' of frequency lists, which contain hapax legomena (words that appear only once in a corpus), as a way of identifying creative lexical items in source texts.

Frequency lists for different texts or corpora can also be compared to identify keywords. **Keywords** are items whose frequency is significantly high (or low in the case of negative keywords) in one text or corpus compared with their frequency in another text or corpus, which is used as a reference. Most corpus processing software will create lists of keywords automatically using statistical tests to indicate the likelihood that the distribution of frequencies has or has not come about by chance. Wordsmith Tools, for example, can create lists based on probability measures such as chi square and log likelihood. The corpus analysis tool Wmatrix extends the keywords method to key grammatical categories and key semantic domains. In her study of the translation of lexical creativity, Kenny (2001) obtained writer-specific forms (i.e. words used by one writer only) by comparing the frequency lists for each writer with the frequency list for her larger corpus. Winters (2009) compares translations of the same text by two translators and keywords help her identify the distinctive use of modal particles as a stylistic trait of each translator.

Word indexes can also provide basic statistics, such as **average sentence length** and **type-token ratio**. The type-token ratio, the ratio of the number of different words (types) to the number of running words in a text (tokens), can tell us something about the variety of word forms used in a corpus, which can be interpreted as an indication of lexical complexity and specificity. Such ratios are usually standardized, that is, calculated on chunks of, say, 100 or 1,000 words of text at a time and then averaged for the entire text. Otherwise, the results would depend largely on the length of the text and not so much on the variety of vocabulary. Other measures of vocabulary richness that take into account text length are Yule's K and Heap's law (Oakes 2012).

Another useful statistical measure is **lexical density**, the ratio of the number of lexical words to the number of running words in a text. Lexical density can be used to measure information load; the lexical density of written texts, for example, tends to be higher than that of spoken texts (Stubbs 1986). Comparatively low average sentence length, type/token ratio and lexical density have been used as measures of simplification by Laviosa in several studies where she compares translated texts with non-translated texts to test the hypothesis that simplification is a potentially universal feature of translation (Laviosa-Braithwaite 1997; Laviosa 1997, 1998a and 1998b).

Analyses of frequency usually benefit from being supplemented by information on **dispersion**, i.e. on where the words occur within a text or corpus. It may be useful to ascertain whether a word is a regular feature across the text or whether most occurrences are clumped together in a small section (Baker 2006:49).

When comparing statistics in a parallel corpus it is important to remember that source and target texts are not directly commensurable; comparisons of type/token ratio, lexical density and even sentence length are not reliable across languages because they do not take into account particularities of each language in terms of morphology or optional and obligatory syntactic elements. Other techniques that are being increasingly used in CL are those broadly known as machine-learning methods, commonly used in text classification and stylometry studies. The idea behind text classification techniques is that a collection of data is automatically divided into sub-collections, with all items in the same group sharing some characteristics. Baroni and Bernardini (2006) use a text-categorization technique known as support vector machines (SVMs) to differentiate between translated text and non-translated text in a corpus of Italian articles from the geopolitical domain. Ke (2012) was able to differentiate translations that were accepted and those that were rejected in a translator's examination at the Norges Handelshøyskole (Norwegian School of Economics). Similar techniques have been used in stylometry – the study of measurable features of literary style – in particular for authorship attribution, i.e. for identifying a text's author. Some of the most successful attributive methods rely on the frequency of the most frequent common words to automatically classify texts by different authors. These methods have also been tested on translations (Burrows 2002; Rybicki 2006; 2010; 2011; 2012). Rybicki (2012), for example, has applied a procedure known as Delta to study the extent to which (statistically significant) traces of translator style may be identified. In most cases, translated texts are grouped (clustered) by author rather than translator, which suggests that the author's style comes across clearly enough in the translations and any textual traces of the translators' own style are not marked enough for these methods to attribute 'translatorship'.

Lists of words and statistical techniques based on word frequencies present linguistic data isolated from their co-text. Hence, while they are useful in examining correlations, they do not often help us in providing explanations for the results (see discussion of causality in Chapter 2, Section 2.10.3). In fact, the mechanisms behind the success of some of the text-classification and author-attribution techniques described above remain a mystery (Craig 1999) and they may even lack "any compelling theoretical justification" (Hoover 2005; in Rybicki 2012:233). To make the risky leap from frequencies to meaning, it is still necessary to look at the lexical items in their co-text and to consider texts in their context to establish possible reasons for the patterns revealed.

In order to look at lexical items in their co-text we can use concordances. A **concordance** is a list of all the occurrences of a specified node with its immediate context. Figure 3.6 offers an example of a concordance of the node 'source' using the British National Corpus.[19] The node can be a lemma, word or expression, basically any string of contiguous characters (including spaces). Restrictions can be specified so as to retrieve only concordances fulfilling certain conditions. In the example in Figure 3.6, one of the conditions specified was that the word 'single' should appear within 4 words to the right or to the left of the node. The words to the right and left of the node are known as the co-text. When using POS-annotated corpora, concordances can be filtered to retrieve only words belonging to a certain POS category, for example, all adjectives used in the co-text of 'source'. **Regular expressions** can be used to make more complex searches. Regular expressions are patterns of characters where wildcards are used to allow for further flexibility: so, for example, the regular expression "colou?r" matches 'color' and 'colour', and "[a-z]+" matches any non-zero sequence of lower case letters.

Once retrieved, concordances can be ordered in a variety of ways, for example by words appearing in the co-text of the node (e.g. according to the first word to the right of the node), or by filename, thus facilitating the search for linguistic patterns concerning the use of the node as well as patterns in terms of the type of text where a certain node tends to appear. In Figure 3.6 the concordances are sorted alphabetically following the first, second and third words to the left of the node.

Concordances are useful in identifying patterns such as collocations, colligations, semantic preferences and semantic prosodies. Collocations are the "characteristic co-occurrence patterns of words in a text" (McEnery and Wilson 1996:7). Collocates are those words that tend to appear in the environment of another word more often than we would expect to happen by chance. The collocational profile of a word can tell us something about the grammatical and semantic environment in which that word is generally used, and is useful in identifying meanings and connotations that are not always reflected in dictionary definitions. For example, the ten most frequent adjectives occurring in the

---

[19] The concordance was obtained using the interface provided by Brigham Young University: http://corpus.byu.edu/bnc/ [Last accessed 7 November 2012].

context of 'source' in the British National Corpus are: 'main', 'major', 'important', 'only', 'other', 'single', 'new', 'useful', 'primary' and 'light'.

economic platform so that you needed er a single authoritative	source	of currency for example er and a single source of er er
most new book orders should be based upon a single base	source	. The base source need not be used unsupported . Once it
selection of newly published books is linked to a single base	source	of information (see Chapter 8) and wherever possible decisions
obvious bias , at least initially . Even a single biased	source	can be useful . There is great scope for the study of
many librarians prefer to select from a single bibliographical	source	(see Chapter 8) , cross-checking to publishers ' catalogues if
in an emergency . Mothers were the single most frequently cited	source	of help (Bradshaw and Holmes , 1989) . While parents
the more they are likely to derive from a single common	source	. This of course is what inspired Thor Heyerdahl 's dramatic
etc . Unlike an industrial accident involving a single emission	source	, the pollutants contributing to an urban smog are emitted from
total which is a uniquely dominant share of a single energy	source	. The Urengoy field , which lies in Western Siberia , inside
, along with hydro-electricity , the largest single energy	source	. In Canada , gas resources are not a limiting factor .
of sources within the organization . The single most important	source	is the Management Accounting department , which is responsible

Figure 3.6. A concordance of the node 'source' obtained using the BYU-BNC interface for the British National Corpus

A number of statistical tests are used to obtain collocates, based on the frequency of the words in the corpus and the relative number of occurrences in the context of the node (the word being investigated). We discussed above some of the problems of using statistical tests in corpus analysis; these are characteristic of the computation of collocates as well. Some measures, such as mutual information, artificially inflate the importance of collocates that have a low frequency in the corpus; others, like T-score, draw attention to high frequency collocates (see McEnery *et al* 2006 and/or Oakes 2012 for an explanation of the differences among the various tests). The best technique, then, depends on whether the researcher is interested in high frequency function words or low frequency content words (Baker 2006:102).

Tognini-Bonelli and Manca (2002) propose a methodology for identifying functional equivalents across languages by identifying the collocates of a source word, then examining the prima-facie equivalents for each collocate in the target corpus and their collocational range, with a view to locating the lexical and grammatical patterns that more characteristically encode the function of the original node word. They test this methodology in two corpora of web pages in the comparable fields of 'Agriturismo' and 'Farmhouse Holidays'. They observe that the word 'welcome' usually collocates with 'children' and 'pets'; in these co-texts, however, 'welcome' does not necessarily convey warmth and friendliness but reminds users that children and pets are usually categories of exclusion. The prima-facie Italian translation equivalent 'benvenuto' is rarely used in the Italian corpus, and two other words – 'ammettere' (admit) and 'accettare' (accept) – are suggested as better translation choices for 'welcome' when used with 'children' and 'pets' as collocates.

Colligation is the relationship between a lexical item and the grammatical classes of the items in its environment. Colligational information can be extracted automatically from lemmatized and POS-annotated corpora. Sketch Engine, a corpus analysis tool, produces 'word sketches' which are automatic summaries of collocations and colligations associated with a word. Figure 3.7 shows a sketch for the word 'source'.

source (noun) British National Corpus freq = 15519 (138.3 per million)

object_of	2247	1.2	subject_of	950	0.9	modifier	9531	1.8	modifies	839	0.2	and/or	1700	0.7
cite	30	7.28	confirm	24	5.75	main	324	8.23	code	156	8.62	primary	13	6.99
tap	23	7.27	claim	36	5.4	alternative	131	8.15	marker	19	7.63	destination	10	6.21
quote	40	7.26	indicate	17	4.76	renewable	75	7.96	node	15	7.39	application	47	5.62
trace	24	6.91	say	275	4.66	major	253	7.81	text	46	6.54	package	12	4.67
identify	69	6.58	report	24	4.61	primary	128	7.8	material	103	6.49	newspaper	7	3.88
constitute	23	6.45	insist	6	4.42	potential	101	7.6	rock	41	6.48	oil	8	3.86
locate	23	6.42	deny	8	4.35	energy	172	7.53	file	18	5.21	source	13	3.77
disclose	12	6.22	estimate	6	4.32	secondary	79	7.48	module	8	4.65	cause	6	3.43
Say	6	6.14	reveal	10	4.14	reliable	63	7.44	income	17	4.52	library	6	3.39
exploit	12	6.05	influence	6	4.03	light	83	7.38	licence	6	4.32	method	10	3.35
eliminate	11	5.97	state	7	3.95	valuable	67	7.35	index	6	4.27	nature	9	3.2
provide	181	5.96	supply	6	3.77	useful	91	7.24	region	12	3.93	energy	6	3.12
consult	10	5.78	mention	6	3.75	important	225	7.22	language	14	3.69	language	9	3.01
integrate	9	5.71	describe	14	3.57	principal	62	7.19	study	18	3.33	use	13	2.84
remain	58	5.7	tell	34	3.49	external	68	7.18	unit	10	3.1	detail	6	2.82
discover	25	5.62	suggest	13	3.41	only	156	7.14	book	13	2.8	datum	6	2.75
protect	21	5.47	add	8	2.84	documentary	45	7.06	datum	6	2.79	material	7	2.57
Use	6	5.38	provide	17	2.57	other	625	7.06	name	6	1.83	type	8	2.49
become	116	5.34	remain	6	2.48	various	109	7.04	form	7	1.73	information	11	2.47
reveal	23	5.25	produce	6	1.9	biographical	36	6.88	level	6	1.48	record	6	2.45

Figure 3.7. A Sketch engine profile of the word 'source'

Semantic preference is defined by Stubbs (2001:65) as "the relation, not between individual words, but between a lemma or word-form and a set of semantically related words". Based on the word sketch in Figure 3.7, we could say that 'source' shows a preference for words involving verbal reporting ('cite', 'quote', 'confirm', 'claim', 'say', 'report'). A related concept is that of **semantic prosody** (also referred to as 'discourse prosody'), which refers to the way in which the collocates of a word can be suggestive of speakers' attitudes (Louw 1993). We saw above that the adjectives that collocate with 'source' are positive and suggest importance. This is confirmed by the word sketch in Figure 3.7. Taken together with reporting verbs such as 'claim' and 'confirm', we could suggest that there is an aura of authority associated with the word 'source'. The concept of semantic prosody suggests that senses and connotations are never restricted to a single unit; they are, as it were, contagious, they spread to co-textual units. Munday (2011) discusses the implication of the study of semantic prosody for translation and notes that certain lexical items (in his example, the English 'loom large' and the Spanish 'cernerse') may have similar meanings and equally negative semantic prosodies but be used in different semantic structures and with different collocates.

One of the advantages of using corpus analysis tools is that we can easily account for all the instances of an item in a corpus. This can help to make the analysis comprehensive which, as explained below, is an important requirement both in CDA and CL. However, we also need to bear in mind the limitations in terms of what a concordance can retrieve automatically, which is based on a search for surface forms. A concordancer will not retrieve instances where the same concept is referred to using a euphemism or a pronoun, for example. The kind of detailed analysis of referring expressions that is to be found in Kang (2007) is not possible using corpus tools. Kang examines how North Korea is (re)constructed in translations of *Newsweek* stories published in *Newsweek Hankuk Pan* (Korean edition). In the source text, a number of referring expressions (e.g. the North Korean dictator, the "Great Leader") are used to refer to the North Korean Head of State. In the target text, he is simply referred to by his name, or the pronoun 'he' – choices which mitigate or neutralize the negative opinion evident in the source text – and using his official title, 'Chairman', which is not used in the source text.

We will finish this overview of corpus-analysis tools with three cautions. First, concordances can facilitate the observation of language patterning, but it is still the analyst who has to recognize patterns and explain them. Sometimes, patterns in concordances will be immediately obvious, but analyzing concordances does require some skill (we recommend using Sinclair 2003 as a practical guide). Second, concordances need to be interpreted in terms of linguistic features and discourse categories which are ultimately interpretative constructions, and the responsibility for interpretation lies with the researcher. And finally, although the use of corpus analysis tools can help us to find patterns faster and across a larger number of texts, thereby potentially allowing us to generalize from our results, it can also arguably make the analysis more superficial, both in terms of accounting for co-textual information and in terms of the range of linguistic features that can be analyzed.

3.5.4   *Addressing issues of quality in critical discourse analysis and corpus linguistics*

Wood and Kroger (2000) identify a list of requirements that can help ensure validity (or, to use their alternative concept, warrantability) in CDA. These requirements were presented in Chapter 2 because they are applicable to qualitative research in general. They can be briefly summarized here as the need for the analysis to be systematic, well documented and transparent (orderliness, documentation and accountability); based on evidence; comprehensive; coherent and plausible. A further requirement is that the analyst should be able to offer new insights and identify implications for future work. In Section 3.2.3 above we discussed some of the criticisms directed at CDA and CL (lack of replicability, risk of circular arguments and assumption of privileged knowledge). These problems can be addressed by following the criteria for warrantability elaborated by Wood and Kruger, and in particular, by adopting a self-reflective stance.

In this section we will discuss in more detail and illustrate with reference to good research practice in translation studies two principles that are particularly important for a systematic and well-supported textual analysis using either a CDA or CL approach: the first is the need for a comprehensive analysis and the second is the requirement for contextualization. A **comprehensive analysis** means that when making a claim, an effort needs to be made to account for every instance relevant to that claim. There are two related aspects to this requirement. First, we need to account for what is present in the discourse as well as what is absent from the discourse; i.e. at the same time as considering salient features, it is important to consider what is not there: alternative phrasings, a break in punctuation, a missed opportunity for clarification. Second, we need to account for the exception as well as the norm. Exceptions "must be accounted for by showing how they can fit the claim, by adjusting or modifying the hypotheses, or by showing that they are outside of the claim, that is, they involve a different pattern or claim" (Wood and Kroger 2000:119). Textual studies of translations often reveal that translation strategies are not consistent, and evidence of inconsistent practices need to be highlighted as part of the "fragmentary nature of the translation strategy" (Tymoczko 2002:20).

In Pöllabauer (2004), we find an illustration of how what is absent from the discourse – and is, at the same time an exception – can be explained by relating it to another pattern. As reported above, Pöllabauer looks at interpreters' behaviour in asylum hearings and observes that interpreters use several strategies to save face. In one case, however, the officer comments that the asylum seeker's account is too vague and the interpreter reproduces the statement without attempting to attenuate it, thereby putting the asylum seeker's positive face in danger. There is nothing remarkable in the interpreter's choice, since she is simply rendering the officer's statement; however, taking into consideration the interpreter's attempt to save the other participants' face in similar situations, or at least mark the authorship of face-threatening remarks, this example is seen as a case of deliberately avoiding such a strategy. This is explained in relation to another pattern, where interpreters' solidarity with officers leads them to assist such officers in reaching their communicative goals, to the point where they – the interpreters – assume the role of "auxiliary police officers" (*ibid.*:157).

In Saldanha (2004), the negative results of a hypothesis-testing corpus-based experiment are used to generate a new hypothesis concerning a different but related phenomenon to the one initially chosen. The study had been designed to test the existence of gender-related linguistic patterns in translations by men and women. The hypothesis was that because women's language is considered to be more conservative, and so is translators' language, the use of split-infinitives, which is discouraged by style guides, would be less common in translations by women. The results showed that there was no correlation between the use of split infinitives and the gender of the translator. However, a qualitative analysis of concordances, taking into account the type of split-infinitives and how frequently they appeared in translations by the same translator, indicated that they could potentially reflect stylistic preferences of individual translators.

Concerning the principle of **contextualization**, a common problem is that contextual factors are highlighted but not brought to bear on the analysis itself. Generally, if a particular contextual feature is important, we should be able to see this in some way or another in the discourse. Accounting for context cannot be reduced to making links with a set of dimensions that are external to the text (time, location, authors, etc.); we need to be able to demonstrate which relevant aspects of the context are activated by the authors/translators by reference to the choices made in the text itself. This can be done by showing that there is a systematicity in choices when looked at from one perspective, a systematicity that is lacking when we look at the same data from a different perspective.

In CDA, the link between the text and its external context is often established through an analysis of **intertextuality**. All texts are intertextual, in that they echo and allude to other texts, but analysis is not intertextual unless it takes account explicitly of the intertextual references within the text. According to Fairclough (1992:194)

> intertextual analysis shows how texts selectively draw upon *orders of discourse* – the particular configurations of conventionalized practices (genres, discourses, narratives, etc.) which are available to text producers and interpreters in particular social circumstances (...)

To conclude this section we will describe a particularly solid piece of research that serves to illustrate the requirement for contextualization and the notion of intertextuality as understood by Fairclough. The study in question, Harvey (2003), was mentioned above in relation to text selection. As already explained, the aim was to "trace" the "various French discourses predicated upon the adaptation and absorption of American gay in the 1970s" (*ibid.*:3). The centrepiece of the research is the analysis of three source texts and their translations. The texts selected are *Dancer from the Dance*, mentioned above, as well as two other American gay novels translated into French within a period of eighteen months, which are comparable in terms of genre, setting and theme. The translational analysis is preceded by an in-depth investigation of how 'American gay' was portrayed in a wide range of textual sources (journalistic commentary, polemic, travel writing, ethnography and original French novels) and is followed by an examination of what Harvey calls the bindings of translations, understood literally and metaphorically to include the paratextual material that surrounds the text (covers and blurbs), reviews and literary criticism.

The aim of the contrastive analysis of the translations is to consider the ways in which the translators negotiate the challenges of the source texts within the context of the transfer of American gay into French. The analysis of French discourses allows the researcher to draw up a profile of the 'horizon of expectations' into which the translations were produced. The themes emerging from this analysis, such as the tension between a need for a distinctive community versus the dangers of 'ghettoisation', the use of effeminacy, and the relevance and desirability of American models, are used to identify aspects of the translation that are of particular relevance for the project. Harvey (2003:128) chooses to focus on "passages of dialogue which crystallize – sometimes in their subject matter, always in their functionality – the problematic of identity and community" and "[v]erbal utterances and exchanges exemplifying the categories of camp and parodic femininity". In terms of linguistic and stylistic features, the analysis draws upon a range of resources, such as the use of grammatical gender, italics, innuendo, register and word play.

What at first sight may appear as a context-text-context research design, whereby text analysis is contextualized by reference to non-translational textual resources, is actually subverted in practice by an analysis that insists on the mutual determination of text and context, so that the three parts of the study are presented as all contributing to an inherently translational process of the formation of homosexual discourse by adopting and opposing discourse categories from different cultures.

Thus far, this chapter has described two approaches to researching the products of the translation process, translated and interpreted texts. Given how they can be and are interlaced, we grouped CDA and CL together. Section 3.6 addresses the topic of product-focused translation research through the lens of quality assessment.

3.6   Research on translation quality assessment: Introduction

Evaluation of translation can involve an examination of the process, the context, and/or the product. To date, the majority of research on **quality** in translation studies has focused on the assessment of the translated product, hence the decision to include our discussion of research on translation quality assessment in this chapter. While CL could be used to facilitate translation quality assessment and CDA could potentially be used as an approach to the study of the same issue, both CL and CDA – as discussed above – are driven broadly by a descriptive/exploratory focus whereas quality assessment is, by its nature, primarily evaluative.

Translation evaluation is a task that has been carried out for centuries, with the initial focus being on the concepts of equivalence, literalness or freeness of the translation and evaluation criteria being mainly subjective. As translation became established as both a profession and an academic discipline, **evaluation** has evolved and become even more complex, while often remaining a subjective exercise. The scope of evaluation as an area of research is enormous, and there is a vast body of literature on the topic in general that should be referred to before any quality-related research is initiated (e.g. House 1997; Nord 1997; Schäffner 1998; Gouadec 2010). Martínez Melis and Hurtado Albir (2001) offer a good overview of quality assessment in translation studies and call for more rigorous research in this domain.

The terminology associated with translation quality can be confusing. Some authors write about quality evaluation, others about quality assessment or even quality assurance. Quality assurance normally refers to systems and processes used to help create or maintain quality. We understand the term evaluation to be a more general term relating to the testing of quality, whereas quality assessment, or QA, is a term frequently used in a professional context to describe the step in the translation process that involves the counting and classification of translation errors. For the sake of consistency here we will use the more specific term quality assessment (QA).

Many models of quality assessment have been developed in translation studies. Martínez Melis and Hurtado Albir (2001:274) summarize these as ranging in focus from technical procedures in translation on the segment or sub-segment level, such as modulation or transposition, to criteria at the textual level (intratextual, extratextual factors), to the socio-cultural context, and stress that no model has brought textual, contextual and functionalist criteria together, nor has such a model been validated through empirical-experimental research. This serves to highlight the complexity of the topic as well as the need for very careful consideration during the research design stage.

3.6.1   *Strengths and weaknesses*

Quality is a very important topic in translation, both in professional and pedagogical settings, and research involving quality assessment is also of importance since it allows us to measure the impact and effect of different variables on the translation product and process and to subsequently change our techniques, training, or tools in order to better meet quality requirements.

Some quality assessment models allow for the reporting of quantitative results using pre-determined categories, which can appear to be objective. However, one of the main criticisms of such models is that they can be reductionist, i.e. they take what is essentially a very complex process that is influenced by many factors and try to account for all of those factors by, for example, counting and categorizing translation errors. Lauscher (2000) comments on how quality will depend on a variety of diverse factors and on how, therefore, it is unreasonable to expect one QA model to be valid in all possible circumstances or to account for all parameters that influence the process and product of translation. She critically evaluates a number of translation QA models, suggesting that many of these models, although useful up to a point, suffer from a lack, or fuzzy definition, of their core concepts and/or fail when applied outside the text type(s) for which they were developed.

Translation QA models that seek to go beyond **reductionism** and take account of a wider range of factors – such as translator competence, text type, text function, target cultural expectations, end user competence, and so on – would clearly be highly complex. On the other hand, quality assessment of sub-segments of translation without any consideration of the situation in which the translation was produced and the end user requirements is too simplistic. Lauscher (2000:161) argues that QA models need to be flexible enough and yet precise. These are the issues that must be faced head on by researchers who wish to engage in translation quality assessment; they are explored in more detail below.

3.6.2   Design

Prior to conducting research that involves translation quality assessment, there are a number of questions that may be asked which will help the researcher to clarify in his or her mind the exact nature and purpose of the quality assessment component of the research project. We have divided these initial considerations into the following topics: setting, status, genre, purpose and focus.

Martínez Melis and Hurtado Albir (2001) identify three possible settings for quality assessment: (1) literary or sacred texts, (2) professional, and (3) pedagogical. QA in the first setting involves an exercise that is akin to literary criticism. But this three-way classification is questionable since both literary translation and the translation of sacred texts can be 'professional', and the purposes of those two genres can differ significantly. On the other hand, it seems to make sense to differentiate between professional and pedagogical settings for quality assessment. This brings us to the consideration of the status of the translators whose work will be assessed for quality. Multiple combinations are possible from different communities such as students, professionals and amateurs. Martínez Melis and Hurtado Albir (2001: 277) outline three purposes of assessment: (1) the diagnostic function, which highlights abilities and shortcomings in the group being assessed; (2) the summative function, which is used to determine end results or knowledge acquired following the application of a particular process (such as a translation course), and (3) the formative function, where assessment is integrated into a learning process and is used to enhance learning. The status of those being assessed should guide the nature of the assessment and, in turn, the assessment model. Clearly, a formative assessment model would be highly suited to a group of students but less suited to a group of professional translators.

The next decision to be made when designing a research project is which genre (see Section 3.5.1) of translated text we wish to include in the quality assessment. The QA criteria will depend on the genre and function of the original text and those of the translation. For example, stylistic criteria may be more important for literary texts and less important (though not necessarily unimportant) for technical instructions. The QA criteria should match the genre specifications for both the source and target genres. Genres conventions are closely related to the functions texts are expected to fulfill in the source and target environment. Translations are ideally conducted according to the instructions in a translation brief, where the text function should be specified. Thus, it is important to consider the genre, the text function(s) and the translation brief together in order to select relevant QA criteria.

The purpose of research involving translation quality assessment should be very clear from the outset. A common purpose is, obviously, to assess and compare the quality of one or more translations and the outcome of this exercise usually involves a pronouncement on the level of translation quality, sometimes in comparison with other translations. To produce reliable results, we need to be sure that the QA model or criteria selected are valid or, to put it more precisely, they need to demonstrate measurement validity, as discussed in Chapter 2. For this reason, the validity of quality assessment models and tools is a research area in its own right (involving meta-evaluation). One example is Waddington (2001), who analyzes the criterion-related validity of four different QA models, two different error-based models, one holistic model, and one which combines error analysis with holistic criteria. Interestingly, he found that all four ways of assessing the quality of student translations possessed criterion-related validity. In other words, all models were valid ways of assessing translation quality among students. However, he emphasizes that this result could be explained not only by the validity of the models themselves, but also 'by the fact that they were carefully designed, tested, and applied' (Waddington 2001:324).

Depraetere and Vackier (2011) is another example of meta-evaluation. They compare the evaluation metric developed for assessing student translators' work (i.e., used in a pedagogical setting) with that of a semi-automated tool used in industry for translation QA (QA Distiller) in order to see what correlations exist between the two models. Testing for ease of application is an important endeavour because many quality models proposed to date contain an enormous number of error categories, which, if utilized, might take so long to apply as to be completely impractical. Gouadec (1981, 1989), for example, proposed a scale in which there are 675 potential error types, which would clearly give a detailed account of errors, but might take an inordinate amount of time to apply in a large-scale research project. More recent work relating to the assessment of student translations (Delizée 2011) includes such granular categories that if they were to be applied to multiple translations for multiple students, assessment could be unrealistically onerous on the translation teacher.

As mentioned in the introduction to this section, quality assessment might focus on the product (the translation itself), the process (the means by which the translation is produced) or the user (the reception of the translation). Research involving QA might very well include all of these aspects, but the scope of the research project will usually force a focus onto one aspect, and it is reasonable to expect that the nature of quality assessment will be dictated by the focus. If we are interested in translation as product, it is quite likely we will elect to use a product-oriented QA model in our research project. Product-oriented models are primarily, though not exclusively, error-oriented; that is, the translation(s) is/are compared to the source text and errors in meaning, transfer, terminology etc. are identified, categorized and assigned penalty scores. In some cases, highly creative translations are rewarded with positive points, though this is relatively rare in professional settings (O'Brien 2012) while being more common in pedagogical settings (Waddington 2001). An example of a product-oriented model is the LISA QA model,[20] which was identified by O'Brien (2012) as being a common source for customized error-oriented quality assessment in the IT translation industry in

---

[20] LISA stands for the Localisation Industry Standards Association, which, at the time of writing, no longer existed. The LISA QA model, however, lived on and is in common usage in the localization industry.

particular. The SAE J2450 is yet another example of a product-oriented model.[21] This metric was developed by the American Society for Automotive Engineers in collaboration with the automotive company General Motors (for a brief description see Secară 2005). Process-oriented QA models are quite different from product-oriented ones since they focus on what needs to be put in place in a company in order to ensure high quality translation from a translation process perspective (for example, hiring qualified translators, or ensuring that a terminology management process is in place). An example is the EN15038 standard.[22] There exist also models that seek to be more holistic, such as the one described in Delizée (2012). This model seeks to go beyond the criteria traditionally used in student translation evaluation. It includes seven categories, some of which are commonly applied in a pedagogical scenario – for example, linguistic skills in the source language, translation skills, linguistic skills in the target language, discipline (which refers to the use of domain knowledge, terminology and style) – and others which include broader evaluation categories, i.e., professional skills (broadly meaning ability to work in professional conditions), methodological skills (involving skills in background and terminological research) and technical skills (ability to use the tools of the trade).

Product and process QA models, to a greater or lesser extent, implicitly include the end user of the translation, but QA measures exist that have a strong focus on the end user, measured, however, through text analysis. According to House (2009), text-based approaches may be informed by linguistics, comparative literature or functional models. Nida and Taber (1969) are credited with introducing a focus on the end user through their concept of dynamic equivalence. This is a 'response-oriented' evaluation, which has been criticized because the criteria for assessing equivalent effect are not made explicit. This focus was then extended by skopos theory (Reiss and Vermeer 1984) and the functionalist school (House 1977, 1997, Nord 1997). In skopos theory, the purpose of the translation is foregrounded and translations are evaluated according to their level of adaptation to appropriate target text and cultural norms.

House (1997, 2001) built on the foundation set by skopos theory and developed a functional-pragmatic model which "provides for the analysis of the linguistic-situational particularities of source and target texts, a comparison of the two texts and the resultant assessment of their relative match" (House 2009:224). House's model of translation quality assessment requires a profiling of the source text according to situational dimensions. She distinguishes between two main situational dimensions: the dimension of language user and the dimension of language use. The former includes aspects such as geographical origin and social class; the latter covers medium of communication, social role relationship and social attitude, among other factors. A basic assumption in House's model is that the target text addressees form a basically similar sub-group in the target language community to the sub-group formed by the addressees of the source

---

[21] See http://www.sae.org/standardsdev/j2450p1.htm [Last accessed 7 November 2012].
[22] See http://qualitystandard.bs.en-15038.com/ [Last accessed 7 November 2012].

text in the source language community. Another important assumption is that both the source text and the target text share the same function. The basic requirement for quality in House's model is equivalence of function. House does recognize that on occasion a special secondary function is added to the target text, but argues that these are no longer translations and need to be defined as *versions* of the source text.

Additional end-user focused quality measurements include **readability, comprehensibility, acceptability** and **usability**. Each of these concepts is intricately linked with the other and it is difficult to establish clear-cut distinctions between, for example, acceptability and comprehensibility. What they all have in common is that they focus attention on quality from the point of view of the individual user and, consequently, QA research involving these measurements necessitates a consideration of individual user attributes, such as reading skill, or motivation for reading the translation. This differentiates them from a functionalist-oriented QA exercise which largely assumes one typical end user. QA research focusing on readability of the translated text might use a readability index[23] and a survey; research focusing on comprehensibility might use a recall test; research focusing on usability might use eye tracking and measures such as task time or task efficiency (for an example, see Doherty and O'Brien 2012); whereas a focus on acceptability might use a ranking scale (where 1 could mean unacceptable and 5 completely acceptable, for example). What this hopefully demonstrates is that the research focus, whether that is on the product, the process, the user or a combination of these, should be determined during the design phase with a view to identifying the most appropriate measurement models and tools.

3.6.3   Which QA model(s)?

Having answered design questions pertaining to setting, genre, purpose, focus and status, as outlined above, more specific decisions can be made about the research design. The most obvious question is which specific QA model (or models) will be applied. While the existence of previously proposed models should not be ignored, there is a justifiable tendency to either customize them or dismiss them as inappropriate in a new research context. It may also be the case that no pre-existing model suits the needs of the researcher, though there are so many to choose from that this is rather unlikely and the motivation for creating a new model should be clearly outlined. Customization generally involves the addition or removal of categories. The motivation for such customization ought to be explained in detail in any subsequent research report. Generally speaking, we would recommend offering a detailed critical overview of the relevant QA models that exist and have been applied in similar research contexts and, where appropriate, their re-use. This has the advantage of testing further the validity and reliability of the model and of creating comparable results across studies.

---

[23] For a list of readability indices see http://www.readability.info/info.shtml [Last accessed 7 November 2012]. Note, however, that the adequacy of some of these indices is questionable.

There are models, generally proposed within academic – as opposed to professional – contexts, that rely on linguistic analysis, such as the model outlined by Kim (2007) and the one developed by House (1997), both based on a systemic functional grammar approach. House's model relies on a Hallidayan register analysis using the categories of field, tenor and mode described above (Section 3.5.1). The model involves producing a profile of the source text on the basis of register analysis with the aim of determining the text's function. The same process is then carried out for the target text and a statement of mismatches is produced. The degree to which the two profiles match is then taken as an indicator of quality (House 2009:224). A distinction is made between **dimensional mismatches**, which are pragmatic errors that have to do with the dimensions of language users and language use mentioned above, and **non-dimensional mismatches**, which are mismatches in the denotative meanings of original and translation elements and breaches of the target language system at various levels. House's model of translation quality assessment has enjoyed particular success in the academic domain, especially because students appear to find it highly accessible and amenable to implementation. There is little evidence, however, that the model has gained traction in quality evaluation in professional scenarios. The model measures quality according to how well the source and target text functions match, measured through linguistic means; this has attracted criticism from Lauscher (2000:154), who argues that the function of a text is attributed to it by its readers in specific contexts, and not solely through linguistic means.

By far the most common type of QA model adopted in the translation profession and in pedagogy is based on **error typology**, as in the case of the LISA QA metric, the J2450, or the models described in Waddington (2001) and Hansen (2009), or those developed by the MeLLANGE project (Multilingual eLearning in Language Engineering[24]). Typically, the typology has a list of error types (e.g. language, terminology, style), which are sometimes categorized as major or minor, are awarded penalties and are weighted, with some errors considered more serious than others. Such models also tend to have thresholds for penalty points; once the threshold is reached the translation is deemed to have failed. The fact that such models are common across pedagogical and professional settings means that students can be prepared for working in a professional context; it means that there is a common currency, so to speak.

While a list of specific errors, penalties, weightings etc. has the allure of being somewhat objective, there are a number of problems associated with error typologies. They can take a lot of time to apply and so are problematic for very large-scale QA tasks. Even though error categories can be well-defined, it is often a matter of subjective judgement as to whether an error falls into one category or another, e.g. whether something is a 'lexical' or a 'terminology' error, a 'stylistic' or a 'fluency' error. Likewise, the classification of an error as major or minor is

---

[24] See: http://corpus.leeds.ac.uk/mellange/about_mellange.html [Last accessed 13 November 2012].

subjective, even if definitions are provided. For example, some companies might specify that an error is to be classified as major if it runs the risk of damaging the brand image of the company, but the evaluator can only speculate as to the impact of an error on the company's image. In the case of doubt, the J2450 metric urges evaluators to err on the side of caution by assigning the category 'serious' rather than 'minor' to an error. Error classification, especially in large-scale exercises, can be tedious, leading to mistakes by the human evaluator. Thus, while they are widely used, the researcher should consider the appropriateness of error typologies, taking into account the scale of the QA exercise and the risks involved with potential subjectivity and mistakes. Measures should be taken to ensure that there are clear guidelines on how to apply the typology and clear definitions for error categories. It is recommended that the evaluators receive training and practice in the application of the typology and that they have the opportunity to discuss the classification with the researcher. As mentioned above, Waddington (2001) found that training the evaluators had a positive effect on the QA task.

Ranking of translation is another method for quality assessment, but this is more common in the field of machine translation quality assessment where a number of candidate translations might be produced by one or more machine translation systems and the evaluators are asked to rank them according to specific criteria (e.g. fluency, adequacy, comprehensibility). This model has some advantages over the error typology since it is likely to be less time-consuming per source language word evaluated because the evaluators do not have to identify and classify specific errors. It also gives immediate information on which translation, translator and/or machine translation system are the best. However, unless there are clear differences among the translations, the evaluator may have difficulties deciding which one is to be ranked higher. Ranking models can cater for such instances since translations can be rated as being equal according to the assessment criteria. Aziz *et al* (2012), for example, use a ranking scale for post-editing effort with the following ranks: 1 = requires complete retranslation, 2 = requires some retranslation, but post-editing still quicker than retranslation, 3 = very little post-editing needed, and 4 = fit for purpose. Where there are ties, two or more candidate translations can be ranked with the same number. Subjectivity is also an issue with ranking scales, especially if the criteria expect evaluators to estimate how much effort might be involved in revising, or post-editing, each translation, as in the example above. Clearly this type of ranking is not a direct measurement of post-editing effort and so should not be presented as such. A disadvantage of the ranking scale is that you do not gain any insight into the nature of the errors encountered, which means that it is not suitable as a diagnostic tool, or for formative purposes. The following example may help to illustrate the point. The source text is in French, with three translations in English generated by free, online machine translation engines. The context is a report on a scientific study carried out on the correlations between the national rate of chocolate consumption and the number of Nobel Prizes won by that country.

> **Source Text:** *On y apprenait qu'il existait un lien de corrélation extrême-ment significatif entre la consommation de chocolat par un pays et le nombre de prix Nobel que le dit pays décrochait.*[25]
>
> **Candidate Translation A:** *It is learned that there was a highly significant correlation link between the consumption of chocolate by a country and the Nobel Prize number as that country won.*
> **Candidate Translation B:** *We learned that there was a highly significant correlation between the consumption of chocolate by a country and the number of Nobel Prizes that the country clinched.*
> **Candidate Translation C:** *It was learned there that there was an ex-tremely significant bond of correlation between the chocolate con-sumption by a country and the number of Nobel Prize that the aforementioned country took down.*

Clearly, none of the above translations are perfect. If we were to rank them for fluency in the target language, we might rank them as B first, followed by a tie between Candidates A and C. But this only tells us which candidate transla-tion was the most fluent, according to a subjective evaluation. Ranking does not oblige us to report on the nature of the errors, and hence no insight is gained into that aspect. Also, if we rate for fluency we might assume that we are intrinsically rating the level of post-editing required to fix each sentence. This is, however, not necessarily the case since we are only guessing that the most fluent will take less time and less keyboarding effort to fix. In fact, the errors in candidates A and C are so obvious that we might be able to fix them quickly, whereas we could linger a long time over the appropriateness of, and possible substitution for, the word 'clinched' in Candidate Translation B, which raises questions of ac-ceptability in terms of collocation.

In Chapter 4 we discuss the use of eye tracking in translation process research in detail. We will therefore limit ourselves here to mentioning that eye tracking can also be used as a mechanism for measuring translation quality. Eye tracking allows the measurement of cognitive load during reading via measures such as fixations (focus of the eyes on one area for a period of time) and reading re-gressions (re-reading of text). It stands to reason that a poor quality translation will demand more cognitive load over a high quality translation, that is, more fixations and more regressions, and thus tracking reading behaviour will provide insight into translation quality. Doherty *et al* (2010) tested eye tracking as a tool for measuring machine translation quality, and Doherty and O'Brien (2012) then built on that to study the usability of machine translated technical instructions. The advantage of using eye tracking for QA is that the researcher can see the direct impact of quality issues on the potential end user, or reader, something that could only be speculated on in models proposed by the functionalist school in the 1980s and 1990s. Additionally, it is useful to combine eye tracking with other

---

[25] Source: http://passeurdesciences.blog.lemonde.fr/2012/11/21/le-chocolat-engendre-t-il-des-tueurs-en-serie/ [Last accessed 25 November 2012].

measures that can offer insight into translation quality, for example, comprehension tests or recall tests that can be administered after the eye-tracked reading session. Researchers could also ask participants to think aloud while reading and to focus their comments on aspects of quality (see Chapter 4 for a discussion of thinking aloud as a research method in translation process research).

Translation quality can also be assessed through traditional research instruments such as surveys. Respondents may be asked to consider an entire text and to answer questions on the overall quality of the text, making use of Likert scales, closed and open questions. Additionally, respondents may be asked to consider translation on a sentence-by-sentence basis and to answer questions on each sentence. A limited survey approach is frequently adopted in machine translation quality assessment where the concepts of **adequacy** and **fluency** have been subjected to Likert-type scales for some time now (White *et al* 1994, LDC 2002). Adequacy refers to the amount of source text meaning preserved in the translation and is usually rated as follows: 5 = all, 4 = most, 3 = much, 2 = little, 1 = none. Fluency refers to the extent to which a translated sentence reads naturally and is usually rated as follows: 5 = flawless, 4 = good, 3 = non-native, 2 = disfluent, 1 = incomprehensible.

While adequacy and fluency have been popular constructs for quality assessment in machine translation in particular, they are not without flaws. As with all QA models, there is still an element of subjectivity. Application of the scale is also time consuming, though, as with ranking, it is less so than the application of a detailed error typology. The approach has also suffered from the proliferation of terms that completely or partially overlap with adequacy and fluency, such as intelligibility, acceptability and comprehensibility.

To compensate for cost and time issues in human assessment of translation quality, **automatic evaluation metrics** (AEMs) have been developed and applied in machine translation research. The past decade has seen a proliferation of AEMs, each one trying to improve on the other. Perhaps the most famous metric, as it is credited with being the first, is BLEU (Bi-Lingual Evaluation Understudy, Papineni *et al* 2002). The basic premise of the AEM is to compare a machine translated sentence with one or many 'gold standard' or 'reference' sentences which have been translated by a human translator and to give the machine translated sentences a score, based on how similar they are to the human translations. Here, similarity with the reference sentence is an indicator of quality. It is beyond the scope of this section to delve into detail on the pros and cons of AEMs.[26] We can state here that, initially, they were met with much skepticism in the translation studies community, especially due to the questionable construct within the AEM of there being one gold standard human translation against which the machine translation candidate translation was compared. Moreover,

---

[26] For further reading on this topic, the online machine translation Archive has many publications on machine translation research in general, and automatic evaluation specifically: www.mt-archive.info [Last accessed 13 November 2012].

it was not always clear that the human translations being used as references had been assessed for quality in the first place, and the fact that human translations were needed as references did nothing to remove the problem of cost in quality evaluation. Perhaps the most problematic aspect of AEMs, however, was that it was difficult, if not impossible, to interpret what the scores actually meant (e.g. how good was a translation that scored 0.53 on an AEM scale?). This criticism, along with some of the others listed above, has been tackled by the machine translation research community by directing significant attention to research into the correlations between human quality assessment and AEMs (see, for example, Coughlin 2003; Agarwal and Lavie 2008). While AEMs are not without flaws as measures of machine translation quality, there is no doubt that they will become more and more robust as time evolves and could be appropriate for some translation quality research projects.

3.6.4   Data collection

Additional factors in the choice of QA model include the scale of the research project. Sampling is discussed in general in Chapter 2, so we will relate the discussion here specifically to QA research. As mentioned previously, QA, especially the application of detailed error typologies, can take a lot of time, which, in turn, will dictate how much translated text can be assessed. Sometimes the quality assessment is only one part of the research project and other factors also need to be measured. Unfortunately, there are no hard and fast rules about how many words should be evaluated in order to produce valid and reliable results. The guiding principle is 'the more you can assess, the better', but of course time and cost play a significant role. As multiple evaluators may be required (see below) and may also need to be paid for their time, the cost of the QA exercise becomes an important factor in the decision on sample size. Researchers can refer to sample sizes used in related studies as a parameter for comparison when making decisions. Another important issue to consider is how the actual sample itself is selected for quality assessment. The sample selection will be dictated by the research purpose and design: one might wish to randomly select sentences from a large corpus of text, or it may be more appropriate to select coherent passages of text, or text that demonstrates specific linguistic features. The most important point here is that due consideration should be given to sample selection in order to ensure a high level of validity and reliability of results, and that the decisions made and motivating factors be clearly reported.

The importance of the criteria used for selecting evaluators to perform the quality assessment should not be overlooked. A number of questions arise: suitability of evaluators, number of evaluators, training and consistency. Given that it is a frequent issue in research design, it is important to state that those selected for assessing translation quality should be suited to the task. Recruiting computer programmers who happen to have some knowledge of a second language to rate translation quality is questionable, unless the focus of such a study is on the ability of such a community to reliably rate translation quality. The key factor to take into account is whether the evaluator's ratings could be treated as valid assessments of translation quality in a standard professional context. Similarly, research focusing on translation quality assessment in a pedagogical setting should recruit evaluators who are practised in performing QA in a pedagogical setting. For an interesting comparison between the performance of different types of evaluators (teachers, translators, bilinguals), see Colina (2008). A second question that arises here is whether the researchers themselves should act as evaluators. A researcher may fit the criteria set for recruiting evaluators, but it is advisable to separate the evaluation from the data analysis, so that the researcher's own expectations do not influence the evaluation results. So, where possible, researchers should remain independent of the quality assessment exercise.

A frequent mistaken assumption in quality assessment is that no training is required prior to application of the QA model. It may be assumed that every professional translator is familiar with an error typology such as the LISA QA model, mentioned above. This is not always the case since not every translator conducts quality reviews (though most will have their work submitted to such a review). Similarly, a teacher of translation may use a different QA model from the one applied in a research project focusing on pedagogy. It is therefore worthwhile to train evaluators prior to the application of the QA model and allow them time to clarify any doubts they might have with the researcher.

Similar to the question of sample size, the question of how many evaluators to use is an important one. A typical design is to have multiple versions of translation (produced by several individual translators) rated by a number of evaluators, the assumption being that the more evaluators one employs, the more reliable the QA results will be. Cost and time will again play a role in this decision, but researchers should be extremely cautious in cutting corners as it has been documented time and again that QA is such a subjective exercise that evaluators rarely agree with each other (see Stymne and Ahrenberg 2012 for example). As Bayerl and Paul (2011:713) remark,

> The higher the number of annotators who are able to agree, the less bias and distortion can be expected in the data and the more stable and comparable the results are likely to be. Reaching high agreement with a larger number of annotators would thus indicate a higher trustworthiness of annotations.

When doing quantitative analyses, inter-coder agreement is frequently calculated using a measure called Cohen's kappa (1960) or Fleiss' kappa (1971). **Cohen's kappa** is used to measure agreement between two coders, while **Fleiss' kaapa** is used for measuring agreement between more than two coders. If coders are in complete agreement, then the kappa score is equal to 1. If there is no agreement, other than that which would be expected to occur by chance, then the kappa score is 0. The closer the score is to 1, the higher the level of agreement.[27] On the basis of their meta-analysis of inter-coder agreement, Bayerl and Paul (2011:719) produce some recommendations that could also be useful for research involving translation quality assessment. Most notably, they advise using few categories (rarely the case with translation error typologies!) and evaluators with the same level of expertise. They also recommend intensive training (as mentioned above), and the use of five or more people for 'very critical tasks' (where very high quality is critical) and three or four for 'less critical scenarios'.

3.6.5 Analysis

The nature of the analysis will be dictated by the QA model, or models, applied in the research project. For the QA models outlined above, a typical analysis would be quantitative, with perhaps some qualitative aspects too. The error typology lends itself well to the use of descriptive statistics, reporting and comparing, for example, percentages of specific error types and sub-types using tables, graphs and/or bar charts. As mentioned earlier, the error typology often comes with penalty points, weights and thresholds, so quantitative scores can also form part of the analysis. Where the QA model is holistic, making use of reflective reports on processes used during translation in a pedagogical setting for example, the analysis might move more in the direction of a qualitative one involving the coding of student reports for evidence of awareness about quality issues. For QA models that employ Likert-scales for concepts such as adequacy and fluency or ranking, again descriptive statistics reporting average ratings for each construct are adequate. The AEMs produce their own scores, which are usually reported as an overall average for the corpus being tested. The AEM scores' correlation with human judgements may also be reported using standard correlation measures such as Spearman's rho or Pearson's r (see Chapter 5, Section 5.3.6 for a detailed discussion of these measures). Where eye tracking is used as a measure of translation quality, typical eye tracking measures of cognitive load can be employed – total number of fixations during a reading task, the average length of a fixation, total number of regressions during reading (see Chapter 4 for a detailed discussion) – as well as some usability-type measurements such as total task time, comprehension scores, recall scores, satisfaction ratings, etc.

Perhaps the most important part of the analysis in the context of QA research for which rating or coding is required, though, is inter-coder agreement, because without an acceptable level of agreement, the trustworthiness of results is questionable. If inter-coder agreement is low, researchers might consider adding more evaluators to the task and/or interviewing evaluators in order to understand why agreement is so low. This could then lead to a refinement of the design (e.g.

---

[27] A full explanation of the formula used for the kappa scores is beyond the scope of this book. However, there is a clear explanation and online calculator available at http://www.stattools. net/CohenKappa_Pgm.php [Last accessed 17 February 2012].

fewer error categories, clearer definitions for error types, more refined criteria for the recruitment of evaluators, better evaluator training, etc.) and a reapplication of the QA model with new evaluators. As with all methods, whether they are product, process or people-oriented, researchers will aim for transparency, giving necessary details on the QA model, methods of evaluator recruitment and training, in order to facilitate replicability. We end this section with a quotation from House (2009:225), which summarizes the core concern in QA:

> Future work on translation quality assessment needs to develop beyond subjective, one-sided or dogmatic judgements by positing intersubjectively verifiable evaluative criteria on the basis of large-scale empirical studies.

3.7 Summary

This chapter has described three approaches for researching the products of the translation process, translated and interpreted texts. Given how they can be and are interlaced, we grouped CDA and CL together. We started by explaining the principles underlying each approach, their strengths and weaknesses, and argued that some of their respective weaknesses may be addressed by combining the two approaches. We looked at the type of research question that is often addressed using these two methodologies and discussed the benefits and disadvantages of different research designs, highlighting the need for comparative data. The most common types of corpora used in translation studies (parallel and comparable) and key issues in corpus compilation were outlined. In the analysis section we introduced some of the linguistic concepts used in CDA and CL and illustrated them with examples from translation studies research. An overview of the most common tools and techniques used in translation research using CL was provided, together with examples of research where they were applied. We then also discussed two key principles to ensure validity in CDA: the requirement for the analysis to be comprehensive and the requirement for contextual factors to be brought to bear on the analysis itself, for example by showing how the text draws selectively upon different orders of discourse.

Research on translation quality assessment was addressed separately, though we explained that some concerns are shared across all three approaches. For QA, we focused on translation quality assessment in product-oriented research. We highlighted the initial considerations for designing QA-based research, such as the setting, status of those doing the translation, genre, purpose, and focus. Attention was drawn to typical examples of assessment models, some of which are product-oriented, some process-oriented and some more holistic, as well as to measures that are segment-, text-, and end-user oriented. We have also highlighted the necessity of selecting and testing valid models and of training evaluators in order to increase inter-coder and intra-coder agreement.

Chapter 4. Process-oriented research

4.1 Introduction

Translation process research seeks to understand translator or interpreter behaviour, **competence**, **expertise**, the **cognitive processes** that orient these, and the relations between cognition and the translated or interpreted product. Furthermore, since translation is not divorced from social context, process research seeks to understand the effect of the context on the process. Individuals, with their specific traits and ways of processing, are also a central focus. Hence, while translation process research is frequently understood to mean investigating the mental operations involved in translating, in fact it encompasses a much broader object of interest.

Process research dates from the 1980s, with some of the earliest studies focusing on both interpreting (e.g. Tommola 1986) and translation (e.g. Krings 1986a, 1986b, 1988) processes. In the last decade or so, a growing body of research on translation processes has emerged, with several volumes of collected work being published since 1999 (Hansen 1999; Tirkkonen-Condit and Jääskeläinen 2000; Hansen 2002; Alves 2003; Göpferich 2008, Göpferich *et al* 2008 and 2009, Mees *et al* 2010; Shreve and Angelone 2010; O'Brien 2011a). While process-oriented research in interpreting has not stagnated, the written translation process appears to have attracted increasing attention in recent years, most likely because of the new research tools that have been adopted by researchers. While some of the methods discussed here can be applied to interpreting, our focus is primarily on methods for investigating the written translation process. It is worth noting that research in written translation also encompasses various processes that are relatively new and which have come to the forefront as a result of technological evolution within the translation profession, such as the increasing use of machine translation and translation memory technologies. One such process is **post-editing**, which has attracted attention in translation process studies (see, for example, O'Brien 2006, 2011b). On the periphery, but also of importance, are new studies of interaction within the translation process and with translated text. For example, the EU-funded 'Casmacat' project[1] seeks to model translator behaviour using computer tools in order to build a cognitive model of the translation process, while Doherty (2012) has investigated the **readability** of machine translated text from a cognitive effort standpoint.

Despite the recent advances in translation process research, the authors of published findings are often keen to point out that results are 'preliminary'", the projects are 'pilots', and hypotheses and models are 'tentative'. Research methodology has evolved and there is currently consensus on the necessity of **triangulation**, the comparison of results from various methods, and a focus on process complemented by product analysis or vice versa. In the search for more

---

[1] www.casmacat.eu [Last accessed 19 July 2012].

reliable and innovative methods, researchers have raised the bar considerably by adopting methods which generate more data than a single researcher can analyze in a reasonable amount of time (thereby increasing the necessity for better research **asset management**[2]), and by increasing the requirements for technological know-how and more sophisticated statistical analysis. To move translation process research to the next level, the research community needs to continue embracing these new challenges, but what is more likely to result in substantial maturation in a shorter time-frame is increased collaboration among translation researchers as well as with experts from outside translation studies; these might include eye-tracking experts, psycholinguists, cognitive scientists, computational linguists, experts in human-computer interaction, writing and reading process experts and neuroscientists, all of whom tend to have more ex- perience than translation scholars in the application of specific research methods in cognitive and computer science.

Muñoz Martín (2010) argues that the notion of 'translation process' should be understood on three levels. The first level is fundamental and pertains to the mental states and operations at play during the act of translating. The second, related, level encompasses the sub-tasks that are executed during the mental act of translating (e.g. reading, typing, research). The third level refers to the **situatedness** of the translation process and includes everything and every agent engaged in the period of time from contact by the commissioner of the transla- tion to receipt of the final translated product by the addressee. Muñoz Martín further argues that research on this third level should not be ignored since our knowledge of the situated nature of the translation process could enhance the ecological validity of research (see Chapter 2, Section 2.10.1) on the other two levels. In other words, the process-oriented methodologies described in this chapter should be combined more often with the type of context-oriented re- search described in Chapter 6.

Toury once wrote that "process-oriented empirical studies normally make use of elicited manifestations of the *gradual* emergence of a translated utterance, to the complete neglect of its final version" (1988:47). More recently, however, this neglect of the translated product in process research is being redressed. After all, "the establishment of a product not only marks the end, but also forms the very *raison d'être* of the problem-solving processes which translating is" (Toury 1988:60, emphasis in original). As an example, Alves *et al* (2010:110) favour product-oriented research being combined with process-oriented research:

> Both research foci are interrelated in that what we observe as the specific characteristics of translated texts may, at least to some degree, be corre- lated with behavior directly or indirectly observable during the translation process ... both product and process research still face major challenges which can best be overcome through a combined approach.

---

[2] See, for example, Alves and Vale (2009) and Göpferich (2010).

In particular, Alves *et al* argue that corpus-based research can complement process-based research (see Chapter 3). As an example of good practice in combining translation products and processes, Alves *et al* (2010:123) mention the CORPRAT project. The CORPRAT project collected five data types for comparative analysis: keystroke logs, eye-tracking metrics, audio recordings, screen recordings and annotated target texts. All data types are triangulated in order to analyze the grammatical shifts that occur during the process of (de)metaphorization during translation.

The call to combine process data with product data necessarily raises the question of quality assessment (see Chapter 3, Section 3.6), which has formed part of only a few process-oriented studies to date. It is sometimes declared in reports on process-driven studies that product quality assessment is beyond the scope of such projects, but we would argue that correlating quality assessment with process findings is essential for a better understanding of the translation process (for a more detailed discussion of this issue, see Hansen 2010a). The source text as a product of the writing process also deserves careful attention. We deal summarily with source text selection for process research below.

We agree with Muñoz Martín's broad definition of translation process research and with the contention that a combined process- and product-oriented approach provides a richer analysis and understanding of translation. Given this broad understanding of translation process research, both qualitative and quantitative methods are clearly appropriate. Since at least some research methods for investigating Muñoz Martín's 'third level' are dealt with elsewhere in this book (cf. Chapters 5 and 6), and methods for investigating the translation product are also dealt with elsewhere (Chapter 3), we will mostly limit ourselves in this chapter to discussing methods that are relevant for investigating Muñoz Martín's first and second levels.

In section 4.1.1 we sketch what the main objects of inquiry have been to date in translation process research but we do not claim to provide an exhaustive list of research topics.[3] Then, since many of the methodological issues are relevant for all methods used in process research, we present a general discussion of these issues separated into questions of research design, data elicitation, analysis and reporting (Section 4.2). Following this, we discuss specific issues pertaining to the most common research methods currently in use (verbal reports, keystroke logging, screen recording and eye tracking). The chapter concludes with a summary of additional methods that could be useful for translation process research in the future.

4.1.1 Common topics

One of the core objects of inquiry in translation process research to date has been **metacognition**, that is, what translators know about their translation processes,

---

[3] For an extensive discussion of the topics translation process researchers have preoccupied themselves with so far, see Göpferich (2008). For an example of interdisciplinarity in translation process research, see the Special Issue of *Target* published in 2013.

how they allocate resources during the task of translation, how problems are recognized and solved, how uncertainty is managed, what strategies are used, etc. (Shreve 2006). Translation and, in particular, interpreting process research has also been interested in how the brain handles the bilingual process, with models of **working memory** (WM) capacity (notably Baddeley's model: Baddeley 1986, 1992)[4] playing an important role, as well as Gile's effort model (Gile 1995). In interpreting, the focus has been on comprehension, production and the simultaneous management of these two processes.

The **cognitive rhythm** of translators, i.e. 'bursts' of creativity in between pauses, has also been recorded and measured. The profiling of cognitive rhythm necessarily involves the analysis of **pauses**, which has been attempted by several translation process researchers to date (see Dragsted 2004:64-71 for an overview; see also Jakobsen 2005; Alves 2005). Other aspects that have been included in the analysis of cognitive rhythm are how the translation process is divided into phases (such as orientation, drafting, revision), what time is spent on various text production activities such as typing, insertions, deletions, cursor repositioning and revisions, and the use of information resources, including reference works and online resources.

The nature of the translation task and how it differs from related tasks is another popular topic, with differences between written and sight translation being investigated (Shreve *et al* 2010), along with differences between translation processes and monolingual writing, revision and reading. The notion of **creativity** has also attracted attention (Bayer-Hohenwarter 2009), as has the challenge of translating metaphors (Sjørup 2011). The effect of the task type and time pressure during the task on the quality of the product is now gaining more attention. Yet another focus is the impact of technology on the translation process and, in particular, the impact of technology on the **unit of translation** (Dragsted 2004) as well as on processing effort (O'Brien 2006, 2008).

By far the largest focus in translation process research to date, though, has been translation **competence** and its acquisition. Researchers have tried to model, insofar as possible, **expertise**, as exhibited by professional translators and to contrast this with non-experts, frequently bilinguals with no translator training, or novices, who are at the early stages of their training, or semi-professionals, often understood to be students who have undergone rigorous translator training, either at undergraduate or postgraduate level and who are about to embark on careers as translators. Two large-scale, longitudinal research projects deserve mention here. The PACTE research group at the Universitat Autònoma de Barcelona has conducted cumulative research since 1998 with a focus on translation competence, translator training and the impact of new technologies on translation.[5] The TransComp project commenced in 2007 and

---

[4] See Rothe-Neves (2003) for an example of research on working memory and translation process.

[5] For a list of all publications see: http://grupsderecerca.uab.cat/pacte/en [Last accessed 4 December 2012].

is a process-oriented study that explores the development of translation competence in 12 students of translation over a period of 3 years and compares it to
that of 10 professional translators.[6] One of the core challenges encountered by
researchers interested in the modelling of translation competence is the definition of the terms expertise, professional and semi-professional. This is a topic
we will return to in Section 4.2.

As alluded to earlier, the growth of translation process research in the last
decade or so can be attributed, in no small part, to the research methods adopted
by researchers. In the early days of translation process research, it was introspective methods such as verbal reports recorded in **think-aloud protocols (TAPs)** that
were mainly applied. More recently, new tools such as **keystroke logging software**, **screen recording** and **eye tracking** have opened up new research avenues.
These tools have often been applied in conjunction with introspective methods,
and this development has necessitated a discussion of the validity of the previous methods used as well as of the newly adopted ones. The remainder of this
chapter will highlight relevant questions, challenges and some solutions.

4.2   General translation process research issues

In our introduction, we mentioned that there are many questions around
translation process research that pertain to all methods used. We discuss these
general questions in this section under the headings of design, data elicitation,
analysis and reporting. This is followed by a consideration of specific methods.
What should be kept in mind throughout this chapter is that the focus of translation process research is often the cognitive processes involved in executing the
task but that no research method can give direct access to cognitive processes.
Some methods are heavily mediated by the participants themselves (e.g. verbal
reports), while others depend on psycho-physiological competences (e.g. keystroke logging) or on individual eye movement patterns (e.g. eye tracking). Even
methods that scan brain activity (e.g. **fMRI** or functional magnetic resonance
imaging) do not directly measure cognitive processes. Therefore, all research into
translation processes is essentially an indirect measurement of these processes.
Having said that, indirect measurement is still valid and valuable.

4.2.1   Design

In a summary of TAP-based translation process research in 2001, Bernardini concluded that the research conducted at the time of writing was very problematic.
She summarizes the problem thus (2001:251):

> Most of the research reports ... describe the research design summarily,
> present findings in an anecdotal fashion, do not provide any statistical

---

[6] http://gams.uni-graz.at/fedora/get/container:tc/bdef:Container/get [Last accessed 4 December 2012].

analysis of their data (and sometimes not even the data themselves) and leave central theoretical assumptions unexplained. The reader thus finds it difficult to assess the validity of the results obtained. Besides, experimental conditions are often relaxed without as much as a hint that the researcher is aware of possible consequences.

She also highlights the excessive reliance on **between-subject designs**, used to compare the performance of professionals with that of semi-professionals and/or non-professionals. The between-subjects design allocates each individual participant to one group only and compares the results across groups. The common approach in translation process research is to allocate all professional translators to one group and all semi- or non-professionals to another group and to compare results across the two. This is a controversial design because each participant is measured only once, which means that to produce valid results very large numbers of participants are required, something that has not yet been achieved in translation process research. Given the idiosyncratic nature of translation, confirmed regularly by translation process research findings, Bernardini recommends the adoption of **within-subject designs**, where one participant's translation process is examined under different task conditions, rather than multiple participants being compared with each other. Undoubtedly, within-subject designs have benefits in that they reduce the requirement for a large number of participants, but they also have drawbacks, the most significant of which is the **carry-over effect**, where the repetition of a task has an effect on tasks presented later in a sequence of tasks. Randomization of task sequence is usually recommended to counterbalance this effect. We do not recommend the abandonment of between-subject designs; rather, we would urge a deep consideration of the objectives of the research, the number of potentially available qualified participants and the adoption of a design that is appropriate to the research objectives.

We mentioned earlier the problem of the terms used in translation process research to designate specific groups of participants (professionals, experts, semi-professionals, novices). Unfortunately, these terms have been used variously by translation process researchers to date, with different definitions being applied to each term. A 'professional', for example might be somebody who earns a living from commercial translation practice and who has ten years of experience, or it might be an MA student who has completed one year of translator training and who is about to launch their translation career. Clearly, cross-study comparisons cannot be made with such varied definitions, and this state of affairs seriously hampers the building, testing and validating of models and theories in the discipline. Since the focus of translation competence research is often pedagogical, it also hampers the development of pedagogical theory and practice, and so the problem cannot be understated. Until the discipline comes to an agreement about how to designate participants, individual researchers should pay significant attention to their own use of terms and definitions and should aim to be transparent. We also need to avoid loose interpretations. For instance, it might seem acceptable to call somebody an 'expert translator' if they have earned a living working as a translator for ten years or more, but their competences may not actually comply with a formal definition of expertise (see Jääskeläinen 2010a and Englund-Dimitrova 2005 for a more detailed discussion of these problems). Additionally, we cannot necessarily assume that two translators with the same professional profile will produce equal quality within the same timeframe, and attention thus needs to be paid to this aspect when selecting participants by, for example, pre-qualifying participants through translation tests, questionnaires or interviews prior to their acceptance onto a study. As an example, the notion of time pressure and performance is one that is of importance to translation process research and study designs often have an element of time pressure built into them. What stands for 'pressure', however, is assumed to apply equally across all participants, but this does not account for natural differences in pressure thresholds. To account for this, Jensen (2011a) proposes testing natural speed under no time pressure in a warm-up task, which is then taken as a baseline for applying varying, personal time pressure conditions for each participant.

On the issue of participant selection, translation process research presents particular challenges. Professional translators do not easily give of their time (for understandable reasons), with the consequence that process research often needs funding to engage translators. Where funding is limited, as it often is, convenience sampling (see Chapter 2, Section 2.10.1) is the only avenue open to us. However, even if we need to resort to convenience sampling this does not justify using participants who do not match our requirements, such as using students when we want to study professional translators. Moreover, the recruitment of student translators raises ethical questions, in particular when the researcher is also a teacher of the students in question (see also Chapter 2, Section 2.11).

The next design-related global issue is **task descriptions**, their validity and impact on the process itself. The importance of the **translation brief** has been discussed in general in translation theory (Nord 1997). In the early days of translation process research, the provision of a translation brief in a study was rare. However, since the task description has been found to leave its mark on professional translators' products (Jääskeläinen and Tirkkonen-Condit 1988), there is increasing evidence to suggest that translation process researchers have more recently taken the validity of the task description seriously. Closely associated with the translation brief is the question of target text quality. Participants in translation process research are commonly told to aim for a level of quality that would be expected by a client. However, quality expectations will vary among clients, and it is difficult to establish whether or not research participants are, in fact, aiming for the quality that would be expected of them in a commercial contractual scenario. To at least partially address this, participants can be paid the standard rate of pay and ought to be given a credible translation brief. It might also help if they are told that the translated product will be assessed according to a specific translation quality assessment framework (see Chapter 3, Section 3.6).

Also related to the translation brief is the concept of a 'routine' vs. a 'non-routine' task. Whether the task is routine, i.e. performed regularly and without much variation in the steps, has significant implications in process research because it forms part of the assumptions associated with participants' abilities to reflect on their processes (see Section 4.3). The challenge in process research then is how to operationalize 'routine' in the domain of translation. This has been controversial to date and Bernardini (2001) suggests that directionality (i.e. L1-L2 or L2-L1) could be used as an operational parameter to separate routine from non-routine tasks. While this goes some way towards operationalizing the concept, it does not seem to be precise enough. Dimensions such as the domain, sub-domain and text type a translator routinely works with may also need to be factored in.

It is obviously necessary to consider, during the design stage, what data elici-tation techniques will be used.[7] According to Lörscher (1988), six major factors characterize the data obtained from verbal reporting as a research tool, and these six factors can be applied to data elicited from many research tools used in translation process research. They are:

- number of participants
- research context ('when', 'where' and 'how')
- recency of the event[8]
- mode of elicitation and response (oral vs. written instructions)
- formality of elicitation, and
- degree of external intervention.

These six factors would seem useful for any researcher who wants to characterize the data obtained in translation process research and, if implemented by many, might even form a high-level basis for cross-study comparison.

Having identified participants and data elicitation techniques, we might next turn our attention to selecting appropriate texts for the task. It is rather too easy to select texts in a subjective manner. In research carried out to date, texts have frequently been sourced from newspapers, popular science or travel literature. While these are legitimate text types for translation, the three domains do not represent the extent and breadth of domains in which translation occurs, and we cannot build more sophisticated process models on evidence from newspa-per texts, popular science and travel literature alone. We would like to argue in favour of expanding the text types used to include, for example, user manuals, patents, annual reports, poetry, short stories, and so on.

Judgements on the degree of complexity or difficulty of texts can be rather arbitrary and are usually based on the researcher's opinion, not the appropriate-ness of the text for the participants' competences or the translation brief. Some notable exceptions to this are: Alves *et al*'s proposal to use rhetorical structure

---

[7] Note that we deliberately use the term 'elicitation' here, rather than the term 'collection', because process research usually requires the active stimulation of participants to create research data.

[8] Englund-Dimitrova (2005:66) distinguishes between 'online' and 'off-line' modes, with online referring to concurrent thinking aloud and off-line referring to interviews, for example.

theory as a means of measuring the complexity of any text to be translated (Alves *et al* 2010), Göpferich's Karlsruhe comprehensibility concept (Göpferich 2009) and Jensen's use of readability indices in combination with word frequency and the number of non-literal expressions in the text (Jensen 2009, 2011b). It should be noted, however, that the use of readability indices as measures of text translatability is still highly questionable (O'Brien 2010a and Jensen 2011a, 2011b) and the field is in need of more accurate techniques for text profiling.

The length of texts also needs careful consideration. Due to the fact that the research methods used in process studies generate substantial volumes of data for analysis, that multiple participants are typically included in the research design, that research is often carried out by lone researchers, that funding is limited, and that triangulation is a common strategy, the tendency is to select short texts. For example, Angelone (2010) employs a text of 50 words; Dragsted (2010) one of 100 words; Alves *et al* (2010) use a text 318 words in length and in Shreve *et al* (2010) the mean length is 167. That such short texts could elicit all relevant strategies or processes, or give full indications of all participants' competences, is of course questionable, and usually acknowledged. However, this hurdle needs to be overcome, rather than just acknowledged. We can, for example, consider Bernardini's call for more within-subject designs, which would enable us to give longer texts to participants. We can be more rigorous in our selection of texts, ensuring that they are suitable for the research design, and we can also aim for having more research collaboration, so that the data generated can be thoroughly analyzed, making it possible to have longer and more appropriate texts.

Translation process research often seeks to compare texts for the translation effort or strategies they demand, and the design therefore has to cater for more than one source text. We might 'treat' a text in a particular way, to make it theoretically more or less complex using one of the above-mentioned measuring techniques, for example, and then test the effect on translation effort. As mentioned above in our discussion of within-subject designs, this raises a question about the sequence in which texts are presented to participants. If text A is always presented first and text B second, will there be a carry-over effect for participants? In other words, will text B inevitably be easier to translate, because of the 'effect' of translating text A? The only way to control for this is to randomize the presentation of texts, i.e. some participants get text A first, others text B first, and so on.

The research design might be even more ambitious than described above, including several **factors** (often used synonymously with 'variables', see Chapter 2.8.1) and one or more **conditions**. Factors and conditions are then crossed leading to what is called a multi-factorial research design. An example of such a design in translation-related research using eye tracking is Fougner Rydning and Lachaud's (2010) study. They were interested in investigating two factors: context (the presence/absence of context, i.e. co-text) and expertise (professional translation/non-translator bilingual) and the impact these had on the creativity of participants. By crossing factors, they created a four-condition design which involved: (a) translators transcoding text (understood as the alignment of word correspondences out of context), (b) translators translating text, (c) bilinguals transcoding text, and (d) bilinguals translating text. Randomization of conditions would be necessary in such multi-factorial designs, in order to rule out effects caused by the sequence in which tasks are performed or texts processed.

We have already alluded to the fact that translation process researchers tend to favour triangulation (Alves 2003). As Shreve and Angelone explain, "[t]riangulation has come to be regarded as a desirable 'best practice' in process-oriented research" (2010:6). However, Hansen (2010b:189) warns against simply collating data via different methods without considering how the data and their interpretation can be integrated. She argues for an "integrative description", by which she means a multi-paradigm approach that focuses on translation as a process and a product and on texts in situations (*ibid*.). Although the approach is called 'integrative', she also cautions that the descriptive, reflective and explanatory parts of any such research should be kept apart so that eventual readers can make their own interpretations of the data collated. The importance of terminological consistency is also emphasized by Hansen (*ibid.*:205). Her contention that description, reflection and explanation should be kept apart also raises the not insignificant challenge of data management, which we discuss more fully in later sections.

A final, global issue in translation process research is that of ethics. Since we deal with ethics in some detail in Chapters 2 and 5, we will not discuss the topic at length here. However, we feel it is important to reiterate that undisclosed screen recording, keystroke logging or covert observational tools like cameras would generally be considered inappropriate. While process experiments require an element of control, the ethical basis and possible repercussions of telling participants that the object of inquiry is one thing when in fact it is something else should be given serious consideration in advance. The use of students as participants has very particular ramifications, in particular when account is taken of the power relations between the researcher and the student (see Chapter 2, Section 2.10.5). And, even if an academic institution does not require a researcher to obtain ethics approval prior to conducting translation process research, we would urge all researchers to give thought to potential ethical issues during the research design phase and to implement best practice such as seeking informed consent, protecting identities and giving participants the option of opting out at any time, without repercussions.

4.2.2   Data elicitation

The impact of the research setting on the validity and reliability of results is of particular interest to process-related research, given its interest in human behaviour. Moreover, some of the risks identified in Chapter 2 are quite significant in this context. For example, an unfamiliar environment might have an impact on participant behaviour; an environment that is too 'laboratory-like' may result in what is known as the **whitecoat effect**. Data collated in the classroom may impact on student behaviour, even if they are not in a formal 'class'. Even unfamiliar keyboards, monitors and software may interfere with routine behaviour.

A second global issue pertaining to the elicitation of process data is the time of data elicitation. If we are interested in comparing novice with expert performance, we have to deal with the problem that expert performance is often only achieved after very long periods of time, often 10-20 years (for detailed discussion on the concept of expertise in general, see Smith and Ericsson 1991 and Dreyfus and Dreyfus 2005). This makes longitudinal studies quite challenging (how many people will sign up for a research study spanning 20 years?). **Longitudinal studies** of expertise can employ methods such as interviews with identified experts as well as diary-keeping by said experts, methods that worked well for Ericsson *et al* (1993) who investigated expertise in music performance. The data acquired through diary-keeping and interviews act as supplementary data to the tests of expert performance. A **quasi-longitudinal design** can also be adopted, where, instead of following the same participants over a number of years, different participants are selected from different stages of development and their data are compared. As an example, one could select first-year and third-year undergraduate students as well as postgraduate students and collect data from them simultaneously, but analyze it from a quasi-longitudinal viewpoint, treating the participants as if they were the same people being tracked over five years of training. Clearly, this is not as precise as a truly longitudinal study, but it is one way of overcoming the drawbacks of the latter. Longitudinal studies also carry the risk of participant drop-out. In designing our research, we should consider the risks of drop-out and how we might mitigate against them.

The acquisition of data can be threatened by technical failure, which is a high risk in translation process research, especially when multiple tools are used simultaneously to collect data streams (e.g. screen recording + eye tracking + keystroke logging + verbal reports). Ensuring that the computers used to collect the data are equipped with powerful enough processors and testing the simultaneous use of technology over long time intervals in pilot stages is essential for minimizing these risks.

4.2.3   Analysis

The main challenge posed during analysis of process data is perhaps the units of analysis, i.e. what exactly are we to measure? Consideration of the unit of analysis in process research inevitably introduces the concept of the **unit of translation** and the question: what is the difference between these two concepts? As the discussion by Kenny (2009) illustrates, the unit of translation has been seen from many different perspectives, with perhaps the two most common approaches being product-oriented and process-oriented. The product-oriented approach tends to view the unit of translation as a linguistic entity, often using the source text as a basis of determination. The process-oriented approach, on the other hand, tends to view units of translation as being dynamic and impossible to determine *a priori*. As Alves and Gonçales (2003:10-11) put it, a translation unit "is a segment in constant transformation that changes according to the translator's cognitive and processing needs". Alternative, product-oriented definitions include: "the simultaneous/consecutive comprehension in the SL and production in the TL of a text segment the size of which is limited by WM [working memory] capacity and the boundaries of which are identifiable through pauses" (Dragsted 2004:274), and "TL segments produced between pauses" (Englund-Dimitrova 2005:29). As can be seen, there is no one accepted definition of a translation unit in process research and there is not necessarily a correspondence between translation unit and unit of analysis since the interests of process research are not necessarily limited to linguistic segments but also encompass cognitive indicators, such as focus of attention or cognitive effort.

One of the most common units of analysis in process research is the **problem indicator.** Angelone and Shreve (2011) use the concept of a problem nexus to develop a model that involves metacognitive bundles consisting of problem recognition, solution proposal and problem resolution, which are then mapped onto three different parameters – the textual level, the behavioural locus, and the translation locus – each with its own set of sub-classes. However, Jääskel-äinen (1993:102) states that she avoids using translation problems as a unit of analysis because the term 'problem' is vague and has multiple meanings in translation studies.

The **strategy,** defined by Lörscher (1991:76) as "a potentially conscious procedure for the solution of a problem which an individual is faced with when translating a text segment from one language to another", is another common unit. Again, Jääskeläinen (1993, 2010b) explains how this term carries varied meanings and why Lörscher's definition of the term, and its restriction to conscious processing and problems, is too limited. She proposes a broader definition of strategy: "a set of (loosely formulated) rules or principles which a translator uses to reach the goals determined by the translating situation in the most effective way" (1993:116). However, this broad definition risks making operationalization even more difficult. Chesterman (1997) holds yet another, text-level, notion of strategy, in which strategies are seen as shifts in the target text when compared with the source text. The latter is clearly a product-oriented definition of 'strategy' and could be used in process research where process and product analysis are being combined, as discussed earlier.

The **attention unit** is another popular unit of analysis. Bernardini (2001:249) maintains that "attention units are better defined in hierarchical rather than sequential terms, with smaller units being processed within larger units". Here, she refers to linguistic units, with the clause, for example, qualifying as a smaller unit, and the text as a larger unit. Similarly, Alves and Vale (2009, 2011) discuss macro and micro units, but, unlike Bernardini, they do not define them as linguistic units but rather as the flow of continuous target text production separated by pauses. The use of pauses inevitably leads to a **temporal unit** of analysis. This typically entails dividing process indicators (such as text production, deletions, insertions) into units delimited by pauses of specified lengths. The pause lengths selected by researchers to date have tended to be arbitrary, for example 2 seconds (Lörscher 1991), 2.4 seconds (Jakobsen 2005), 4 seconds (Jensen 2000), 5 seconds or more

(Jakobsen 2003; Englund-Dimitrova 2005). It is assumed that pauses that are longer in length are indicative of cognitive processing, as opposed to shorter pauses which may be just indicative of physiological constraints, such as the speed with which a participant can type. However, we have little evidence to suggest that a pause of 2 seconds is more or less valid than a pause of 5 seconds, and researchers tend to experiment with different pause lengths to see what their data tell them. Perhaps the best we can do with this type of unit of analysis is to ensure transparency and aim for replicability.

As this short overview suggests, a variety of units of analysis have been availed of in translation process research. Thus far, no one unit has gained more traction than another. Each researcher has to decide which unit(s) of analysis is/are the most appropriate for their own research objectives. Decisions can be made during the research design stage, and it is recommended that a detailed operationalization of the unit of analysis is determined upfront. At the same time, some flexibility might be required to allow researchers to react to the structure of their data during analysis.

Shreve and Angelone (2010:11-12) identify two major challenges for translation process research in the future. The first is the development of "a strong, commonly-accepted model (or even viable competing models) of the translation process" (*ibid*:12). The second challenge, and the one we wish to comment on here in the context of data analysis, is data volume. As mentioned above, in our attempts to engage in more valid research through triangulation, and in the adoption of new tools and methods, we are now faced with massive data streams to manage and analyze, which are often not synchronized with each other. Recently, attempts have been made to tackle this problem via research asset management systems (see, for example, Göpferich 2010), which are databases containing the various data streams produced during a research project, such as keystroke logging files, think-aloud protocols and eye-tracking recordings, which can be annotated and made available to groups of researchers. This is perhaps one solution to the challenge. A second solution is to work towards more collaborative efforts so that teams of researchers can analyze different data streams from one research project, as happens in other fields. However, researchers may still have to (or want to) work alone and without the aid of an asset management system, in which case a data management plan may be useful. Depending on the time available, this may simply mean looking at only one data stream at a time and moving on to the next data stream in a serial manner, with evolving hypotheses and results as more triangulation occurs.

Large volumes of quantitative data generally benefit from statistical analysis. In earlier process-related research, findings were often reported without any statistical analysis, or, at best, using central tendencies such as mean, median and mode. Nevertheless, researchers would claim significant differences in results between groups, even though the term 'significant' was subjective and not at all in keeping with the statistical concept of **statistical significance**. When units of measurement are as precise as milliseconds and millimetres, as they can be in process data, then we are in a position where we can perform more robust statistical tests on our data, and this is a trend we have seen in the past few years. Researchers have started reporting results from tests such as Anovas (Analysis of Variance between variables) and tests for correlations (e.g. Pearson's correlation co-efficient) (see, for example, Jakobsen 2003; Jensen 2011a; O'Brien 2011b). Reporting the results from such tests is an important requirement for the validity and reliability of experimental, quantitative research (but see Section 4.5 on eye tracking for further discussion; also see Chapter 5, Section 5.3.6, where these statistical measurements are discussed in more detail).

One of the major challenges, however, is that translation process data tend to be derived from small groups of participants and is often not normally distributed. This situation forces the use of statistical tests for so-called non-parametric data, that is, data about which no initial assumptions can be made or models applied. We discuss Anovas, correlation tests and statistical tests suitable for non-parametric data under Section 5.11 in Chapter 5 and refer the reader to that section for a more detailed discussion. However, a full description of the statistical tests that can be applied is beyond our scope. We refer readers instead to Rasinger (2008), who dedicates an entire volume to the question of statistics in linguistics-related research. We return to this topic briefly when discussing the analysis of eye-tracking data in Section 4.5.2.

In this section we have now outlined some of the most important global challenges in translation process research along the parameters of design, elicitation, analysis and reporting. These challenges arise and have to be addressed no matter which methods are used in a translation process research study. In the following sections, we discuss the strengths and weaknesses of specific methods commonly applied in translation process research as well as specific issues of design, data elicitation and analysis pertaining to those methods. These sections are organized in a loose chronological manner, according to the timeline in which specific methods were introduced and applied in process research.

4.3   Introspection

The method of **introspection**, broadly meaning self-observation and reporting, was developed in the field of psychology by the Würzburg school (Lörscher 1988) and verbal reports, or talking about what one is thinking, belong to this method. Thinking-aloud is seen as a special case of introspection and the resulting transcript is known as a 'think-aloud protocol' (**TAP** for short).[9] Verbal reports can be produced concurrently or retrospectively. For retrospectively produced verbal reports, one might include a cue of some sort (a screen recording of the task activity, for example), in which case the outcome is termed a **cued retrospective protocol**. Retrospective verbal reports, although usually oral, can also be written. In **written protocols**, the participant writes introspectively about the processes

---

[9] Note that Göpferich (2010) suggests the use of the term Translation Process Protocol (TPP) that covers a broader understanding of the translation process than TAP, including the use of reference works, for example.

they engaged in while completing a task, alone or in dialogue with another research participant. A special case of written introspection is the 'integrated problem and decision report', or IPDR, a diary of sorts containing information about problems encountered during the translation process, solutions considered, resources used and the final solution (Gile 2004; Pavlović 2009). IPDRs can be created retrospectively or concurrently with the task.

It is suggested that one of the primary weaknesses of introspection is that it has an effect on the very processes it seeks to investigate. Ericsson and Simon (1980, 1999), working with the hypothesis that human cognition is information processing, developed a model for how research participants verbalize information and tested the effect that thinking aloud might have on cognitive processes. They concluded that thinking aloud does not change the structure of the task process but that it might slow down the process.[10] A second conclusion was that, in the act of verbalizing, participants report the *products* from cognitive processes (Ericsson and Simon 1999), with the consequence that the researcher has to infer the actual cognitive processes from the verbal reports. Ericsson and Simon also contended that thinking-aloud studies were good for hypothesis generation but not for hypothesis testing.

A further characteristic of the thinking-aloud process observed by Ericsson and Simon was its incompleteness, due to the fact that some cognitive processes are unavailable for verbalization. There are types of behaviour, especially habitual behaviour, which happen without any reportable thoughts (Ericsson 2010:247). This concept is frequently referred to as **automaticity** in expertise studies and has also been considered in translation process research. For example, Jääskeläinen and Tirkkonen-Condit suggested that the lack of verbalizations in some of their protocols might be indicative of automaticity (1988:91). A final point worth highlighting is that Ericsson and Simon's tests of the method were based on tasks with socially agreed performance characteristics. These are tasks where there is general agreement on the criteria for successful completion of the task: "[b]y restricting the research to tasks with socially agreed performance characteristics, it appears that the structure of the task imposes the constraints for functional mental representations and successful thinking" (Ericsson and Simon 1998:182). This raises a critical question about the method's appropriateness for translation-related research since translation – unlike chess, for example – does not have the luxury of socially agreed performance characteristics as an examination of the literature on translation quality assessment will reveal (see Chapter 3, Section 3.6).

Despite these limitations, translation scholars have still employed thinking aloud as a valid data elicitation method for translation processes. As long as the

---

[10] Ericsson and Simon (1999) differentiate between various levels of verbalizations, Levels 1, 2 and 3, with Level 1 being termed talking aloud and Levels 2 and 3 being termed thinking aloud. Some translation scholars opt for not making this distinction (see, for example, Englund Dimitrova 2005), but researchers interested in using TAPs should read more about the important distinction made by Ericsson and Simon.

reported slow-down effect is not an issue in the research design, thinking-aloud has been seen as a useful tool for learning about translation competence, about how professional translators work, and for building models of the translation process that could be used in translator training. Translation scholars began experimenting with introspection in the mid-1980s (Jääskeläinen 2002). Until recently, this was the main research method used in translation process research. Nevertheless, the adoption of thinking aloud as a method in translation has not been without its critics, and sometimes its main proponents are the first to point out its weaknesses. Ericsson himself notes that several studies have demonstrated that participants' verbal reports can be inconsistent with their observed behaviours (Ericsson 2010:247). Toury (1995) highlights the potential for distraction during the verbalization task, and Fraser (1996a and 1996b) questions a lack of systematicity in her review of TAP-oriented studies. Jääskeläinen (2011) recently went as far as questioning the validity of the method for translation research.

4.3.1   *Design*

The most important question for translation process research is whether thinking aloud is an appropriate method for one's research objectives and what impact it might have on the data elicited. These questions can be explored during the design stage. The most obvious impact on data is the slow-down effect, which has been confirmed by some scholars in translation studies, such as Krings (2001) and Jakobsen (2003). Therefore, if translation task time is an important unit of measurement in the research design, then concurrent thinking aloud is inadvisable and retrospective verbalization might be more appropriate. On the other hand, if task time is not an important variable, there might be some advantages to using concurrent thinking aloud. In fact, Angelone (2010) argues that the slowing down effect might even be beneficial when researching translation problem handling because it forces participants to stop and think more carefully. Deffner (1984, cited in Lörscher 1988) also highlights the benefits of concurrent thinking aloud for problem solving. Comparing participants who were thinking aloud versus those who completed a task while thinking silently, Deffner found that those who thought aloud were more systematic problem solvers and that the thinking aloud group were also more successful problem solvers. However, it is important to draw attention to the possibility that there is a difference in the type of verbalizations alluded to by Angelone and Deffner and those that require participants to report directly on thought processes. As Ericsson and Simon (1998:182) point out, "[w]hen participants are thinking aloud, their sequences of thoughts have not been found to be systematically altered by verbalization. However, when participants are *asked to describe and explain their thinking*, their performance is often changed – mostly it is improved" (our emphasis). In other words, if we ask participants to reason about what they are thinking, this may very well have an impact on thought processes and may result in task improvement. While this might be a desirable effect for teaching translation competence, it may not be the effect we want while researching and may compromise the ecological validity of the research.

The slow-down effect also applies to **dialogue or conversational protocols**, where two or more participants talk aloud about a shared task (see Pavlović 2009 for an example of how this is applied in translation research). Not only will task time be affected, but the processes themselves, as well as their outcomes, are also likely to change. As Bernardini (2001:243) points out, "conversation involves reworking thoughts to make them conform to socially established norms, a process which might sensibly alter the information attended to". A dialogue protocol affords insight into how two people might negotiate the task of translation and, therefore, might be appropriate for researching translation collaboration strategies, but such a protocol cannot adequately represent the outcomes of the cognitive processes of an individual translator at work.

Perhaps less obvious and less verifiable is the effect thinking aloud might have on the task product. Jakobsen (2003) and Krings (2001) both suggest that the thinking-aloud method had an effect on the translation and post-editing processes in their studies. In addition, Englund-Dimitrova (2005:74) mentions a study by Stratman and Hamp-Lyons (1994) which found an effect of TAPs on revision processes and products.

Cued retrospection, in particular when supported by recorded keystroke activity and/or overlaid with screen recordings with eye movement data (see discussion of eye tracking in Section 4.5), can provide very powerful reminders to participants about the nature of their engagement in a task. The obvious disadvantage is that retrospection relies on memory, with its inherent weaknesses and consequences for accuracy (Englund Dimitrova 2005), and that the cues provide only surface-level evidence of the processes, not deep representations of the cognitive processes engaged in during the task. While cued retrospection offers a visual reminder of what the participant was doing during the task, the cues themselves can also be distracting or can cause items to be made more salient during recall, with the result that the participant comments on their typing skills or on their eye movements and not on their processes.

Written reports have the benefit that a written task (translation) does not have to be re-encoded in oral form (as is the case for verbal reports), something that was highlighted by Toury (1988) as another potentially confounding factor. However, if written reports are compiled after the task they also suffer from memory limitations. If, on the other hand, they are compiled during the task, they undoubtedly interrupt the very process they are supposed to document.

During the design stage the nature of the study participants also requires consideration. It is often assumed that anyone who meets the specific criteria for inclusion in a study could be included in that study (for more discussion about sampling criteria see Chapter 5, Section 5.4.2). However, if verbal reporting is to be used as a data elicitation method, we should consider the possibility that not all otherwise qualified participants will be good at verbal reporting. Verbal reporting is an uncommon activity for most people. Moreover, to be asked to carry out a task and talk out loud about it at the same time is not a trivial demand. Some individuals may feel quite uncomfortable with such a task, and this is likely to impact on their task performance. Even if researchers expect participants to be comfortable with thinking aloud, some warm-up exercises and training should be given in advance.

It has been suggested that cultural background influences the propensity for verbal reporting. Clemmensen *et al* (2008) report on numerous studies demonstrating that thinking aloud hampers participants from Eastern countries (which they broadly define as "people from China and the countries heavily influenced by its culture" (*ibid.*:2)), whereas solving problems in silence appears to hamper those from Western countries (defined as "people from Western Europe and U.S. citizens with European origins" (*ibid.*:2)), although the authors also acknowledge that cultural differences can exist between peoples of different countries and not just between East and West. Drawing on Nisbett (2003), Clemmensen *et al* (2008:7) argue that "the language in which verbalizations are made affects their content" and conclude:

> Our analysis of the TA method by use of Nisbett's cultural psychology suggests that culture influences how instructions are acted upon by users, how users verbalize, how evaluators read users, and how the overall relationship between evaluators and users develops. These influences have implications for practitioners and for researchers, in particular those wishing to do cross-cultural work. (*ibid.*:10).

The authors provide some guidelines for researchers who wish to use thinking aloud, especially with Western and Eastern participants (albeit for usability research, but the instructions could be applied to other domains).

Although the validity of verbal reports as actual and accurate representations of cognitive processes has been questioned, the method has still been applied in many research domains (including education and human-computer interaction for instance.) and has been used sucessfully to generate interesting hypotheses. Whether or not verbal reports should be used in translation process research will depend on the objectives of the research and, more specifically, on the variables to be examined. If the purpose is to spur participants into more creative problem-solving modes, then concurrent verbal reporting and/or dialogue protocols might be appropriate. The propensity of participants to produce TAPs that help to answer the research question might need to be tested and the impact of culture should also be considered. Finally, the impact on study variables of re-encoding a written task in an oral manner needs to be considered.

4.3.2 *Data elicitation*

We mentioned above that it is to be recommended that training and warm-up tasks be given to qualified participants prior to collecting the study data (Ericsson and Simon 1998:181). The instructions given to the participants prior to data elicitation are also of considerable importance. In this relation, we would like to draw attention to one of Ericsson's (2010:247) comments on the validity of the thinking-aloud method:

> Within the cognitive science community, there has now evolved a consensus that with appropriate verbal-report instructions participants provide valid concurrent and retrospective verbal reports on their cognitive processes that match other evidence for the associated performance and process-trace data.

The phrase "that match other evidence" points to the desirability of triangulation. Appropriate verbal-report instructions are discussed in some detail by Ericsson and Simon and examples provided (1999:375-379). The instructions given to participants for producing verbal reports should also be consistent across participants and well documented, so as to ensure transparency and replicability: "investigators should document their verbatim instructions and exact descriptions of any scripted interactions between the experimenter and participants" (Ericsson 2002:986).

It is not unusual for participants to fall silent for periods of time during verbalization. When this occurs they should be reminded by the experimenter to keep talking (Ericsson and Simon 1999). However, we should be cognizant of the fact that this might interfere with automatized processes (Englund-Dimitrova 2005) and that a problem-solving process which is so cognitively demanding may leave little or no capacity for verbalization. Prompting also carries the risk of reminding the participant that they are being monitored. On that risk, Ericsson and Simon (1999:375) remark that participants "get so involved in the task that little notice is taken of the environment, and situational factors have no real effects". We, too, have observed participants being so involved in a task that they seem to lose awareness of the fact that they are participating in a controlled experiment. Nonetheless, we cannot naively assume that reminding them to verbalize their thoughts has no effect on processing. A trade-off is inevitably required between collecting no data at a certain point in the task, because the participant has fallen silent, and influencing the data through prompting.

Prior to data elicitation, a decision has to be made on which language participants will use for verbalization. There are numerous pitfalls awaiting the researcher with this decision. First, the choice of language might impact on the ability of the participant to verbalize, especially if they are using a second or third language. Second, in the case of translation, the participant is already engaged in a bilingual processing task, so there may be interference between source and target languages and the language used for verbalization – participants are very likely to produce **bilingual protocols**. While this is not a problem in itself, it adds to the complexity of the data analysis. Third, if the choice of language is left up to the participant, the researcher may have to analyze verbalizations in two (or more) languages, which makes annotation and coding more complex. For the sake of consistency in reporting, a researcher would have to translate the verbal report, introducing another layer of mediation and putting even greater distance between the cognitive processes and products, on the one hand, and the protocols on the other, thus reducing the validity of the research findings. Resolving these issues is by no means straightforward. Providing the participant with the means to produce the most valid protocols is probably the most important consideration. If this means having to deal with multilingual protocols, then that is something that needs to be considered by the researcher. Cued retrospective protocols might reduce linguistic interference and stress but then recall capacity and saliency – the relative importance of an item for the participant or the making prominent of an item through some form of highlighting in a software program, for example – become potentially interfering variables.

4.3.3   *Transcription*

Before we can analyze verbal report data, they first have to be transcribed. Here we provide an outline of some of the key issues involved in **transcription** (see McLellan *et al* 2003 for a more in-depth discussion of these issues). Transcribing is a long, time-consuming process, which is why some researchers, assuming they have the funds, might decide to pay a professional company (or a research assistant) to transcribe the data. However doing the transcription oneself has the advantage that it allows one to get to know the data thoroughly and helps to inform decisions that have to be taken regarding the subsequent coding of the data. There are several computer programs that can be used to digitize recorded speech and that can help transcribing, for example by pausing automatically every few seconds, repeating previous segments or slowing down the recording. Express Scribe, Transcriber, HyperTranscribe and Voicewalker are some popular ones at the moment. Transana is an open source transcribing software package that also integrates tools for the management and analysis of digital audio and video files (see Chapter 6, Section 6.6.3). Transcribing software can also work together with speech recognition software. Because voice recognition works better with voices the software has been trained to recognize, some researchers use it by listening to the recordings, repeating the words into a microphone and having the software generate the text.

The importance of the transcription process should not be underestimated because it already imposes a layer of interpretation on the language used by participants (Bucholtz 2000). The choice of what to transcribe and annotate is one way of determining what is meaningful or not. Transcribers also bring in their own language ideology into the task, for example by standardizing (or not) grammar as well as the spelling of lexical variants, or simply by the way they use punctuation. One of the key decisions to make before transcription is how much detail (verbal and non-verbal) to include and what conventions to use. A **denaturalized transcription** attempts to retain features of the oral language, such as prosody, false starts, filler words and pauses, which can all be meaningful and are particularly useful if the transcript is to be submitted for linguistic analysis. However, the result may be difficult to interpret, particularly for those not used to encountering oral features in written language. A **naturalized transcription** is one in which oral discoursal features are omitted and the result reads more like written language (for an example of a naturalized transcription see Chapter 5, Section 5.9, Table 1). Such transcripts run the risk of failing to call enough attention to the possible change in meaning in the transformation from speech to writing. In any case, for purposes of replicability, it is important to choose a set of conventions to follow and specify clearly the criteria used to select what was transcribed and annotated.

Göpferich (2010) discusses the issue of transcribing data collected during translation process research. Figure 4.1 gives a small snapshot of some transcribed denaturalized process data collected in her TransComp project. The conventions for a speech transcription system for German (GAT or Gesprächsanalytisches Transkriptionssystem – Selting *et al* (1998)) are used here where non-lexical utterances, e.g. 'hm', are transcribed and the lengthening of a vowel or other sound is indicated by one to three colons, e.g. 'hm:::'. Audible inhalations and exhalations are also coded, e.g. '.hh', and '( )' indicates incomprehensible utterances. Apart from this, standard orthography is used, but dialect is transcribed as it is spoken (as in the example in Figure 4.1, which is in Austrian German) (Göpferich, 2010:113).

---

bedeutung von f psychischen faktoren oder konditionierung bei
mit physischen stoffen wird der süchtige durch sein starkes verlangen daran gehindert
mh:: .h aha
in spite of the importance of psychological or conditioning factors in addiction
ASO! .hh mhm. jetzt verSTEH i des erst also psychologie: hh .hh psycho no psychologie
oder konditionierung
.h
haben zwar
.h
bei sucht und gewöhnung
( )
durchaus ihren stellenwert,
.h
der süchtige
m m m m doch h
doch der süchtige
mh
wird
durch sein starkes verlangen daran gehindert seine sucht aufzugeben ein altes chinesisches sprichwort besagt
mn mn mn mn mh:. .hh ( )

Figure 4.1 Example of TAP transcription from the TransComp project (http://gams.uni-graz.at/fedora/get/o:tc-095-201/bdef:TEI/get), post-phase_2, participant: Professional AEF, Source Text A1

4.3.4 Analysis

Having transcribed verbal reports, we then need to code the data for analysis. Here we offer a brief introduction to the coding process and discuss specific characteristics of TAP coding; see also Chapter 5, Sections 5.5 and 5.9 for a discussion of coding quantitative and qualitative data (respectively) in participant-oriented research. To reiterate an important point made by Ericsson and Simon (1999:204), processes cannot be coded directly from verbalizations but must be inferred from the data. A preliminary coding scheme may be developed prior to the actual act of **coding** (and this is where transcription by the researcher himself is useful as it may act as a catalyst for the dynamic development of a coding scheme during transcription) and fitted to the data. Alternatively, the coding scheme may be driven by the data, emerging and evolving during the data analysis. Developing a coding scheme in advance of its application has the benefit that we establish *a priori* analysis categories and variables that are appropriate to our research question. It also enables the re-use of existing coding schemes, allowing for the testing of replicability. However, this approach also carries a substantial risk of moulding data to fit our analysis categories, rather than allowing categories to emerge from the data. By adopting a data-driven coding approach, we are freer to react to the data, but our coding scheme could become unwieldy and overly complex. Of even greater concern is the impact the latter approach can have on existing or emerging theories. Ericsson and Simon (1999:286) offer advice for reducing the impact of existing theories on data coding. They suggest, for example, that the researchers' theoretical commitments should be "kept as small and weak as possible" (*ibid.*), that theoretical assumptions and presuppositions should be made explicit and that objectivity, consistency and reproducibility should be given precedence.

Verbal protocols can be coded at macro, micro or both levels. Macro-level coding and analysis is useful for comparing general approaches to a task or problem and can involve, for example, episode-level or solution-step analysis (Ericsson and Simon 1999). An episode is a collapsed view of steps taken and solution-step analysis involves the unfolding of the episode to view specific steps, which in turn can be unfolded to view the specific (micro) processes making up each step. An example of a macro-level analysis mentioned by Ericsson and Simon (*ibid.*:202) is Goldner (1957), who categorized approaches to problem solving (though not with reference to translation) into two, i.e. 'whole', if participants considered all information given, and 'part', if participants focused on part of the information given; the approach was also categorized along the dimension of 'flexibility-rigidity', depending on participants' ability to use varied approaches. Since translation is often viewed as a problem-solving task, and flexibility is a construct of particular interest to translation process researchers (Jensen 2011b; Bayer-Hohenwarter 2009), this approach to micro- and macro-level coding and analysis could be useful.

To date, translation process studies have preferred a micro-level analysis of verbal report data. One of the main challenges for micro-level coding and analysis is segmentation, i.e. where does a **process indicator** start and end? The markers normally used include pauses, intonation and syntactical markers. When results from verbal report analyses are being triangulated with other types of data, we also have to consider the question of segmentation according to other data types. For example, if we are gathering both verbal and keystroke data (see Section 4.4), a pause in verbal reporting might not coincide with a pause in typing and therefore the segments, or units of analysis, will not be aligned – the benefits of triangulation obviously come with important methodological challenges. While micro-level segments from different types of data may not be directly compara-ble, we may be better able to compare results from macro-level analyses.

Ericsson and Simon (1999) emphasize the importance of the replicability and validity of verbal report coding. According to them, the usual procedure for this is to develop a coding manual, which gives guidance on the categories to be applied and/or on how to create categories, and to provide practice for coders. Ideally, multiple coders will be engaged to code the same data, after which **inter-coder reliability** is measured and reported.[11] Inter-coder reliability is a measure of how often coders agree on the allocation of categories to specific data segments. Fifty percent agreement, for example, is considered to be low while ninety-five percent agreement is high. A common measure for inter-coder agreement between two coders is **Cohen's kappa** (Cohen 1960), while **Fleiss' kaapa** is used for measur-ing agreement between more than two coders (Fleiss 1971) – see discussion in Chapter 3, Section 3.6.4. For translation process research, though the use of multiple coders and testing of their agreement levels is still rare.

As Englund-Dimitrova (2005:82) points out, the coding and analysis of TAPs is not standardized in translation process research:

> ... no *single*, widely accepted model for coding and analysis exists. There is no *a priori* unit for analysis, since it depends on the purpose of the analysis, nor is there any *a priori* way of transcribing the protocols, since this also depends on the purpose of the analysis. (emphasis in original)

This lack of a standard approach is problematic as it prevents the pooling of research resources, such as corpora of tagged TAPs, for analysis from different perspectives by multiple researchers. While in some cases it is important for the coding to emerge over time, depending on the specific research objectives, in others it is worthwhile considering whether coding models used by prior re-searchers could be adopted and, if necessary, adapted. For example, Englund Dimitrova reuses the verbalized problem representations of monolingual text revisers for the coding and analysis of problem representations in translation revision (2005:122-124).[12] Bernardini (2001:260) also encourages **standardization** of coding schemes, emphasizing that this would aid the systematic analysis and description of TAPs. A first step in the direction of standardization has already

---

[11] See Chapter 5 for a discussion of intra-coder reliability.
[12] For a list of the coventions used in Englund Dimitrova's TAPs, see (Englund Dimitrova 1995:80).

been made by Göpferich (2010), who proposes the use of an asset management system to make translation process data accessible on the Internet, as well as a text annotation system, based on the **Text Encoding Initiative** (TEI), for **translation process protocols**.

To summarize, then, the primary issues that we need to consider in the analysis of TAPs relate to who transcribes the data, what transcription convention to use, how to cope with multilingual TAPs, the choice of coding scheme and whether to create them in advance or allow the data to drive the coding process, the comparability, or lack thereof, of micro-level data, and the use of multiple coders as well as their level of agreement.

4.4   Keystroke logging

Keystroke logging involves the use of a special software program that records all keys pressed on the keyboard, as well as mouse movements and pauses between key presses during a text production task. As translation production is now primarily a computerized task, the validity of using keystroke logging as a tool for recording the task has increased. While other tools were and are available (for example, **Inputlog**),[13] the development of the **Translog** tool (Jakobsen and Schou 1999) for use in translation process research in particular has provided an important impetus for the method of keystroke logging. In comparison with other keystroke logging tools that integrate with word processing programs, Translog has its own user interface which is specially designed for translation with source and target language windows.

Keystroke logging tools produce a log file containing a record of all the keys pressed during a task, such as text production characters, punctuation symbols, navigational characters (up and down arrows, right and left arrows, etc.) as well as pauses and their duration, and text and revision indicators such as deletions, cut and paste operations, and so on. Figure 4.2 illustrates the type of data one can expect from a Translog log file (known as a linear representation). Navigational keys are in square brackets; square brackets with figures preceded by an asterisk indicate pauses over 10 seconds in duration; single asterisks '*' indicate one second pauses; typed text appears as normal text and ⊠ indicates a deletion.

[Ctrl←][:11.13][Ctrl→][Ctrl→][ShftCtrl→]***[ShftCtrl→][ShftCtrl→]*[ShftCtrl→]⊠****[Ctrl→][Ctrl→]*Be fehl•[*:14.07]wird•über•die•lokal•[ShftCtrl→][ShftCtrl→][ShftCtrl→][ShftCtrl→]⊠[Ctrl→]⊠⊠•[Ctrl →][*:26.96][Ctrl→]*Handbuch•⊠s•"[Ctrl→]*User's•Guide[Ctrl←][Ctrl←][Ctrl←]⊠⊠*I[Ctrl→]⊠⊠⊠ ⊠⊠⊠⊠⊠⊠⊠⊠→→→→→→→→•und•Referenz[Ctrl→]*[Shft⇨][Shft←]angz⊠ezeigt.→*→

Figure 4.2 Example of Translog linear data

The log file can also be used to replay a screen recording of the text production process. This can be played at 100% speed (at the same speed with which the

---

[13] http://www.inputlog.net/index.html. [Last accessed 4 December 2012].

text was first produced) or it can be slowed down, sped up and paused when necessary to facilitate analysis. In Translog, the researcher can view the actual text being produced and the corresponding dynamic linear data can be viewed in a parallel window. Since keystroke logging tools also record on-screen activity, the line between keystroke recording and screen recording as research methods is fuzzy. Similarly, other tools such as eye trackers (see Section 4.5) record keystroke and mouse activity, and screen activity in addition to gaze data. It is therefore difficult to discuss them in isolation of each other. Here, for purposes of clarity, we will focus in each case on the primary function of the tool, i.e. keystroke logging in the case of Translog.

4.4.1   Design

Keystroke logging records various aspects of the product of translation processes on both the macro and micro levels. On the macro level, keystroke logging tools record:

- Total task time
- Time spent in the orientation, drafting or subsequent revision stages (Jakobsen 2002)

On the micro-level, they record:

- Pauses, their frequency, duration and positioning, all of which can be inferred to represent cognitive effort (Jakobsen 1998; Wengelin 2006)
- The number and length of text production units
- The number, nature and timing of revision actions, which could also be seen as being indicative of cognitive effort.

Thus, the use of keystroke logging results in quite a rich data set for analysis. Its advantage over verbal reports is that the method of keystroke logging itself does not slow the task down, nor does it interfere with the task by putting extra demand on participants' cognitive resources. Given that it records only the products of cognitive processes, on the other hand, it is recommended that it be coupled with at least one other data elicitation method, such as verbal reporting or eye tracking, in order to increase the ability of the researcher to make inferences about translation processes.

Translog has obvious strengths and limitations, and its appropriateness for the research objectives ought to be analyzed during the design stage. For example, Translog requires that the translator works within the keystroke logging environment only. That is, when Translog is used, any activity outside the Translog environment such as querying of Internet resources is not recorded. Restricting participants to an environment which is (a) unfamiliar to them and (b) curtails their usual translation routines will obviously have an impact on research validity. In addition, since there are no spell-checking or formatting features in the current version of Translog, these aspects of the translation production process cannot be captured. A tool such as Translog also limits the possibility of analysis of interaction with other translation technologies, such as translation memory tools.

Other keystroke logging tools, e.g. Inputlog or BB FlashBack,[14] record keystroke data independently of the word processing environment, giving the researcher greater flexibility in the choice of software programs that can be included in the study design. On the other hand, one loses the source text/target text set-up that is specific to Translog. Tools such as Inputlog and BB FlashBack also allow for voice recording, which enables the simultaneous capture of keystroke and verbal reporting data. It is also possible to integrate Translog and Inputlog with an eye tracker, allowing for simultaneous acquisition of keystroke and eye-tracking data.

Tools such as Translog and Inputlog are free to use for the academic community, easy to install and easy to learn. They are generally stable, but since their development is often (understandably) not the main focus of their developers, improvements and updates are slow to be introduced.[15] Some character encoding, platforms or operating systems, for instance, may not be supported. Bugs might also take some time to fix. It is therefore imperative that the researcher who intends to use such a data elicitation tool thoroughly tests the scenario in which the tool will be employed in advance.

In Section 4.2 we highlighted some issues on participant profiling in general. A particular participant profiling question emerges where keystroke logging is concerned: do all participants possess equal keyboarding competences? Some participants might be very skilled touch typists, others might be very fast typists, but not touch typists, some might be very skilled at using keyboard shortcuts while others will favour the mouse. In a setting where pauses of between 2 and 5 seconds are used as segmenters for units of analysis, it would seem obvious that keyboarding skills might have an impact on the data at that level. Therefore, profiling of participants' keyboarding competences (as well as their translation competences, as mentioned above) is an important parameter in the design stage.

4.4.2   *Data elicitation*

As we have established above, the choice of keystroke logging tool will depend on the research objectives, which have to take account of the strengths and weaknesses of each tool. Another parameter in the decision-making process is the location of data elicitation. If ecological validity is of high importance in the study design (see Chapter 2, Section 2.10.1), then collecting data on-site, at translators' workplaces, might be necessary. The setting of the data elicitation task in a translator's workplace will, in turn, influence the choice and combination

---

[14] http://www.bbsoftware.co.uk/bbflashback/home.aspx. [Last accessed 4 December 2012].

[15] The main developers of Translog are translation process researchers and translation studies scholars.

of methods used. For example, a translator could not be expected to produce a verbal report in an open-plan, bustling office.

When using keystroke logging in the translators' workplace, we are obliged to ascertain whether the appropriate platform and operating systems are pre-installed on the computers to be used and to seek permission to install the necessary software on those computers. The issue of varying computer processors, platforms, operating systems and so on should not be underestimated. Testing of the keystroke logging tool on each computer is probably a wise step in the pre-elicitation stage. A not-insignificant step in this stage is to secure permission from the translator or translator's employer for the screen recording and keystroke logging. In this context, it is not uncommon for researchers to be asked to sign non-disclosure agreements, which specify that they will only record information pertaining to the particular text in the study and that confidential information will not be disclosed. For example, it would not be unusual for a translator to pause in the middle of a translation task in order to check email, which could disclose confidential information that is captured by the screen recording tool.

The alternative setting of the research facility certainly appears to have some advantages over the on-site scenario: the researcher has complete control over the computer(s) used and can test in advance; variation in platforms, operating systems and so on is not a concern; there is no hurdle of a non-disclosure agreement; the setting can be selected so that the translator can produce a verbal report and/or interact with an eye tracker. In short, the researcher has much more control. Of course, the unfamiliar scenario reduces ecological validity, as does the use of unfamiliar computer configurations and software. Moreover, the use of a different physical keyboard and, potentially, different keyboard layouts might have a significant impact on the translators' keyboarding behaviour (researchers should ask about keyboard layout preferences in advance). Finally, it may be more difficult to recruit participants if they have to travel to another facility. Again, the pros and cons of each data elicitation location and combination of methods will have to be weighed up during the design stage.

4.4.3 Analysis

Keystroke data allow us to make concrete measurements in relation to specific macro-level tasks in the translation process. For instance, we can measure and compare total task time across participants, or the total amount of time spent on a particular segment (Jakobsen 2003). We can also measure the amount of time spent in different stages of the process (Jakobsen 2002), though their delimitation is not altogether straightforward (when does orientation end and drafting begin? Can the translator orientate herself and draft at the same time?). On the micro-level, the number of pauses can be captured (O'Brien 2007), but this measure is subject to the varied definitions of pause duration. Additional concrete micro-level measures include the number of cuts/pastes, character deletions/insertions, navigational keys used, and so on.

As mentioned above, on its own, keystroke data only allow us to infer hypotheses about translation processes. In combination with other data streams, we are in a better position to validate (or challenge) those inferences. If, for example, we combine keystroke logging with eye tracking, we can learn about the focus of attention at any point in the process: on the source text, target text or on both (**parallel processing**, for example, when the eyes are on the source text but text is simultaneously being produced in the target window) or, indeed, on something outside the source and target texts (such as information sources) (Jensen 2011b).

A second challenge in the analysis of keystroke logging data has already been alluded to in Section 4.2: what is the unit of analysis? As we stated above, process researchers, in general, tend to have very different concepts of units of analysis varying from problem indicators (which could be verbalized or indicated by a pause of a specified length, see Angelone 2010), to attention units (length of time spent looking at the source text or target text and/or typing target text, see Jensen 2011b), to temporal units (such as any data enclosed between five-second pauses), to linguistic units (such as the sentence), to less well-defined units (such as the translation unit). We can only reiterate here that the validity of the unit of analysis will depend on the research objectives and on a credible operationalization of the variables. Transparancy, validity and replicabilty are, as usual, of high importance.

4.5   Eye tracking

Eye tracking is the process of recording the point of gaze of a person and the movement of the eyes from one point to another. An **eye tracker** is the apparatus used to make such recordings. In their early instantiations, eye trackers were built into helmets which were placed on a participant's head. The helmet contained two protruding cameras which tracked eye movement. Such head-mounted apparatus is still in use today, especially for research that requires very precise measurements. The eye tracker then evolved into a device that resembled and behaved like a standard computer monitor. This type of eye tracker has discreet, built-in infra red light diodes, which reflect light off the eyes, enabling the eye-tracking software package to calculate the precise X and Y co-ordinates of the eyes on the monitor on a millisecond basis. The dilation (widening) or constriction (narrowing) of the pupil is also measured in pupil diameter per millisecond as are the rapid eye movements from one point to another (known as '**saccades**'). More recently, eye trackers have evolved into specialized spectacles, which can be worn like normal spectacles, but which also have built-in light diodes that record eye movement. The latter are particularly useful for research that requires the participant to be mobile, for example marketing research in commercial environ-ments. It is the second type of eye tracker, i.e. the computer monitor, that has been most commonly used in translation process research to date.[16]

Eye tracking is predicated on the '**eye-mind hypothesis**' formulated by Just

---

[16] At the time of writing, the most common brand of eye tracker in translation research was the Tobii monitor: http://www.tobii.com/. [Last accessed 5 December 2012].

and Carpenter (1980) which posits that there is no significant time-lag between what a person fixates on and what the brain is processing. The data gathered by the eye tracker can be used to infer cognitive effort (usually correlated with pupil dilation) or to determine the focus of attention via **fixations**, defined as "eye movements which stabilize the retina over a stationary object of interest" (Duchowski 2003:43). Eye tracking data can also be used to visualize the **gaze path** – the sequence of fixations on a stimulus over a period of time. Such data have proved to be useful in different domains, including information processing, assistive technology for people with special needs, accessibility, usability, readability, psycholinguistics, emotion research, gaming, language learning and, not least, translation process research. Figure 4.3 shows a screen shot of some fixations on English instructions as they are being read by a participant. The numbers indicate the sequence of fixations.

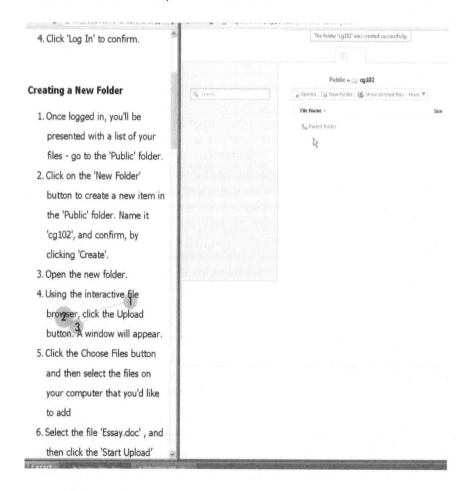

Figure 4.3 Example of fixations during a reading task from a study by Doherty and O'Brien (2012)

In the field of translation process research, eye tracking has been used to in-vestigate many different topics such as cognitive effort and translation technology (O'Brien 2006, 2008, 2011b), different types of reading tasks – e.g. reading for comprehension, reading while typing a translation (Jakobsen and Jensen 2008; Alves *et al* 2011), effort in metaphor translation (Sjørup 2011), processing effort in subtitled material (Caffrey 2008), processing effort in translation directionality (Chang 2009) and uncertainty management during translation (Angelone 2010), to mention just a few.

4.5.1   *Design*

The issues of participant and task profiling as well as translation and typing competences, discussed above under Sections 4.2.1, 4.3.1 and 4.4.1, all apply to the use of eye tracking as a research method and will therefore not be revisited here. We concentrate instead on the specific issues that enter into the equation when eye tracking forms part of the research design (for more discussion on methodological challenges of eye tracking in translation process research, see O'Brien 2010b).

Eye trackers can be portable, especially eye-tracking helmets or spectacles, but these portable devices are currently less suited to translation process re-search than the desktop eye trackers normally used because they are either more invasive than we would desire for a naturalistic task, as with the head-mounted ones, or less accurate, as with the spectacles. The desktop eye trackers are considerably heavier than a standard computer monitor and, although they are mobile, moving them from one location to another is not trivial. What is more, the computer connected to the tracker also needs to be moved because the tracking software is installed on it. Alternatively, the researcher must install the software on another computer, first ensuring that a suitable operating system and graphics card are installed. Thus, by far the easiest solution is to maintain the eye tracker in one location and ask participants to visit that location. This has an impact on the ecological validity of the research design and also raises issues regarding familiarity with software packages, keyboards, etc. (see Section 4.4). Until portable eye trackers become more accurate (which will undoubtedly happen), we will have to compensate for potential impacts caused by inviting participants to visit university laboratories for translation process studies.

On the other hand, there are advantages to maintaining the eye tracker in one location. One such advantage is that the researcher can control, at least to some extent, the light and sound variables. It is well known that light has an effect on pupil size, with the pupil constricting in high-intensity light environments and dilating in low light. If pupil size is being used as an indicator of cognitive effort (see sections 4.5.2 and 4.5.3), then variation in light intensity during the task is undesirable. Some control over the lighting is required and all participants would ideally carry out their tasks under the same lighting conditions. Additionally, sound is known to have an impact on pupil dilation and should also be controlled. Unfortunately, few translation researchers have access to sound-proofed rooms, but this can be somewhat overcome by selecting a room that is far from the madding crowd, or by conducting sessions when the traffic in corridors is likely to be quieter (taking account, of course, of safety for all involved).

Pupil size is also known to be sensitive to emotions – something that is impossible to control – and to certain physical substances. For example, caffeine (or stronger stimulants!) can affect pupil size. Heavy eye make-up might also present problems. Ideally, participants would be made aware of these facts prior to taking part in an eye-tracking session.

Eye tracker manufacturers claim that contact lenses and glasses for normal corrected vision do not have an impact on the collection of gaze data but more significant vision impairment could lead to a reduction in data quality or to a failure in data elicitation. With or without glasses, some participants may just not be suited to the collection of **gaze data**. This is normally established at the calibration stage, where participants sit in front of the tracker and follow a moving dot on the screen with their eyes. The tracker then reports the quality of the data capture. If the calibration is recurringly poor, there is a strong chance that your participant is (inexplicably) just not suitable. Even when calibration is fine, subsequent data capture can be poor. Factoring a warm-up task into our design can help identify these issues at an early stage. During design, it is not unwise to assume that some of the data captured will be of dubious quality and that some participants, or parts of their recordings, will have to be eliminated from the study. Therefore, if the study requires 20 participants as a minimum, at least 25 should be recruited.

Yet another physical aspect of the design is the necessity for head control. More specifically, when using a desktop tracker, the participants would ideally be seated at exactly the same distance from the monitor and they should not alter their head position significantly, once they have been successfully calibrated. At the same time, they do not need to behave like statues because modern eye trackers can compensate for small variations in head position, but participants should be made aware that they need to control their head movements more than usual during the research task. A practical way of preventing substantial changes in head position (apart from instructing the participants) is to provide a non-swinging chair, but one that is adjustable for height. Participants should also be instructed to hold their position between calibration and the onset of the task as we have observed participants holding their positions very well during calibration and warm-up tasks and, once the actual task commences, adjusting their position as they 'relax' into the task! Yet another way of ensuring limited head movement is to use more invasive eye-tracking equipment. For example, in psycholinguistic research, where measurements are often taken on a millisecond basis, an eye tracker with a built-in chin rest is commonly used. The chin rest allows the participant to rest their chin in one location, thereby maintaining the same head position throughout the task. Of course, the suitability of this arrangement for ecologically valid translation production tasks is highly questionable.

An important decision in the design of a research project that makes use of eye tracking is the source text(s) to be used. We have discussed issues regarding text selection above but we also need to highlight specific questions arising in the eye-tracking scenario. Three constraints force the selection of relatively short texts for eye-tracking research. The first has to do with the amount of data: an eye tracker collects a large variety of data types, which are discussed in more detail in Section 4.5.2. If the researcher is working alone, the data analysis is consequently quite time-consuming. The second reason pertains to the size (in terms of bytes) of data collected. Since the eye tracker is recording screen and keyboard activity, in addition to gaze data, the size of the recordings can be very large, even for a short (let's say 30 minute) session, which can slow down the computer as the task progresses. Only powerful processors would support longer tasks and texts.[17] Thirdly, translation process research is often interested in the duration and number of fixations on a particular part of the screen (where the source text, target text or glossary windows are situated) or even on particular text fragments or words. Measures such as **fixation count** (the number of fixations on an area of interest per participant/task), average fixation duration (the average length of fixations per participant/task measured in milliseconds) and **observation length** (the average length of all observation time during a task) are typical in eye tracking studies. The analysis is relatively straight-forward if these **areas of interest** (commonly abbreviated to 'AOIs') do not move about on the screen. However, a longer text will require scrolling, thereby moving the AOIs and making the analysis more complicated. If we take into account that translation typically involves longer texts, the requirement for short texts leaves the researcher with a dilemma concerning ecological validity.

The dilemma of text length is further complicated by the fact that translation process researchers are often interested in fixations on particular sentences, phrases or words, but eye trackers cannot show which word was fixated on with 100% accuracy.[18] For this reason, the font size has to be made considerably large in order for the fixation data to be more reliable. There are no standard guidelines for font sizes but researchers have tended to use 14-16 point font size to date. Double line spacing is often applied for the same reason, and it is recommended that the text does not extend to the very right or left of the monitor, as fixations on those points could be lost. All of these measures should be tested in a pilot stage of the study. When the font size, line spacing, and no scrolling controls are implemented, we are left with rather short texts. Nonetheless, we should point

---

[17] How powerful a processor needs to be is dependent on the type of research. For example, research employing media files (films or games) will need more powerful processors than research using text only. We recommend discussing requirements with eye tracker suppliers.

[18] To tackle this problem, a tool known as the 'Gaze-to-Word Mapper' was developed as part of an EU-funded research project (Eye-to-IT). The Gaze-to-Word Mapper theoretically allowed the researcher to more accurately map fixations onto specific words, but its accuracy is also limited (80% accuracy reported by Dragsted and Hansen 2008, 65-75% accuracy reported by Jensen 2008). A new version of Translog (Translog II) has now been developed which can integrate data from the Tobii eye tracker into Translog log files (see: http://openarchive.cbs. dk/bitstream/handle/10398/8435/Michael_Carl_2012.pdf?sequence=1 [Last accessed 20 April 2012).

out that the constraints on text length for eye tracking do not necessarily apply to other parts of a study. An excerpt from a longer text can be used for the eye-tracking stage, while the longer text might be used for triangulation purposes. This undoubtedly limits the direct comparability of results, since we would not be comparing the exact same text, but it allows for a flexible research design where hypothesis generation is followed by exploration or testing, for example.

4.5.2 Data elicitation

What eye trackers are perhaps best used for in translation process research is the elicitation of attentional and cognitive effort data. The eye tracker has a dynamic replay function (**gaze replay**) which overlays eye movements, in the form of a coloured dot, across the screen over the duration of the task. This is visible retrospectively, not during the actual task itself. The gaze replay shows where the translator looked at any point in time during the task. When coupled with immediate retrospective verbal reports (see Section 4.3), gaze replay acts as a powerful cue for the participant, leading to an enrichment of the eye-tracking data. However, we should sound a note of caution here: since many translators have not (yet) encountered gaze replays, they can be over-awed by the novelty of the replay and might find themselves distracted by the colourful dot bouncing around the screen, leading to exclamations about their eye movements instead of verbalizations about the process. To reduce this risk, the researcher can show a replay in advance or use the replay during a warm-up session in order to reduce the novelty aspect and increase focus on the verbal reporting.

The gaze replay demonstrates saccadic eye movement too. The number of backward saccades in particular is seen to be an indicator of cognitive effort in reading (see Rayner 1998 for an extensive review of eye tracking and reading research). There are different types of forward and backward eye movements, each of which, it is claimed, is representative of different types of text processing tasks. For example, Kaakinen and Hyönä (2005:243) differentiate between first-pass re-readings and "look-backs from subsequent text to re-read the relevant text information after the first pass". The former reflect initial integrative and comprehension processing, while the latter reflect a need to restore information from working memory (*ibid.*).

Eye-tracking software also produces static representations of attentional data in the form of **hotspots** (also called **'heatmaps'**), static screen shots of the user interface with colour-coded 'heat' marks overlaid on the parts of the interface that received most attention. For example, with the Tobii eyetracker and its associated software, the part of the interface that received the most attention is coloured with red in the heatmap, followed by yellow and then green to indicate decreasing intensity of gaze. This data type is useful for discovering what parts of a user interface are most attended to during a task and is commonly used in usabilty and web browsing studies.

In addition to gaze replay and hotspots, eye trackers produce attentional data in the form of fixations. The position of specific AOIs, such as the source text window, can be manually defined by the researcher and the number and average duration of fixations can be automatically estimated for each AOI. Fixation count and duration give not only an indication of the attentional focus during the translation process but are also indicative of cognitive effort (Just and Carpenter 1980; Rayner and Sereno 1994; Rayner 1998).

Attentional data are taken to indicate, in an indirect way, cognitive processes; that is to say, when the gaze replay indicates that a translator is reading the source text, we assume that the cognitive task of reading is actually taking place. Also, as we explained above, fixations are indicators of cognitive effort – the more fixations there are and the longer the average duration, the more effort is deemed to be required. Changes in baseline **pupil size** have also been shown to be an indicator of cognitive effort (Hess and Polt 1964), and this measure has been applied in translation process research. However, we should point out that translation researchers have sometimes found pupil dilation not to correspond with other indicators of cognitive effort (see, for example, Doherty *et al* 2010). Also, changes in **pupil dilation** in response to a stimulus have been found to occur with a delay of 100-200 milliseconds (Beatty 1982), something that should be factored into the data analysis for this indicator.

An eye tracker is useful for recording temporal data for specific text levels, such as paragraphs, sentences, segments. While this can also be done using screen recording or keystroke logging tools, the gaze data add another, more visible, layer of evidence. During eye tracking the screen activity is automatically recorded. If translators switch between different programs (from a text processing tool to a web browser, for example), this action is also captured. Likewise, some eye-tracking analysis software collects keystroke logging data and align that data type with pupil measurements and eye position on the XY coordinates. In summary, then, eye tracking collects multiple data streams and types and provides the researcher with a vast amount of data for analysis. This is both a strength and weakness, as we discuss in the next section.

4.5.3   *Analysis*

A first point relating to the analysis stage of a study involving eye tracking is the consideration of what to do with poor data quality. As eye trackers are not consistently 100% accurate in the capture of gaze data, especially the desktop monitors where there is more freedom of head movement, there will inevitably be parts of a recording for some participants that are of lower accuracy than other parts. Eye-tracking programs have indicators for signalling data quality. For example, Tobii Studio gives a % quality rating for recordings where 100% means that both eyes were found consistently throughout the recording and 50% means that either one eye was found for the full recording or both eyes during half the time. In addition, the raw data file can be consulted; this contains validity codes for the tracking of right and left eyes on a millisecond basis. Both of these mechanisms allow the researcher to establish the quality of the recording at particular points in time for each participant. This information should be used to exclude either entire recordings (if absolutely necessary), or parts of recordings. Again, there are no standards in place, and researchers therefore have to use their own judgements and should take care to report the thresholds used to filter out low quality data. Moreoever, some researchers and eye-tracking manufacturers use different terminology for the same measures. It is therefore important that the specific meaning of each measurement is spelled out in a transparent way when reporting results.

4.5.3.1 ANALYSIS OF TEMPORAL DATA

Temporal data captured via an eye tracker can be analyzed on the macro and micro levels. A macro-level analysis is straightforward: The eye tracker automatically captures the total task time per participant, which is then easily compared. Micro-level analysis of temporal data is also possible by segmenting the task into researcher-defined segments. For example, we might want to know how much time in total was spent translating and revising a particular segment. To do this, we would have to isolate the time slots during which the translator was 'paying attention to' this segment (attention would be determined by specific operationalization definitions such as fixations occurring on the segment), merge all time slots together and calculate measures such as total fixation duration and total fixation count for that segment. This type of analysis requires manual segmentation of the eye-tracking recording. Some eye-tracking programs enable automatic segmentation into time slots, but to avail of this, unique 'actions' within the task must be defined. As an example, if a unique keyboard shortcut (e.g. Ctrl+Shft+↑) is used to open or close a segment in a Translation Memory tool, that could be used as the automatic segmentation key by the eye-tracking software. If consistent unique actions are not identifiable, manual segmentation is required. Once the time slots have been identified, the software usually permits automatic analysis of the relevant indicators.

4.5.3.2 ANALYSIS OF ATTENTIONAL DATA

Attentional data, the focus points for participants' eyes, are obviously indicated through fixation counts. Additionally, the gaze replay function allows for an analysis of the flow of attention. By replaying the eye movements overlayed on the screen and the task, we see what the translator focused on at any particular point in time and also the transitions, how often they move between source and target text, translation window and information searches and so on. With this replay, we can also measure the number of backward saccades, i.e. the number of times the eyes re-read a portion of text. However, not all eye trackers allow the researcher to measure the number of saccades automatically, so this measurement may have to be done manually. Another layer of information can supplement the analysis of attentional data if the participant records a retrospective report while watching the gaze replay. Finally, as mentioned above, the hotspot images produced automatically by some eye trackers also provide a visual representation of the areas that received most attention during a task.

4.5.3.3 ANALYSIS OF DATA PERTAINING TO COGNITIVE EFFORT

By defining AOIs, eye-tracking software enables automatic macro-level calculations of data such as fixation duration, fixation count, visit duration and so on for
the source text, target text and glossary window. While some of the measures
mentioned above are effectively temporal measures, they are seen as being indicative of cognitive effort: the more fixations you have, the longer the fixation
time, the more visits to an AOI, the greater the cognitive effort. As mentioned
above, typical measures in translation process research include fixation count,
fixation duration, observation length. The pupil diameter measurement is
sometimes reported as an average pupil dilation per task/participant, but what
is perhaps more accurate is to record the average pupil dilation for a relevant
baseline task and to compare that with the change in average pupil dilation for
a comparative task. As mentioned earlier, a delay in changes to pupil size of
between 100-200 milliseconds (known as 'latency') has been noted by researchers and ought to be factored into the analysis of pupil data (see Jensen 2011b
for an example of how this is applied). However, it is possible that the lack of
control, in the form of sound proofing, controlled lighting, or chin rests makes
this measurement somewhat problematic for translation-related research that
also seeks to be ecologically valid.

What translation process researchers using eye tracking are mostly interested in is differences across conditions. A simplistic example is: is Text A easier
or more difficult to translate than Text B for different populations (students vs.
professionals)? It is not sufficient to report averages in this regard, but rather
tests for statistical significance are required. The type of test to be performed
depends on the nature and quantity of the data you are working with. If your
data are normally distributed you can perform certain statistical tests. If not,
you are confined to tests for what is known as non-parametric data (such as the
Mann Whitney-U or the Wilcoxon signed rank tests). We discuss these tests in
relation to the analysis of questionnaire data in Chapter 5 (Section 5.11). Since

the discussion is relevant to eye-tracking data too, we refer the reader to that section, rather than repeat ourselves here.

We should note, however, that the tendency to use tests such as Anovas has come under criticism in translation process research as such tests assume a high degree of control over all variables. In naturalistic environments, such as those in which translation is carried out, we do not have a high level of control over variables and, consequently, the use of Anovas has been questioned (Balling 2008:176). **Linear mixed effects modelling** (or LMER), one technique within the approach generally known as **multiple regression analysis**, has been put forward as an alternative that can cope with the lack of control over variables (*ibid.*; Jensen 2011b). According to Balling (2008:177), "multiple regression techniques make it possible ... to investigate multiple correlations of both central and more control-oriented independent variables with the dependent variable at the same time". The technique allows the researcher to investigate whether differences in groups are significant over and above differences between individuals (Balling 2008:183). It is beyond our scope to delve into this in more detail here, but we recommend reading Balling (2008) and Jensen (2011b), the latter being an example of the theory put into practice for translation process research.

4.5.3.4 ANALYSIS OF LINKED DATA

By linking the many different streams of data (temporal, attentional, cognitive) produced in eye tracking we obtain a potentially very rich analysis of translation processes. Adding layers of keystroke, verbalization or product data enriches the analysis even further. Some researchers have already made attempts to combine such data streams in their analyses to produce what is termed 'user-activity data' (Carl 2010). The combination of so many data streams brings with it not only richness, but also a great deal of complexity, and the resulting analysis task should not be underestimated. As the field matures, we will hopefully see the development of better analysis tools that will help us make sense of such rich data sets.

4.6 Complementary methods

Translation process research can benefit, and has benefited, from research methods other than the mainstream ones listed above. We briefly discuss some of these methods below, as these can be seen as alternatives for, or complementary to, the methods described above or, indeed, the methods described in the other chapters in this book.

4.6.1 *Contextual inquiry*

Contextual inquiry is an ethnographic technique where researchers observe and interview participants in their natural working environment. It originated in the field of systems design (Bayer and Holzblatt 1998), but has recently been applied to translation research (Désilets *et al* 2008, 2009). The focus in translation-related research has so far been on translators' use of computer-aided translation tools and online resources, such as Wikis. Specifically, researchers who use this method are interested in understanding how resources are being used in reality, rather than in how users *think* they are using the resources (the two often diverge). The original objective was to enable the development of new or better systems in order to better serve the needs of users (in our case, translators). Computer aids are now an important component of translation processes in specific contexts, and contextual inquiry is therefore an appropriate research method for translation processes supported by computers.

The contextual inquiry method involves observation of a participant while a standard task is being performed in a naturalistic setting. The researcher can take notes and interrupt the user to ask for explanations for particular actions, and this interaction can be recorded for future analysis. The participant may be asked to think aloud while engaging with the task and their screen activity may be recorded, both of which are then available for later analysis. Désilets *et al* (2008) describe one implementation of this method where translators' verbal reports were transcribed and synchronized with screen recordings, then notes were added, and an open coding system was implemented, using a grounded **theory** approach (see Chapter 5, Section 5.9), in order to develop recurring themes. The data were then analyzed by a translation researcher and a technologist, in order to bring both perspectives to the analysis. The authors conclude that this method was "very useful for grounding Language Technology R&D in the actual needs of translators" (*ibid.*:344), and we suggest here that its use could be extended beyond the language technology domain to more general translation process research.

The contextual inquiry method could be supported by the theory of **situated, embodied cognition** (Clark 1997, 2008). Risku (2010) discusses the relevance of this theory for translation and technical communication. She describes the situated, embodied cognition approach as one that "considers human beings as partners, players, artists, architects or other creative beings who are dependent on their physical and psychological circumstances (i.e. bodies and situations)" (2010 95). With respect to cognition, she goes on to say:

> We now no longer simply ask what actually goes on in the human brain;
> we widen the scope of the question to include the whole human being
> and his/her individual history and *environment. (ibid.,* our emphasis)

The emphasis on the individual (i.e. the user in terms of contextual inquiry) and the environment would seem to make the theoretical approach of situated, embodied cognition a useful underpinning for the method of contextual inquiry.

4.6.2 *Personality profiling*

In Section 4.2, we highlighted the need for describing the profile of participants in translation process research as well as for screening of their competences.

It has been suggested that **personality profiling** could be used, not only to screen participants but also to draw inferences between personality traits and translation competence and strategies (Hubscher-Davidson 2009). In much of the translation process research published to date there are consistent observations of *individual differences* within groups. Clearly, no matter how controlled the experiment, the translator's individual personality, experience, attitude and so forth will have an impact. Personality profiling might be a useful method for exploring this in more detail.

Personality profiling is performed via **psychometric tests**, which are defined as "standardised forms of questionnaires designed to measure particular traits or personality types" (Langdridge and Hagger-Johnson 2009:108). This form of testing has had its ups and downs in history (see Matthews *et al* 2003 for a review) and while it is generally accepted that tests are reliable, they are not necessarily accepted as being valid (for a discussion of reliability vs. validity, see Chapter 2; see also Hubscher-Davidson 2009). Nonetheless, there is general agreement that five personality traits can be identified, known as the 'big five', and most tests work off more or less detailed scales that test these five traits (listed as neuroticism, extraversion, openness to experiences, agreeableness and conscientiousness by Langdridge and Hagger-Johnson 2009:109). Langdridge and Hagger-Johnson list a number of 'big five' personality inventories *(ibid.:*108), stating that the NEO-PI-R and NEO-FFI[19] are the most popular in psychological literature. Both tests are available online and free of charge at The International Personality Item Pool (IPIP) website.[20]

Hubscher-Davidson (2009) is an example of one of the very few translation researchers who have applied psychometric testing in translation process research to date. Her aim "was to gauge whether and how students' personalities affected their decision-making processes when translating texts, and whether some of their personality traits and individual differences would be perceivable in some way to their target audience" *(ibid.:*176). She used a test for measuring Jungian personality traits: the Myers-Briggs Type Indicator (MBTI). Acknowledging the weaknesses in personality testing, she argues for a mixed-methods approach and uses pre-task questionnaires, think-aloud protocols and traditional quality assessment procedures (for example, scores for stylistic features, grammar, idiomatic renderings as determined by four assessors in this case) in conjunction with the MBTI test. Her results are interesting because they suggest that personality tests can be used along with other methods such as quality assessment and think-aloud protocols to gather insights into the role of personality and translation competence. There appears to be scope for implementing this method to a greater extent in translation process research but, as Hubscher-Davidson points out, training in the administration of these tests and in the background theories is important prior to implementation. We also need to consider the impact of culture and gender in psychometric testing. Matthews *et al* (2003:52) review

---

[19] NEO – Personality Inventory – Revised & NEO – Five Factor Inventory.
[20] www.ipip.ori.org/ipip [Last accessed 5 December 2012].

some of the research on the universality or cultural-specificity of psychological traits and point out that "there are potential obstacles to establishing trait universality. Cultural specificity may be strong enough to substantially alter the relative importance of traits".

4.6.3   *Physiological measurements*

We have tried to emphasize throughout this chapter that many of the research methods used for translation process research measure the product of cognitive activity but cannot directly measure cognitive events. Techniques do exist, however, to record brain activity and to investigate correlations between such activity and external physical events (such as word or image processing). Examples of these techniques include **electroencephalography** (usually abbreviated to EEG), **functional magnetic resonance imaging** (fMRI), and the **galvanic skin test**, to name but a few. EEG measures electric variations generated by the activity of neuron assemblies via pads fixed to the scalp (Lachaud 2011). fMRI measures blood flow and oxygenation in the brain, while the galvanic skin test measures the flow of electricity through the skin, which increases when perspiration increases as a response to specific emotions or mounting cognitive effort. All three tests are used in the measurement of brain activity and, of interest to translation process researchers, in the measurement of cognitive effort (see, for example, Chang 2009).

Although the interest in these neurological measurements in translation studies dates back to the 1980s (Göpferich 2008), the EU-funded Eye-to-IT project was the first to combine the techniques of keystroke logging, eye tracking and EEG. The simultaneous use of all three (or even of two) of these techniques is not a trivial matter. Lachaud (2011:136) describes the difficulty well:

> EEG requires situations which do not promote eye movements, blinks, motor activity, and any cerebral activity other than the one being studied. Therefore, reading and typing while translating represent sources of artefacts that one would like to avoid, making it meaningless not only to use EYE and KEY together with EEG, but to use EEG for studying translation.

He goes on to say: "[h]owever, the improvement of mathematical algorithms allows extracting useful information from EEG with artefacts, opening its application to new research areas" (*ibid.*), and he successfully combines EEG and eye tracking in his study, albeit at the level of the word. There are clearly significant hurdles in using methods for capturing brain activity in translation research. Nonetheless, we expect that we will see more of this type of trans-disciplinary research in the future.

4.7   Summary

Although translation process research commenced in the 1980s, it is still in its infancy in terms of methodology and there is a great need now for increased standardization, collaboration, rigour and transparency. Having said that, great strides have been made in the last thirty years, helped especially by the creation and implementation of new technologies such as screen recording, keystroke logging and eye tracking. New methodological avenues remain to be exploited, with triangulation being a primary concern. The combination of process and product research will most likely lead to a greater understanding of the cognitive aspect of translation. The addition of other dimensions, such as personality profiling and ethnographic studies, could lead to an even richer understanding of the factors that influence the translation process and the impact those factors have on the process and product.

Chapter 5. Participant-oriented research

5.1 Introduction

Ever since the publication of Douglas Robinson's *The Translator's Turn* (1991) there have been calls for more attention to be paid to the human agents in the translation process, in particular, to translators and interpreters. In 2009, Chesterman suggested adding a branch called 'Translator Studies' to Holmes' famous map of the discipline. In the last decade or so, this trend can be linked to the development of a new sociological approach to the study of translation, with several publications proposing new theoretical frameworks in order to explain the interaction between human agents, translated texts and their context of production and reception from a sociological perspective (Inghilleri 2005a; Chesterman 2006; Wolf and Fukari 2007; Wolf 2011). Much of this research is conceptual, discussing how concepts and theories from sociology and neighbouring disciplines can offer new and productive ways of understanding translation. However, some of it is also empirical, as attested by many of the studies used in this chapter to illustrate participant-oriented research.

The methods described in this chapter (questionnaire surveys, interviews and focus groups) are staples of sociological research and therefore, we argue, are crucial for the development of a truly encompassing sociology of translation. However, these methods are also not restricted to sociology and, in translation studies, they have also been extensively used in applied research without resorting to social theories in order to explain the results.

The methods described here are oriented towards participants in two different but complementary senses. First, they can be used to study the participants (more commonly called 'agents') involved in the process of translation: translators, trainers, students, commissioners and so on. Second, the research requires the participation of human beings in the research process. A note on terminology is called for here. Our use of the term 'participant' is in line with new developments in research involving human beings which attempt to recontextualize the research by presenting it as a collaborative process between the researcher and the people who are invited to participate in it. The aim is to recognize the contribution made by those whose views we request and to highlight the fact that, for the research to be valid, they need to be fully informed stakeholders whose consent is free and revocable. This view is better suited to a social constructivist epistemology whereby knowledge is seen as constructed among the research participants rather pres-existing in the mind of 'subjects', from where researchers need to extract it using scientific methods (see Chapter 2, Section 2.2).

Other terms occasionally used in this chapter to refer to participants are 'respondent' and 'informant'. A respondent is any person who responds to a questionnaire or to questions presented by an investigator. An informant is seen as a partner in the research and has a more active involvement in constructing the knowledge that is to be the outcome of the research process. When referring to examples from the literature, our policy is to retain the term used by the authors of the research report.

This chapter is divided into two main parts, one discussing questionnaires (Sections 5.2 to 5.4) and another discussing interviews and focus groups (Sections 5.5 to 5.7). These two parts follow a more or less parallel structure, starting with strengths and weaknesses of each method, followed by issues of design and data collection/elicitation. At the analysis stage, the key factor is not so much whether the data have been elicited from interviews, questionnaires or focus groups but whether the aim is to derive quantitative or qualitative results. Accordingly, we have two sections focusing on analysis: Section 5.8 on qualitative data and Section 5.9 on quantitative data. Section 5.10 then offers a discussion of mixed methods approaches, which suggests ways in which data from the three methods discussed can be integrated into one research project.

5.2 Questionnaires

5.2.1 Overview

This section discusses questionnaires as research instruments. A questionnaire is defined by Matthews and Ross (2010:201) as "(1) a list of questions each with a range of answers; (2) a format that enables standardized, relatively structured, data to be gathered about each of a (usually) large number of cases". The term 'survey' is often used as a synonym for 'questionnaire'. However, here we agree with the differentiation proposed by Langdridge and Hagger-Johnson (2009:88): "[t]he term 'survey' is used to describe a study design where the questionnaire is the primary focus". Throughout this section, therefore, 'survey' will refer to the study design and 'questionnaire' to the instrument used in such a study.

Questionnaires have been used to some extent in research on translation, most notably to research topics on the translation profession, technologies or to survey translation student opinions about teaching and learning (see, for example, Chan 2010; van Dam and Zethsen 2008, 2010; Bernardini and Castagnoli 2008; Lagoudaki 2008; Sela-Sheffy 2005; Fulford and Granell Zafra 2004). We will draw on some of these examples throughout this section to illustrate issues and solutions. Unfortunately, there is only limited evidence of good questionnaire design and of serious consideration of the questionnaire as a research instrument in the translation-related research published to date. There has been little discussion of how questions address construct validity (see Chapter 2, Sections 2.9 and 2.10.1, and Sections 5.3.1 and 5.3.6), how questionnaires have been tested for reliability (see Chapter 2, Section 2.10.2, and Section 5.3.6 below), how sampling methods are chosen and sampling errors calculated (see Chapter 2, Section 2.10.1, and Section 5.4.2 below), on the effect that low response rates have on the conclusions (see Section 5.4.3), or on ethical considerations (See Chapter 2, Section 2.11, and Section 5.3.7 below), to mention just a few issues. However, for valid and reliable research results as well as ethically-sound research conduct, significant consideration ought to be given to the design and administration of a questionnaire.

Before proceeding, we should note a distinction between the use of question-naires to do research on translation and interpreting and the discussion about the validity and reliability of *translated* questionnaires. There is a significant body of research, notably in the domains of medicine and psychology, which addresses the question of the validity and reliability of standardized questionnaires that have been translated from one language into another (see, for example, Sperber 2004 or Hanson *et al* 2000). Although this is an interesting question in and of itself for scholars in translation studies, and although translation scholars might themselves make use of translated questionnaires for their own research and therefore be confronted with questions of validity, we will not focus on this is-sue here but concentrate on the use of questionnaires for translation studies research.

5.2.2   *Strengths and weaknesses*

A questionnaire may be used to collect background information on research participants; to collect data on facts, opinions, attitudes, behaviour, etc. or to combine the collection of both. Questionnaires are popular research instruments, since they appear to offer a means of collecting structured data on a large scale and, in theory, they consume less time than individual interviews. The structured nature of the data makes analysis somewhat easier, when compared with un-structured interview data, for example (see Chapter 2, Section 2.7, and Section 5.6.1 below). Moreover, because of the possibility of acquiring large amounts of quantitative data, and assuming the population sampled is appropriate (see Sec-tion 5.4.2), generalizations can be made about the larger population (see Chapter 2, Section 2.10.3). There are, however, some drawbacks to questionnaires: it is quite easy to get the design and administration of a questionnaire wrong (see Sections 5.3 and 5.4 below) and although questionnaires are good for collecting exploratory data they are not the best instruments for collecting explanatory data (for example, about emotions, opinions and personal experiences) unless they are followed up by more in-depth interviews. To illustrate, Pavlovič (2007) was interested in researching Croatian translators' and interpreters' attitudes towards directionality in translation (translating into one's first or second lan-guage). 73% of Pavlovič's respondents stated that more than 50% of their work was into the second language (L2). However, when asked whether they agreed with Newmark's statement (1988:3) that translation into L1 was "the only way you can translate naturally, accurately and with maximum effectiveness", as many as 42% of the respondents agreed or strongly agreed with the statement that is in such sharp contrast to their everyday practice (Pavlovič 2007:89). As Pavlovič mentions, it would be necessary to follow this questionnaire-based study with an explanatory study which sought to explain this contrast between attitude and praxis. For an example of a research design in translation studies where a questionnaire is used for collecting quantitative and qualitative data, followed by an explanatory phase based on interviews, see van Dam and Zethsen (2008, 2010).

In Chapter 2, Section 2.10.1, we discuss validity threats posed by research participants, including the Hawthorne effect, which occurs when people alter (usually improve) their normal behaviour because they are aware that they are being studied. Participants will often respond according to how they think the researcher would like them to respond (perhaps this explains Pavlovič's dilemma above?) or they might select what they think is the 'nicest' answer because it will reflect well on them. These issues are termed 'social desirability' and 'impression management' respectively (Langdridge and Hagger-Johnson 2009:96). The tendency towards socially desirable answers is also culture-dependent: Rasinger (2008:63) notes findings from Johnson *et al* (2005) who conclude that general cultural behavioural patterns can be seen in response styles. Johnson *et al* (*ibid.*) noted that respondents in individualistic and high power-distance cultures are more likely to give extreme responses while respondents from cultures that value conformity are more likely to give acquiescent responses.

Additional drawbacks include that participants are somewhat constrained in their responses, the risk of low response rates and – what is perhaps the most important challenge – how difficult it is to secure an appropriate sample of participants to enable researchers to draw conclusions on their research questions (see Section 5.4 on data collection below for a more detailed discussion). Four types of error can be associated with the survey research method. The first is a coverage error; this refers to when some part of the population is not included in the study. The second is a sampling error: when some parts of the population have a higher probability of being included in a survey than other parts of the population. The third error type is known as a nonresponse error, which arises when members of the sample do not answer the questionnaire at all or answer only some questions. The fourth error type is a measurement error, which occurs when the actual response (i.e. the answers given) differs from the 'true' response (i.e. the facts or beliefs of the participants). This can arise if the participants give answers not in-keeping with their true feelings because of the sensitivity or ambiguity of the question or because of researcher bias effects (see Chapter 2, Section 2.10.1).

5.3 Designing questionnaire surveys

5.3.1 *Operationalization*

The design stage for a questionnaire is arguably the most important stage since, if we get the design wrong, we may jeopardize our entire research project. The most important question we can ask ourselves when considering which questions should be included in our questionnaire is: how will this question help answer my research question?

Having clarity on the construct we wish to investigate is of the utmost importance. In Chapter 2, Section 2.9 we referred to operationalizing our research question(s). When designing a questionnaire, we need to refer back to our operational definitions to ensure that the questionnaire is really addressing the research question(s). If, for example, we want to investigate the perceived status of translators in the workplace in a particular country, we will have to operationalize 'status' first and then construct questions that directly link to that operationalization. A good example of this in translation studies is the research carried out by van Dam and Zethsen (2008, 2010), mentioned above, which had the objective of studying the status of different groups of translators in Denmark. Van Dam and Zethsen first discuss how the construct 'status' is not easily definable – "status cannot be viewed as an absolute notion but is a complex, subjective and context-dependent construct" (2008:74) – and then describe how they operationalized this difficult construct by drawing on Danish studies of occupational status in which status was broken into four main parameters (a high salary, a high level of education/expertise, visibility/fame and power/influence). The researchers then devised questions which addressed each of these parameters, allowing them to comment generally on the perceived status of the sample population. This is a good example of how an abstract construct can be operationalized and how a questionnaire can then be designed to focus specifically on that construct.

5.3.2   *Number and phrasing of questions*

Some general, but important, principles of questionnaire design, notably the length and the language used, should be discussed before going into the more technical details. Questionnaires should be as short as possible so as to avoid non-completion. There is no ideal number of questions for a questionnaire. Besides, different types of question will take different amounts of time to answer. The questions a researcher should ask regarding the number of questions is: (1) Am I asking the right questions and no more and no less than I need to get data on my research question, and (2) How much time will it take to answer the questionnaire and is this a reasonable demand of my target population's time? A progress indicator can be included (even in paper-based questionnaires) so the participants can see how much more time they might need to dedicate to the questionnaire. Filter questions, designed to allow participants to skip questions that are not applicable to them, can also be included, rather than making participants read questions that are not applicable to their specific cases.

It is not uncommon to commence a questionnaire with the fact-finding, background questions which elicit personal data. However, the inclusion of such questions within one questionnaire raises ethical questions (see Section 5.3.7 and Chapter 2, Section 2.11), and it is recommended that questions eliciting personal data should be separate from the other questions. Interestingly, research on self-stereotyping has shown that self-evaluation becomes more stereotype-consistent when a person's in-group versus individual identity is made salient (Sinclair *et al* 2006), and so asking participants to classify themselves according to pre-defined categories might influence their subsequent responses to questions.

If sensitive questions are to be asked, the participant should be alerted to this in advance (see 5.3.7 below for more discussion). Including sensitive questions may cause consternation among participants, causing them to opt out, answer untruthfully, or even to lodge a complaint. Chan's (2010) questionnaire included seemingly innocent questions that, on further analysis, may have led to unreliable responses. For example, question number four was "In which country does your company mainly operate?". Notwithstanding the fact that for multi-national companies this is a difficult question to answer, it also raises questions about whether companies will want to state the truth of the matter. Some may have a large number of employees in one country but be officially registered in another for tax purposes. Questions five to eight asked about how many freelance and in-house translators each respondent's company had. This information would be considered highly sensitive and competitive by many, and Chan himself comments on how some responses to these questions appeared to be unreliable. By piloting a questionnaire in advance with appropriate respondents, issues such as these can be highlighted and dealt with.

Concerning the language used in formulating questions, the main principles to bear in mind are clarity and sensitivity towards the participants. Importantly, questions often seem unambiguous to the questionnaire designer but turn out to be ambiguous to respondents. Ambiguity can be especially problematic if non-native speakers of the questionnaire language are included in the sample, though the problem is not limited to non-native speakers. Double negatives should be avoided because they tend to be ambiguous. For example, if a participant answers 'no' to a question such as 'Do you think that not many publishers would be unwilling to commission translations?', the researcher cannot be sure whether the participant did not actually mean 'yes'. Jargon should also be avoided, even in cases where the researcher expects that the participants would be familiar with, or even users of such jargon. For example, in Chan's questionnaire (2010) relating to the perceived benefits of translator certification for the translation profession, country-specific certification programmes such as 'MCIL', 'NAATI' and 'CATTI' were offered as examples of certification programmes without further description of what each one stood for. It is doubtful that all respondents (including company CEOs and Operations Directors from several different countries) would have come across these abbreviations prior to answering the questionnaire.

To make sure the answers truly reflect the participants' views, they should not make implicit assumptions. For example, if the question is 'what aspects of the programme do you think need improving to better prepare students for working as professional translators?', then there is an implicit assumption that the programme needs improving, while it may be the case that the participants think the programme is fine as it is. The wording should also be neutral, rather than leading. A leading question is one that suggests the answer the researcher is looking for. In van Dam and Zethsen's research (2008), where Likert scales (see below for more details) were used, they deliberately chose to facilitate 'high-status' rather than 'low-status' answers by ordering multiple-choice answers in descending degrees, with the highest degree placed at the top. Their motivation for this was that the assumed general position of translators was one of 'low status' and they "wanted to ensure that if this were confirmed ... it would not be a consequence of the way we represented the choice of responses" (2008:78). While this decision seems very well motivated, it also raises the issue of whether responses were biased the other way by presenting high-status answers first. A potential solution to this problem is to change the sequence of responses question by question and to alter the phrasing (negative followed by positive, for example, or high-status responses first followed by low-status responses in the next question) in order to reduce any potential bias introduced by the wording of questions or the sequence of multiple-choice answers. The obvious drawback is, of course, that the participant expects a pattern and often answers as if there is one, even if the pattern has been deliberately reversed. For Likert scales (see Section 5.3.4 below), questions can be phrased in opposite ways (positive followed by negative), but we should keep in mind that the scale itself might also need to be reversed (see Rasinger 2008:75 for a discussion and example).

Only one question should be asked at a time. If participants have two different responses to each sub-question they have no way of recording the relevant differences when two questions are rolled into one. For example, a participant might have two different answers to the following double-barrelled question: 'Should translator certification be required by law in all countries and would this, in your opinion, contribute positively to the status of translators: Yes/No'? A participant might very well answer *no* to the first part and *yes* to the second part, or vice versa, but may not have the opportunity to signal these opposite answers when two questions are rolled into one. Moreover, the first question is problematic because the participant's answer might be along the lines of 'not in all countries but in specific ones such as...', but they have no way of indicating this response if given only the option 'Yes/No'. Multiple choice questions, where only one answer is allowed, should be written carefully to ensure participants find only one answer applicable. Catchalls are another type of question that attempt to capture too much information in one go and can end up not providing any useful information at all. Questions such as 'what is your greatest problem as a literary translator? or 'what do you think is absolutely essential for a literary translator?' may be interpreted very differently by each participant, and the result is little comparability across participants. Such questions may first appear attractive to the researcher because they seem to empower the participant to a significant degree, but they pose analytical difficulties – which means they are not actually useful.

Answers to questions that require comments on hypothetical situations (for example: 'how would you feel if an author criticized your translation?') are not reliable, because they tend to elicit idealized or socially-desirable responses. Likewise, questions that could be interpreted as face-threatening or where a particular answer may reflect negatively on the participant may also lead to unreliable answers. For example, a question such as 'do you approve of manipulating a text in translation for an ideological goal?' is likely to be answered negatively, because the word 'manipulating' in common parlance has negative connotations.

5.3.3 Open and closed questions

A questionnaire typically includes both closed (or 'structured') and open questions. Closed questions restrict the possible responses from participants to answers like Yes/No/Not Applicable (used to categorize participants) or to Strongly Agree/Agree/Neither Agree nor Disagree/Disagree/Strongly Disagree (used to measure opinion), for example. Other types of closed questions include fact-finding questions about gender, age category, nationality, length of employment, etc. (used for quantification). A closed question might ask the respondent to select one item from a list or all that apply, or may even ask them to rank an item in a particular order. Open questions, on the other hand, allow participants to write their responses to a question in a text box (which is often restricted in size, thereby restricting the length of the response). An example of a free-form question might be: 'What, in your opinion, are the causes of the perceived low status of translators?'. An open question will allow participants to explain their choices for the closed questions, to add further opinions, or to highlight an opinion they hold and which is not addressed in the questionnaire. It is considered to be good practice to include an 'anything else you wish to add' box at the end of a questionnaire. Although responses to this item might not contribute to answering the research question, it gives participants a level of satisfaction to communicate thoughts to the researcher and can diffuse frustration over questions that do not have the right focus, according to the participant's opinion.

Both question types have advantages and disadvantages. Closed questions lead to structured data that can be analyzed quantitatively but they curtail the responses participants can give and do not allow for nuanced thoughts to be expressed. By offering pre-defined categories from which to select, there is a risk that none of the categories are the appropriate response for a participant, yet there is nothing the participant can do but select an inaccurate response or skip the question, unless you provide the option of 'other' with a free text box in which the participant can elaborate. Open questions allow the researcher to collect qualitative data and to compensate, to a small extent, for the restricted nature of the questionnaire. On the other hand, the inclusion of open questions will increase the time required for completing the questionnaire and participants often skip them (due to a lack of time or because they do not have a well-formed response). Responses to open questions can also be difficult to interpret (see 5.8 below).

5.3.4 Likert scales

A very common device in questionnaires is the 'Likert scale', which was developed by the American psychologist Rensis Likert. A Likert scale commonly offers a series of five, seven or nine responses along a continuum of 'strongly agree to strongly disagree'. Some researchers favour an even-numbered scale which, they believe, prevents respondents from conveniently selecting the mid-point on the scale (usually 'neither agree nor disagree' or 'not sure'). The tendency for respondents to select this mid-point is quite problematic for researchers because it limits answers to the research question. If the majority of respondents are 'unsure', then we cannot say very much about their opinions towards the research construct, except that they are unsure!

Chan (2010) uses a Likert scale to investigate the perceived benefits of translator certification to stakeholders in the translation profession. Of the 34 statements offered in his questionnaire (some of which are on translator certification, some of which are fact-finding), many of the responses are spread evenly across the five-point Likert scale of agreement leading to a mean around '3' for most statements. For example, on the statement 'A person with translator certification receives higher pay', the mean response is 3.08, reflecting a range of responses from strongly disagree to strongly agree of 16.67%, 13.64%, 27.27%, 30.30% and 12.12% (*ibid.*:106). Although not all responses are so spread across the scale, many are. Chan concludes that "[t]ranslation companies generally welcome a system of translator certification, as it provides a relatively reliable signal of applicants' linguistic ability, and this has made the recruitment process easier and more time-efficient" (*ibid.*:110). However, if the responses are generally spread across the range of strongly disagree to strongly agree, one might rather be tempted to conclude that the sample population are, at best, ambivalent about the benefits of translator certification in the translation profession.

5.3.5   *Pilot testing*

Questions regarding the appropriateness and comprehensibility of the wording, the best scale to use, the appropriate responses to offer, etc. should be considered in detail in advance of distribution of a questionnaire. An important step in the design phase is the piloting of the questionnaire, meaning the testing of it with an appropriate sample (by which we mean respondents who are part of your sample population and not family, friends, or colleagues who may not meet the criteria for inclusion in the sample). Piloting should assess numerous aspects such as the time required to fill out the questionnaire, its usability, clarity and so on. As researchers, we should endeavour to elicit rich feedback on pilot questionnaires by discussing the questionnaire experience with the pilot participants in detail. This offers an opportunity to remove or rephrase ambiguous questions and to refine questions (for an example of piloting a questionnaire in translation studies research see, for example, Lagoudaki 2008).

One question we can ask of our pilot respondents has to do with the appropriateness of the order of questions. The order of questions should be logical and the link between questions should be obvious to the participants. Rasinger (2008:70-71) suggests that simple questions should be placed first, followed by the more complex ones, and that a questionnaire could be considered somewhat like a story, with a beginning, middle and end.

5.3.6   *Reliability and validity*

One of the main concerns in the design stage, as we have mentioned, is whether the questionnaire is both reliable and valid as an instrument for measuring the research construct. We discussed these two concepts in general in Chapter 2 and will revisit them here in the context of questionnaire design. We have already touched on reliability and measurement validity to some extent above when discussing the composition of questions that allow the researcher to address the research question and the piloting of a draft questionnaire. There are other, more quantitatively formal methods for testing questionnaire reliability, including the split-half, test-retest, and parallel forms methods, which we will discuss here in some detail (Rasinger 2008).

Questionnaires are designed in such a way that they record multiple responses to the research construct. An assumption is made that by answering multiple questions on the construct participants provide data from which conclusions can be drawn about their responses regarding the construct. **Correlation tests** exist which allow the researcher to test the internal consistency (and, therefore, reliability) of questionnaires that measure a single construct. One such test is the **split-half method**, which involves dividing the questionnaire into two equal halves, giving a group of respondents the first set of questions and then giving the same group of respondents the second half of the set of questions. Responses can be recorded as numeric scores (using Likert scales, for example) and the correlation between these scores calculated. A typical correlation measurement is known as the Cronbach alpha measure; this is based on the split-half method only it is repeated for every random pair of question splits. In other words, the split-half reliability is calculated, as described above, then the questionnaire items are randomly divided into two alternative halves and the test is reapplied. This makes the Cronbach alpha measure a more robust measure of reliability when compared with the split-half test. The scale goes from negative infinity up to 1 (highest possible correlation).

If we revert to the example of Chan's questionnaire on translator certification, with 39 statements, we can imagine that this questionnaire could be divided into two parts, one with 20 and the other with 19 statements. Let us imagine that we perform a Chronbach alpha test on the responses to these two halves and the result is 0.70. This number typically indicates that there is a high level of correlation between the two halves on the questionnaire (Langdridge and Hagger Johnson 2009:101). If the result of the test were 0.35, on the other hand, there is a low level of correlation and we have a problem with internal consistency in our questionnaire.

The test-retest method, which measures a type of reliability also known as 'temporal stability', involves giving the entire questionnaire to a set of respondents and then giving the same set of respondents the same questionnaire after a period of time has elapsed. The researcher then calculates a Pearson's correlation coefficient between the two sets of results. **Pearson's product moment correlation** (also known as Pearson's r) is a test used for parametric data (where the measurement scale is interval or ratio and the data are normally distributed – see also 5.11) and can have a value of between -1 and 1: 1 indicates a perfect positive correlation and -1 indicates a perfect negative correlation. A value of +0.7 would suggest a 'strong' positive correlation, whereas a value of -0.4, for example, would suggest a weak negative correlation. For non-parametric data (where the measurement scale is nominal or ordinal and/or data are not normally distributed), the **Spearman's rho** correlation test is used instead. If the questionnaire is reliable, we should see a high positive correlation (a value of at least 0.70 to 1). However, this test is clearly problematic when working with humans since humans learn from their experiences and change over time. Having completed a test or questionnaire once, respondents might remember the answers they gave and simply give the same answers again. At least three months' time difference is required between test and retest, but it is suggested that the longer the time lapse the better since respondents are less likely to remember their previous responses when a greater amount of time has passed since the first application (Langdridge and Hagger-Johnson 2009:102). On the other hand, we should also bear in mind that opinions can actually change over such timeframes.

Another option for testing questionnaire reliability is the **parallel forms test** which involves creating two questionnaires that test the same construct, through different wording. Pairs of equivalent items are created during questionnaire design and one set makes up one version of the questionnaire, while the other set contributes to the second one. The two versions are given to the same set of respondents on two separate occasions and, if the correlation of scores is high, the questionnaire can be seen as reliable. This technique may also overcome the problem of memory effects that applies in the test-retest scenario. Given the history and importance of the concept of 'equivalence' in translation studies, we are aware of the problem in assuming that one can create items that are 'equivalent' in a questionnaire. We cannot delve into a discussion of this here but it is worth highlighting the importance of considering whether or not the rephrasing of a question actually addresses an equivalent construct. For example, the concept of 'readability' is sometimes used in translation studies to indicate that a translation is good or of high quality. If we ask respondents to rate the quality of a translated text on a scale of 1 to 5, where 5 means 'excellent' and 1 means 'very poor', and then retest this with a question asking them to rate the readability of a text, where 5 means 'very high readability' and 1 means 'very low readability', the obvious question that emerges is whether or not the two actually measure the same construct, i.e. is 'quality' the same as 'readability'?

It is worth considering for a moment the interaction between reliability and validity (see also Chapter 2). As Langdridge and Hagger-Johnson put it (*ibid.*:104):

> a scale can be reliable but not valid. However, a scale cannot be valid if it is unreliable! Reliability is the bread, and validity the butter, of scale development. You can eat bread on its own, but not butter. A good test is comprised of good items, reliable and well validated.

They also warn that it takes a lot longer to demonstrate the validity of a questionnaire than it does to demonstrate reliability.

In Chapter 2, we mentioned a number of different types of validity and their appropriateness for quantitative or qualitative research. Arguably the most important type of validity for questionnaire design is **construct validity**, which is the extent to which the questionnaire measures what it purports to measure, but Langdridge and Hagger-Johnson warn that "[n]o single research study can provide all of the necessary evidence that a scale has reached the 'gold standard' of construct validity" (*ibid.*).

A second type of validity is known as **concurrent validity** and is achieved if our results confirm the findings of other studies that investigate the same question. Replication of research in translation studies is still in its infancy (at best), and a consideration of this type of validity is therefore rare, but that is not to say that it is not desirable. For example, Alves *et al* (2011) make a step in this direction when they seek to replicate a study regarding reading modalities in translation conducted by Jakobsen and Jensen (2008), but generate different findings which they then seek to explain by referring to differences in participant profiles and methodological procedures, such as differences in the filters and eye tracking software used in the two studies. By asking questions that seem 'sensible' to the respondent, we are addressing a third type of validity known as **face validity**. A lack thereof might cause respondents to skip questions or even drop out of answering the questionnaire. **Convergent validity** is a fourth type; it seeks to establish the validity of responses by asking the same question in different ways and comparing responses (e.g. What age are you?, In what year were you born?). This is a simplistic example, and one that has the potential to irritate respondents, but we can aim for convergent validity by wording several questions which effectively address the same concept, in different ways. This recalls our discussion above of the parallel forms test, which measures reliability (the 'bread') while convergent validity addresses the 'butter', to re-use the metaphor above.

5.3.7   *Ethical considerations*

Earlier we mentioned the problem of including questions about personal data and how this might cause participants to be reticent in filling out the questionnaire because they see clearly that their personal data is linked with their other responses. This problem touches on the wider question of ethics in questionnaire design and administration. We discussed the basic tenets of confidentiality, anonymity and informed consent in Chapter 2, Section 2.11, and they also apply to questionnaire design. It is difficult for a researcher to guarantee anonymity if identifying details are embedded in a questionnaire. In particular, when a sample size is very small (see Section 5.4 below), and especially if the questionnaire is given to a community with limited and known members (e.g. in a translator training environment with limited numbers of students), there is a risk that inferences can be made about the identity of the participants, based on their responses. Care should be taken then that, where possible, there is an adequate number of people in the sample size so that individuals cannot be identified.

Another recommendation for overcoming the problem of identification is to collect the background, factual, biographical information in a shorter, separate questionnaire. This is perhaps a little more complicated for the researcher, who has to be able to link the two sets of data without risk of error, but it will reassure participants that their personal data cannot be linked by anyone else to their responses and should, therefore, contribute to the reliability of their answers. An alternative approach is to collect all data in one questionnaire and to assure participants that the information will be separated out before data analysis, but this is perhaps less reassuring to participants who might be sensitive to this issue. As with other research instruments, the researcher ought to apply a unique identifier to each participant in order to identify them, but the connection between that identifier and the participant's real name should be available only to the researcher and ideally should be password protected (if in electronic format) or stored very securely (if not in electronic format). Participants can feel reassured if procedures for protecting their identities are outlined prior to answering the questionnaire.

Informed consent should be sought from all participants. We have discussed this in detail in Chapter 2, Section 2.11.3, so suffice to say here that even if participants have agreed in principle to answer a questionnaire, informed consent in the form of a signed sheet is still to be recommended and should be provided with the questionnaire. It is good practice to reiterate the goals of the research either at the beginning of the questionnaire (but briefly) or in the informed consent form and to thank participants for taking the time to fill it out. The informed consent form can be used to remind participants that they are making an important contribution to a researcher's project and it offers a researcher the opportunity to indicate that some of the questions may be sensitive in nature. Such advance warnings have the benefit of not taking participants by surprise and risking an abandonment of the exercise or possibly causing offence. The form can also be used to offer participants the possibility of talking over any sensitive questions in advance with the researcher.

When considering the sample population, we should keep in mind that questionnaires can be exclusive. For example, those who cannot read or write, or those who do not speak the language of the questionnaire, are automatically excluded from answering it, and those without technological skills or access to computers or the Internet are excluded from answering online questionnaires. Where researchers are administering questions in a face-to-face situation, we need to be aware of the power relationships at play and how they can affect participants' answers (see Chapter 2, Section 2.11.5, for further discussion).

Whereas in the past questionnaires might have been posted out to a sample population or administered in a face-to-face situation, electronic administration is now very popular. There is ongoing debate as to whether a new set of guidelines is specifically required for such online research or whether the ethical guidelines for traditional research settings can be applied to online research. Eynon *et al* comment that "confidentiality, anonymity, disclosure, and informed consent, concepts at the core of ethical governance in the social sciences, are cast into uncertainty when it comes to research online" (2008:27). They argue that Internet research ethics need to be tailored to different contexts. Vehovar and Manfreda (2009:187) add that new ethical issues arise for Internet-based surveys: "The most prominent among them include the problem of unsolicited e-mail invitations, privacy and security threats, obtaining of informed consent online, combining data from different sources, and surveying children and minorities, among others". Codes and standards for Internet-based surveys exist (see, for example, ESOMAR (online) and CASRO (online)) and as researchers we have a duty to make ourselves aware of these standards during questionnaire design. We will discuss Internet-mediated questionnaires further in Section 5.4.4.

To close on this section about questionnaire design, we should of course mention the layout and formatting of the questionnaire. We have covertly dealt with many of the issues, such as the inclusion of informed consent and brief research objective information at the start, the separation of personal from other data, the order and phrasing of questions, and so on. In addition, the questionnaire itself ought to be laid out in a clear and non-fussy manner, using standard fonts, a limited number of font sizes, formatting and colour, for example. It should be easy to navigate (whether it is online or not). If required, instructions on how to complete and return the questionnaire should be given. We will return to the topic of layout and formatting in online questionnaires when discussing data collection below.

5.4   Data collection using questionnaires

Data can be collected in different ways using questionnaires. One of the main differentiators is whether the researcher is present or not during the completion of the questionnaire. Typical examples of where the researcher is absent is when a questionnaire is sent by post or e-mail to potential participants or is posted on a website (we will discuss specific issues relating to Internet-mediated data collection below). When the researcher is present, the participant can either answer the questions without (much) interaction with the researcher or the researcher can use the questionnaire as a tool for interviewing the participant (making it akin to a structured interview, see Section 5.6.1). Absence of the researcher means that participants might feel freer with their responses while also allowing for a far-reaching dissemination of the questionnaire. However, it is more likely to lead to abandonment of the questionnaire or the skipping of particular questions. When the researcher is present, on the other hand, power relations might influence responses, but the advantage is that contextual clues through non-verbal communication and tone are available to the researcher and clarifications can be sought for responses to open-ended questions. The researcher can collect this information in a research diary (see Chapter 6, Section 6.6.2). Which data collection method is most appropriate will have to be determined by the researcher, with reference to the research objectives.

5.4.1   Sampling

One of the key issues in collecting data via questionnaires is the sampling method. As mentioned in the introduction to this section, questionnaires are commonly used to collect relatively structured data from a large number of cases. This allows the researcher to make some statistical inferences about the research question (see Section 5.9 below). It is usually impossible to include the entire target population as participants, and the researcher thus has to locate a representative sample of the population, though this is so much easier said than done (see Chapter 2 for more detailed discussion). There is always a trade-off between the amount of data collected and the accuracy of the data. A representative sample means that we assume that the results we obtain from the sample data would be the same if we were to survey the entire population in question.

To be able to make reliable inferences from a sample, we must draw the sample in such a way that we can calculate appropriate sample statistics and their standard errors (a measure of the variability of a statistic). To do this, a probability-based sampling method (also called 'random sampling' – see Chapter 2, Section 2.10.1) can be used where the probability with which every member of the population could have been selected and included in the sample is known. Researchers ought to then report confidence intervals and confidence levels with their results. These are mechanisms by which we can indicate, respectively, the potential margin of error in our results, given that we have not surveyed the entire population, and our own level of confidence in the results (see section 5.9 for further discussion). One of the main questions asked about sampling is: how many people do I need in my sample in order to be fairly confident of my results (referred to as the 'confidence level') and fairly accurate (the 'confidence interval')? As Langdridge and Hagger-Johnson note (2009:57-58), there is usually a trade-off between size of sample and time and cost. The kind of analysis one might wish to conduct and the likely response rate need to be considered too. It should also be noted that the figure of 1,000 respondents is often used by market research polls since it is generally accepted that the level of accuracy does not increase substantially by adding respondents over and above 1,000. Some online calculators exist to help researchers calculate the number required for samples, given specific confidence intervals and levels (see, for example, Creative Research Systems [online]).[1]

Non-probability sampling (also called 'convenience sampling') was discussed in Chapter 2, Section 2.10.1. To recap, this occurs when participants are selected purely on the basis of easy accessibility to the researcher. Convenience samples have been the most common in translation studies research to date, but they generally do not allow for statistical inferences. That is not to say that such sam-

---

[1] To illustrate, the website mentioned above calculates a sample size of 1,067 when 95% confidence level and 3% confidence intervals are specified along with an unknown total population size. With a known population size of 500, a 95% confidence level and a 3% confidence interval, a sample population of 341 is calculated.

pling is always a bad idea; they can be useful for developing research hypotheses, for example. An issue arises, however, when a convenience sample is used and generalizations are made to the population at large.

A large and ambitious online survey was carried out by Lagoudaki (2008) on the topic of Translation Memories (TMs), their penetration in the translation community and patterns of use. The objectives of the survey were in fact quite broad since it sought to:

1. establish the needs of translation professionals via their practices and working habits during the translation process;
2. reveal the tasks related to TM use;
3. distinguish the profiles of different TM user groups according to criteria such as the type of tasks they perform, their professional status, their years of working experience, their computer usage competence, etc.
4. provide an insight into the work environment in which translation professionals carry out the translation activities today;
5. estimate the TM technology penetration in the translation market;
6. help understand the reasons behind low usage of TM technology and discover missed opportunities for reaching potential users;
7. uncover user satisfaction levels for existing TM systems;
8. open the way to new ideas about future systems and identify possibilities for expanding the functionality and scope of use of TM systems.

While the results of this survey provided useful information regarding potential trends in the language industry, these were not conclusive because convenience sampling was used; 28% of respondents said TMs were not suitable for their work and a further 16% had TM software but had not learned how to use it. This means that 44% of the sample were not in a position to provide data on items (2), (3), (7) and (8) above, i.e. over half of the survey objectives. It is not so uncommon to assume we have targeted the right people, but for it to transpire that they do not actually fit our pre-determined criteria. Van Dam and Zethsen (2008) discuss a rigorous process of respondent elimination based on specific criteria and communication with the Human Resources departments of 50 Danish companies, which got pared down to 13 companies in the end and, even then, they had to eliminate five respondents due to the fact that they did not meet the researchers' pre-defined criteria.

5.4.2 Response rate

Having determined the type of sampling to be used and the criteria for inclusion in the sample, the next, quite important, concern is the response rate. This is perhaps one of the most serious drawbacks of using questionnaires since response rates are notoriously low: 25% is typical for a postal questionnaire, according to Matthews and Ross (2010:215). Langdridge and Hagger-Johnson (2009:97) provide a list of ways in which to increase response rates:

- Keep your questionnaire as short as possible
- Stick to a clear, relatively conservative layout
- Include a pre-paid envelope with postal surveys
- Send a reminder after one or two weeks have passed
- Give advance warning
- Offer a small incentive if possible

Some would argue that the last point is ethically unsound, so clearance on the ethical front is essential, keeping in mind different cultural attitudes towards incentives (see Chapter 2, Section 2.11, and Section 5.3.7 above). We might add to this list that timing also needs to be considered. For example, if you target a population during their busy or vacation time, this will obviously impact on the response rate.

Face-to-face sessions are good for response rates, but clearly take time and effort in setting up and limit the researcher to participants who are geographically near. However, Fricker and Schonlau found that "face-to-face interview question-naires tend to get more socially acceptable answers than online self-completion questionnaires" (2002, cited in Matthews and Ross 2010:301). A third alternative is the use of Internet-mediated questionnaires, which are discussed in detail in the next section.

5.4.3   *Internet-mediated collection methods*

By Internet-mediated questionnaires we mean any questionnaire that is sent by e-mail, either in the body of the e-mail or as an attachment, or a question-naire that is hosted on a website. Not unlike postal questionnaires, this method increases the distance between the researcher and the participants, which has both positive and negative implications; when the researcher is physically close to the participants (possibly even in the same room) power relations may come into play which are perhaps reduced when there is greater distance; on the other hand, distance can be one reason for a lack of response. Nevertheless, there are many advantages associated with Internet-mediated questionnaires: they are good for finding 'hidden populations' (groups who are not easy to identify) by posting information about and links to questionnaires in various online forums, for example, which are then forwarded to other potentially relevant sites; it is also possible to filter questions and therefore avoid those that are irrelevant for specific participants, making the overall experience less time-consuming (for example, a questionnaire might ask if a translator has taken any continuous professional development courses in the last twelve months. If the answer is 'Yes' the next question might look for details on which courses were taken. If the answer is 'No' the participant would be redirected to the next logical ques-tion for them); the researcher can get an update on the response rate on a daily basis; there is a lower possibility of 'researcher effect' (as is also true of postal questionnaires); and self-administration via the computer also has the advantage of allowing the participant to answer when they wish, increasing their sense of privacy, again an advantage shared with postal questionnaires.

Although there are clear advantages, we should give some consideration to the challenges. Vehovar *et al* (2008:181) warn us that "unsolicited e-mail invitations and intercept surveys that interrupt users' tasks might breach professional standards". They also report on a meta-analytical study which demonstrated that "on average web surveys gain lower response rates (from 6 percent to 15 percent lower) than other survey modes when comparable implementation procedures are used" (*ibid.*:184), but this could be compensated for by the potentially larger number of respondents to an online survey. The online method can result in exclusion (only participants who have online access can respond) and poor representativeness through self-selection. Furthermore, it is difficult to ensure informed consent electronically. Perhaps more serious still is that it is more difficult to confirm the identity of people who respond and it is difficult (thought not impossible) to prevent people from responding more than once, with different identities used each time (this is referred to as 'subject fraud' in Best and Krueger 2009:221).

On the pragmatic level, Internet-mediated questionnaires delivered via e-mail introduce security threats – viruses can be transferred from the respondents' computers to the researcher's or vice versa. As people have become more aware of these threats, they may be less willing to open an e-mail attachment. We should also keep in mind that not every computer user is comfortable with opening, saving, editing and re-attaching attachments in e-mail programs. One method for overcoming this barrier is to embed the questionnaire into the body of an e-mail.

If opting for an online questionnaire, we also need to consider its formatting. Something that looks nicely formatted in one e-mail program/word processor/web browser might look untidy in alternative programs. While this might seem a trivial problem, Best and Krueger (2009:218) warn that

> [w]ithout instrument uniformity, data quality suffers. Measurement error increases as the uniformity of the instrument decreases, because the diverse presentation of the question may affect responses. Moreover, non-uniformity also may damage the generalizability of the data.

Obscure fonts should be avoided as those with older computers or program versions may not be able to display them. The Arial and Times New Roman fonts are highly backwards-compatible, and 12 point size is considered to be most readable (*ibid.*:224). Symbols should generally be avoided, with words being spelt out instead (e.g. 'euros' instead of '€'). We should test how long it takes to download the file. With low band-width Internet connectivity, large files that take a long time to download might cause participants to abandon the effort. These are some of the restrictions that should be considered before the researcher opts to carry out research using the Internet; for a more detailed discussion of the broader key issues, see Hewson *et al* (2003), and for a discussion of design issues in Interned-mediated research see Hewson and Laurent (2008) and websm.org [last accessed: 1 October 2013].

5.5   Interviews and focus groups

5.5.1   *Overview*

Edley and Litosseliti (2010:176) describe interviews as a mechanism by which one party (the interviewer) extracts vital information from another. They note that within the social and human sciences, as part of a general shift from quantitative towards qualitative methods, and in response to a growing disenchantment with positivistic and laboratory-style experiments, the use of interviews has increased significantly, to the point that it has become *the* method of choice in some quarters (*ibid.*:156). Interviews have always been important in interpreting studies research, both as a tool for eliciting data and because much of the interpreting material available for analysis is in the form of interviews, particularly in the public service domain (police departments, social welfare centres, hospitals, schools, etc.). Here we focus on the use of interviews for eliciting data about translators and interpreters, rather than on the analysis of existing, interpreter-mediated interviews.

In studies focusing on (written) translation, interviews have not been used as widely as in interpreting research. The use of interviews has been particularly common in research on community interpreting, as is evident when we look at the proceedings of the Critical Link conference series. Several examples from this area are used here (Angelelli 2007; Tipton 2010; Weber *et al* 2005). Compared to translation, which is often seen as a more isolated activity, the activity of interpreting itself has a more prominent social aspect, which might make the use of research methods borrowed from the social sciences a more obvious choice. However, interviews and focus groups are as applicable to the field of translation as they are to the field of interpreting, and they are becoming increasingly important in all domains of translation studies. This tendency is expected to continue as the discipline expands beyond the realm of linguistics, literature and cultural studies, and takes upon itself the task of integrating the sociological dimension of translation. Areas that have already been explored using interviews include feminist translation (Wolf 2005); translator style (Saldanha 2005); translator training (Mirlohi *et al* 2011); translator competence (Károly 2011), and the revision part of the translation process (Shih 2006).

Like questionnaires, interviews are often seen as straightforward research tools. Interviews are part of our daily life: we hear them on the radio, on television, and they are part of the process of applying for a job. However, as we show below, the use of interview data for research purposes presents some specific challenges which need to be thought through in designing the project. In addition, the actual interviewing process itself and the moderation of focus groups require careful preparation.

5.5.2   *Strengths and weaknesses*

Interviews and focus groups are time consuming not only for the researcher, who needs to conduct, transcribe and analyze them, but also for the participants. Recruiting relevant participants who are willing to take the time and who are accessible is one of the big hurdles in this type of research. As a result, interview and focus group studies often rely on small numbers of participants which do not often constitute representative samples of the population. This means that results obtained from interviews and focus groups can rarely be generalized to a wider population.

The main benefit of interviews is that they give privileged access to a person's thoughts and opinions about a particular subject, which are difficult to access through direct observation of behaviour. Traditionally, the interview and/or focus group data have been seen as "essentially free-standing or independent of the (discourse of the) interviewer/moderator" (Edley and Litosselitti 2010:178). When interviews and focus groups are viewed in this light, as fact-finding exercises, one of the problems presented by this type of research is the potential bias created by the proximity between interviewer and interviewee. Issues such as researcher bias effect (Chapter 2), social desirability and impression management (Section 5.2.2. above), and the risks of interviewers 'going native' (See Section 5.9 below) may affect both the validity and reliability of the results. From this positivistic perspective (see Chapter 2), the solutions to the problems tend to involve using techniques that ensure the interviewer remains as neutral as possible, such as minimizing intervention and using structured interview schedules (more on this below).

A more radical solution and one that is more in line with an interpretivist approach to research is to acknowledge that the interactive aspect of interviews cannot be ignored and consider it as a valid part of the research exercise. In Chapter 3 we saw that discourse analysts see language as a form of social practice that not only reflects the social context in which it is produced but is also constitutive of that context. This view of language is not exclusive to discourse analysis but is a key premise of a wider school of thought known as social constructionism which has pervaded research in all areas of the social and human sciences (see also Chapter 2). According to this view, in order to provide a valid analysis of the language used in an interview, we need to understand how it is influenced by the social context in which it is used – for example, the relationships among the participants involved – and we need to consider the effects language has upon that context, in helping to construct social identities and relations. In other words, interviews and focus groups are not considered as ways of eliciting meanings that had been previously 'stored' in the mind of the interviewee/s but as a space where opinions are (re)constituted rather than reported, and these are taken as indicative or illustrative of particular social phenomena (Edley and Litoseeliti 2010:173).

The interpretivist perspective sees interviews not only as useful but imperfect sources of referential knowledge, but also as spaces where both interviewer/

moderator and participants can *do* things (see Section 5.7.1 below). For example, a participant may change their views about a topic in the process of a focus group, and these changes need to be taken into account as part of the data generated.

We saw in Chapter 3 that current language research favours the use of naturally occurring language, that is, language that is produced independently of the research process. This is generally not the case for interview data, unless the topic of research is actually the interview itself, as in the case of interpreter-mediated interviews mentioned above. In other cases, the researcher sets the agenda in a more or less overt fashion, and this results in a series of constraints regarding the content of what is to be said and the manner in which the participants express themselves, which compromises the spontaneity of the language used. However, while this criticism is very relevant for the investigation of language use, it is less so when we want to find out about people's opinions and thoughts. In this case, the fact that the researcher sets the agenda helps the discussion to be focused in such a way as to extract precisely the information that will help the researcher answer his or her research question.

Another counter-argument to the criticism that interviews do not reflect naturally-occurring language is that it is difficult to think of situations where language production is not constrained by someone's agenda. The problem in a research context is that there may be a conflict of interest in that the researcher sets the agenda and also interprets the results, which could lead us to question the validity of the conclusions reached. However, some degree of subjectivity is inherent in any type of research and self-reflection can help researchers be mindful of their own influence on the participants' discourse.

As mentioned above, interviews and focus groups give access to people's thoughts and opinions. However sincere, these should not be taken at face value. Interviews and focus groups offer insights into what participants *say* they believe or do, not into what they *actually think* or do (Edley and Litoseeliti 2010:173; Gillham 2000:13-14). In semi-structured and structured interviews (see below), where interpreters have the opportunity to discuss certain issues at length, their contradictions can become evident in the course of the interview. Examples of this can be found in Clifford (2004, discussed below) and Torikai (2011). Torikai conducted interviews with interpreters with the aim, among other things, of exploring their perception of their role as cultural mediators, and found that interpreters "did not necessarily abide by the norms they expressed" (*ibid.*:89). Although they occasionally compared their role to that of machines and emphasized the need for invisibility, their own accounts of their practices showed them acting in a much more active mediating role.

Despite the problems described, when it comes to finding out about peoples' conscious thoughts about a certain topic, interviews and focus groups have few rivals in terms of methods. The subjective nature (and inter-subjective nature in the case of focus groups) of the participants' accounts is indeed a crucial element in the choice of these methods over others. In this regard, it is worth quoting here at length Tipton's reflections on the choice of focus groups to investigate issues of trust in interpreter-mediated social work encounters. The choice was made partly on the basis of the conclusions reached by previous research which had shown that "trust involves belief about the way that other people, and even institutions, are likely to behave" (Edwards *et al* 2005, in Tipton 2010:191). Tipton (*ibid.*) then reports that

> [t]his observation has served, in part, to inform the choice of methodology for data collection in the present paper, since the use of focus groups is designed to foreground the intersubjective nature of trust in social relationships through the elicitation of practioners' perceptions *about* practice and the beliefs that shape their professional relationships with interpreters. This approach draws on Möllering's (2011) reflexive approach to trust and his contention that trust research should concern the subjective reality as interpreted by the person who trusts; this contrasts, for example, with a behaviourist approach to cause-effect relationships of trust which assumes that trust is a stable, observable, variable.

5.6   Designing interviews and focus groups

This section discusses issues of research design when using interviews and focus groups. Many of the issues discussed above in relation to the design of questionnaire surveys are valid here too; these include the need for operationalization, the language used to formulate questions, the advantages of piloting, and ethical considerations. These issues are therefore not discussed here in detail, except where the particularities of interviews and focus groups bring up questions not discussed above. Instead, we focus on the interview and focus group format, the language in which interviews and focus groups are conducted, and on interview and focus group schedules.

We said above that when designing questionnaires it is essential to refer back to the operational definition of the research construct to make sure that the questions included help answer the research question, and this is true for when we design interview schedules too. When concepts that are key to the research construct are discussed in the interview, it is important to ensure that the way in which participants are using the concepts correspond to how they are understood by the researchers. The problems arising from mismatches in this area are illustrated in Torikai (2011). Torikai interviewed five Japanese/English diplomatic and conference interpreters. The interpreters' role in bridging cultural gaps was one of the key topics explored in the interviews. Torikai found that the interpreters were dismissive of cultural differences and the challenges they can pose to interpreters, with one being strongly opposed to the notion of cultural mediation (*ibid.*:75). Torikai reflects that one plausible reason for what she calls a "blasé attitude" towards the cultural aspects of interpreting is that "the meaning of 'culture' in the interview questions was too broad" (*ibid.*:79). In fact, the participants seem to discuss cultural issues at length, but they do not appear to seem them as relevant to 'culture' in the sense that Torikai understands it.

5.6.1   Types of interviews and focus groups

One of the first decisions to make when designing a study based on interviews is what type of interview to use (structured, semi-structured or unstructured) and whether to interview one person at a time or organize focus groups. In **structured interviews**, the interviewer goes through a series of carefully prepared questions ensuring that the order in which they are asked and the wording is exactly the same in each case. Closed questions tend to be used (see Section 5.3.3 above). The advantage of this type of interview is that it ensures the same topics are covered in all cases and facilitates comparability across responses from different participants, as well as quantification. The disadvantage is that the data collected will remain within the boundaries predicted by the researcher, and the interview does not allow space for new insights which might emerge in the process of interviewing. Researchers may miss a whole area of concern just because they did not think of asking questions about it.

Unstructured interviews are characterized by a free-flowing process, where the interviewer uses a series of guiding questions at their discretion so as to elicit the required information in the manner that best suits the particular circumstances of the interview. The goal is generally to see the research topic from the perspective of the interviewee and to understand how and why they come to have this particular perspective. Interviewers are allowed to improvise and open-ended questions allow participants to say as little or as much as they like, actively shaping the course of the interview. As a result, the data collected tend to reflect more accurately the concerns of the participants themselves, although this is at the expense of comparability. The analysis is more difficult and time-consuming because it requires more interpretation. Quantification is never an aim in this type of research but it can be used, for example, to highlight the recurrence of some topics.

Unstructured interviews were used in a project entitled 'Health Care Inter-preter Services: Strengthening Access to Primary Care' (Clifford 2004). One of the goals of the project was to better understand the ways in which healthcare services were being provided to people in Canada who have limited knowledge of English or French, based on data obtained from a series of qualitative interviews with over 150 healthcare professionals and providers of interpreting services in Canada. The interviewers would start with a basic question to launch discussions with the informants, such as 'What can you tell me about your clinical work with patients who don't speak English or French?' or 'What can you tell me about the interpreting you've done in primary healthcare?'. Informants were then allowed to steer the conversations to topics that were important for them. This approach enabled the researchers to gain a deeper understanding of their informants' experience of interpreting in healthcare (Clifford 2004).

Semi-structured interviews, as the name suggests, are somewhere in-between the two types already described. As in structured interviews, an interview sched-ule tends to be used, but more of the questions are open-ended and there is more flexibility to allow variation in the order in which the questions are asked, as well as to introduce new questions. This is the format chosen by Torikai in her oral history research involving life-story interviews with English/Japanese interpreters mentioned above. Life-story interviews are personal narratives about one's life told as a result of a guided interview. The aim of Torikai's research was to find out how interpreters acquired the linguistic, communicative and cultural competence needed for interpreting between Japanese and English; what specific efforts were exerted in trying to bridge the gap between those two different languages and cultures; and how interpreters perceived their roles: as "invisible conduits" or "cultural mediators" (Torikai 2011:76). These aims are too broad to be covered in a structured interview, where the interpreters would not have the opportunity to go into the details they may feel are particularly relevant. On the other hand, an unstructured interview may have left some of those questions unanswered.

Deciding what type of interview is best suited for our research purposes depends on our research question(s). As a general guideline, structured interviews are useful when there is a focus on factual information and the researcher knows in advance the type of information the participants will be able to provide, while unstructured interviews are more suitable for explorative research, when we want to let the participants choose the themes that emerge from the discussion, as in the study reported by Clifford (2004) above. Semi- and unstructured interviews (and focus groups) tend to shift the balance of power away from the researcher and towards the research participant, allowing for the co-construction of knowledge. As a result, participants can feel empowered by the role they are taking and change their behaviour accordingly. For this reason, interviews and focus groups are often used in action research (see below).

Focus groups are groups of typically 6 to 10 participants which are brought together to engage in a discussion that is 'focused', that is, centred around a small number of issues. The discussion generally lasts approximately 1 to 2 hours when conducted face to face (as opposed to online, where it can be asynchronous). Focus groups are similar to collective interviews, but there is greater emphasis on the interactive nature of the activity: "a group takes shape by – indeed depends on – the synergistic dynamics of participants responding to and building on each other's views" (Edley and Litoselitti 2010:167). There is no 'interviewer', but rather a facilitator or moderator. Focus groups can also be more or less structured, and the role of the moderators will change accordingly: in structured discussion the role is more directive; in others the moderator initiates topics but then lets the discussion flow in whatever direction participants choose (Edley and Litosselitti 2010). Napier (2011:65) reports on a study of sign language interpreting using focus groups and mentions that the facilitator only intervened in the discussion for the following reasons: "(i) to clarify a comment from a participant; (ii) to link a comment to that of another participant; (iii) to allocate a turn to a participant if needed; and (iv) to bring the discussion back to the point of signed language interpreting".

Focus groups present many advantages. A group discussion discourages habitual or semi-automatic responses. Since other group members may challenge an answer, individuals tend to be more analytical and thoughtful.

The possibility of observing participants interacting can give researchers an insight into inter-professional discourse and hierarchies. However, focus groups are generally considered a poor way of recording existing knowledge shared by an entire group: you only learn what the most knowledgeable person in the group knows. Fear of losing face will silence those who know less or are less confident. Edley and Litosselitti (2010:171) note that researchers often come to focus groups with the expectation that they will be able to pin down certain opinions but find that opinions are emergent and dynamic, rather than established and fixed. It is in the nature of this type of research that it cannot be exactly replicated, because even if we were to gather the same participants a second time and give them the same questions, the discussion would take a different course.

By making diversity of opinion more manifest, groups can stimulate ideas or promote reconsideration. Therefore, apart from consolidating existing knowledge about participants' views, attitudes and beliefs, and finding out about why people think or feel the way they do, focus groups are often used as a way of brainstorming and generating new ideas (Edley and Litosselitti 2010:170) and are particularly useful for action research. **Action research** is described by Burns (2010:81) as a piece of research designed to bring about change and improvement in the participants' situation, generate theoretical as well as practical knowledge about the situation, engage participants and establish an attitude of self-development and growth. For example, it can be used to conduct research on the impact of modifications made to a training programme (e.g. the introduction of a new module) or to a translation workflow process in a translation agency (e.g. the introduction of new technologies) so as to decide whether to retain the modifications made in their current state or make further modifications. Weber *et al* (2005) use focus groups in an action research project involving medical interpreters. One of the focus groups brought together qualified interpreters who had not had much practice; participants were interviewed twice, the second time after they had increased their working experience. In this way, researchers could see how the interpreters' attitudes had changed throughout that period and could evaluate the impact their own intervention might have had on the interpreters.

5.6.2   *Designing interview and focus group schedules*

The points made above about the language used to formulate survey questions are also applicable to interview questions. In brief: questions should be unambiguously phrased (avoiding jargon and double negatives); they should not make assumptions or be leading; they should not attempt to elicit more than one piece of information at a time (double-barrelled and catch-all questions should be avoided); and questions that present hypothetical scenarios or lead to potentially face-threatening statements should similarly be avoided.

Regarding the order of questions, it is normally best to open with a question the participant can answer easily, such as requests for factual or descriptive information. In focus groups, asking the participants to introduce themselves may help break the ice and provide information on the basis of which they can relate to each other. More difficult and sensitive questions should be held back for when the participants are more relaxed. Both closed and open questions can be used in interviews, although closed questions tend to be used more rarely and only in structured interviews.

It is important to point out here that although it may be less detailed, an interview schedule may also be useful in unstructured interviews, where it can contain a list of topics to be covered to make sure nothing is left out by accident. This might consist of a few ready-made, appropriately-worded, probe questions which the interviewer can resort to if needed and a template for the opening statement to make sure that nothing crucial is left unsaid. The demands placed on the interviewer/facilitator are considerable and having to deal with an unexpected situation could easily mean that the interviewer/facilitator forgets something important. Napier (2011), for example, uses a list of prompt questions which were sent to the focus-group participants one week in advance. During the discussion, the facilitator did not pose these questions but used them as a guideline for monitoring the discussion and making sure that the range of themes were covered. Napier's study focused on practitioners' and consumers' attitudes towards sign language interpreting, and the prompt questions were designed to elicit these attitudes. The questions for consumers, for example, touched on issues such as what they liked or disliked about working with interpreters, the benefits and challenges of working with interpreters, best and worst interpreting experiences, criteria for using interpreters in different situations, and whether interpreters should attend training/professional development (*ibid.*:65).

We have stressed earlier (in Chapter 2) that research questions should not be too general and abstract; however, even appropriately-formulated research questions would be too broad and complex to be asked directly in an interview or focus group. Instead, they can be used as a basis for developing a more specific set of questions and probes. Imagine that the research questions are as follows:

- To what extent do recently-graduated postgraduate students feel sufficiently prepared to start a career as translators?
- To what extent do postgraduate students feel that the course they have taken has helped them prepare for a career as translators?

These questions could be broken down into four more specific questions to be used in semi-structured interviews:

1) Can you please describe the course from which you have graduated?
2) Are you planning to start a career as a translator in the near future? If so, what are your main concerns?
3) What aspects of your course do you feel were most useful in preparing you for a career as translator? Why do you think they were useful? Probe: a particular skill acquired? A particular module or topic?

4) What aspects of your course do you feel were least useful in preparing you for a career as translator? Why?
5) Generally speaking, do you feel a course like the one you have taken is sufficient preparation for working as a translator? Please explain.

The information potentially obtained from question 1 may also be available from other means (such as course and module descriptors available from the training institution) and may be more detailed and/or accurate. However, this is a question that demands a descriptive response and provides a good starting point because it is easy to answer and would help the participant relax. Besides, it may still be helpful to find out what aspects of the course they highlight when describing it. Question 2 seeks to address the issue of 'preparedness' but is more open than that so as to allow the students to come up with what is at the top of their minds without constraining them by requiring them to make a (rather difficult) judgement as to what the essential requirements to start a career as a translator might be and whether they have acquired them. Questions 3 and 4 address the notion of preparedness that is key for the research construct but make it more specific for the participants by linking it to aspects of the course they took in preparation for their professional career. Since the research focuses on graduates, the results should allow us to link the degree of preparedness to the course they have recently finished. Note that the probes are rather general and do not actually mention a particular module or topic, because otherwise they would be leading questions. Provided relevant information was obtained in question 3, probes should not be needed for question 4 because question 3 would have already prepared the ground. It may be that the answer to question 5 is already clear from the two previous questions, and in a semi-structured interview the interviewer may choose to omit it, but note that it introduces the concept of sufficiency, which may not have been addressed, and it provides a way of summarizing what the interviewee has said. This last question also offers the participants the opportunity to comment on issues that affect how prepared they feel but may not have been covered in previous questions.

In some cases it may be best to structure the discussion around issues crucial to the research construct but without bringing that construct *per se* to the attention of the participants as the main focus of the discussion. This can be useful as a way of avoiding self-censoring on the basis of participants' assumptions regarding the researcher's expectations. This is the approach adopted by Tipton (2010) in her focus-group research in interpreter-mediated social work encounters. As mentioned above, the focus of the research was 'trust' and, in particular, the socio-cultural norms that impact the interpreter-mediated interaction and levels of trust created therein. The participants were social-work practitioners and the aim of the focus groups was to allow them to "articulate and evaluate their experiences of practice" (*ibid.*:188). Tipton used a semi-structured approach, and the concept of trust informed most of the discussion points; however, trust was not foregrounded as the main feature of the sessions because the researcher "wished to gain as great an insight as possible into the range of practitioner experiences" (*ibid.*:192).

5.6.3   Language issues

For interviews and focus groups, a crucial decision to make is which language to use when the interviewer and the interviewee could potentially choose from several ones. Saldanha (2005), a native speaker of Spanish with English as a language of habitual use, interviewed two translators who were native English speakers and translated from Spanish and Portuguese. One of the translators was at the time residing in Spain and had Spanish as his language of habitual use. The interviews could have been conducted in either English or Spanish with adequate levels of fluency. The researcher opted for English on the basis that the data would later be described in English, at least in the first instance. Conducting the interview in Spanish would have resulted in an extra layer of interpretation imposed by the researcher when analyzing the data in a different language and translating any quotes to be used in the report.

More difficult situations arise when the participants (interviewer and interviewees) do not speak the same language with a similar degree of proficiency. Wherever possible, participants should be allowed to express themselves in the language in which they feel most at home talking about the topic of the interview (which may not necessarily be their native language). This does not mean, however, that the interviewer should use the participants' language wherever possible: if the participants do not understand the question presented by the interviewer, no matter how fluent their answer is, it will not be useful.

If the report is going to be written in a language other than the language of the interview, it is often necessary to translate the transcripts; for example, if the interviewer and researcher are not the same person, or if the transcript is to be included as an appendix in a PhD thesis. Translation imposes another layer of interpretation on the data. There is no need to explain to a readership of translation studies students and scholars the risks to the validity of our results if we use translated texts to make inferences about someone's attitudes, knowledge, opinions, etc. However, the problems do not only concern validity and interpretation. Temple and Young (2004) offer a useful discussion of some of the issues involved from an exclusively methodological point of view, with particular reference to the use of sign language. They point out that whether a transcript is translated or not will matter more to some researchers than others, according to their epistemological stance: researchers who take a positivist stance and believe in the objectivity of the research project are more likely to be comfortable with using a translated text, because they will also assume that it is possible to be a completely neutral translator. Temple and Young claim that this is the predominant model in much cross-language research where "[r]esults are presented as if interviewees were fluent English speakers or as if the language they used is irrelevant" (*ibid.*:163).

A key issue when translation is involved in the research process is whether it is carried out by the researcher or by someone else. In the first case, it can even present some advantages, since the translation process "offers the researcher significant opportunities for close attention to cross cultural meanings and interpretations and potentially brings the researcher up close to the problems of meaning equivalence within the research process" (*ibid.*:168). However, any potential bias the researcher has towards the participant is likely to become embedded in the data as well as potentially affecting the analysis itself. This is particularly problematic because, while the analysis is, at least to some extent, scrutinized by other researchers, the translation will not be so open to scrutiny.

When the translator is other than the researcher, we have the added problem that bias can be exerted from two different sides, which affects not only validity but reliability. As a way of addressing this from an interpretivist epistemological perspective, some researchers who use translators have begun to reflect on their practice and explore ways in which the translators could be made more visible, for example by inviting them to participate in the interpretation of results. Temple and Young cite the example of Edwards (1998), who argues that translators should be seen as key informants rather than neutral transmitters and encourages the translator to use the third person rather than to translate literally, as a way of marking the account as in part constructed by the translator.

Apart from having an impact on validity, the use of translation can present ethical dilemmas too when there are differences between the power and hierarchy of the languages involved. In the case of sign language, for example, Temple and Young note that "the expediency of translation reinforces the invisibility of the source language – an issue that is both political and methodological" (*ibid.*:166). Temple and Young conclude that the problem is not the use of translation *per se*, but how translation is executed and integrated into research design (*ibid.*:175).

5.6.4   *Piloting*

Piloting interviews is more difficult than piloting questionnaires because they are more time consuming. If only a small number of participants are to be interviewed, then using one or two interviews as pilots is not cost effective. In larger studies pilots are crucial to refining research questions at an earlier stage, allowing the researcher to subsequently focus on collecting and analyzing data by using a more stable set of questions, minimizing the to-ing and fro-ing that almost inevitably happens in qualitative research because we start analyzing data at the same time as we are collecting them. The less predictable format of semi-structured interviews means that pilot runs are not as helpful as in structured interviews; however, experience is a key asset in becoming a good interviewer, and a few trial runs will therefore prove invaluable. We strongly recommend that researchers test their interviewing skills in advance and that they record and transcribe their trial runs in order to self-evaluate their performance. When piloting is not possible, it is essential nevertheless to obtain feedback about the questions prepared, if possible from people who fit the profile of the participants. As in other qualitative research (see Chapter 5), any changes made to the interview questions on the basis of the pilot study need to be declared and discussed.

5.6.5 *Ethical considerations*

Interviews and focus groups are fraught with the type of ethical issues which were discussed in Chapter 2 and above in relation to questionnaire surveys. Kvale (1996) offers an in-depth discussion of the ethics of interviewing. Here we touch upon the main points. Apart from the usual requirements of informed consent and confidentiality, because of the direct contact with participants it is likely that ethical authorization will be required from the institution to which the main researcher is affiliated and possibly from other organizations, such as the participants' employers (see Chapter 2). For example, in order to recruit participants from social services in the Greater Manchester region, Tipton (2010) had to request authorization from Manchester City Council. Many large institutions have a dedicated contact person who deals with research requests and who will request a research protocol for review before permission is granted to contact individuals about arranging interviews. Researchers should always make an effort to establish the relevant requirements of the institution and follow them. Establishing good relationships will benefit both sides and the research community in the longer term.

Online interviews and focus groups do not involve direct contact but bring in a whole set of other issues regarding privacy, unsolicited contact, etc., mentioned above and in Chapter 2, and discussed by Mann and Stewart (2005) in some detail in relation to qualitative research. In all cases, it is important to be able to demonstrate that the data were collected with the knowledge of the participants and for the specific purpose of the research project at hand (rather than using data collected previously for a different project, in which case fresh permission needs to be sought). Researchers should therefore obtain signed forms where all relevant information is available (see Mann and Stewart 2005 on obtaining consent in Internet-mediated research). Confidentiality needs to be respected by keeping recordings and transcripts in a safe location and by removing names and other identifying features from transcripts (see also Chapter 6 for a discussion of similar issues in case studies).

Issues relating to the balance of power between researcher and participants are particularly relevant when the two parties enter in face-to-face contact. It is important that individuals invited for the interview do not feel pressured to participate (not only for ethical reasons but also because the interviewee's willingness affects the quality of the data). Therefore, it is important to state clearly in the invitation that while the study is important and their participation would be much appreciated, taking part is completely voluntary and non- participation will not affect them negatively, and to reassure participants that they will not be identified (where this is relevant).

While it is often possible to collect questionnaire data anonymously, this is not the case in face-to-face interview and focus group studies, even if the data can be anonymized at a later stage. Using the Internet, however, it is possible to conduct an interview where interviewee and interviewer know nothing about each other's identity or biosocial attributes (Hewson *et al* 2003:45).

Anonymity is not necessarily a requirement or an advantage, particularly in unstructured individual interviews, in cases where the participants may have been chosen because the information sought can only be provided by them and not someone else. Saldanha (2005, 2011a, 2011b, 2011c), for example, studied the style of two literary translators and used interviews to elicit their thoughts about the stylistic features revealed in a previous corpus-based analysis. In this case, it was essential to be able to name interviewees in the report itself. Any aspects of the data obtained that have not been cleared for permission should be treated with utmost confidentiality. The participants should always be offered the opportunity to comment on a draft of the relevant parts of the research report and told what kind of feedback about the study they can receive and when they are likely to receive it.

Another difficulty that can arise in interviews is whether interviewers have the right to ask certain questions because they are relevant to their research even if they may concern rather private aspects of a person's life. Remember that translators, and particularly interpreters, deal with confidential material. In these cases anonymity and reading of drafts are no guarantees, and it is best to avoid probing around sensitive issues unless these are crucial to the research. Demands on those being investigated can be quite high, not only because of the level of disclosure, but also because the researcher can have a considerable impact (positive or negative) on the subjects of research (Stake 2005:459):

> Those whose lives and expressions are portrayed risk exposure and embarrassment, as well as loss of standing, employment, and self esteem. Something of a contract exists between researcher and the researched: a disclosing and protective covenant, usually informal but best not silent, a moral obligation.

5.7   Eliciting data using interviews and focus groups

This section first discusses the process of sampling and recruiting participants, and then moves on to the basic principles and challenges of the actual process of interviewing and moderating focus groups. Brief consideration is also given to interviews and focus groups conducted online.

5.7.1   *Sampling and recruiting participants*

Although it is possible, in theory, to apply random sampling methods in large studies based on interviews, the aim is rarely to generalize to wider populations but rather to provide rich and diverse information from key participants. To achieve this goal, purposive sampling, where participants are selected on the basis of principled criteria so as to cover the key aspects of the research question, is more effective (see Chapter 2). A clear and interesting example of purposive sampling guided by both theoretical and pragmatic criteria is provided in Bourdieu's (2008) paper on the literary publishing field in France. The research was based on thirty-eight extensive (and sometimes repeated) interviews with publishers and series editors in every sector of the field, as well as interviews with translators, critics, administrative agents, press attachés, and foreign rights managers. Other methods were also used, such as bibliographic research and statistics gathered from archives and publishing houses. What concerns us here is how publishing houses were chosen. The aim of the research was to map the structure of the French literary publishing field. The 'literary publishing field' was defined as "a relatively autonomous social space – that is to say one capable of translating all external forces (economic and political) according to its own particular logic – in which the principles governing editorial strategies become manifest" (*ibid.*:127). This way of operationalizing the research construct required choosing only those publishers who were "autonomous enough to have developed their own editorial policy" (*ibid.*). The degree of autonomy enjoyed by decision-makers is difficult to measure, especially in the case of subsidiaries of larger companies, and varies over time, which required examining subsidiaries in detail and on a case-by-case basis, relying on information provided by interview participants and documented sources (*ibid.*:128).

Another decision was to focus on publishers who exerted an influence on the structure of the publishing field. Therefore, small-scale publishers who had a 'nominal existence' and those who had not yet made a name for themselves and had "yet to exercise any real influence in the field" (*ibid.*) were excluded. Likewise, publishers specializing in the social sciences, paperback editions, fine arts, practical works, dictionaries or encyclopedias and schoolbooks, as well as book clubs, were left out on the same grounds. In the end "a sample of sixty-one publishers of literature written in French or translated into French, all of which published between July 1995 and July 1996" (*ibid.*:127) was retained for the analysis. However, only thirty-eight interviews were carried out with publishers and series editors. Although Bourdieu does not elaborate on how the specific interviewees were selected, he mentions certain difficulties which had an impact on the recruitment of participants, such as "the extremely secretive attitude of a professional milieu that is ill disposed to the prying questions of outsiders" (*ibid.*).

Purposive sampling is not always possible in translation and interpreting research, so convenience sampling is also widely used. Napier's (2011) focus-group study, mentioned above, was designed to elicit views on sign-language interpreting among three groups of stakeholders: interpreters, deaf consumers and hearing consumers. The recruitment was done through a flyer that was sent to "personal contacts of the researcher, distribution lists for various interpreting agencies, the peak body representing deaf signed language using people, and various organisations providing services to deaf people that rely on signed language interpretation services" (*ibid.*:64). As mentioned above, a convenience sample is not a problem *per se*, provided the limitations in terms of generalizability are acknowledged. Napier (*ibid.*:80-81) discusses the ways in which using this recruitment method could have influenced the results in her study, noting in particular that

(i)   All participants were self-selected, and thus more highly motivated to discuss issues related to interpreting.
(ii) The majority of interpreter participants were studying in, or had completed, the only university training program for signed language interpreters in Australia — at the university of the author. Thus they may have had a natural bias in their discussions to display a certain attitude towards their work.
(iii) The majority of the deaf participants were university educated and working in professional contexts, and therefore had very clear ideas of what they wanted from interpreters and why.

It is interesting to note, however, that the availability of participants may add a random element to the final sample, particularly in focus groups, where date and times need to be agreed to suit the majority of participants.

As already mentioned, focus groups and interviews are intensive in terms of commitment from the participants, which means that response rates can be low. For this reason it is often a good idea to approach participants individually. Generally, the participant selection process remains open as long as possible so that after some initial data have been gathered, additional participants can be brought in to fill gaps in the initial description, expand or even challenge it (Dörnyei 2007:126). Ideally, the iterative process of analyzing and collecting data should go on until a 'saturation point' is reached, which occurs "when additional data do not seem to develop the concepts any further but simply repeat what previous informants have already revealed" (*ibid.*:127).

Often, in studies where interviews are used to expand on results previously obtained from questionnaires, participants are asked to indicate in the questionnaires whether they are willing to be interviewed at a later date. This self-selection process does limit the potential bias exerted by the researcher in approaching participants but may introduce another bias in that there is often a reason why some participants volunteer for interviews while others do not (which can range from a simple matter of availability to complex personality issues).

Focus groups typically consist of between six and ten participants. Having fewer than six participants may result in a lack of diversity of opinions, which stifles discussion, while groups of eight or more people tend to fragment into smaller groups. However, some of those who initially agree may fail to turn up, and hence over-recruiting is sometimes used to avoid the risk of ending up with a group that is too small to function adequately (personal reminders are a good strategy to avoid this too). Alternatively, if participants are members of existing teams (who work together or form a reading group) this problem can be avoided if the researcher comes and meets them at their usual meeting location (during their lunch hour, for example).

Dörnyei (2007:145) suggests that a project should involve four or five groups as a minimum so as to achieve adequate breadth and depth of information, and to mitigate any idiosyncratic results that occur because of unexpected internal or external factors affecting the dynamics of the group. Including friends, partners, relatives or colleagues in the same group may not be a good idea in that they can enter into private conversations, it can discourage disagreement, and there's a tendency to assume shared knowledge (Edley and Litosselitti 2010).

The key decision to make in terms of focus group composition is whether to have homogenous or heterogeneous groups. A heterogeneous group of people of different ages, gender, social backgrounds, etc. could be useful if we are interested in establishing the common denominators among a diverse group; however, large gaps between participants in terms of, for example, professional background, may make some of them less willing to share their opinions, out of deference for those they consider more knowledgeable or out of fear of offending. Sometimes, discussion can be more fluid in a homogenous group, in which case each group is selected so as to represent a particular constituency and thus capture a wider range of perspectives. This approach is adopted in the study by Napier (2011), mentioned above, where focus groups were organized per stakeholder group (hearing consumers, deaf consumers, sign language interpreters). Each group was then balanced wherever possible for gender and age. In addition, deaf participants were also balanced according to whether they were native or non-native signers; hearing participants were balanced for level of experience in terms of working with interpreters; and interpreter participants were balanced for level of interpreting accreditation.

Interviews and focus groups can be used together as methods of data elicitation within the same research project. Each type of method may provide different insights and suit different types of participants. Sometimes the decision to use one method instead of another has to be made in the course of the data collection process. This is the case in the study by Angelelli (2007), who used focus groups to evaluate, from a cultural point of view, the validity of medical exchange scripts to be used for testing interpreters. The scripts were based on authentic medical exchanges with Spanish, Cantonese and Hmong-speaking patients, and they were then presented to focus groups with the aim of validating the scenarios and the adaptations of the script. Focus groups also discussed the main cultural issues among their ethnic group. Angelelli (2007) uses focus groups that are heterogeneous in terms of professional background (community members, interpreters and healthcare providers) but homogenous in terms of ethnic background. In this way, the validity of the script was assessed from the point of view of all interested parties. In some instances, Angelelli reports, community members felt more comfortable revealing personal information and experiences on an individual basis, and one-to-one interviews were conducted in these cases (*ibid.*:75).

In qualitative research of this type, because the sampling is not done using procedures that are tried and tested to ensure they are representative, it is important to be explicit as to the procedures for sampling and recruiting participants, since reliability will depend to a great extent on the transparency of the data elicitation process. For this reason, it is recommended that a research diary is kept for this purpose (see Chapter 6 for a description of this and other research aids).

5.7.2 Interviewing and moderating: Basic principles and key challenges

As discussed above, at the start of an interview or focus group it is important to remind participants of the purpose of the interview, reassure them of confidentiality and obtain informed consent. Apart from this, it is useful to remind participants of the approximate duration of the interview and make sure they have the time required, so as to avoid rushed answers. In face-to-face interviews that are being recorded or video-taped, it is crucial to check that the equipment is working as it should, to avoid losing any data because of technical problems.

Ending the interview and focus group also requires some tact; it is generally a good idea to signal that the end of the interview/focus group is approaching by mentioning that there are one or two questions left (in a structured interview), or by summing up the main points (in an unstructured one). It is not a good idea to end on a bad note, so steering away from difficult issues at that point is important. Finally, asking the participants whether they want to add any other comments and offering the opportunity to ask questions is usually considered good manners as well as good research practice, and so is thanking the participants for their time.

When undertaking structured interviews, interviewers should be very familiar with the schedule of questions and very clear as to what each of them is meant to tap into, so that if the participant fails to provide relevant information at first, they can probe further. All questions should be posed to all participants, even if the interviewer thinks they already know what the participant is going to say or if they think the question has already been answered.

Generally speaking, interviews are characterized by an unequal power relationship between interviewers and participants, which can affect participants' answers. In particular we need to be aware of the potential for researcher personal attribute effect (see Chapter 2 Section 2.10.1). Issues of social desirability and impression management discussed in relation to questionnaires (see Section 5.2.2) above are even more prominent in interviews and may lead participants to say what they think the interviewer/moderator wants to hear. A clarification at the beginning of the interview to the effect that the interviewer is not searching for particular answers and is interested in recording the whole range of possible answers is often a good idea. Problems of bias and manipulation can also be caused by the researcher unintentional expectancy effect, where an interviewer unwittingly leads participants directly in terms of what they say (see Chapter 2).

Even if we agree with the interpretivist perspective according to which interviews and focus groups never provide a true objective account of meanings existing in the participants' minds, we can see neutrality, understood as a means of "creating appropriate space for the interviewees to share their experiences with us freely, regardless or any social, moral, or political content" (Dörnyei 2007:141) as a goal to aim for. This, however, should not prevent interviewers and moderators from developing an empathetic approach where appropriate. Interviewing effectively requires that the interviewer sees what is happening from the interviewee's point of view and establishes rapport with them. In brief, a self-reflective, open-minded and socially-aware attitude on the interviewer's part is likely to create an environment that encourages cooperation from participants.

Diplomacy is a key skill in interviewing and moderating focus groups; it can help interviewers negotiate common difficulties such as lack of responsiveness and over-responsiveness. If interviewees are not very willing to talk, they should be allowed to take their time. Silence is a strategy used by good interviewers to indicate they want to hear more, although the silence need not become uncomfortable. The over-communicative interviewee may digress often, and a possible strategy for interrupting politely and getting them back on track is to ask them to expand on something said earlier which was relevant for the research. Interviewers should be prepared for challenging answers: participants may express opinions they disagree with, or may question the research or the value of their questions, and in these cases it is best to remain as detached as possible.

Sometimes people fail to say what is taken for granted. This means that, particularly in semi-structured or unstructured interviews and focus groups, it is important to probe for concerns that the researcher expected to hear voiced but have not been mentioned. Likewise, interviewers should not take any specialized knowledge for granted and should not be afraid of clarifying the meaning of even basic terms at the beginning of the interview. Otherwise, we risk running whole interviews where the participant and interviewer talk at cross purposes – see the example provided in Section 5.7 concerning the use of the word 'culture' in the interview study conducted by Torikai (2011).

The focus group presents some specific challenges. As mentioned in Chapter 2, there is a risk of inter-subject bias in these situations. This can result in **false consensus,** which occurs when some participants with strong personalities and/or similar views dominate the discussion while others remain silent (Edley and Litosselitti 2010:172). Another common aspect of group dynamics is **group polarization**, where a group may respond collectively in a more exaggerated way than any individual member normally would (*ibid.*).

All participants should be allowed equal opportunities to express their views. Generally speaking, it is more difficult to keep discussion on track without inhibiting the flow of ideas in a group than in a one-to-one interview. Discussions can become rather intense in a group setting, and it is important for the moderator to avoid taking sides or giving the impression that they are biased towards one or the other view. Some of these problems can be addressed through careful planning and skilful moderation. Eye contact and gentle probing can be used to minimize the influence of dominant participants, for example by not looking at the dominant speaker. In order to support a minority view so that it can be expressed more fully, the interviewer can mention that a similar view was expressed in an earlier group (Breakwell 1990:77). A good overall strategy is to establish a code of conduct at the start of the discussion asking people not to interrupt and to respect each others' views.

The collection of data is accompanied by a continuous process of analysis and interpretation of the data being collected, which may (if at a very early stage) even lead to changes to the research design (for example, to the interview schedule or to focus group composition). This is one of the reasons why it is not usually recommended to gather too much data at the initial stage. It is best to schedule interviews at regular intervals, rather than all or most on the same day, for example, allowing time for transcription and reflection in between.

When the researcher him- or herself carries out the interviews and transcribes them, the fact that they are immersed in the process of data elicitation from the beginning can help them get a feel for how the data is shaping up, which may result in ideas as to how best to organize (code) the data during the analysis stage. In order to keep track of how the theory is developing and also to encourage self-reflexiveness and awareness, there are a number of techniques that the researcher can use. **Vignettes** are short narrative (story-like) descriptions of events (interviews/focus groups) and participants. **Interview profiles** are more substantial accounts of participants' contributions, in their own words (i.e. in the first person). Both vignettes and interview profiles can help the researchers refresh their memory at the point of analysis. Vignettes can also be used to record impressions about the interview; for example, whether a defensive attitude was noted, whether the interviewee seemed to have an agenda, etc. Interview profiles can help the researcher to see the narrative from the participants' viewpoint.

5.7.3   Face-to-face, telephone and Internet-mediated interviews and focus groups

Most interviews and focus groups are conducted face-to-face, and the analysis is based either on notes or transcripts of the recorded interview. It is generally agreed that for interviews to be really useful they need to be recorded; taking notes presents a problem of fidelity, does not allow the capture of nuanced responses and disrupts the interviewing process. Recording is generally straightforward, but even with the use of this basic technology there are many things that can potentially go wrong. At the very least, it is crucial to try the equipment at the beginning of the interview, to make sure there is enough power and a back-up power source, to make sure the recordings are appropriately labelled and to have back-ups. By recording only voice, a number of non-verbal clues are lost, such as facial expressions, gestures, posture. However, video-recording is more difficult and more intrusive, so it is only justifiable if one is specifically concerned with the coordination of discourse with other activities.

Telephone interviews are also possible. This medium is acceptable for short interviews – 15-20 minutes maximum (Breakwell 1990:84) – and can work quite well with structured interviews. Semi- or unstructured interviews are more difficult because the interviewer lacks non-verbal feedback and complex questions can prove to be more difficult to answer on the telephone. Unless the call is made using a computer, which often presents problems of quality, recording telephone interviews also presents considerable technical challenges that need to be taken into account. Transcribing is a crucial part of the process of data collection in recorded face-to-face and telephone interviews and focus groups. We discuss some of the issues involved in transcription in Chapter 4, Section4.3.3.

The use of the Internet to conduct **interviews or focus groups** is becoming more common; however, online qualitative research is a methodology that is still being experimented with and the lack of examples of actual practice in translation studies research means that any discussion can only be speculative. Therefore, for a detailed discussion we direct readers to reference works in other disciplines, for example Mann and Stewart (2005), Hewson *et al* (2003), James and Busher (2009), Fielding *et al* (2008) and Salmons (2010). Here, we will restrict ourselves to briefly outlining how interviews and focus groups can be carried out online and discuss the main advantages and disadvantages.

One of the key choices to be made when using the Internet for conducting interviews and focus groups is whether asynchronous or synchronous communication is to be used. Asynchronous interaction can take place using email (for interviews) or discussion forums (for focus groups). Synchronous interaction can take place using Voice over Internet Protocols (VoIP) – which works in a similar way to the telephone – as well as chat and conferencing software. There are also purpose-built websites and specialist online facilities for focus group (used mainly in marketing research). The choice of virtual environment is linked to the choice of a written or verbal mode of communication. Each environment offers opportunities and entails limitations, and the decision will depend on the requirements of the study context (for example, whether a more or less structured approach is preferred) as well as the availability and characteristics of the participants. While synchronous communication brings people closer and is more spontaneous, the opportunity for reflection between message and response has the potential for the development of sophisticated thinking. Synchronous and asynchronous interaction also differ in terms of privacy, cost and potential for interruption (see Mann and Stewart 2005 for a more detailed discussion).

Although an online medium can affect recruitment negatively among populations that for socio-economic, political or age-related reasons do not have easy Internet access, it facilitates the participation of people who are hard to reach otherwise, such as people living abroad or busy professionals, and keeps costs down. Online interviews and focus groups are less time consuming, in particular because they save transcription time. The automatic logging of data is also a key advantage because it removes one layer of data interpretation that is more often than not an unintended effect of transcription. However, researchers need to bear in mind that Internet-mediated communication has its own peculiarities in terms of language use which will be reflected in the texts collected, and this needs to be taken into account when analyzing the data. The impact of Internet-mediated communication on language use is a topic of research in its own right and cannot be discussed in any detail here, but see Baron (2008) for a comprehensive discussion and Walther (2012) for an overview of current research.

The lack of extra-linguistic cues can be a further disadvantage of the online environment, although it offers other linguistic and typographical cues (punctuation, capitals, 'smilies' and acronyms). On the one hand, an Internet-mediated environment may be a space where many people feel at ease; it has been argued that the Internet often facilitates the discussion of sensitive topics, because of the more anonymous nature of the interaction (Hewson *et al* 2003:45; Mann and Stewart 2005:18). On the other hand, how at ease participants may feel will depend on their computer literacy and how familiar they are with the specific electronic environments (email, chat, complex websites) in which the interviews or focus groups are conducted. Interviewers and moderators do have to be highly computer-literate and familiar with both the technicalities and the 'netiquette' of the specific online environment in which the research is conducted. **Netiquette** refers to the conventions that structure online interaction as well as the standards of politeness that apply in that environment.

Compared with traditional interview methods, the email interview may be less spontaneous and flowing, but it allows participants to answer in their own time and at their own convenience, which may encourage more detailed and carefully considered answers (Hewson *et al* 2003:45). Participants may also be more ac-curate in answering factual questions for which they need to check information, enhancing the validity of the data obtained (*ibid.*) The email interview also makes it easier for interviewers to come back for clarification at a later stage. However, overall, researchers who have carried out semi-structured interviews online are divided about their success (Mann and Stewart 2005:76).

5.8   Analyzing qualitative data

This section explains how to analyze qualitative data collected through question-naires, interviews and focus groups; however, much of this discussion is relevant to the analysis of data obtained by other means, such as transcriptions of audio and video recordings, diaries, letters, field notes, etc. The common element in these cases is that we are dealing with verbal data and not with numbers, and that the analysis is not 'linguistic', in the sense that it does not make use of lin-guistic knowledge and tools in order to go beyond the surface meaning of texts. Here, the analysis of language is a means to an end, rather than the end itself as was the case in Chapter 3. Of course, as noted in Chapter 3, nothing prevents us from analyzing interview data linguistically, using discourse analysis or any other tools; the choice, as always, will depend on the research question.

As mentioned above, qualitative interviewing is fraught with bias and so is the data analysis. Self-awareness is key to identifying what kind of biases are at play. Some of the common risks are confirmation bias, noting the exception rather than the norm, elite bias and going native. **Confirmation bias** refers to the tendency to notice and to look for what confirms one's beliefs. Researchers need to be careful not to focus on the details that confirm the hypothesis, neglecting those that disconfirm it. On the other hand, when we do not have strong expectations, we risk **noting the exception** and not the norm. It is important to ask to what extent are opinions or attitudes typical and make sure claims are made only on the basis of observing an adequate number of events. **Elite bias** occurs when too much weight is given to participants who are more articulate and better in-formed. Interviewers should be careful not to overlook the contributions made by the less eloquent participants. Finally, **going native** involves getting too close to the participants, to the point where it is not possible to think independently;

researchers feel compelled to share the informants' view. This risk is particularly strong when dealing with highly emotive issues.

We mentioned above that structured interviews allow for some basic quantification, for example, to say how many within a category of participants chose each option; or to offer average ratings where participants had to rank options. These figures are generally too low to benefit from any statistical processing, but they provide a way of summarizing the data and facilitate the observation of patterns.

In semi-structured or unstructured interviews and focus groups, the process is less straightforward: it does not begin with units assumed as a given and preconceived categories or variables but tends to follow an inductive and iterative pattern. This process is similar to analyzing data in discourse analysis, corpus linguistics and case studies (see Chapters 3 and 6). Numerical data does not start to make sense until we have quite a lot, but the more complex and rich verbal data that is obtained from interviews or focus groups is likely to trigger an analysis process at a very early stage (this is particularly the case in small scale projects where the interviewer/moderator and the researcher are the same person). The first thoughts about possible ways of organizing (coding) the data will tend to occur during the data collection and transcription, and this may lead the researcher to rethink the phrasing of some questions. This is why it is important to keep a systematic research diary from the beginning, where all these ideas and any changes made to the process of collecting data are noted.

The process of **coding in qualitative research** is different from that described above in relation to the analysis of quantitative questionnaire data and it involves organizing the data around themes. More specifically, coding involves identifying units of analysis, i.e. segments of text which contain one piece of information that is relevant to answering the research question, and then applying labels, for example in order to group broadly similar statements, or identify features that may need closer attention. These labels should help the researcher retrieve and group the units of analysis in such a way that patterns are highlighted.

Generally speaking, in qualitative research that follows an inductive approach the categories are not predetermined but derived from the data. The research questions act as a prism through which to view the information and choose relevant items, but do not provide the researcher with a set of pre-defined topics to look for. It is possible, however, to apply a **coding template** that was designed before the analysis, for example on the basis of the interview schedule (in structured and semi-structured interviews), or on the basis of previous research. It is important, however, to remember that the flexibility and emergent design that are typical of qualitative analysis are very likely to be compromised by the use of template coding.

There are several approaches to coding qualitative data, such as thematic analysis, content analysis or grounded theory. Given that the length of responses to open questions are often (and ideally) restricted in questionnaires, thematic analysis is most appropriate. **Thematic analysis** is described as "[a] process of working with raw data to identify and interpret key ideas or themes" (Matthews and Ross 2010:373). In some cases, an index of themes is established initially, but with the restricted nature of questionnaires an index may not be necessary. Thematic analysis of open-ended responses means working with 'chunks' of data, which might consist of several paragraphs, a sentence, a phrase or even single words or terms. Answers to open-ended questions might refer to more than one idea (or 'theme') and so multiple codes might be assigned to one response.

Qualitative content analysis is a broad term used to describe analytical moves which consist of identifying themes, looking for patterns, making interpretations and building a theory (explanation) (Dörnyei 2007:246).[2] Coding in qualitative content analysis moves gradually from superficial to more abstract (and interpretative) labels. Unlike grounded theory (discussed below), it does not require the researcher to follow a specific set of steps. Here, as an example, we describe the levels of coding (initial and second-level) suggested by Dörnyei (2007) as one way of approaching this process. **Initial coding** requires clear and transparent labels that are descriptive of the meaning of the code. Sometimes using key words from the actual passages is helpful. **Second-level coding** goes beyond description and notes emerging patterns, for example, by clustering similar categories under a broader label and introducing hierarchies. Once the coding is completed, it is important to review the data to cross-examine the codes applied, identifying overlap between coding categories or grey areas.

Concepts derived from the theoretical framework used to account for the data can also be deployed to provide coding categories. Saldanha (2005; 2011a, 2011b, 2011c) used both analytical theoretical concepts and emergent codes in her study. As already mentioned, semi-structured interviews, paratexts and metatexts produced by two translators were used in order to explain individual stylistic traits found to be common across several translations by the same translators. A first level of coding identified themes that emerged from the texts and the interviews and used descriptive labels such as views on foreignization and domestication, translators' visibility, translators' subjectivity, translation as compromise and conceptions of readership. For the next level, Saldanha used more abstract categories, drawing on Berman's concepts of 'translator's project', 'translator's position' and 'horizon of translation' in order to establish links between the units of analysis identified. Within one of the categories derived from Berman's model, the translator's position, Saldanha identifies another layer of coding. This sub-layer is, again, descriptive and identifies aspects of convergence and divergence among the views expressed by the two translators. The examples in Table 5.1 consist of two units of analysis identified in the interviews, each belonging to a different translator, and is followed by the codes assigned at the three levels described above.

---

[2] Note that sometimes thematic and content analysis can be considered as a type of discourse analysis (see Napier 2011, for example). Here, we consider them as three different methods of analysis.

Source	Interview-Translator 1
Unit of analysis	I mean, you can have oddity in a translation but not an oddity that looks like a translation oddity. If the author uses language in a strange way then you have to find some way of being strange as well but it doesn't have to be the same way.

Level of coding	Code label
1	Views on foreignization
2	Translator's position
3	Aspect of convergence

Source	Interview-Translator 2
Unit of analysis	What I have to do is to try and create a style that is original in English in the way that his style is original in Spanish, so it actually disturbs the reader, out of normal patterns of thinking about language and about narrative and so on.

Level of coding	**Code label**
1	Views on foreignization
2	Translator's position
3	Aspect of convergence

Table 5.1 Examples of coding of semi-structured interview data

Another quite popular technique for carrying out qualitative data analysis is **grounded theory**. Despite the name, this is actually not a theory but a research method, and more specifically a mode of data analysis. It is based on two basic principles. The first is that the data analysis should be based on empirical findings (grounded) and follow a specific sequential coding system. The second is that the analysis should produce some 'theory' as an outcome of the investigation, that is, it needs to go beyond a description of the phenomenon under consideration and propose a coherent and contextualized explanation for it. The best-known aspect of grounded theory is its three-level coding system, consisting of open coding, axial (or theoretical) coding, and selective coding. **Open coding** involves segmenting the data into units of analysis (anything from one line to a short paragraph) and assigning *conceptual* categories to the segments, based both on the data and on the researcher's conceptual knowledge. A key difference with other systems is that categories are abstract and conceptual rather than descriptive, responding to questions such as: What does this piece of data illustrate? What principles underlie these statements? In other words, these categories already involve some interpretation. **Axial coding** involves connecting and grouping these first order concepts into more encompassing concepts that subsume several subcategories. The last stage, **selective coding**, consists of selecting a core category that will be the centrepiece of the theory proposed. This core category needs to be sufficiently abstract to subsume as much of the relevant data as possible. Typically, a core story is selected which is then written up as a proposed 'theory' (with explanatory power), by contextualizing it within the existing literature. Grounded theory was used in the project 'Health Care Interpreter Services: Strengthening Access to Primary Care' which was mentioned above as an example of research using unstructured interviews (Clifford 2004). One of the main objectives of the project was to understand the ways in which healthcare services were being provided to people in Canada who have limited knowledge of English or French. Clifford (2004) focuses on only one aspect of the project and does not describe the full coding process, but it is interesting to see how the themes evolve throughout the iterative process. Clifford explains that three themes were first extracted inductively from the interviews with participants involved in the provision of interpreting services. The emerging themes were the low status of community interpreters, the state of community interpreting as a profession and the issue of bringing practitioners on board. This third topic, which reflected managers and interpreters' concerns with collaboration from the healthcare professionals, guided a second stage of the analysis, focusing on interviews with healthcare professionals. Here, the researchers identified two main positions taken by the informants: those who expect interpreters to act as a neutral 'conduit', transferring information faithfully from practitioner to patient, and those who expected interpreters to act as part of the same team, providing expertise in a different area. The 'theory' developed in the context of the study reported in Clifford (2004) concerns how healthcare professionals evolve from one view to the other, and is discussed in more detail later in this section as an example of a successful self-reflective account of how conflicting views are integrated into one explanatory framework (the 'theory' in grounded theory terms).

When interpreting semi-structured or unstructured interviews, apart from coding what is *there*, it is useful to look for themes that you expected to find in the answers but are surprisingly *absent* from them. One of the first observations made by Weber *et al* (2005) in their project on the relevance of gender in medical interpreting is that during focus group discussions, neither interpreters nor patients mention the fact that the lexical and grammatical systems of the different languages (French and Albanian) render gender differences in different ways, and this is despite the fact that a period of ten minutes of the discussion was devoted to the importance of gender in the consultations. However, remember that we mentioned above that people can sometimes fail to state the obvious.

As Dörnyei (2007:125) points out, in qualitative research there are no explicit restrictions as to what counts as data, which means that any comments on the topic of the research can be potentially relevant. As a result, one of the difficulties in analyzing qualitative data is knowing where to stop. The concept of **saturation**, which was used in our discussion of sampling, can help us here, where it means that the iterative process stops producing new topics, ideas and categories (*ibid.*:244). This is the point where the researcher can decide what is relevant and sufficient to address the research question. It often means that other possible avenues of research need to be left out as they are beyond the scope of the current project, to be explored at a later date. How quickly the saturation point is reached will depend on how homogenous the sample is – the more homogenous, the quicker the saturation point will be reached.

As our interpretation will ultimately lead to conclusions, a high level of self-reflexivity is recommended at the stage of analyzing the data, whether we have chosen to use thematic analysis, content analysis or grounded theory. Categories will emerge throughout the entire data analysis process and researchers will revise the codes as they progress through the data. At the time of reporting and justifying our decisions, it will be important to remember how decisions were made and on what basis. There are several research aids that can help us to achieve this, such as research diaries, analytical memos and visual data displays, all of which are described in more detail in Chapter 6.

Qualitative data analysis and interpretation is about bringing flexible and insightful order into rather messy data. Because of the nature of the data, we cannot really expect it to always fit into neat categories, but the researcher's interpretation needs to be based on systematic and transparent procedures in order to be convincing. In other words, to apply the post-postivistic concept of validity described in Chapter 2, the researcher needs to demonstrate that the inferences made are justifiable on the basis of the evidence gathered. This, in turn, will depend on the reliability of the research, in particular, on the depend-ability of the data collection and analysis methods.

Two principles of code checking are often used to measure reliability: stability (or intra-coder reliability), which requires that a coder's judgements should not change over time; and reproducibility (or inter-coder reliability), which means that different coders should agree on the coding (see also the discussion in Chapter 4, Section 4.3.3). If it is not possible to have all the data coded by more than one per-son, or twice by the same person, having a small percentage of the data recoded can still provide a good indication of how reliable the coding has been.

Because of the rather messy nature of the data, one of the challenges in qualitative data analysis is how to account for conflicting accounts of similar events. Contradictions often emerge within the discourse of the same participant, as in Torikai's study (2011) described above, where interpreters reported not experiencing difficulties dealing with cultural issues and then went on to report examples of such experiences. In other cases, participants are consistent within their own narratives but we get a range of contradictory views from different participants which are difficult to reconcile. It is worth describing here one such case reported by Clifford (2004) because it also provides an interesting account of how the researcher eventually came to explain the contradictory views. Clifford's research question was "why does the conduit model continue to be promoted as a viable and necessary model for the role of the interpreter?". The responses from healthcare professionals were baffling at first. In Clifford's own words (*ibid.*:107):

> When we looked at our interviews with healthcare practitioners more globally, a confusing picture began to emerge. We seemed to be getting

different responses from different informants, and these responses were often contradictory. "Train interpreters to just repeat what I say and what the patient says," one informant might tell us, while another might indicate that she is "counting on the interpreter to help her understand the patient better." It was difficult to understand these differences, as they did not appear to be related to any easily identifiable variable, such as the informant's age, background, or place of professional practice.

Interestingly, a potential explanation for the contradictory views was offered by one of the participants who was among the last to be interviewed, and who expressed the two opposing stances within the course of the interview. When the apparent contradiction was brought to the participant's attention, he explained it by describing the way in which trust develops among healthcare professionals, across three phases: it starts from a position of lack of confidence when the professionals do not know each other, then moves to relying on the information provided by each other and, finally, ends in being able to ask each other for assistance (*ibid.*:108). When the data obtained in the course of the study was viewed in this new light, the researchers were able to see that it was those healthcare professionals who had little experience working with interpreters who seemed to see interpreters as neutral 'conduits', which seems to suggest that the three-phase process applies to the interaction between healthcare professionals and interpreters more widely. Thus, on the basis of a comment made by one participant, an explanatory framework starts to develop, which through further reflection and theoretical contextualization, becomes the grounded theory presented by the researcher.

5.9   Analyzing quantitative data

Interview and focus-group data are generally qualitative in nature, although structured interviews can be analyzed quantitatively. Questionnaire data might be quantitative (from our closed questions) or qualitative (from our open questions) and so different analysis methods will be required. Here, we focus on the analysis of quantitative data. The data analysis step involves coding and then trying to find relationships between variables that are worth being reported. We will discuss the issue of small or no response below, but first we will focus on the general aspects of data analysis.

During analysis, our focus should be on answering (at least partially) the research questions posed at the outset, or on generating hypotheses that will then be followed up by further research. Questionnaires and structured interviews may consist of multiple questions addressing multiple variables that make up our research construct (recall, as described earlier, how van Dam and Zethsen (2008) operationalized 'translator status' using the four variables of salary, level of education/expertise, visibility/fame and power/influence), but each question should correspond to only one variable (e.g. salary) and each variable will have a range of answers (e.g. different salary ranges), which will need some identification during analysis. This is what is known as **coding in quantitative analysis**: "[a] way of identifying a specific answer or characteristic. It may be numeric or alphabetic" (Matthews and Ross 2010:327). Some responses will be pre-coded, such as the numbers on a Likert scale (1-5, 1-7, or 1-9). Other responses will have to be converted into codes for the purpose of analysis. For example, if you ask participants which languages they translate into and you present them with a list of, say, ten languages from which to choose, each language would be assigned a numeric code from 1-10 for the purpose of analyzing the responses. If questions have been skipped, a special code can be assigned to such a response (e.g. '99').

For the analysis of quantitative data, descriptive statistics are often used, as well as inferential statistics. Descriptive statistics allow us to understand and report our data in terms of minimum and maximum values, means, medians and modes, standard deviations, frequencies and distributions. There is not a strong tradition of statistical analysis in translation studies research. However, if we seek quantitative data, then we have to perform analyses that are appropriate to such data. Simply reporting the 'average' value is not sufficient, and even the seemingly simple concept of 'average' is not without its complications (see Rasinger 2008:113-23 for a detailed discussion). While we do discuss some of the more important statistical measures relating to quantitative data in this section, the overview is necessarily brief, and it is recommended that readers consult more comprehensive guides for a more detailed picture: for example, Rasinger (2008) and Woods *et al* (1986).

The main challenges arising out of questionnaire and structured-interview data analysis are:

- Inappropriate questions
- Very small samples
- Incomplete data
- Inconsistent or conflicting data

The first problem occurs when we have asked questions that do not contribute to answering our research question. Having concentrated on a questionnaire design that specifically focuses on the research question, we should hopefully not be faced with data that do not necessarily contribute to answering our question.

Small samples are useful for pilot testing a questionnaire, generating hypotheses for further research or following up on qualitative research with a quantitative stage. However, as we have already explained, a small or convenience sample is generally not ideal for drawing conclusions that are applicable to larger populations. This should be kept in mind while we are analyzing data. Moreover, as mentioned above, some statistical measures are predicated on there being 'normal distribution' of data, which, although not impossible with a small sample, is not very likely.[3]

---

[3] Rasinger (2008) has a good chapter on this entitled 'Analysing Dodgy Data: When things are not quite normal'.

For many reasons, some participants may not answer all questions and we are then faced with the dilemma of having to eliminate one participant's response from the data analysis, reducing our response rate, or including it and risking a reduction in the validity and reliability of our conclusions. This is, however, mostly problematic for questionnaires using Likert scales to compute an overall score for a single construct. Good questionnaire design should hopefully result in a questionnaire where questions are not inappropriate, irritating or frustrating to such an extent that participants skip them. Also, our sampling and ethical considerations should allow us to target an appropriate sample who will not abandon ship half way through! Nonetheless, we might still be faced with a lack of response. We have given a pragmatic suggestion above for the coding of non-responses ('99') and this is perhaps the best we can do in the face of non-responses. However, if a large number of participants skipped the same question(s), we need to ask ourselves why that might be and reflect on it during data analysis and reporting.

Another issue we might be faced with during data analysis is how to reconcile inconsistent, conflicting or 'don't know' responses. In Section 5.3 we have discussed how to design questions so as to avoid the human tendency of giving a non-committed response. Of course, there are very legitimate cases where participants might be unsure about a response, but large-scale 'don't know' values are quite uninformative for the researcher and should be avoided. Conflicting responses are quite common, as seen in the discussion of qualitative data above. In relation to questionnaire data, we have also mentioned Pavlovič's (2007) dilemma above. Van Dam and Zethsen (2008:87) were also faced with some conflicting responses when core employees assessed translation as needing a 'fairly high level of expertise' but also rated it as being 'relatively highly associated with secretarial work'. As the above-mentioned researchers propose, one solution for unravelling such contradictions is by following up with interviews, something that obviously demands a significant amount of commitment from the participants.

We have already highlighted the measures of **central tendency** that are frequently used for questionnaire data, i.e. mean, median, mode, minimum and maximum values. We can of course delve deeper into statistical analysis, if this is appropriate: there are a number of statistical concepts and tests that can be applied to quantitative data from questionnaires, which are presented here briefly.

For some **statistical tests**, such as tests of significance (see below), it is important to take into account the shape of the data distribution around the central tendencies. **Normal distribution** occurs when data are "distributed symmetrically around the mean point in a 'bell shape'" – also called a 'bell curve' (Matthews and Ross 2010:353); see Figure 5.1. In such a distribution, mean, median and mode are all at the central point. However, in translation studies research, where small samples or case studies are more common than in other areas such as psychology, for example, data are often not distributed normally. The data (and the bell curve) may be skewed to the left or to the right and the mean, median and mode are all different values. The lack of normal distribution has implications for the statistical tests that can be run on the data to test for the significance of the results (see below) as many tests assume that data are normally distributed.

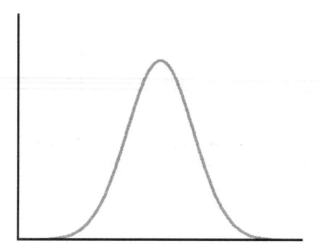

Figure 5.1 Example of bell curve in normal distribution

Related to the concept of normal distribution is that of **standard deviation**, which is "a measure of the dispersion of the cases around the mean" (Matthews and Ross 2010:354). The standard deviation is easily calculated using tools such as Excel and is an important piece of information because it shows us how dispersed the data set is. The lower the standard deviation, the less dispersed the data are from the mean. The higher the standard deviation, the greater the data dispersion. This gives us a feeling for how 'spread out' or 'close together' our individual values are. When values are very spread out it is difficult to speak of clear trends or tendencies.

Cumulative frequency tables can be used to describe data in more detail. In such a table, values are divided into groups of four equal parts (a band of values ranging from the lowest to the highest band, called quartiles), five parts (quintiles) or even ten parts (deciles). Dividing data in this way enables us to make descriptive statements about the lowest performers and the highest performers in our data set. For example, if we are investigating the income of professional translators, we could rank our answers into the first 25% (or fourth quartile for lowest income), the next 25% is the third quartile, the next is the second quartile, and so on. In comparison with just reporting the mean value, this distribution into cumulative frequencies gives us a much more detailed view of our data. We could then examine the inter-relation – a process known as cross-tabulation – between years of experience with income per quartile going from lowest to highest. Another example from translation research is Guerberof's analysis of processing times for post-editors working with 'new' sentences (no match), translation memory (TM) matches and machine translation (MT) matches. Since the averages did not allow her to analyze the processing speeds in sufficient depth, she includes data from the first and third quartiles to perform a deeper analysis; see Table 5.2.

Post-Editor	New	MT	TM
Mean	27.05	21.37	23.64
Median	27.81	23.63	24.88
Standard Deviation	11.37	7	7
Max	45.28	29.23	32.68
Min	12.00	12.35	14.28
Range	33.28	16.88	18.40
1st Quartile	19.71	13.67	17.66
3rd Quartile	33.44	27.25	27.44
Diff Quartiles	13.73	13.59	9.78

Table 5.2. Example of quartile data: From processing times measurement in Guerberof (2008:38)

In Section 5.4 above, we discussed sampling and sampling errors and mentioned that when entire populations cannot be sampled we should be prepared to report our confidence levels vis-à-vis our results. Two measures can be reported in this regard: the confidence interval and the confidence level. The **confidence interval** is the expected margin of error. This is reported as 'plus or minus x%'. For example, we can state that a result is accurate to within a range of plus or minus 4%. The **confidence level** indicates how sure we are that our result is accurate. For survey research, a confidence level of 95% is usually acceptable. We could state, for example, that we are 95% confident that the result is accurate. A confidence level of 85% indicates that we are a lot less sure about accuracy of our results. Similarly, if we have a confidence interval of plus or minus 20%, it implies that our results could be off by this rather large amount. It is beyond the scope of this book to discuss the statistical formula used for calculating confidence intervals, which includes the sample mean, the sample standard deviation, the sample size and a value pertaining to the desired confidence level. However, detailed information about the calculation of the confidence interval can be found in the books on statistics mentioned above (Woods *et al* 1986:96-99; Rasinger 2008:160), among others.

While the measures of central tendency tell us something about our results and their differentiation into cumulative frequency tables gives us a more detailed picture, none of these give any indication of the *reliability* of those results. It is quite common to read reports of questionnaire data (as well as quantitative data generated via other instruments) that make claims such as 'there was a significant difference between variable X and variable Y'. In such contexts, 'significant' usually means 'substantial' or 'large'. However, how large the difference is remains subjective to the researcher and provides no indication of the reliability of the results. To make claims about reliability, we are obliged to go beyond subjective judgement and to resort to specific statistical tests. The term 'statistical significance' is used to indicate the reliability of quantitative results, in other words, how *probable* it is that the results happened by chance. As Rasinger puts it (2008:159):

> Significance in statistics refers to the probability of our results being a fluke or not; it shows the likelihood that our result is reliable and has not just occurred through the bizarre constellation of individual numbers.

Statistical significance is expressed in terms of a 'p-value' which represents the *probability that our results happened by chance*. The lower the p-value, the more confident we can be that our results did not occur just by chance. A p-value of equal to or lower than 0.05 is generally considered acceptable but in the hard sciences researchers would aim for p-values close to or below 0.01.

A variety of tests can be used to calculate statistical significance; their full description is beyond the scope of our discussion here. The array of tests can be baffling, especially for researchers who have little or no training in such matters. However, with some investment in time one can learn and understand what each test is appropriate for and the effort is generally worth it. Which test should be applied is generally dependent on two factors: (1) the type of data collected, and (2) whether the data are normally distributed.

When data are nominal or ordinal (see Chapter 2, Section 2.7), a **Chi-squared test** (denoted by 'X^2') can be applied to test for statistical significance. The Chi-squared test is "essentially based on the comparison of the observed values with the appropriate set of expected values" (Rasinger 2008:145). It compares the recorded frequencies against a set of *expected* frequencies and calculates the probability that the recorded frequencies occurred by chance. The usual starting point is the Null Hypothesis (see Chapter 2, Section 2.5), that is to say, the assumption that there is *no* difference between the expected and actual frequencies. The aim is to determine whether we can reasonably *reject* the Null Hypothesis by testing the probability that our results occurred by chance. If the Chi-squared test returns a result of p<0.05, this means that the probability that our results occurred by chance is less than 0.05 (or 5%) and, with such a level of probability, we can fairly confidently reject the Null Hypothesis and claim a statistically significant result.

To illustrate further, imagine that our questionnaire recorded whether respondents were male or female and whether they used translation technology in their daily work. Our results might tell us that 70% of the female translators use translation tools daily, while 50% of the male translators do so.[4] We can immediately

---

[4] Note that we are talking about percentages here but the Chi-squared test is run on the raw frequencies recorded, not on overall percentages.

see that there is a difference, but is the difference statistically significant? Our Null Hypothesis is that there is no difference in the rate of translation technology use between male and female translators. Imagine our Chi-squared test returns a value of p=0.01. This means that the probability that these results occurred by chance is only 1% (i.e. very low), so we can confidently reject the Null Hypothesis and claim a statistically significant difference in the use of translation technology between the male and female translators in our sample.

Other tests work according to the same basic principles. **ANOVA** (or Analysis of Variance) is used for nominal data, while **paired t-tests** are used on ratio or interval data for paired groups with *normal distribution*, and the **Wilcoxon signed-rank** or **Mann-Whitney U-tests** (for example) are used for data that are not normally distributed (non-parametric data).

We might also be interested in reporting the correlations between two variables and, specifically, the direction of the relationship (negative or positive) and the strength of the relationship (strong, moderate, weak). For this type of report, we will need to make use of **Pearson's product moment correlation coefficient** (when data are normally distributed) or **Spearman's rank correlation** rho (when data are not normally distributed or the sample is smaller than 20) (Matthews and Ross 2010:368). As previously mentioned, both of these values can be calculated using Excel or other statistical analysis software programs.

As mentioned previously, both Pearson's r and Spearman's rho return a value of between -1 and +1 with a value of -1 indicating a highly negative correlation between two variables, a value of +1 indicating a highly positive correlation, and a value of 0 indicating no correlation. As described above, we have to report p-values along with Pearson's r and Spearman's rho to indicate the probability of the results occurring by chance.

Imagine that, in a questionnaire, we collected data on the year in which a participant graduated from a translator training programme and the extent of use of translation technology. Our null hypothesis would be that there is no correlation between these two variables. However, our alternative hypothesis is that more recent graduates would demonstrate a higher level of adoption of translation technology, because technology training is now better incorporated into translator training programmes. Imagine now that Pearson's r returned a value of r=0.90, p=0.05; this means that there is a strong positive relation between year of graduation and rate of technology use (the more recent the year, the higher the use of technology) and there is only a 5% chance that these results occurred by chance, so we are 95% confident about our result.

Reporting values such as confidence levels, correlations and so on can give a more detailed and convincing report on questionnaire results. However, it is important to point out that such measures do not tell us anything about *causality* (for a more in-depth discussion of causality see Chapter 2, Section 2.10.3 on causal mechanisms and causal effects, and Chapter 1, Section 1.3). In the example above, we can speculate that it is the increased focus on translation technology in translator training programmes that *caused* the higher rate of use of translation tools among more recent graduates. However, other factors might also be at play here, such as demands from employers or clients, marketing campaigns, peer influence, and so on. The cause of relationships between variables cannot be determined through statistical analysis, and this is where the qualitative analysis of open-ended responses or the use of other explanatory instruments is vital in order for the researcher to reach a more complete understanding of the factors at play.

5.10 Data analysis in mixed methods research

So far in this chapter we have discussed questionnaires as a mainly quantitative method and interviews and focus groups as a mainly qualitative method. In this section, we offer examples of how both quantitative and qualitative data can be combined when using questionnaires, interviews and focus groups as research instruments. Integrating both quantitative and qualitative data is generally seen as a way of combining the best of both paradigms and overcoming their weaknesses (much of what was discussed in relation to qualitative and quantitative textual data in Chapter 3 is also relevant here). A combination of questionnaires and interviews, for example, is most productive when we are interested at the same time in both the exact nature (qualitative) of a phenomenon and its distribution (quantitative) (Dörnyei 2007:45); for example, to answer a question such as 'why are professional translators so dismissive of translation theory and how extensive is the perception that it is of no use to the profession?'

Alternatively, mixed methods can be used purely for triangulating purposes, as a way of corroborating findings so as to ensure validity. The problem, as Dörnyei (2007:163) points out, is that we may well find out that our results do *not* converge, in which case we cannot speak of triangulation but can still explore the results fruitfully in order to problematize our assumptions and open up new avenues for research.

In terms of research design, a range of mixed methods typologies have been proposed according to two organizational principles: the sequence in which the methods are used and their dominance (see Creswell *et al* 2003 for a comprehensive overview). Focusing on sequence and in very general terms we can distinguish three different designs. The first is a **sequential** approach whereby qualitative data collection and analysis is undertaken first, followed by quantitative data collection and analysis (or vice versa). The second is the use of **concurrent** strategies, which involve data collection using both quantitative and qualitative approaches simultaneously, for example when a questionnaire contains both closed and open-ended questions. Finally, **transformational** strategies, as the name suggests, involve transforming one type of data into another.

A sequential approach where quantitative methods are used before qualitative ones often takes the form of quantitative data being used to identify candidates that fulfill certain conditions for interviews, so that certain cases can be explored in more depth. This may or may not be a planned outcome of the research. Sometimes the results of quantitative data point to extreme cases (see Chapter 6, Section 6.4.1), where values stand out as particularly inconsistent with a dataset, which are then submitted to further, more intensive qualitative analysis to understand the reasons for the deviance. Qualitative approaches can also be used to supplement quantitative results when these may allow us to establish a relationship but may reveal little about the nature of the relationship, so follow-up interviews can explore questions of how and why (see Chapter 2, Section 2.10.3).

This type of sequential approach was adopted in Mirlohi *et al* (2011), in a study designed to measure the degree to which trainee translators experienced 'flow' in the process of translating texts from three different genres. 'Flow', a concept developed by Csikszentmihalyi (1975, in Mirlohi *et al* 2011:252), describes an optimal learning experience "characterized by a skills-challenge balance and by a person's interest, control, and intense focus" (*ibid.*). In the first place, the degree of flow experienced by a group of fifty-six students was measured quantitatively by a questionnaire consisting of 14 items in the Likert format. Students then filled in an open-questions questionnaire and, for further corroboration that scores measured by questionnaires were indeed indicative of the students' experience, four of the students were interviewed. The students interviewed were chosen on the following basis: one male participant was selected randomly, a female participant was selected because she had flow scores with minimum distance between them, one was chosen for his lowest flow score on the narrative, and another participant for her highest flow score on the descriptive text. Mirlohi *et al* (2011) do not specify whether interviews were structured or not. The quantitative results show that flow was experienced for only one of the three translation tasks, and data from the open-ended questionnaire and the interviews supported the numerical data. Analysis of the open-ended questionnaires and interviews brought to the fore the issues that students might have experienced as barriers to flow, such as topic, level of language, individual students' interests and linguistic characteristics of the texts.

Mirlohi *et al* (*ibid.*:256) explain that the reasons for supplementing quantitative with qualitative data is that "using recalls as the only source of data supplies only self-report data that may or may not reflect participant's [sic] true experiences". The fact that recall is prompted in three different ways may help to strengthen validity but only to a certain extent, since all instruments still rely on recall. However, it is clear that the qualitative data in this case were crucial in identifying the reasons why a certain text was more flow inducing than others, something that the researchers would not have been able to explore on the basis of the first questionnaire.

A typical example of sequential methodology in the opposite direction, where a qualitative study precedes a quantitative one, is when qualitative interviews are used to formulate hypotheses and establish key categories, which are then tested using quantitative methods applying the categories developed in the first part of the research. For example, if we were to study readers' preconceptions about translation, we could start with a focus group study trying to identify some key preconceptions and then do a large survey to see how widespread those preconceptions are. The study by Clifford (2004) described above concludes by suggesting that future research could take the form of a survey using a representative sample of healthcare practitioners in order to discover whether practitioners are generally in agreement with the three-phase process of trust-building between healthcare professionals and interpreters which was used to explain the results from his own qualitative investigation.

Concurrent methods, where both quantitative and qualitative data are collected simultaneously, are particularly useful to examine phenomena that have several levels or involve different populations that need to be approached differently. An example is provided by Bourdieu (2008), in the study mentioned above, where interviews were used together with statistics gathered from archives and publishing houses, in order to map the structure of the literary publishing field in France. Five groups of variables (a total of sixteen) were used to carry out a multiple correspondence analysis (MCA). The five categories of variables were: legal and financial status (e.g. company size, legal status), financial or commercial dependency on other publishers (investment in other publishers, distributors), weight on the market (books appearing in bestsellers lists, ability to obtain national prizes), symbolic capital (publisher of Nobel Prize winner, foundation date) and importance of foreign literature (percentage of translated titles, source language). The results are presented in a 'map' that locates the publishing houses along an axis that represent these groups of variables. This statistical analysis is supplemented by a discussion presenting more detailed, narrative profiles of certain agents who stand out in the field because they represent extreme positions, such as the (male) CEO with no literary background whatsoever and little in terms of formal education who runs a purely market-driven business attempting to reach the widest possible readership, and the (female) owner of a small publishing house "condemned to literature virtue", who has extensive literary knowledge but no powerful contacts (Bourdieu 2008:138).

Data transformation can involve either **quantitizing** or, less frequently **qualitizing** data (Dörnyei 2007). Quantitizing data means producing numerical tabulations of certain aspects of qualitative data, for example in the form of scores (how many times a theme comes up). While words and themes and concepts can be counted, it is more difficult to transform numbers into the kind of rich interpretation typical of qualitative research without risking over-interpretation. Dörnyei (2007:271) suggests two legitimate ways in which quantitative data can be used to produce qualitative results. The first involves using data from questionnaires collecting demographic information (age, gender, etc.) about the participants and integrating them into qualitative accounts of the interviews/focus groups. The second involves using the answers to questionnaires to develop a narrative profile of certain participants, as a way of developing a fuller understanding of a person and their responses.

Quantitizing is generally used as a useful way of reporting results in qualitative studies in a precise manner, indicating, for example, the frequency with which a specific theme occurs and its distribution or relationship with other variables (also called 'cross-tabulations' – e.g. relationship between a specific attitude and nationality or age group). These figures can be indicative of potential patterns but are not, in themselves, grounds for generalizing (unless, of course, the sample was representative of a certain population). This technique is used by Napier (2011) for the content analysis of focus-group data. As mentioned earlier, the aim of the study was to elicit stakeholders' (interpreters, hearing and deaf consumers) attitudes towards sign-language interpreting. Napier devised a list of 15 key lexical items (attitude, challenge, problem, trust, comfort (comfortable), understand, need, professional, flexible, quality, standard, communication, language, culture, role) and using qualitative analysis software (see Chapter 6, Section 6.6.3), obtained frequency counts of these items to indicate areas requiring further qualitative content analysis. The discussion then centred on the five lexical items that were most frequently mentioned.

As stressed throughout this book, the choice of method should be appropriate to the research question. The framing of the research question, however, is in part shaped by the epistemological stance of the researcher; some researchers are interested in questions that can be answered in a particular manner. Quantitative researchers may hold the view that the questions asked in qualitative research are too context specific and possibly uninteresting because they cannot be generalized. For their part, qualitative researchers may view the kind of questions used in quantitative research as overly simplistic and decontextualized. We hope that this brief section on mixed methods will have demonstrated that combining methods may offer creative possibilities for addressing research questions from different angles.

5.11 Summary

In this chapter we discussed research methods that are useful for the investigation of the participants in the translation process, focusing specifically on the use of questionnaires, interviews and focus groups. We discussed issues of validity and generalizability in relation to these methods, contextualizing the discussion within a quantitative framework in the case of questionnaires and within a qualitative framework in the case of interviews and focus groups. We stressed, however, the advantages of combining these approaches where possible and discussed ways in which this could be done in the section on mixed methods.

As already mentioned, questionnaires and interviews are methods to which we are exposed in our daily lives and this familiarity sometimes leads researchers to think that they are more straightforward than they really are, at least in a research context. We highlighted the importance of ensuring that the research question is properly conceptualized and operationalized within questions in questionnaires, or in structured or semi-structured interviews or, indeed, within plans for focus groups. We discussed issues of language, both in terms of the choice of language for questionnaires and interviews and in terms of formulating questions. The benefits of running a pilot test, where possible, were also highlighted, and so were the difficulties of recruiting participants and obtaining representative samples. We looked at different techniques for analyzing data and suggested ways in which statistics can be used to report quantitative data. Finally, but importantly, ethical considerations pertaining to the administration of questionnaires and the conducting of focus groups and interviews, in particular the power relations between researcher and participant, were identified.

Chapter 6. Context-oriented research: Case studies

6.1   Introduction

Most translation studies research today claims to pay attention to context. Koskinen notes that "[i]t has rather become a truism to say that translations do not take place in a vacuum, that they need to be interpreted and evaluated in their relevant context" (2008:72). A novel development, however, has been the use of ethnographic models that take a more material approach to the notion of context and consider more mundane physical settings in addition to the textual and ideational contexts. The focus in this chapter is on how to investigate external factors affecting individual translators, the circumstances in which translations take place and how translations influence the receiving culture. Examples include political, economic, social and ideological factors, such as the impact of state censorship on translations or how the reception of translations is influenced by a particular intellectual or economic climate.

Context-oriented research falls within what Marco (2009) calls the culturalist and sociological models. The first is described as aiming to uncover "the complex social, political, cultural and ideological forces which shape translation practices" (2009:15). The second has similar aims, the main difference between them being the disciplines they draw on – cultural studies in the first case and sociology in the second – and the fact that methods employed in cultural studies are more eclectic. Marco claims that "unlike scholars in the DTS paradigm, those working within the culturalist approach aim to go beyond description and uncover the socio-economic and political motives hidden behind norms" (*ibid.*:26). However, as stated in Chapter 1, we do not believe in a clear-cut distinction between descriptive and explanatory research. Any research that attempts to place a certain phenomenon in context, even though its main aim may be descriptive, will inevitably establish links between different factors influencing that phe-nomenon and in that way will create a descriptive model that prioritizes certain explanations over others.

Two important characteristics of cultural studies research are its engaged, political nature and its rejection of the ideal that scientific research leads to the creation of objective knowledge of social reality. Partly because of the abstract and eclectic nature of its object of study and partly because of the philosophical principles underlying theoretical thinking in cultural studies, which has been heav-ily influenced by poststructuralism and postmodernism, there is no one method or group of methods that can be said to be characteristic of this discipline. In fact, some cultural studies scholars simply reject the idea of methods. Saukko cites the example of Savigliano (1995:14, in Saukko 2003:182), who argues that "these 'tools' alienate intellectual workers from their labour and politics". However, this does not mean that these scholars do not follow certain methodologies, in the sense that they conform to research practices that are informed by certain ontological and epistemological assumptions (see Chapter 2).

Sociology is a discipline with a long-standing tradition which has developed a variety of research methods, many of which have also been used in translation studies (see Chapter 5 for examples). However, in terms of context-oriented research, the impact of sociology has been felt not so much in terms of research methodology but in the conceptual frameworks and explanatory procedures borrowed from that discipline. Pierre Bourdieu, Bruno Latour and Niklas Luhman are probably the most influential examples of recent applications of sociological approaches in translation studies (Inghilleri 2005b, 2009b).

Although the disciplines that have traditionally informed context-oriented research in translation studies are cultural studies and sociology, there is work in a much wider range of disciplines, including political science, anthropology and psychology, that is relevant to the study of contextual factors in translation. It is not possible within the scope of this book to describe all the methodologies that could potentially be used to account for contextual aspects of translation; we have chosen to focus on the case study method because of its popularity among all the disciplines mentioned above and because of its flexibility in terms of drawing on a wide range of sources of data.

According to Susam-Sarajeva (2009), case studies are the most common method used in postgraduate research in translation studies. This is probably because 'case study' is often used as a label to describe any study focusing on a single unit of investigation. However, 'case study' also describes a particular research method and, in the interest of consistency, we will only use the term when that particular method has been used. Susam-Sarajeva also notes that the use of case studies in translation studies is characterized by a significant lack of discussion about their characteristics and requirements, which suggests the method is "taken for granted" *(ibid.:*37). In fact, looking at the publications that claim to be case studies, the almost complete absence of documentation in terms of procedures for data collection and analysis may lead to the mistaken impression that this is a free-form research method. However, despite allowing a certain degree of flexibility, the case study does have some important requirements, and carrying out a good case study is not an easy task, as this chapter will attempt to demonstrate.

Throughout this chapter we use three pieces of research for illustrative purposes: Koskinen (2008), Susam-Sarajeva (2006) and Sturge (2004). These three studies are introduced here briefly and then referred to as the need arises. Koskinen (2008) focuses on the Finnish translation unit at the European Commission as a case study of translation in an institutional setting. Susam-Sarajeva explores the role of translation in the 'travelling' of literary and cultural theories across linguistic and cultural borders. She focuses on two cases, the work of Roland Barthes and of Hélène Cixous, in two different contexts of reception (Turkey and Anglo-America). Sturge examines different attitudes of the Nazi regime to translation and relates these to translation practice from 1933 to 1944, in terms of the range of texts translated as well as the translation strategies applied.

6.2   Definition of case study

Gillham (2000:1) defines a *case* as "a unit of human activity embedded in the real world; which can only be studied or understood in context; which exists in the here and now; that merges in with its context so that precise boundaries are difficult to draw". Yin defines the *case study* as "an empirical inquiry that investigates a contemporary phenomenon in depth and within its real-life context, especially when the boundaries between the phenomenon and context are not clearly evident" (2009:18). There are a number of overlapping characteristics in these two definitions, which suggests that what distinguishes this method from others are those aspects that make a 'case' a rather unique unit of investigation. Note the emphasis on contextualization and a real-life setting. It is these aspects that make the case study so appropriate for what we call context-oriented studies. The above definitions serve to differentiate the case study from other methods such as the experiment, where a phenomenon is studied under controlled conditions and deliberately divorced from its context so that attention can be focused on a few, clearly defined variables; and from textual analysis, where there is a clearer boundary between the object of enquiry and its context. Historical research, like case study research, exercises no control over the events it focuses on and also requires the examination of a wide range of sources (for a fuller discussion of researching translation history, see Pym 1998). Both Yin and Gillham make a clear point of restricting case studies to contemporary events, and Yin suggests that this is the main distinction between historical and case study research. According to Yin, historical research is the obvious choice when events are in "the 'dead' past – that is, when no relevant persons are alive to report, even retrospectively, what occurred, and when an investigator must rely on primary documents, secondary documents, and cultural and physical artefacts as the main sources of evidence" (2009:11). The case study, on the other hand, has access to techniques such as direct observation and systematic interviewing which are not available in historical research. However, here we take a different view from Yin and Gillham, in that we see no reason why the case study cannot be used in studying historical phenomena and be considered a method within the broader field of historical research. Two of the studies used here for illustrative purposes, Susam-Sarajeva (2006) and Sturge (2004), focus on historical events.

As we will see below, a crucial step in designing a case study is to establish boundaries to the unit of analysis, i.e. the case. This need underlies a key aspect of the definition of 'case': it should be a real-life phenomenon, not an abstraction such as a topic, an argument, or a hypothesis (Yin 2009:32). On the basis of the above definitions we can establish that a case can be anything from an individual person (translator, interpreter, author) or text (note that text fragments cannot be cases because of the requirement of contextualization), to a whole organization, such as a training institution or a translation agency, and even a literary system. A case can also be a process or an event. For example, a case study may look at the process of training, in whichever way you want to delimit that process, for example, from the moment a student is registered on a translator training course to the moment where they enter the job market. An event can be a particular historical moment, the onset of a war, the election of a president, a change in legislation, all of which will trigger a series of translations or a change in translation policy. It should be noted, however, that a case study also requires some form of conceptual structure. We cannot choose an institution or an event as the *aim* of our analysis; the study needs to be organized around research questions or issues. So, rather than studying 'an institution' we choose to study 'how the introduction of new technology affects the translation output and working environment within an institution'.

Another useful way of identifying what constitutes a case is describing what a case is not. A case is not a sample or an example (Susam-Sarajeva 2009). A sample is a small part of a group that is taken to be representative of the whole group, and therefore studying the sample allows the researcher to make inferences about the whole group (see the discussion on sampling methods in Chapter 2). An example is a single instance that is used to illustrate what is typical of a more general group or rule; therefore, using examples requires the prior identification of a group (of people, texts, strategies, etc.) that shares certain characteristics, or of a norm, a behaviour that tends to occur given certain circumstances. The example is used when constraints of space or time do not allow for a description of the whole group or several instances of the norm in action. Cases, on the other hand, are complete and interesting on their own merit. They are, in one way or another, a unit that is part of a larger population (of translations, translators, training institutions, literary systems) and we investigate them because we are interested in that population. However, the case study is not carried out with the assumption that it will enable us to generalize the results to the larger group of which the case forms a part.

Before we move on to explain when and how to use case studies, a final clarification is needed on the difference between case study and **ethnography**. Above, we described case studies as a method where novel ethnographic approaches can be applied. However, ethnography and case studies are traditionally different methods, even though they are closely related and the terms are now sometimes used interchangeably (White *et al* 2009). Ethnography is "a holistic study of a particular culture, or community, and the aim is to attend to both the everyday details and routine text production as well as to the wider social context" (Koskinen 2008:37). The term also includes the writing that emerges from the fieldwork data (Madden 2010:34). Traditionally, an ethnography required the direct observation of human behaviour within a particular 'culture' to allow the researcher to understand social reality from the perspective of those belonging to that culture; for this purpose, a persistent and prolonged immersion in the everyday activities of the participants was recommended practice (Starfield 2010). However, some contemporary ethnographies can exclude observation altogether and work on the basis of written documents or qualitative interviews, and even virtual ethnographies are possible (Hine 2000). In other words, ethnography has ceased to be a clearly defined method: the term refers to a methodological approach where multiple sources of data and techniques of analysis are acceptable, and this is where the boundaries with the case study start to blur. Both case studies and ethnographies share a holistic philosophy according to which human behaviour is best understood as lived experience in the social context, and both involve gathering rich, detailed data in an authentic setting. Some may argue that the difference is more theoretical or paradigmatic than practical: the case study belongs to a more conservative or postpositivist tradition (Guba and Lincoln 2005), where issues of validity, reliability and objectivity are still at stake, while ethnography belongs to a postmodernist paradigm where the experience of the researcher is formative of the research process (see Chapter 2). In practical terms, the distinction is not always clear cut but we can still say that there is a difference in focus. The cornerstone of the ethnographic approach is the methods of inquiry which require a high degree of personal involvement from the researchers, such as participant observation and ethnographic interviewing. What is crucial in case studies is the specificity and boundedness of the case. Stake (2005:443) goes as far as arguing that case study is defined by "interest in the individual case, not by the methods of inquiry used". The case study therefore uses a more eclectic range of sources and tools, which may or may not include those used in ethnographic research. In this sense, we can talk about case studies that use an ethnographic approach, as Koskinen (2008) does, where the sources favoured are those used in ethnographic research.

In brief, ethnography is understood here as a methodological orientation that can be adopted in case study research as well as used on its own. The distinctive characteristics of this orientation are "engagement with the object of study – going into the field – and a willingness to learn from those who inhabit the culture" (Koskinen 2008:37) as well as a focus on the researcher's personal involvement with the data; in Koskinen's words, "*my* observations, *my* interpretations, *my* knowledge and understanding, as well as *my* personal contacts and *my* skill in eliciting information (and *my* limits in all these) delineate the research" (*ibid.*, emphasis in original).

6.3   When to use case studies

One of the purposes of a case study is to consider elements that are specific to the particular case, and therefore different from all others. Because of the multiple nature of causality, generalization from one piece of research to other cases is always done under the assumption of all other things being equal. In case study research it is difficult to generalize to other cases because the individuality of the case generally prevents us from making assumptions that all things can be equal in a different scenario. Therefore, the case study belongs to the group of qualitative research methods described in Chapter 2 that can make contributions to knowledge beyond the particular in three different scenarios: (1) in exploring questions of *how* and *why*, (2) for hypothesis generating (as opposed to hypothesis testing), and (3) for testing the viability of a theoretical framework.[1]

---

[1] Note that quantitative methods can be used as part of the case study methodology, to investigate one particular aspect of the case, but the generalizability of any statistical results will be limited to that aspect.

When exploring questions of how and why, we often find that mechanisms of causation are far more complex than an abstract probabilistic prediction may suggest. Koskinen (2010:177) warns that while case studies yield interesting results on causal relations, "they also easily entangle the researcher into a complex cobweb of conflicting motivations and interrelations". Koskinen (2008) looks at the mechanisms behind the choice of preliminary and operational norms in institutional translation. She describes how the drafting and translating of EU documents results in shifts that reveal competing tendencies: towards readability on the one hand and towards 'institutionalization' on the other. 'Institutionalization' is understood here as the process of adding complicated, bureaucratic expressions and buzz words with the effect of pushing the role of the institution to the forefront (*ibid.*:131, 141). She also shows how translators favour readability in their practice even though they complain about not being able to take the reader into account. These tensions between the translators' feelings about their work on the one hand and their practice on the other are revealed by triangulating data from a comparative textual analysis of the translations with focus group interviews of the translators.

Susam-Sarajeva (2006) provides an example of the use of case studies to formulate hypotheses in translation theory. She is interested in exploring the role of translation in the 'travelling' of literary and cultural theories across linguistic and cultural borders. Her assumption is that the power differentials at play in each situation influence the reception of theories in the target system. The study enables her to make suggestions as to how the importation of theories may differ from that of, for example, literary texts.

The third scenario where case studies can contribute to general knowledge is when they are used to test the viability of a new model, or in order to test the limits of more established ones. Hanna (2006), for example, uses Arabic translations of Shakespeare's great tragedies in order to explore the possibility of applying the sociological model developed by Bourdieu to the field of drama translation. Paloposki and Koskinen (2004) use a case study of retranslations into Finnish to test the retranslation hypothesis, according to which first translations tend towards domestication and retranslations are closer to the source text. The results falsify the hypothesis, showing that the picture is considerably more complex than predicted.

A case study can also challenge established theories and it may point to the need for a new theory in areas that have not received sufficient scholarly attention. Thus, the application of theory to cases is one way of providing feedback to the theorist, and may lead to additions or modifications to existing theories in order to accommodate puzzling aspects of a case. Researchers often engage in case study research when they have hunches about what modifications could be made to existing theory, or how different findings from those reported in the existing literature could be obtained (Gillham 2000:10).

Gillham (2000:3) argues that the evidence provided by case studies is similar to the evidence used in judicial enquiries. The findings may not be generalizable, but some of the insights may help us, under certain conditions, 'solve' a similar case, as happens in courts or in criminal investigations. In other words, the evidence may be transferable (see Chapter 2, Section 2.10.3). If the context in cases A and B is similar, information about case A may be used to formulate hypotheses as to what factors are responsible for certain characteristics of case B. As explained in Chapter 2, the degree of transferability is a direct function of the similarity between the two contexts, what Lincoln and Guba call 'fittingness' (1979/2000:40).

A case study does not need to be an isolated instance of research: a series of cases can be conducted to construct increasingly plausible and less fortuitous regularity statements (Eckstein 1992/2000:129). Below, we explain the different 'formats' that research using multiple case studies can take. Case studies can also help to identify subjects and insights that are then subsequently explored by larger scale comparative studies from which statistical generalizations may be derived (see discussion of mixed-methods research in Chapter 3).

6.4   Case study design

Case studies have what Gillham (2000:6-7) calls an 'emergent design', which means they are open-ended and flexible in terms of research questions and design; in other words, modifications can be made as the research progresses. There are, nevertheless, some decisions that need to be made in advance, such as whether to focus on one or several cases. Another important decision concerns the boundaries of the case(s) identified. And finally, it is important to have identified the main sources of information on which we will rely, and how these are to be used, before the research starts in earnest. The factors to be considered in making each of those decisions are described below.

6.4.1   *Types of case studies*

A small survey of translation studies research carried out by Susam-Sarajeva (2001) suggests that there is a tendency to focus on one unit of analysis, generally one text. When more than one unit is analyzed, it is often the perceived links and analogues between units that makes them eligible for analysis in the first place; conclusions also highlight similarities (*ibid.*:172). According to Susam-Sarajeva (*ibid.*:173) leaving out differences results in:

> ensuring the material's suitability for testing a given hypothesis, support-ing an argument, or arriving at certain generalizations. Differences that arise from contrastive perspectives are not referred to, because they are either irrelevant for the purposes of the arguments put forward, or (even worse) they would have weakened the argument.

Susam-Sarajeva argues that we should not focus on similarity at the expense of contrastive studies using multiple units of analysis because this precludes the possibility of seeing translation from a wider range of perspectives and "[s]uch comparative and contrastive work may ultimately protect us from easy generalizations derived from single units of analysis" (*ibid.*:175).

Choosing between **single** and **multiple cases** depends on whether the population of existing cases is heterogeneous or homogeneous (Gerring 2007). Data from several similar cases can help us present cumulative evidence about a single phenomenon. Even when using heterogenous cases, the logic of **cross-case analysis** is premised on some degree of cross-unit comparability (unit homogeneity). When adjacent cases are heterogeneous, studying more than one case is 'expensive' in the sense that a wider range of factors may have to be taken into consideration, and harder because it is more difficult to establish meaningful comparisons, since what is relevant in one case may not be relevant in others. However, depending on time and resources, cross-case studies of heterogeneous cases can provide a particularly rich picture. See Glaser and Strauss (2004) for an interesting piece on 'theoretical sampling', i.e. the process of selecting sources for data collection within an emergent theory design.

Susam-Sarajeva (2006) chooses a multiple case study format to explore the role of translation in the importation of literary and cultural theories across linguistic and cultural borders, and across power differentials. The cases in question are the importation of Barthes's works into Turkish and of Cixous's works into English. Although quite close in chronological terms, the cases are separate in spatial terms (see discussion of spatial boundaries below). The reasons why they were chosen initially had to do with the perceived similarities and differences between the two. Among the similarities listed by Susam-Sarajeva are the fact that "[b]oth writers stood in metonymic relationship to entire schools of thoughts" and "both received parallel criticisms because of the prevailing political and cultural agendas in the relevant receiving systems" (*ibid.*:2). Differences included the fact that "attitudes towards language in each case were … very different: in Anglo-America language was not something to be tampered with, while in Turkey it could be actively moulded", and that "the dominance-dependence relationship between the source and receiving systems were [sic] drastically different" (*ibid.*:2).

The cases chosen by Susam-Sarajeva are different enough to make the comparison expensive in terms of the range of sources to be explored, and therefore it is understandable that only two cases are chosen, despite the fact that one of the aims of the study is to address a rather wide gap in the literature on the translation of theories. If we think of a population of cases as in all the important theories ever disseminated across cultures and languages — assuming such a population could indeed be defined — we can see that with such a heterogeneous pool of cases it is impossible to establish *a priori* variables and parameters of similarity that would allow us to conduct reliable large scale studies in any systematic manner. On the other hand, the elements of similarity between the two cases chosen are striking enough to make the comparison worthwhile.

Sometimes it is possible to identify sub-units of analysis, such as several translations of one piece of work, or several individuals constituting a group of translators who share certain characteristics such as a political agenda. In this case we have an **embedded case study**. Sturge (2004), for example, takes into consideration all translations published or censored during the Nazi regime, which forces her to discuss them in very general terms; but she also uses two embedded case studies where she considers certain translations in more detail. One of these is the case of an approved and recommended translation, which allows her to examine in more depth the interaction between evaluative statements and translation strategies. The other focuses on a specific genre that was strongly rejected by the regime: detective novels. This allows her to examine how certain disapproved books escape censorship and to what extent they conform to or subvert the official literary policy.

There are types of cases that, because of their unusual nature, tend to require single case research. These are: extreme cases, deviant cases, crucial or critical cases and revelatory cases. **Extreme cases**, as the term suggests, are those where one aspect is particularly striking (extreme) when compared to similar cases. Sturge describes her study of literary translation under Nazi Germany as "an extreme case of translation's implication in the construction of nationalist literary boundaries" (2004:20), where translation policies required imported literature to "define the *völkisch* specificity of the Germans by a process of contradistinction to the foreign *Volk* of the source" (*ibid*.). **Deviant** cases are those where something unexpected happens. In medicine, researchers are keen to investigate those individuals who, despite repeated exposure to a virus such as HIV, do not become infected. **Revelatory** cases offer an opportunity to investigate a phenomenon previously inaccessible to scientific investigation. These, by their very nature, do not occur very often, but when they do they raise particularly interesting issues.

The **crucial** or **critical case** was introduced to the social sciences by Eckstein in 1975 as one "that *must closely fit* a theory if one is to have confidence in the theory's validity, or, conversely, *must not fit* equally well any rule contrary to that proposed" (1975:18, in Gerring 2007:115). If we have a theory that has specified a clear set of propositions as well as the circumstances within which the propositions are believed to be true, we could identify one case that meets all the conditions. Alternatively, we can identify a scenario where a prediction is least likely to be fulfilled, and reason that if it is fulfilled here, it must be fulfilled elsewhere. This case offers a most difficult test for an argument and thereby provides what is perhaps the strongest sort of evidence in a non-experimental setting. It involves a risky prediction that is highly precise and runs counter to expectations, which is why it is unlikely to be explainable by other causal factors. A frequently cited example is the first important empirical demonstration of the theory of relativity, which took the form of the prediction of a single event in relation to a solar eclipse. Einstein predicted that gravity would bend the path of light toward a gravity source by a specific amount and, as a result, during a solar eclipse stars near the sun would appear displaced, and predicted the amount of apparent displacement. No other theory had made these predictions, and there was no plausible competing explanation for the predicted result, hence the test was strong and gave the theory considerable credibility.

Sometimes cases are not selected because of their unusual nature but, on the contrary, because there is nothing particularly striking about them and they can be considered **typical**. Koskinen, for example, focuses on translation in the European Union institutions as a "prototype case of an institutional setting" (2008:7). Gerring (2007) defines a typical case as one that is representative and can tell us something about the general population. In our view, however, it is extremely unlikely that a 'representative case' can be reliably identified (see also the discussion about translator idiosyncrasies in translation process research, Chapter 4). Large scale research of a comprehensive nature would need to have been conducted in order to establish the defining characteristics of the population, and a fair amount of information about this case would need to be available to establish that it has all those characteristics and nothing else that makes it in any way deviant from that population. Therefore, we would advise refraining from claiming that a case study is representative and from making generalizations on that basis. The research can be designed on the understanding that the conclusions may potentially be true of a larger population, but proceeding with caution and documenting carefully the specificities of the case at hand.

Because of the looseness of the predictions and theories in the humanities and social sciences, one does not commonly find case studies that fit tightly into any of the categories described above (extreme, deviant, critical, revelatory or typical). However, the framework can still be useful because the principles underlying the classification are more general than a brief sketch of case types would lead us to think. In relation to crucial cases, for example, Gerring (2007:119) argues that

> the deductive logic of the 'risky' prediction may in fact be central to the case study enterprise. Whether a case study is convincing or not often rests on the reader's evaluation of how strong the evidence for an argument might be, and this in turn – wherever cross-case evidence is limited or no manipulated treatment can be devised – rests upon an estimation of the degree of 'fit' between a theory and the evidence at hand.

It is also common to find cases where two or more of the categories described above overlap. Koskinen (2008:5) describes her choice of the Finnish translation unit within the European Commission in the following terms:

> For a Finnish researcher, selecting the Finnish translation unit for a case study is a convenient choice, but it also has wider implications. As a non-Indo European language, Finnish can be used as an 'acid test' for the translatability of texts or new terms …. And as a 'small', non-procedural language within the Commission, Finnish represents the majority of the official languages, and joins ranks with all the new languages of the 2004 and 2007 enlargements, none of which can hope to achieve a 'working language' status. There is thus reason to believe that Finnish can function as a typical and telling example.

To sum up, then, when choosing case studies it is important to think about how they are typical of the population we are interested in, or – if they are unusual – how they can challenge or test our assumptions about that population. In many cases, because of time constraints and limited resources, convenience will also play a part in our choices, but it is always important to select a case that is likely to be revealing, on some basis or other. When multiple cases are chosen, it is important to consider the homogeneity or heterogeneity of the population, that is, in what ways they are similar or different. Choosing, for example, two cases that are similar in all respects except the variable of interest allows for an intensive study of that variable.

Before moving to other aspects of case study design, a final cautionary note should be introduced in relation to the choice of case type. Even though cases are not samples, as explained above, the selection can still be more or less biased: we tend to choose cases that will prove our preconceived notions of what translation is or what translators do. A very widespread feeling about translations, even among translation researchers, is that they are not as good as the original. As a result, most studies of translations focus on what translators did wrong or could have done better. Another reason for this bias could be that it is easier to spot translation problems or 'inaccuracies'. These tend to stand out, while all the creative solutions either go unnoticed or attract criticism as a result of their creative nature. This bias, in turn, helps to reinforce the notion that translations are nothing more than poor reproductions of original work. In fact, choosing bad translations to analyze is one way of avoiding risk in our predictions and finding all too predictive results, which seriously undermines the contribution we make to existing knowledge.

6.4.2   Delimiting case studies

Once a type of study has been chosen, it is important to establish clear boundaries for the case or cases identified, or at least for the aspects of the case on which we will focus. We can see this as part of the process of operationalizing our research construct (see Chapter 2). Paradoxically, the fact that cases tend to have blurred boundaries makes it even more important for the researcher to impose certain limits, while acknowledging that this may involve leaving out potentially interesting aspects of the case. Otherwise, as we move on from the core to the periphery of our case and delve further and further into the context of our case, there is a risk that the study will simply never be completed. Indeed, the lack of clear limits is often one of the main reasons why sometimes brilliant research ends up languishing in drawers and never sees publication.

In order to impose limits, it is helpful to think along three dimensions: social, spatial and temporal. **Temporal boundaries** are self-explanatory: we can choose to look at contemporary or historical situations, at translations published in the last ten years or in the first decade of the twentieth century, etc. We can also conduct a study that focuses on a specific moment in time or a longitudinal one that looks at changes over a period of time, for example, following changes in novice translators' behaviour as they become trained.

To establish **social boundaries** it is useful to think in terms of populations of cases, i.e. groups of cases that share the key characteristics that make our case one of a kind, such as literary translators, trainee translators, translation trainers, training institutions, etc. When establishing **spatial boundaries** we can focus on geographical limits, such as particular nations or regions (e.g. the EU, Latin America). However, it is generally more useful to think of the space as a particular (poly)system, in Even-Zohar's terminology, or field, in Bourdieu's terminology. Thus we would consider restricting our study to a particular genre within a nation state, or to types of translation, such as audiovisual translation or machine-aided translation. Often, the system or field is too large to be considered as a whole and some sort of artificial limit needs to be imposed; though artificial, this limit needs to follow rational and transparent criteria.

Koskinen (2008:7) describes how the field of institutional translation is narrowed down, as explained above, to the EU institutions as a "prototypical case". The entire field of EU translation being still far too wide to be covered by one researcher, she then narrows it down to the institution she knows best: the European Commission, and further to the Finnish translation units (which makes sense for a Finnish researcher, see above), and finally to the Luxemburg unit. One document is used to illustrate the drafting and translation processes within one unit, and the translators working in that unit are observed for one week. Koskinen (*ibid.*) acknowledges that "one document and one week represent a minuscule fraction of the work flow of even that one unit, not to mention the entire field of institutional translation", but makes clear that this is a conscious methodological choice driven by the desire to offer a rich and detailed picture observed from multiple viewpoints.

Finally, it is important to identify the main sources of information on which the research will be based, and how these are to be used. For this, a clear aim and a set of clearly operationalized research questions are essential prerequisites (see Chapter 2), since in order to choose sources of information we need to ask how they will help to answer those research questions. It is not unusual that, as we start to interrogate our sources, our expectations of the type of information to be obtained will need revising, which may prompt a rewording of the questions. However, unless we have a clear idea of what we want to find out, we cannot choose how we are going to proceed in terms of collecting data.

Different sources will help illuminate different aspects of the case under study and, here too, we may need to establish some boundaries regarding aspects that require special attention and how much data can be obtained and examined in each case. Sturge (2004) provides a good example in terms of defining clear criteria and documenting the choices made when selecting sources. The temporal boundaries of her case study on translation policy during the Nazi regime were historically determined (1933 and 1944). Spatial (systemic) boundaries were also imposed: only translation of fiction, from any language and published in German. However, analyzing all translated fiction in that period is clearly impossible, so subsets of the data are chosen for detailed analysis. First, a database of published fiction translated into German between 1933 and 1944 is produced and the list of titles is restricted to those advertised in a national bibliography (*ibid.*:47-48). Second, five literary journals are chosen from among over 80 titles in order to explore the official discourse on translation during the Nazi regime (*ibid.*:82-84). Then, one particular translation is chosen as an example of approved translation under the Nazi regime (*ibid.*:126-27). Finally, ten detective novels are randomly selected as illustrative of an officially disapproved genre (*ibid.*:148-68). We could think about the different subsets as building blocks, each looked at through a magnifying glass as a way of constructing a detailed picture of a larger building for which we can only provide an outline.

In sum, when designing a case study it is important to be flexible and re-member that the design may need adjusting as the research progresses. We need to determine whether to look at one or more cases at the same time, and whether there are any sub-cases that may be worth exploring in particular detail. The choice of case needs to be justified; the above list of case types provides a few principles on which we can base our selection criteria. It is important to set some boundaries along social, spatial and temporal dimensions. A clear list of research questions will help us identify the sources of information to be used, by asking how each of those sources will provide answers to the questions. When setting boundaries and choosing sources we want to make sure we cover the topic in enough depth and breadth so as to make our investigation relevant and of general public interest (see also discussion of ethics in Chapter 2). However, it is important to be realistic as to how much can be covered within the time and with the resources available, otherwise we run the risk of producing an unbal-anced piece of research, where one aspect is covered in detail and others are only superficially explored, leaving too many questions unanswered to reach any meaningful conclusions.

6.5   Collecting data

The case study is a broad method which may encompass the use of several types of data gathered and analyzed using different methodologies, both quantitative and qualitative, including all the ones discussed in previous chapters, as well as others. Apart from providing a good way of verifying the reliability of the find-ings emerging from any one of the sources (triangulation), combining multiple sources of data provides a way of compensating for the almost inevitable bias emerging from our sources themselves, be these individual subjects or govern-ment statistics.

The choice of sources will depend on the nature of the research project, the relevance and availability of data from various sources and the skills and background of the researcher(s). Koskinen's case study (2008), for example, presents institutional translation from three vantage points – the institutional setting, the translators, and the translated texts – and uses different sources for each of them. In order to discuss the institutional settings, Koskinen uses official documents as well as ethnographic observation of the physical settings. The translators' perspective is explored using questionnaires and focus groups.

Finally, a comparative study of source texts and translations is used to present a product-oriented perspective.

Below we describe briefly some of the most common types of data used in case studies: written sources, verbal reports, observation, physical artefacts, quantitative data. This list is not exhaustive and many other sources can be used. In previous chapters we discussed in detail how to gather information using questionnaires, interviews and focus groups, verbal reports, keystroke logging, screen recording and eye tracking. We also discussed the use of statistics in analyzing and reporting quantitative survey data (Chapter 5) and methods of text analysis such as discourse analysis (Chapter 3), content analysis and grounded theory (Chapter 5) that can be used to interrogate either pre-existing texts or verbal data elicited through questionnaires, interviews or focus groups. Here, we do not insist on any of the issues previously discussed and focus instead on sources that have not yet been introduced.

6.5.1   Written sources

Texts, and in particular source texts and translations, but also translator's drafts, paratexts (prefaces, footnotes, blurbs) and metatexts (reviews, academic articles) constitute one of the primary sources of information in translation studies research in general, and it is therefore not surprising that case studies of translation are often based almost exclusively on written sources, as is the case in Sturge (2004) and Susam-Sarajeva (2006), who rely mainly on academic sources and translations. This does not mean, however, that the research focuses exclusively on texts rather than, for example, participants. In the case of Sturge (2004) and Susam-Sarajeva (2006), the reliance on written documents is probably due to the historical nature of the research. Susam-Sarajeva, however, does attempt to bring in information about the translators, their biographical details, including their educational background and their professional role in the target systems.

As in any other type of research, a literature review is essential in case studies in order to contextualize our theoretical viewpoint or subject area. In addition, academic literature can be one of our main sources of information (as a type of secondary data, see Chapter 2). In her study of the literary translation system during the Nazi regime, Sturge (2004) contextualizes her case by presenting an overview of the institutions attempting to manage literature in the period using secondary sources, in particular academic work. Note that this is not strictly speaking a literature review but an integral part of the research since information is collated from a range of diverse sources, with different aims in each case. By bringing this information together Sturge charts an area of research that had not been purposefully investigated in any detail prior to her research. Sturge also examines five librarians' journals to provide an overview of state-approved discourses on translation at the time.

Concerning the use of translations *per se*, the analysis can illuminate many different aspects of a case study. Sturge (2004) includes a comparative analysis of several texts where she looks for discrepancies between source and target texts that could be explained by the particular literary and political climate in which the translations were produced. As part of her investigation into EU translation, Koskinen (2008) produced a multi-stage comparative analysis of several drafts of a communication from the EU Commission, as well as the Finnish translations of the last two drafts. The aim was to uncover the institutional factors and interpersonal relations as they were manifested in the shifts of expression between the different draft versions of the original and between the original and the translations. In her case study dealing with the translation of the work of Roland Barthes and Hélène Cixous, Susam-Sarajeva (2006) looks at the problems presented by terminology in the translations and retranslations of texts by these authors, as a way of testing the status and tolerance of the source and receiving systems.

Other types of written sources include documents such as letters, agendas, minutes of meetings, progress reports, etc. commonly used in research focusing on institutions; legal instruments, such as those used in research on court interpreting; syllabi, course specifications, essays, etc. as used in translator training research. Koskinen (2008), for example, makes use of institutional documents which frame and regulate translation work for the European Commission, such as the Staff Regulations of Officials of the European Communities, a White Paper on European Governance, an Action Plan to improve communication by the Commission and selected parts of the web pages of EU institutions.

Sometimes documents are accessed in the form of archival records, which are collected and managed in a systematic manner by an organization. Archives may include most of the documents listed above, but also service records, maps and charts, lists of names, survey data (such as census records), photographs, etc. Public and university libraries usually hold specialist archives, but they are not the only ones. Government departments are another source of written documents (policy, legal statutes, etc.) as well as recordings of conversations (e.g. telephone enquiries). Private companies and organizations may be willing to make available copies of correspondence or audiotapes of telephone calls in exchange for feedback that would complement their own analyses and improve their procedures in several ways.

Archives can be stored in computerized retrieval systems that we may not be able to operate ourselves, or in a format that we may not be familiar with. This is why this type of research needs to be planned carefully in advance; we need to obtain as much information as possible about the archives so as to have a clear idea of what we are going to look for and have a plan in place to make the most of our visit. Among other things, we need a detailed list of questions to guide us while reading the documents to avoid getting easily distracted by less relevant information.[2]

We have seen in this section that written sources can range from translated texts to minutes of meetings and course specifications. These texts can be approached in many different ways. It is useful to recall here the distinction made

---

[2] The University of British Columbia library has a good tutorial on how to conduct archival research: http://www.library.ubc.ca/spcoll/Guides_UBC/Index.html [Last accessed 23 July 2012]

in Chapter 3 concerning the analysis of text as a means to an end or as an end in itself (Baxter 2010). Official documents or texts obtained from archives can be subjected to discourse analysis if we are interested in the discourses these documents reveal, but they can also be used as sources of evidence in themselves. The aim of the analysis of literary librarians' journals in Sturge (2004) is to reveal attitudes in the state-endorsed discourse that are not explicitly stated, and the study thereby benefits from a discourse analytical approach. Other documentary sources used by Sturge, such as indexes of works censored and promoted by the regime, including the national bibliography (*Deutsche Nationalbibliographie*), are used in order to extract information about translations published between 1933 and 1944, and are employed as an end in themselves, for their information value. However, even when using documentary evidence it is important to remember that all documents, even official records, do not contain unmitigated truths. Documents are often edited before being released to the public, and they are written for some other purpose than research and some other audience than the case study researcher. We therefore can never be totally sure of the reliability of the data collection procedures followed by the organizations in charge, who also have their own agenda and targets to meet by compiling the reports (think, for example, of crime statistics by law enforcement agencies). Sturge (2004) points out that some of the gaps in the national bibliography mentioned above occur as a result of ideological biases. The bibliography was the main source of information for the book trade, and it could therefore be used in the interest of censorship, by omitting information on undesirable titles. In sum, it is important to consider documents in their context, taking into account who wrote them and for what purpose.

6.5.2   *Verbal reports*

Interviews (described in detail in Chapter 5) are another staple of case study research. Most commonly, case study interviews are semi- or unstructured (see Chapter 5). Koskinen, for example, uses focus group interviews with translators in the Finnish translation unit at the European Commission in order to find out how the translators negotiate their national and European identities and how their profession affects these identities (2008:82).

Interviews are only one of a range of ways in which we can obtain information directly by talking to people. While conducting observations (see below), we may also gather verbal reports. In addition, when doing case studies, it is not unlikely that we may come across people whom we have not planned to interview but who have relevant information or express interesting opinions. If these encounters occur by chance we may not have a prepared interview schedule or a recording device with us. This does not mean that we cannot integrate them as a piece of evidence; we can still encourage the informant to talk and take notes either during the conversation or as soon as possible afterwards. As with planned interviews, it is important to explain that we would like to use the information provided and request their permission to do so, and to clarify whether their contribution is to be reported anonymously or not (see below). We should give them our details and obtain their contact details in case the first meeting needs to be followed up, and so that they can be sent the relevant sections of the report for comments (see below and Chapter 2, Section 2.11.3).

If a participant offers his or her insights into the phenomenon analyzed and these are taken as a basis for further inquiry, he or she is considered an informant rather than participant (for a discussion of the difference between these two, see Chapter 5). While doing field research we establish interpersonal relationships whose influence on the research may not become noticeable at the time of conducting the investigation. It is important not to become too reliant on one key informant, who may influence the investigator more than others because they are particularly articulate, or seem to be particularly knowledgeable (see Chapter 5, Sections 5.2.2, 5.8.2 and 5.9 for a discussion of potential sources of bias in participant-oriented research).

6.5.3   Observation

Observation is a rather neglected tool in translation studies, but one worth being aware of (see Chapter 4, Section 4.6.1 on how it can be used in process-oriented research). Think of the benefits of being able to observe translators and interpreters at work (for example in interpreting booths), sitting at translation lectures or attending meetings in translation agencies. As part of her study on institutional translation, Koskinen explores the institutional setting in which translators work. This setting is understood both in the abstract sense, referring to norms and regulations governing the role of translators, as well as in the concrete sense, referring to the physical environment and material conditions of their workplace (Koskinen 2008:61). This second sense requires direct observation:

> [i]n order to understand the translations produced by the Commission translators, it can be useful to look at issues such as where they are physically located, and with whom, how their offices are designed and decorated, whether there are indications of eurospirit or mementos of their home country on the walls, and so on. Minute details such as flag stickers or table cloths, and practicalities such as the flight schedules or the location of the lifts can help in creating an overall picture of the production context of EU translations. (*ibid.*:72-73)

Becker and Geer (2004) discuss the advantages of participant observation as compared to interviewing and mention, among other things, the problems posed by different native languages or language varieties and social codes with which the interviewer may not be familiar, an issue which is particularly relevant in a translation studies context. Despite being quite time consuming, observation is particularly effective because it can give us unrestricted access to what people *do* as opposed to what they say they do, or what we infer they do from analyzing the products of their work. However, observing for research purposes is not as easy as it may seem, and becoming an accurate and balanced observer takes discipline and effort. Gillham (2000:47) reports that research on 'witnessing' – what people have seen and what they report – shows observation to be both fallible and highly selective. A common problem is that we forget to report the obvious. This is important because unless something is recorded it cannot form part of our evidence. It is better to err on the side of caution and report as much as we can, and exactly what we have seen (see Gilham 2000:50-51) for an example of a detailed report of an observation). Where possible, given confidentiality constraints, combining observations with either video or audio recording can be useful to ensure that relevant details are not missed, to refresh the researcher's memory when integrating the information gathered into the report and to illustrate the points made when disseminating the research.

Junker (2004) discusses at length the different social roles for observation in a field work situation. In very general terms, we can distinguish two broad types of observation, **detached** and **participant observation**, depending on whether the observer comes to the situation as an outsider or takes an active role within the group, institution or process being observed. In both detached and participant observation, one of the main problems affecting the validity of the research is the inevitable observer or Hawthorne effect (see Chapter 2). People act differently when they know they are being observed, whether they are used to the participant being in the same environment or not. There is no way of avoiding this, but it is important that we constantly consider the effects we may be having and ask other participants for their opinion as to whether the situations observed are characteristic.

We need to be careful not to form particularly close relations with some members rather than others, because this may lead to a perception that we are biased. We need to introduce ourselves to those being observed and explain what we are doing and our purpose. Explaining in general terms what we are studying is important for those being observed to feel at ease and trusted. Trust is important for participants to be open with us. However, this does not mean we should discuss with participants the results or answers we expect to find, because this may influence their behaviour in such a way as to affect the validity of our research (see discussion of validity and the researcher unintentional expectancy effect in Chapter 2, Section 2.10.1).

Detached observation can be much more structured than participant observation, and it will require a schedule listing the key behaviours or events we want to focus on, as well as the aspects of that behaviour/event that require particular attention. If certain behaviours, events or actions are particularly frequent, they may need to be sampled so as to get a good overview. Interval sampling involves checking what the situation is (e.g. how many students are taking notes) every so often. Event sampling involves noting how many times a certain behaviour/event/action occurs over a period of time.

Participant observation is a technique most frequently used in anthropological studies of cultural and subcultural groups, and is a key element of the ethnographic method. When observation is carried out as part of an ethnographic project, it tends to be participant rather than detached observation. In these cases, the researcher must "do as others do, live with others, eat, work and experience the same daily patterns as others" (Madden 2010:16). Participant observation often provides access to spaces that are otherwise inaccessible to scientific investigation, and provides a viewpoint from inside the case study rather than external to it. The observer may be able to manipulate events or situations to some extent, with the required permission, so as to produce a greater variety of relevant situations for collecting data. It is important to bear in mind that, whether deliberately or not, the decisions the researcher takes as a member of the group may well have an impact on the results of the study. This type of observation is less structured because being actively involved prevents the observer from planning or recording the observation in detail. However, it is still a good idea to have some sort of plan and a schedule, for example in the form of a ready-made table that is always at hand and which can be ticked under certain categories when a specific behaviour, event, etc. occurs.

Bourdieu (1990:34) describes participant observation as a contradiction in terms, since observation means a certain detachment, a belief in objectification, while being a participant implies a belief in the benefits of knowing from personal experience. However, as he argues himself, good social research tries to combine the benefits of both objective observation and subjective experience while being aware of the problems inherent in both. In this sense, his technique of participant objectification may provide a useful tool when conducting observations. Participant objectification involves a double distancing from the object of study: the first as part of the process of observation and objectification of the reality observed, which requires withdrawing from the actual experience in order to observe it from above and at a distance. The second is part of a process of objectifying the relation between observed and observer, which calls into question the presuppositions inherent in the position of the 'objective' observer (Bourdieu 1990).

Koskinen's study provides an interesting example of how the observer's position can sometimes be neither fully detached nor participatory. A significant factor in her study is that she herself had worked as a translator for the European Commission before re-entering the field as a researcher. Although personal experience was clearly an asset in terms of access to the translation unit and understanding of the work culture and organization, being both an informant and a scholar posed significant challenges. Koskinen mentions, for example, the difficulty of integrating the tacit knowledge acquired from first-hand experience into research reports, or the difficulty of questioning one's opinions in the same way a scholar questions the opinions of any informant. Her solution is to let the outsider and insider viewpoints enter into a dialogue with each other, and she finds that her personal memories enrich and balance her analytic academic discourse (Koskinen 2008:9). She is careful throughout her report, however, to clearly highlight personal accounts as such when these have had a bearing on the analysis or argumentation, so as "to enable the reader to assess their weight methodologically – or to judge for themselves the extent of my bias" (*ibid.*:54).

6.5.4   *Physical artefacts*

Another source of information is physical artefacts, that is to say, non-textual objects that are revealing of the situation or play an important part in the event or processes studied. These can be technological devices such as tools or instruments, a work of art, photographs, etc. In translation studies, copies of a particular edition of the translation under study are often used. In his study of the translation of American gay literature into French, Harvey (2003) discusses the kind of socio-cultural meanings encoded in the book covers and how they are used to activate certain knowledges in the readers. Physical artefacts are generally used as supplementary information, since they provide insights about very specific aspects of our research. If considerable weight is to be attributed to their meanings, then it is likely that we need to resort to appropriate methods of analysis, such as social semiotics (for an overview of methods of visual analysis see van Leeuwen and Jewitt 2001).

6.5.5   *Quantitative data*

Quantitative data can be derived from several of the sources listed above, particularly archival records. Statistics used in case studies tend to be descriptive rather than inferential. **Inferential statistics** enable you to draw inferences from the data. They involve calculations that derive non-immediate meanings from the data, such as the likelihood that a result could be down to chance; for example, whether the difference between the averages for two populations (trainee translators and professional translators) is 'significant' or not. **Descriptive statistics** simply help you to summarize and compare information; for example, in the form of averages or percentages. Simply arranging data in tables according to categories is a very helpful way of summarizing them, and can help the researcher see more clearly the kind of questions that the data may be able to inform as well as how each set of data may relate to other pieces of quantitative or qualitative information (cross referencing). As mentioned above, Sturge (2004) compiled a database of translations published under the Nazi regime. This database was used to provide descriptive statistics on the number of translations published per year as well as to plot trends concerning source languages and genres and to offer a general profile of the translators.

6.5.6   *Using a database to manage data*

We have described five different types of information that can all form part of a case study. In order to keep track of and manage data from different sources, it is recommended that a database be compiled in order to maintain a comprehensive record of all the data gathered, the sources, date of access, etc. We can think of the database as our own personal research archive. It may include, for example:

- An annotated bibliography;
- A list of documents accessed with dates and place of access;
- An expanded list of names of informants, including details such as date of birth, nationality, background, and other relevant observations;
- Full transcriptions of interviews, together with vignettes and interview profiles, if available (see Chapter 5, Section 5.7.2);
- Detailed descriptions of any coding system used to analyze textual data of any kind, including transcripts;
- The research diary or log book (see below);
- Photographs;
- Emails and letters exchanged with informants, organizations, etc.;
- An index of all the information contained in the database.

The type of qualitative research software described below provides the means for creating highly sophisticated databases where the different elements listed above can be linked. Databases can also be created using electronic spreadsheets (e.g. Excel) for all the list elements of the database and a clear system of filenames to link the lists with documents such as transcripts and photos.

6.5.7 Ethical considerations

Before moving on to discuss the process of data analysis, it is important to highlight some ethical issues that need to be taken into account when carrying out case study research. Case studies aim to provide in-depth pictures of the object of study, often including subjective views and opinions from a range of informants or participants, thereby raising issues of confidentiality. The rules of informed consent outlined in Chapter 2 need to be followed and participants should be allowed to preview the report before it is made publicly available, so as to correct any misinterpretations and confirm that they are happy with the record of their contribution. Any signs of concerns should be taken seriously.

A particular problem of case studies, as Koskinen (2008) points out, is that it is not always possible to anonymize the data obtained, particularly when an ethnographic method is adopted. While the anonymity of the individual translators in Koskinen's study was protected, it was not possible to hide the EU origin of the documents and the language of the versions studied: "the emphasis of locality in ethnography makes it difficult to hide the geographical location of the unit" (2008:56). It is likely that if the case is to remain anonymous, much more than names needs to be removed, since many distinctive characteristics of the case may lead to it being easily identifiable. Whether anonymity is protected or not, it is imperative to treat the data with sensitivity, in full acknowledgement of the moral responsibility of the researcher towards the people, groups or organizations involved.

Issues of confidentiality may also arise when dealing with documentary evidence. The fact that the people involved are not available to provide informed consent (see Chapter 2) means that extra care should to be taken to anonymize any details that are to be made public. Confidentiality is one of the reasons why certain sources are not publicly available; often, we may need to obtain special permission to access archives and again to make copies of any documents consulted. We may also need to consult them within the specific location where they are held.

Koskinen (2008:37) lists "moral responsibility towards the group under study" as one of the fundamental principles of an ethnographic approach. Ethical problems may arise if the topic of the study is controversial, as when the study reports on practices that may be considered substandard, unprofessional or even illegal. As Stake (2005:459) points out, "[b]reach of ethics is seldom a simple matter; often, it occurs when two contradictory standards apply, such as withholding full disclosure (as per the contract) in order to protect a good but vulnerable agency". A question to be considered from a moral perspective is the longer-term implications of the case study research for the participants as well as for any groups or organizations under study (Koskinen 2008:56). We need to ask ourselves, for example, whether they will benefit or suffer from the research, and whether their aims may be advanced or hindered by it. It may not be possible to answer these questions in advance, but they should be given careful thought and revisited as the research progresses.

To sum up this section, in choosing our sources of information it is important to avoid bias by selecting only convenient sources and limiting our analysis to aspects that will confirm our assumptions. Bias is reduced by using multiple sources of information, which also leads to richer descriptions and more convincing arguments. Written documents are a particularly relevant source of information when dealing with translations and can come in many forms: academic literature, translated texts and paratexts, archives, etc., each requiring a different approach. Accessing documents and archival records requires advance planning and we should never forget that all documents, however factual they may appear, are liable to bias: we need to question from which perspective they were written or compiled, under what conditions and for what purpose. This also applies to information obtained from informants, however knowledgeable they may appear. Observation is a neglected tool that can provide first hand primary data as well as being useful in contextualizing primary data obtained by other means. It is important to remember that observers have an impact on the situation observed, and analyzing our own act of observation and interpretation should be part of the enterprise. Physical artefacts are often supplementary sources of insight into the case under study and descriptive statistics can be helpful to visualize possible trends and relations between different sets of data. It is recommended that the data collected should be organized in a database so as to facilitate access to the information throughout the iterative research process and ensure replicability. Finally, we highlighted the need to deal with any confidential information sensitively and consider the impact of our research on the people and organizations involved.

6.6   Analyzing case-study data

This section presents some key principles that should guide our analysis of case study data, then offers some practical suggestions and outlines three types of research aids (research diaries, analytical memos and visual data displays) that can help us identify patterns as well keep track of the development of our ideas. Finally, we describe software that can be used to assist qualitative and mixed-methods analysis.

6.6.1   *General principles*

The research process in case studies tends to follow the iterative pattern of qualitative methods (see Chapters 3 and 5) rather than the linear pattern of quantitative methods (collection → processing → analysis → report). The researcher starts analyzing at the same time as collecting the data, and the analysis informs subsequent data collection and may even lead to adjustments in the research design. It is important, however, not to start theorizing at a too early stage in the investigation, at the risk of over-narrowing our perspective and becoming blind to the new insights that new data can provide. Further evidence may qualify, complicate or even contradict our first impressions. Even at the stage of writing up a report, the researcher may need to go back and review data that have already been analyzed. Having a database (see Section 6.5.6) helps to ensure that information is easily retrievable.

   Case study research requires us to approach the data with an open mind and – paradoxically – our close familiarity with the object of study makes that rather difficult. We know what it is like being a translator, or a translator trainer, we have experienced reading translations and we feel we have a privileged understanding. However, the assumptions that we derive from our experience as to what translators do and readers experience are exactly what can make us biased and unable to appreciate experiences different from our own. Gillham (2000) recommends that we approach our object of study as if we were social anthropologists going to study a culture that is completely different from our own, deferring the interpretation of our findings for as long as possible and never considering it final until we have a fuller picture. He also explains why this is difficult (2000:19; emphasis in original):

> A basic limitation of human cognition is that we feel impelled to understand, to make sense of what we are experiencing. New knowledge is mainly interpreted in terms of what we already know, until that proves so inadequate that our 'knowledge framework' undergoes a radical reorganization. In research this is sometimes known as a *paradigm* shift – a complete change in the way we understand or theorize about what we are studying.

On the other hand, as we start collecting the data, if we do not start filtering and organizing them at the same time, they can soon become unmanageable and we risk diverting our attention too much from aspects that are relevant to the research question.

The non-experimental nature of case studies means that variables cannot be easily controlled , i.e., confounding factors cannot be easily eliminated. We tend to make observations about different factors, but these are generally not comparable along the same dimensions. As often happens in detective work, one piece of evidence suggests something, whereas another piece suggests something else. A good researcher is adaptive and flexible, able to turn unexpected or confusing outcomes into opportunities rather than obstacles, for example, by using them as reminders to actively look for more discrepant data along the same lines and thus challenge previous assumptions.

We can think of analyzing case study data as trying to find an explanation that makes all pieces of evidence fit together as part of a large puzzle, but always remembering that the pieces are not regular. The strength of the argument will depend on whether alternative configurations of the puzzle can be built. This is why in the process of analyzing the data it is important to identify viable alternatives (what, under the circumstances, were the options?) and play out various scenarios. Another important skill is being a good 'listener', literally, for those doing interviews, but also in relation to the inspection of documentation: being capable of assimilating large amounts of information without prejudging, paying attention to the choice of words and understanding the perspective from which the information is conveyed.

One way of making sure that the puzzle does indeed map the complex reality underlying it is having a good grasp of the issues being studied, both theoretical and factual. We need to make sure we have a comprehensive understanding of the context in which the phenomenon under study takes place and an in-depth understanding of the theoretical model on which our explanation is based. If it is pointed out to us that an element of the puzzle is missing, we can respond by showing how it can be integrated or why it has been left out. Case study research is, by definition, difficult to replicate. However, we can still attempt to ensure that if someone looks at the same case and follows the same steps, they would come to a similar conclusion, or at least see that our conclusion makes sense. Transparency and detailed documentation of the process is absolutely crucial for this purpose.

The data analysis process is one of inductive theorizing, i.e. making sense of what we find after we have found it (Gillham 2000:6). Our representations of the raw data are always interpretative, the process of rendering the data into a linguistic description involves applying a multiplicity of complex conceptual structures, which are likely to superimpose upon, or overlap with, one another. This process is partly deliberate and often determined by a previously chosen conceptual framework, and is partly unconscious and determined by our world-view and by presuppositions we may not even be aware of.

The system of coding described in Chapter 5 can be useful in helping us interpret case study data. As described in Chapter 5, the codes can be descriptive categories that follow the data's 'natural' organization and are grouped into more abstract categories as the analysis progresses. They can follow a pre-existing schedule, such as an interview or observation schedule, or they can be based on a theoretical model that is used to analyze the data. If codes are used to bring together all the data collected from different sources, it is likely that the coding system will remain at a more general level, so that categories can be applied across different types of data. Alternatively, they can be designed to suit specific parts of the project.

In her overview of state-approved discourses on translation during the Nazi regime, and in trying to make sense of the multiple and often contradictory images of translation portrayed by five different librarian journals, Sturge (2004) uses Robyns's framework for analyzing the discursive practice of translations in relation to encounters with the alien, which distinguishes four categories: imperialist, defensive, trans-discursive and defective discourses (Robyns 1992, in Sturge 2004:84). It is the lack of coherence in the data that prompts Sturge to make use of a pre-existing model. The model was not designed specifically to account for the data that Sturge has collected and therefore, despite being useful, has clear limitations, which are duly highlighted (2004:85). In another section of the same study, presenting an analysis of translation strategies in translated detective fiction, Sturge uses ad-hoc descriptive categories that emerge from the textual analysis itself, some of them highlighting the textual effect of the translator's strategy, such as simplification and explicitation, and others dealing with specific genre characteristics, such as strategies affecting characterization and themes (love-interest, the great detective, etc.).

It is important, when trying to apply any sort of categories to our data, to remember that case study evidence is never perfectly tidy or coherent. Our descriptions must therefore stay as close as possible to the data and our claims must be grounded in the evidence, avoiding the temptation to tidy them into abstract models of such perfect coherence that they become implausible. Koskinen (2010:177) warns that when "[l]ooking for causality, the researcher may end up with creating a causal narrative, that is, manufacturing rather than observing connections between facts". Koskinen's (2008) work provides a good example of the kind of tensions that we may find when analyzing our data and how these tensions can be integrated into a useful explanatory model. On the one hand, all her sources (documentary evidence, translators' interviews and textual analysis) point towards a need for and an attempt to increase readability in EU texts. On the other, she finds evidence of a tendency towards institutionalization which works against readability. Koskinen resorts to Toury's concept of translation norms to explain these results and suggests that there seems to be a rift between the preliminary norms concerning translation policy, established at the level of the Directorate General of Translation, which recognize the need for reader orientation, and the operational norms implemented on a day to day basis at the level of the translation units. However, Koskinen does more than simply describe the apparently contradictory behaviour of norms: she looks at how sociological research on the role of habits and routines could explain the tendency towards institutionalization as an accidental outcome of routine behaviour and suggests that the explicit drive towards readability could be a result of the need to counteract that tendency (Koskinen 2008:148-49).

In brief, the process of data analysis starts during the data collection, but we need to proceed carefully, not jump to conclusions, and make sure our analysis remains grounded in the evidence accumulated (see also the discussion of **sensitization** in Chapter 2). Evidence should be examined with an open mind, actively looking for information that is incompatible with the hypotheses that – invariably – we start to formulate as we become acquainted with the data. Our analysis should be based on thorough knowledge of the context of investigation and our chosen theoretical model. The strength of case studies relies on how coherent the argument that we propose to account for the case at hand is; however, the aim of the case study is to provide a rich description and an in-depth analysis of the particular, and reality is messy and complex; it rarely fits neatly into the abstract categories that make up our theoretical models. It is the models that need to adapt to our case, rather than our case to the models.

6.6.2   *Practical suggestions*

Given the wide range of types of data used in case studies, it is impractical to give concrete suggestions here as to how to deal with each of them. The most common sources of information for case study research (such as interviews and texts) have already been discussed extensively in previous chapters, and readers are referred to these chapters for details. Instead, we reproduce here a series of techniques suggested by Miles and Huberman (1994, in Yin 2009:129) for the analysis of case study data:

- Organizing the information in different groups
- Making a matrix of categories (codes) to organize the evidence (see Chapter 5, Section 5.9)
- Creating data displays (flow charts and diagrams) to display the data (see Section 6.5.5 above)
- Tabulating (i.e. recording in a table) the frequency of events (for example, when doing observations, see Section 6.5.3 above)
- Examining the complexity of such tabulations and their relationships by calculating second-order numbers such as means and variances (see Chapter 5, Section 5.9),
- Putting information in chronological order or using some other temporal scheme

Above, we highlighted the need to use a database in order to organize what are often large amounts of data in many different formats. At the analysis stage, there are also other types of research aids that can be helpful to keep track of the ideas that all the different sources suggest and see if any patterns start emerging. These are: the research diary, analytical memos and visual data displays.

In the **research diary** or **log book** we record all our notes, which can be grouped into two broad types: (1) notes on the different pieces of evidence examined, such as remarks during observations, impressions from an interview, observations made in the process of reading a document, etc.; and (2) personal notes on questions we need to reflect on, preliminary hypotheses, ideas for the final report, etc. – see Lofland (2004) for very useful recommendations on how to write notes on field work.

The research diary can be handwritten or typed and stored electronically, or a combination of both. If entries are recorded by hand, it is a good idea to regularly transcribe and back them up electronically. Some people prefer to use a personal recording device and transcribe the notes afterwards. In any case, it is important to make entries immediately (or you may forget important details) and to regularly revise, assess and summarize them. This is essential to keep track of our research aims and make sure our research does not lose direction, as well as to self-monitor our progress.

Analytical memos are notes taken during the process of analysis, especially when coding is used, to help researchers maintain track of how the argument and theory are developing as they do the analysis. These notes are an essential part of the grounded theory approach (see Chapter 5, Section 5.8) and help us to move from first- to second-level coding. Qualitative analysis software (see below) generally allows for these notes to be linked to codes. They are particularly useful when different researchers are working on the same data, so as to keep each other informed of how their thinking is progressing. **Visual data displays**, such as tables, tree diagrams, graphs and charts, are also useful at this stage to help organize ideas and identify patterns, and may also be useful when producing the research report at a later stage.

6.6.3   *Computer-aided qualitative analysis*

Unlike statistical packages used in quantitative research (for example, SPSS) which do carry out part of the analysis, the packages described in this section *do not do any real analysis*; they simply help in managing and organizing the data, rather than analyzing them. Qualitative analysis software includes text processing tools that allow the researcher to segment and code the data to start with and then to search and interrogate the dataset. The Computer-Assisted Qualitative Data Analysis (CAQDAS) Networking Project,[3] based at the University of Surrey, provides a range of information about CAQDAS packages (currently, Nvivo, Atlas.ti, QDA Miner, Digital Replay System, HyperRESEARCH, MaxQDA, MiMeG, Transana, Qualrus) and offers a range of other resources for researchers wishing to work with these tools (see also Lewins and Silver 2007).

Some of the tools (Digital Reply System, for example) include transcribing tools as well and allow the audio and text files to be displayed concurrently. Apart from audio files, other types of multimedia formats such as video and graphics files are also supported. Visual tools are often integrated in order to help with the creation and display of graphs, tables, charts and diagrams. Writing tools

---

[3] http://www.surrey.ac.uk/sociology/research/researchcentres/caqdas/support/choosing/index. htm [Last accessed 11 July 2012]

are also provided so as to enable the researcher to write memos, vignettes, etc. and to link them to other data. These packages also provide basic concordancing tools (see Chapter 3) which allow textual data (keywords and phrases) to be explored in a key word in context (KWIC) format, which can be useful when the use of language is relevant to the research question.

The usefulness of qualitative data analysis computer tools for preserving and managing the data is undeniable, but apart from that, they can help to make sure that coding is systematic and make it possible to interrogate large amounts of data effectively, for example by finding keywords and comparing data grouped under two or more codes. They can be used to establish simple or more complex relationships between codes and represent these relationships graphically in the form of maps, which can help in the development of conceptual models of the data. They can also facilitate the quantification of certain aspects of the qualitative dataset; basic frequencies can be used to produce graphs, tables and charts, which are useful not only at the analysis stage but also for reporting effectively. By supporting different multimedia formats they aid analysis and help towards the preparation of presentations and reports that are richer than the 'text only' format.

Apart from the usual problems with using any type of technical device in research (a steep learning curve, losing all the data if not backed up in several locations, potentially unreliable technical support), such tools also pose some risks to the quality of the research: by facilitating the coding process, they can lead to over-coding, which can result in a fragmented view of the data, and some of the capabilities of the software, for example the possibility of establishing hierarchical diagrams, may influence the thinking process in a way that some researchers may find unhelpful. As the coding progresses, the researcher tends to end up working with increasingly decontextualized chunks, which can be problematic. At the same time, the possibility of integrating different views in one screen (e.g. the transcribed text and a coding diagram) or of listening to an audio file while coding also helps the researcher remain close to the data.

Although these software packages are referred to as 'qualitative analysis tools' they can increasingly be used to manage aspects of mixed methods projects. Quantitative data collected through questionnaires and analyzed using statistical packages such as SPSS can be imported into qualitative software packages.

6.7   Summary

We hope that any preconceptions of case studies as free-form research have by now been dispelled and the advantages and risks of using this method clearly established. Case studies look at one unit of investigation in depth, always treating the unit of investigation as a whole rather than prioritizing certain aspects of it (holistic research) and paying particular attention to the context in which it is situated. The requirement for depth means that researchers working on contemporary topics benefit from using qualitative methods, particularly those used in ethnographic research, such as interviews and participant observation, which allow them to get a handle on rich experience, something that is not attainable with surveys or questionnaires. According to Stake, the "[c]ase study facilitates the conveying of experience of actors and stakeholders as well as the experience of studying the case. It can enhance the reader's experience with that case" (2005:454). This experiential knowledge is extremely valuable, but because critical observations and interview data are subjective, it can be confused with questions of opinion or feeling: "Good case study research follows disciplined practices of analysis and triangulation to tease out what deserves to be called experiential knowledge from what is opinion and preference" (*ibid.*:455).

Researchers working with historical material will not be able to obtain the same type of first-hand experience and will therefore need to resort to alternative ways of sourcing revealing information that allows them to go beyond the superficial aspects recorded in easily accessible historical documents. Archives containing letters, diaries and records of everyday communication can be very useful, but not always available. Paying particular attention to details, close and critical discourse analysis of documents (see Chapter 3) can go some way towards making written documents reveal more than their superficial linguistic content, but the conclusions will always remain more speculative than when a dialogue can be established with living participants.

The holistic and contextualized aspects of the research mean that several sources of information are generally required. The aim should always be to cover all relevant and critical evidence, taking into account alternative perspectives and respecting the integrity of the rather messy data that is typical in social and cultural real-life research. However, it is worth remembering that the amount of evidence can soon become overwhelming, and boundaries therefore need to be established and made clear, including specifically what is *not* included in the case study.

The particularity of cases is another element to be respected and valued. Results cannot be generalized, and it is not useful to force case studies to stand for realities larger than themselves. What Geertz says about the methodological problem of the microscopic nature of ethnography can well be applied to the contained nature of case studies (1973/2010:354):

> it is [a problem] not to be resolved by regarding a remote locality as the world in a teacup or as the sociological equivalent of a cloud chamber. It is to be resolved – or, anyway, decently kept at bay – by realizing that social actions are comments on more than themselves; that where an interpretation comes from does not determine where it can be impelled to go. Small facts speak to large issues.

For our case studies to speak to "large issues", it is important to choose them carefully for their relevance, for the significance of the issues they will raise, the hypotheses that they can help to formulate, their capacity to improve on previous theories, and the insights they can provide into the complex mechanisms through which social, political, cultural and ideological forces shape translations and are shaped by them.

Chapter 7. Conclusion: The research report

7.1 Introduction

Research only becomes useful to the wider community through dissemination, which generally means that it needs to be published. In this final chapter we highlight some of the most important issues to bear in mind when writing a research report. In Section 7.2 we discuss ways of structuring the research report; we consider the advantages and disadvantages of the traditional IMRAD (introduction, methods, results and discussion) structure as well as the principles of chronological and causal sequencing. Section 7.3 focuses on the introduction, literature review and conclusion, which are the key elements that allow us to frame our research and highlight its relevance to the research community. We then move on to general considerations of reporting methods (Section 7.4). Sections 7.5, 7.6 and 7.7 discuss the reporting of results, looking in turn at the specific challenges presented by qualitative, quantitative and linguistic data.

It goes without saying that since dissemination often depends on publication, good writing skills are crucial for the researcher. Offering advice on how to write goes beyond the scope of this book; however, it is useful to bear in mind that different academic traditions may favour different qualities in academic discourse. An ability to write clearly, synthesize, engage and guide the reader is a key skill in English academic writing, but other language communities may favour different writing skills (Bennett 2007).

7.2 Structuring the report

The form of the report will depend, to some extent, on the research design and the nature of the data. Empirical research reports have traditionally followed what is known as the **IMRAD** (introduction, methods, results and discussion) structure.[1] The assumption is that this structure reflects the actual steps of the research process; however, it was famously criticized by a Nobel Prize-winning immunologist, Peter Medawar, as idealizing that process and misrepresenting the dynamic of thought and discovery that is at the basis of the work reported (Medawar 1996). The research process is much less tidy and linear than the report suggests: the IMRAD structure requires the research to be reorganized so that a 'noise-free' presentation of what are generally seen as the most essential aspects of the study is achieved. While the criticisms made by Medawar are valid, the IMRAD structure has an important advantage: it enables readers to quickly scan the paper for the information they need.

If the criticism levelled by Medawar is convincing in relation to research in the natural sciences, it is even more so in relation to some of the methodologies

---

[1] Although the acronym does not reflect it, an overview of previous work, or 'literature review', is also generally included before the methods section.

discussed here, which explicitly acknowledge the rather messy nature of the research process. The iterative process followed in much qualitative research would result in confusion if it were to be faithfully reflected on paper. Writing a report offers an opportunity to step back from the discourse analyzed and consider the implications of the analysis from the reader's perspective. Whether we follow the IMRAD structure or not, the findings need to be presented in a manner that is generally tidier than the way in which they were arrived at, while at the same time being truthful to the nature of the research and its complexity, for purposes of transparency.

The more organized the process of data collection and analysis, the easier it will be to report it. It is generally recommended that the writing process starts as soon as the research starts, in the form of analytical memos, interview profiles, or simply notes on methodological decisions (see Chapter 6 for a description of these research aids). These notes will be essential to provide the necessary level of detail required for achieving transparency. Integrating elements from these notes into the report is also useful to demonstrate the level of self-reflection achieved throughout the research process.

The two sections that always need to remain in place are the introduction and the conclusion. The rest of the report can take many different forms, provided there is some sort of logical sequence to guide the reader. Chronological and causal sequencing are important factors to take into account. When the study covers events over a period of time, it is important to make clear the chronological sequence of such events, particularly if most readers are not likely to be familiar with that sequence. However, for purposes of clarity it is advisable to describe the current situation before moving on to the description of how that situation developed; in these cases, the progression should be clearly signposted, so that the reader knows the historical background will be provided later and is not distracted by trying to guess how the situation came about.

Causal arguments, even when the explanation is presented at the beginning, for example in the form of a hypothesis, tend to start by describing the situation to be explained before moving on to a description of the causes and how the links between them were established. To some extent, this helps to introduce an element of 'suspense' into the report. This can work well in case studies, where readers are provided with the elements of the situation to be explained and will begin considering potential answers while following the development of the researcher's argument. One of the skills of building a causal argument lies in plotting the sequential revisions to our first explanations in a way that demonstrates how the research progressed, building more and more sophisticated explanations as we proceed.

Where multiple sources of evidence are used, as in case studies, it is common and methodologically convenient to divide the report into sections describing findings from each source of evidence separately, as is done, for example, in Koskinen (2008). In these cases, it is important to make sure that the reader can clearly perceive the thread linking what may otherwise come across as separate pieces of research. For this purpose, it is important to retain some flexibility and on occasion "blur the divisions and put the different findings in direct dialogue" (Koskinen 2008:61-62).

When dealing with more than one case study, it may be tempting to organize them in sequential chapters or even larger sections, followed by a section containing the comparative analysis. Despite the seemingly logical nature of this division, it is quite likely that by the time the reader finishes with the second case, he or she will have forgotten quite a lot about the first one. This will require us to devote a considerable amount of space to summaries for purposes of recall. Therefore, smaller sections devoted to each case within a chapter may make the reading experience easier by providing diversity while facilitating a more detailed comparison. On the other hand, moving backwards and forwards from one case to the next within a few paragraphs will also lead to confusion and will not help the reader to remember the key facts about each case. See Susam-Sarajeva (2006) for an example of how the comparative analysis is carried out in stages, while providing a coherent picture of each scenario.

7.3 Framing the report: introduction, literature review and conclusion

The impact of our research depends not only on its quality but on its wider significance; therefore, providing a rationale for our project, contextualizing the research within the academic literature and assessing its contribution in relation to existing knowledge is essential. These are the main functions of the introduction, literature review and conclusion sections. The introduction needs to state clearly the aim of the study and present the research question(s) and/or hypotheses. It is also important to provide a rationale for the project, explaining how we expect the research to contribute to existing knowledge about the topic. Generally, a brief statement to this effect is enough in the introduction, and a more detailed argument can be elaborated during the literature review. A summary of existing research serves to identify the gap in the literature that we are trying to fill and, together with the section on methodology, situates our project within a theoretical framework (see Chapter 2, Section 2.6 for a more detailed discussion of what a literature review entails).

In the traditional IMRAD structure, the literature review comes immediately after the introduction and before the methods section. While it is important to demonstrate awareness of existing literature on the topic early in the report, sometimes it makes more sense to cite relevant literature as the argument develops rather than concentrate it in one section. This is particularly the case in interdisciplinary research where a multitude of subject areas are drawn upon and each may be more clearly explored on its own and in relation to a particular aspect of the research project.

A good literature review should be comprehensive, up to date, coherent and should demonstrate critical awareness. The requirements of coherence and critical awareness mean that it is not sufficient to list references, previous findings and claims: it is necessary to evaluate what each piece reported contributes to the field from the perspective of our own project. The literature review should help us to build an argument, explaining why our research is important.

The conclusion sums up the results and highlights the contribution made by the research, which may be different from what we expected. Often, particularly in longer research reports such as PhD theses and book-length publications, it also includes suggestions for further research. It is crucial that the conclusion explicitly addresses the questions asked at the beginning of the project. Any claims made need to relate to the initial research questions or hypotheses, and we need to demonstrate that such claims are warranted by the evidence gathered throughout the research process.

As researchers, we need to carefully assess the strength of the claims we make: are we in a position to declare that something is indeed the case? For example, that a hypothesis has been supported or otherwise? Or does a claim need to be moderated in the light of counter evidence? This is ultimately a matter of choosing the right language: if we formulated the question in modest terms, we may be able to offer more definitive answers; if our question was rather ambitious, then we may only be able to offer tentative answers. Generally speaking, framing our aims and claims in modest terms is preferred in English academic discourse.

When results cannot be generalized to a larger population, the strength of the argument depends heavily on the researcher's capacity for building a plausible case. Claims need to be demonstrated by discussing potential alternatives and counter claims, and showing that the relationships established are logical despite the possibility of alternative readings. In any case, when drawing conclusions, we have to be extremely careful to specify their scope. Some conclusions will be specific to the case, texts, participants that constitute the object of the study; however, even then there may be aspects of our findings that have implications beyond our particular study. To make these implications clear, we need to position our results in a broader context and, in particular, establish clear links with our literature review and the theoretical framework used to design the study.

7.4   Reporting methods

Any report needs to include a description of the study design, collection and analysis methods. The opportunity for providing detail might be limited, depending on the type of document in which the research is being reported – a journal article will allow more space than a conference paper, for example. Nonetheless, a short statement such as 'we conducted interviews' or 'results were obtained on the basis of questionnaires', with no further discussion, is very unsatisfactory to a reader, preventing them from evaluating the appropriateness of the research design to the aims of the study and from replicating the research. In the interests of credibility and replicability, at least some space needs to be given to a serious discussion of methods.

In the IMRAD structure, methods are reported after the literature review and immediately before the results section. When a study reports on data from a range of different sources, each requiring different methodological approaches and techniques of analysis, we often have several methodology sections that precede those where the corresponding results are presented. This structure is used by Sturge (2006), where chapters combine information from one or two types of sources, each focusing on a different aspect of the case study, and where we find a progression from the general (institutional policy, academic discourses, general patterns in the publication of translations) to the particular (specific genres and individual instances of translations).

One of the key issues in reporting our methods is the choice of sources of data; whether these are texts, participants, archives, etc. In quantitative studies, the discussion of sources of evidence is tied in with the discussion of sampling (see Chapter 3, Section 3.4.1 and Chapter 4, 4.2.1). Mention should be made of the recruitment process and the response rate, where relevant. In participant-oriented research, we should describe the number and key characteristics of participants. When focus groups have been used, we should mention the number of groups and the make-up of each group. A brief profile of the participants is always important, but the details included in such a profile will depend on the research project. If keystroke logging is to be used, for example, we should also pay attention to the profiling of participants' keyboarding competences and their general translation competence. The design of research instruments, such as questionnaires, interview schedules or translation tasks, should also be described in detail and they should be reproduced in an appendix, if space allows.

When reporting oral data (from verbal reports in process-oriented studies or from interviews and/or focus groups), the analysis will often be based on transcribed versions of the spoken interactions, a fact that should be mentioned in the report. If the report discusses transcribed data in any detail, then transcription conventions should also be reported on and some consideration should be given to the method of transcription and the extra layers of interpretation that it imposes on the research process (see Chapter 4, Section 4.3.3).

Product-oriented research requires us to justify the selection of texts (including interpreted-mediated events) for analysis. When corpora are custom-built, it is crucial to describe the criteria for selection of texts along the lines described in Chapter 3, Section 3.4. When possible, complete bibliographical details of all the texts included in the corpus should be published as an appendix. Otherwise, at least the overall number of words, the number of texts, the genre, their sources, the date range in which they were published or accessed, and the name of the author/translator (where appropriate) need to be mentioned. When using already existing corpora, it is sufficient to provide only those details that are relevant for the study at hand and refer readers to more comprehensive descriptions of the corpus on a website or in another academic publication.

A rather difficult task is faced by the critical discourse analyst who has chosen texts because of their significance (compare this with the use of corpora that aim to be representative, for example). Significance is, of course, relative to the cultural context, so bearing in mind that academic research targets an international audience, it may be a good idea to start with a description of the context in which the text is embedded. A good example in this regard is Kang (2007), who offers a concise but clear historical account of both the American and North Korean stances on North Korea before describing how current views are represented in the news articles examined. If possible, it is a good idea to include the whole text(s) upon which the analysis is based as an appendix to the report. In all cases it is crucial to provide details of the provenance of the text, the name of the author/translator or institution responsible for it, the place of publication, and date of publication or date of access when the text is obtained from the World Wide Web.

Apart from choice of sources, a discussion of methods should explicitly justify our motives for the selection of certain measures, themes or discourse features for investigation. When a coding system has been developed for the analysis, it also needs to be described with a certain amount of detail. When describing units of investigation and the categories applied to them, it is important to offer examples from our own research wherever possible. Theoretical models that were instrumental in designing our project should be described and analytical concepts used to identify our units of analysis should be defined. If we carry out a process-oriented study using keystroke logging, for example, we need to explain how the keystroke logging data were segmented and justify our focus on, say, pauses, as well as establish what counts as a pause for the purpose of our study. If we carry out a qualitative analysis of focus group transcriptions we may need to justify our decision to focus on references to cultural mediation and offer a definition of cultural mediation that allows us to identify references to this type of phenomenon. Likewise, a corpus analysis of explicitation needs to be based on a clear set of criteria to determine what counts as explicitation and what does not.

When using specialist software and/or hardware – for example, for keystroke logging, corpus analysis, eye-tracking or qualitative analysis – it is important to mention the specific version number, make and model used. In process- and participant-oriented research, the physical context in which the data are collected – such as the choice of translator workplace rather than a research facility such as a laboratory – also merits detailed discussion, since it may well affect the ecological validity of our results. When participants are required to perform designated tasks, we should explain the instructions given and the nature of the warm-up task, if one was used. In eye-tracking studies, it is also important to state the make and exact set up of the computers used, the lighting and sound controls, the exact settings used in the eye-tracking software (for fixation definition and specific filters used by the eye-tracking software) and the criteria used for measuring the 'quality' of the data captured. This is a long (and probably incomplete) list, but it serves to highlight the fact that there are many factors in the research design that need to be disclosed if other researchers are to be able to replicate our findings.

7.5   Reporting qualitative data

Wood and Kroger (2000:180) suggest that in discourse analysis the section conventionally called 'results' is probably best called 'analysis' since it does not present purely the output of the analytic procedures. The data is presented together with a description of how the analysis has been done. This analysis section will also include elements that might conventionally be viewed as discussion because the analysis is explicitly interpretive. Although it is impossible to reproduce the whole analysis, it is important to choose key moments that capture the logic of the argument, including revisions and exclusions of hypotheses (*ibid.*:170). Often, the analysis will be organized into sub-sections which can correspond to the themes or discourse functions identified.

The discussion of qualitative data obtained from participant-oriented research is equally interpretive and so is that of qualitative results obtained from verbal reports, experts' diaries, reflective journals and field notes from observation studies in process-oriented research. All such data require the researcher to identify and communicate trends in a convincing manner, without over diluting individual differences, or overstating the importance of specific themes. It is important to balance the need to present a coherent overall picture that highlights the relevance of the results with the need to not underestimate the subtleties and details that this type of qualitative analysis reveals. Once the data have been coded, the researcher moves away from the highly contextualized individual responses towards a more abstract level; at some point, particularly if using software to carry out the analysis, the researcher may be dealing only with decontextualized utterances represented by short labels. The report should capture some of the individuality of the original statements, for which purpose quotations are very helpful, as they can illustrate the depth and diversity of opinion expressed. The freedom of expression allowed to participants in semi-structured and unstructured interviews can result in interesting quotes that can make a powerful story when strung together properly. Ideally, these interviews should be reported in such a way as to allow the participants to speak for themselves; the researcher acts more as an editor, selecting those parts that are most eloquent and/or relevant.

We should keep in mind our ethical obligations towards participants (see Chapter 4, Section 4.2.1 and Chapter 5, Section 5.3.7), taking care that individuals cannot be identified through the information we give and making sure not to misrepresent them by quoting them in a different context. As already mentioned, where appropriate, for example in the case of reports based on extensive interviews, drafts of the report should be submitted to participants for their approval.

By their very nature, qualitative data are not easy to summarize and generally result in detailed narratives, which risk being too long or cumbersome. It is best to organize the narrative into small sections with descriptive headings to facilitate reading. Particularly striking pieces of information can be highlighted in separate boxes or in bold in order to make it easier for readers to remember the information presented and facilitate its processing. It is also a good idea to follow sections containing many detailed facts with interpretative sections that sum up the main points and move the argument forward in small steps.

If figures or dates are frequently reported, summarizing them in a table may make them easier to assimilate. Tables and bullet points can also help to list important categories used in the collection of data or in the analysis. Diagrams are another way of helping readers to visualize the logic underlying the picture we have constructed. Photographs and other pictorial elements, such as reproductions of book covers, can also bring our report to life by providing a break from the narrative, and they also function as mnemonic aides, but remember that in most cases reproduction of copyright material requires permission. Some aspects of our observations can be recorded in photographs and videos, which can also be used to liven up our reports. When using photographs, and in general when reporting observations, an important issue to think about is the need for participants (whether individuals or institutions) to remain anonymous (see Chapter 6, Section 6.5.7).

7.6   Reporting quantitative data

Questionnaire surveys and process-related research typically generate quantitative data which can be reported textually and numerically (in tables), but are usually also supported visually by bar charts, pie charts, scatter plots, etc. Graphs and tables are typically used to report quantitative data arising out of keystroke logs (task time, number of deletions, insertions, mouse clicks, pauses), eye-tracking sessions (number and duration of fixations, pupil dilation measurements, number of transitions from one area of interest to another), screen recordings (e.g. number of switches between target text and online information resources, duration of consulting time for information resources, number and type of information resources consulted). Clearly, this volume of quantitative data has to be reported in a manner that is accessible and comprehensible to readers so that they can assess whether or not they agree with the conclusions. While tables are excellent at presenting exact figures, graphs are sometimes better at highlighting a pattern, especially if there are significant differences between individuals or groups.

When the data are obtained using corpus analysis, linguistic patterns are sometimes easy to present using tables and graphs such as histograms and bar charts. Tables embedded in the body of the article, particularly those containing text as well as figures, should include only the necessary amount of data so that patterns can be observed at a glance; readers should not be expected to read through multiple lists of figures to find out key results or trends. Any graphs or tables that need to be examined in more detail should be included only as appendices and only if necessary, so as not to compromise the validity of the report. It is generally useful to summarize data using measures of central tendency, which display the value of the typical data item (such as mean, median and mode), and degrees of variability (range, variance and standard deviation). Oakes (2012) explains how to calculate these values using the R statistical package. However, when working with small samples, we should take care not to just report percentages, but to give specific values too, otherwise we risk giving the incorrect message that there are large differences between variables when in fact the difference might only amount to two or three units.

If concordances are presented these should be in the KWIC (key word in co-text) format, where the node (search words) appears at the centre of the concordance line so that words and co-text appear relatively aligned, which facilitates the observation of patterns (see Chapter 3, Figure 3.4). When used for illustrative purposes, concordances should not take up more than 20 or 30 lines, as a maximum.

7.7   Reporting linguistic data

In product-oriented research, using examples from the texts analyzed is crucial for purposes of credibility but also because it makes the report more readable and helps to bring home any points made. It is important, however, not to rely on the examples to make the point; each example should be described in detail so as to show how it supports any claims being made. Here, it is important to avoid simply stating the obvious, or paraphrasing the example. Examples should be carefully chosen; in short reports, such as journal articles, each example should illustrate a different point being made. For purposes of credibility, it is also important to declare the source of the example.

Reporting the results of linguistic analysis presents a particularly difficult challenge when the object of study is translation because readers cannot be expected to be familiar with the two or more languages involved. Writers need to make sure readers understand the differences in the two (or more) linguistic systems that are relevant for the texts being discussed without assuming knowledge of any languages other than that in which the report is written. There is no easy way around this challenge, except to describe the relevant aspects of the two systems clearly, providing enough but not too much information so as to avoid confusing readers, and providing good examples with glosses in the language in which the report is written.

7.8   Summary

As we hope this chapter has demonstrated, *reporting* research presents a new range of challenges compared to those presented by *doing* research (as discussed in previous chapters). We can summarize these challenges as follows: we need to be able to detach ourselves from the intricacies of our projects and see them from readers' point of view in such a way that readers can follow our thinking; we need to contextualize our aims and conclusions in such a way that their importance is appreciated and their limitations can offer a stepping stone for further research; we should offer enough details about the actual steps taken and the criteria guiding our decisions so that someone doing a very similar project would be able to compare the results meaningfully; a close reading of our report should enable a reader who is familiar with the general area to clearly see the logic of our conclusions in the light of our data while appreciating their complexity.

As researchers, we all want the report to showcase our work in the best possible light. For this reason, it may be tempting to gloss over those aspects of the work that – under close scrutiny – appear less convincing. A more rewarding strategy is to use such opportunities to demonstrate a self-reflective and critically-aware approach to research. One of the most important qualities of a research report is its ability to convince, and in order to be convincing we need to first inspire trust. Thus, transparency should probably be the most important principle to bear in mind when writing a research report.

References

Agarwal, Abhaya and Alon Lavie (2008) 'Meteor, m-bleu and m-ter: Evaluation Metrics for High-Correlation with Human Rankings of Machine Translation Output', in *Proceedings of the Third Workshop on Statistical Machine Translation*, Columbus, Ohio: Association for Computational Linguistics, 115–118.

Ahmad, Khurshid (2008) 'Being in Text and Text in Being: Notes on Representative Texts', in Gunilla Anderman and Margaret Rogers (eds) *Incorporating Corpora: The Linguist and the Translator*, Clevedon, Buffalo & Toronto: Multilingual Matters, 60-94.

Alves, Fabio (ed.) (2003) *Triangulating Translation*, Amsterdam & Philadelphia: John Benjamins.

------ (2005) 'Ritmo Cognitivo, Meta-Função e Experiência: Parâmetros de Análise Processual no Desempenho de Tradutores Novatos e Experientes', in Fabio Alves, Célia Magalhães and Adriana Pagano (eds) *Competência em Tradução: Cognição e Discurso,* Belo Horizonte: Ed UFMG, 109–169.

------ and José Luis Gonçales (2003) 'A Relevance Theory Approach to Inferential Processes in Translation', in Fabio Alves (ed.) *Triangulating Translation: Perspectives in Process Oriented Research*, Amsterdam & Philadelphia: John Benjamins, 3-24.

------ and Daniel Vale (2009) 'Probing the Unit of Translation in Time: Aspects of the Design and Development of a Web Application for Storing, Annotating, and Querying Translation Process Data', *Across Languages and Cultures* 10(2): 251-273.

----- and Amparo Hurtado Albir (2010) 'Cognitive approaches', in Yves Gambier and Luc van Doorslaer (eds) *Handbook of Translation Studies, Vol. 1*, Amsterdam & Philadelphia: John Benjamins, 28-35.

------, Adriana Pagano and Igor da Silva (2010) 'A New Window on Translators' Cognitive Activity: Methodological Issues in the Combined Use of Eye tracking, Key-Logging and Retrospective Protocols', in Inger Mees, Fabio Alves and Susanne Göpferich (eds) *Methodology, Technology and Innovation in Translation Process Research*, Copenhagen: Samfundslitteratur, 267-291.

------, Adriana Pagano, Stella Neumann, Erich Steiner and Silvia Hansen-Schirra (2010) 'Translation Units and Grammatical Shifts: Towards an Integration of Product and Process Research', in Gregory Shreve and Erik Angelone (eds) *Translation and Cognition*, Amsterdam & Philadelphia: John Benjamins, 109-142.

------, Adriana Pagano and Igor da Silva (2011) 'Towards an Investigation of Reading Modalities in/for Translation: An Exploratory Study Using Eye Tracking Data', in Sharon O'Brien (ed.) *Cognitive Explorations of Translation*, London: Continuum, 175-196.

------ and Daniel Vale (2011) 'On Drafting and Revision in Translation: a Corpus Linguistics Oriented Analysis of Translation Process Data', *TC3: Translation: Computation, Corpora, Cognition* 1(1). Available at http://www.t-c3.org/index.php/t-c3/article/view/3, last accessed 9 June 2012.

Angelelli, Claudia V. (2007) 'Assessing Medical Interpreters: The Language and Interpreting Testing Project', *The Translator* 13(1): 63-82.

Angelone, Erik (2010) 'Uncertainty, Uncertainty Management, and Metacognitive Problem Solving in the Translation Task', in Gregory Shreve and Erik Angelone (eds)

Translation and Cognition, Amsterdam & Philadelphia: John Benjamins, 17-40.

Angelone Erik and Gregory Shreve (2011) 'Uncertainty Management, Metacognitive Bundling in Problem Solving and Translation Quality', in Sharon O'Brien (ed.) *Cognitive Explorations of Translation*, London: Continuum, 108-130.

Atkins, Sue, Jeremy Clear and Nicholas Olster (1992) 'Corpus Design Criteria', *Literary and Linguistic Computing* 7(1): 1-16.

Aziz, Wilker, Shiela C.M. de Sousa and Lucia Specia (2012) 'PET: A Tool for Post-Editing and Assessing Machine Translation', in *Proceedings of the LREC 2012 Conference*. Paris: European Language Resources Association, 3982-3987. Available at http://www.lrec-conf.org/proceedings/lrec2012/index.html, last accessed 30 April 2013..

Baddeley, Alan (1986) *Working Memory*, Oxford: Oxford University Press.

------ (1992) 'Working Memory', *Science* 255: 556-559.

Baker, Mona (1998) 'Translation Studies', in Mona Baker (ed.) *Routledge Encyclopedia of Translation Studies*, London & New York: Routledge, 277-280.

------ (2000) 'Towards a Methodology for Investigating the Style of a Literary Translator', *Target* 12(2): 241-266.

------ (2011) *In Other Words: A Coursebook on Translation*, London & New York: Routledge, 2nd edition.

------ and Carol Maier (eds) (2011) *Ethics and the Curriculum: Critical Perspectives*, Special Issue of *The Interpreter and Translator Trainer* 5(1).

Baker, Paul (2006) *Using Corpora in Discourse Analysis*, London & New York: Continuum.

Baker, Paul, Costas Gabrielatos, Majid KhosraviNik, Michal Krzyzanowski, Tony McEnery and Ruth Wodak (2008) 'A Useful Methodological Synergy? Combining Critical Discourse Analysis and Corpus Linguistics to Examine Discourses of Refugees and Asylum Seekers in the UK Press', *Discourse & Society* 19: 273-306.

Balling, Laura Winther (2008) 'Regression Designs and Mixed-Effects Modelling', in Susanne Göpferich, Arnt Lykke Jakobsen and Inger Mees (eds) *Looking at Eyes. Eye Tracking Studies of Reading and Translation Processing*, Copenhagen: Samfundslitteratur, 175-192.

Baron, Naomi (2008) *Always on: Language in an Online and Mobile World,* Oxford & New York: Oxford University Press.

Baroni, Marco and Silvia Bernardini (2004) 'BootCaT: Bootstrapping Corpora and Terms from the Web', in *Proceedings of the LREC 2004 Conference*. Paris: European Language Resources Association, 1313-1316. Available at http://sslmit.unibo.it/~baroni/publications/lrec2004/bootcat_lrec_2004.pdf, last accessed 9 June 2012.

------ and Bernardini, Silvia (2006) 'A New Approach to the Study of Translationese: Machine-Learning the Difference between Original and Translated Text', *Literary and Linguistic Computing* 21(3): 259-274.

------, Silvia Bernardini, Adriano Ferraresi and Eros Zanchetta (2008) 'The WaCky Wide Web: A Collection of Very Large Linguistically Processed Web-Crawled Corpora', *Language Resources and Evaluation* 43(3): 209-226.

Baumgarten, Stefan (2009) *Translating Hitler's Mein Kampf: A Corpus-Aided Discourse-Analytical Study,* Stuttgart: VDM Verlag.

Baxter, Judith (2010) 'Discourse-Analytic Approaches to Text and Talk', in Lia Litosseliti (ed.) *Research Methods in Linguistics,* London: Continuum, 117-137.

Bayer-Hohenwarter, Gerrit (2009) 'Translational Creativity: How to Measure the Unmeasurable', in Susanne Göpferich, Arnt Lykke Jakobsen and Inger Mees (eds) *Behind the Mind: Methods, Models and Results in Translation Process Research*, Copenhagen: Samfundslitteratur, 39-60.

Bayerl, Petra and Karsten Paul (2011) 'What Determines Inter-Coder Agreement in Manual Annotations? A Meta-Analytic Investigation', *Journal of Computational Linguistics* 37(4): 669-725.

Beatty, Jackson (1982) 'Task-Evoked Pupillary Responses, Processing Load, and the Structure of Processing Resources', *Psychological Bulletin* 91(2): 276-292.

Becker, Howard S. and Blance Geer (2004) (including an exchange with Martin Trow) 'Participant Observation and Interviewing: A Comparison', in Clive Seale (ed.) *Social Research Methods: A Reader*, London & New York: Routledge, 246-251.

Beeby, Allison, Patricia Rodríguez Inés and Pilar Sánchez-Gijón (eds) (2009) *Corpus Use and Translating: Corpus Use for Learning to Translate and Learning Corpus Use to Translate*, Amsterdam & Philadelphia: John Benjamins.

Bell, Roger T. (1991) *Translation and Translating: Theory and Practice*, London: Longman.

Bennett, Karen (2007) 'Epistemicide! The Tale of a Predatory Discourse', *The Translator* 13(2): 151-169.

Bernardini, Silvia (2001) 'Think-Aloud Protocols in Translation Research: Achievements, Limits, Future Prospects', *Target* 13(2): 241-263.

------ (2011) 'Monolingual Comparable Corpora and Parallel Corpora in the Search for Features of Translated Language', *Synaps* 26: 2-13.

------ and Federico Zanettin (eds) (2000) *I corpora nella didattica della traduzione. Corpus Use and Learning to Translate,* Bologna: CLUEB.

------ and Sara Castagnoli (2008) 'Corpora for Translator Education and Translation Practice', in Elia Yuste Rodrigo (ed.) *Topics in Language Resources for Translation and Localisation*, Amsterdam & Philadelphia: John Benjamins, 39-56.

------, Adriano Ferraresi and Federico Gaspari (2010) 'Institutional English in Italian University Websites: The acWaC Corpus', in Ángeles Linde López and Rosalía Crespo Jiménez (eds) *Professional English in the European Context: The EHEA Challenge*, Oxford, Bern, etc.: Peter Lang: 27-53.

Best, Samuel J. and Brian S. Krueger (2009) 'Internet Survey Design', in Nigel G. Fielding, Raymond M. Lee and Grant Blank (eds) *The Sage Handbook of Online Research Methods*, California & London: Sage, 217-235.

Biber, Douglas (1993) 'Representativeness in Corpus Design', *Literary and Linguistic Computing* 8(4): 243-257.

Blommaert, Jan and Chris Bulcaen (2000) 'Critical Discourse Analysis', *Annual Review of Anthropology* 29: 447-466.

Bolden, Galina (2000) 'Toward Understanding Practices of Medical Interpreting: Interpreters' Involvement in History Taking', *Discourse Studies* 2(4): 387-419.

Bourdieu, Pierre (1990) *The Logic of Practice*, translated by Richard Nice, Cambridge, UK: Polity

Bourdieu, Pierre (2008) 'A Conservative Revolution in Publishing', translated by Ryan Fraser, *Translation Studies* 1(2): 123-153.

Bowker, Lynne and Jennifer Pearson (2002) *Working with Specialized Language*: A

Practical Guide to Using Corpora, London & New York: Routledge.

Bowker, Lynne and Peter Bennison (2003) 'Student Translation Archive: Design, Development and Application', in Federico Zanettin, Silvia Bernardini and Dominic Stewart (eds) *Corpora in Translator Education*, Manchester: St. Jerome, 103-117.

Breakwell, Glynis M. (1990) *Interviewing*, London: The British Psychological Society & Routledge.

Brotherston, Gordon (2009) 'Script', in Mona Baker and Gabriela Saldanha (eds) *Routledge Encyclopedia of Translation Studies*, London & New York: Routledge, 2nd edition, 249-257.

Brown, Penelope and Stephen Levinson (1987) *Politeness*, Cambridge: Cambridge University Press.

Bucholtz, Mary (2000) 'The Politics of Transcription', *Journal of Pragmatics* 32(10): 1439-1465.

Burnard, Lou (2005) 'Metadata for Corpus Work', in Martin Wynne (ed.) *Developing Linguistic Corpora: A Guide to Good Practice*. Oxford: Oxbow Books, 30-46. Available at http://ota.ahds.ac.uk/documents/creating/dlc/index.htm, last accessed 4 May 2012.

Burns, Anne (2010) 'Action Research', in Brian Paltridge and Aek Phakiti (eds) *Continuum Companion to Research Methods in Applied Linguistics*, London & New York: Continuum, 80-97.

Burrows, John (2002) 'The Englishing of Juvenal: Computational Stylistics and Translated Texts', *Style* 36(4): 677-697.

Caffrey, Colm (2008) 'Using Pupillometric, Fixation-Based and Subjective Measures to Measure the Processing Effort Experienced When Viewing Subtitled TV Anime with Pop-Up Gloss', in Susanne Göpferich, Arnt Lykke Jakobsen and Inger Mees (eds) *Looking at Eyes. Eye Tracking Studies of Reading and Translation Processing*, Copenhagen: Samfundslitteratur, 125-144.

Calzada Pérez, María (2003) 'A Three-Level Methodology for Descriptive-Explanatory Translation Studies', *Target* 13(2): 203-239.

------, María (2007) *Transitivity in Translating: The Interdependence of Texture and Context*, Bern, Berlin, etc.: Peter Lang.

------, María and Saturnino Luz (2006) 'ECPC Technology as a Tool to Study the (Linguistic) Functioning of National and Trans-National European Parliaments', *The International Journal of Technology, Knowledge and Society* 2(5): 53-62.

Carl, Michael (2010) 'Triangulating Product and Process Data: Quantifying Alignment Units with Keystroke Data', in Inger Mees, Fabio Alves and Susanne Göpferich (eds) *Methodology, Technology and Innovation in Translation Process Research*, Copenhagen: Samfundslitteratur, 225-247.

CASRO (Online), *Market Opinion and Social Research – Vocabulary and Service Requirements (ISO 20252:2006)*. Available at http://www.casro.org/ISO/iso_main.cfm, last accessed 1 February 2011.

Chalmers, Alan (1999) *What Is This Thing Called Science?*, Maidenhead: Open University Press, 3rd edition.

Chan, Andy (2010) 'Perceived Benefits of Translator Certification to Stakeholders in the Translation Profession: A Survey of Vendor Managers', *Across Languages and Cultures* 11(1): 93-113.

Chang, Vincent (2009) *Testing Applicability of Eye-Tracking and fMRI to Translation and Interpreting Studies: An Investigation into Directionality*, Unpublished PhD thesis, Imperial College London.

Chesterman, Andrew (1997) *The Memes of Translation: The Spread of Ideas in Translation Theory*, Amsterdam & Philadelphia: John Benjamins.

------ (2000) 'A Causal Model for Translation Studies', in Maeve Olohan (ed.) *Intercultural Faultlines: Research Models in Translation Studies I – Textual and Cognitive Aspects*, Manchester: St. Jerome, 15-28.

------ (2001a) 'Empirical Research Methods in Translation Studies', *Erikoiskielet ja käännösteoria* (VAKKI-symposiumi XX) 27: 9-22.

------ (2001b) 'Proposal for a Hieronymic Oath', *The Translator* 7(2): 139-154.

------ (2006) 'Questions in the Sociology of Translation', in João Ferreira Duarte, Alexandra Assis Rosa and Teresa Seruya (eds) *Translation Studies at the Interface of Disciplines*, Amsterdam & Philadelphia: John Benjamins, 9-27.

------ (2007) 'On the Idea of a Theory', *Across Languages and Cultures* 8(1): 1-16.

------ (2008a) 'On Explanation', in Anthony Pym, Miriam Schlesinger and Daniel Simeoni (eds) *Beyond Descriptive Translation Studies. Investigations in Homage to Gideon Toury*, Amsterdam & Philadelphia: John Benjamins, 363–379.

------ (2008b) 'The Status of Interpretive Hypotheses', in Gyde Hansen, Andrew Chesterman and Heidrun Gerzymisch-Arbogast (eds) *Efforts and Models in Interpreting and Translation Research*, Amsterdam & Philadelphia: John Benjamins, 49-61.

------ (2009) 'The Name and Nature of Translator Studies', *Hermes* 42: 13-22.

Clemmensen, Torkil, Morten Hertzum, Kasper Hornbaek, Quingzin Shi and Pradeep Yammiyavar (2008) 'Cultural Cognition in the Thinking-Aloud Method for Usability Evaluation', *ICIS 2008 Proceedings*, Association for Information Systems: Paper 189. Available at http://culturalusability.cbs.dk/downloads/ICIS2008/icis2008cl emmensen%20et%20al.pdf, last accessed 9 December 2012.

Clark, Andy (1997) *Being There. Putting Brain, Body, and World Together Again*. Cambridge, MA: MIT Press.

------ (2008) *Supersizing the Mind: Embodiment, Action, and Cognitive Extension*. Oxford: Oxford University Press.

Clifford, Andrew (2004) 'Is Fidelity Ethical? The Social Role of the Healthcare Interpreter', *TTR* 17(2): 89-114.

Cohen, Jacob (1960) 'A Coefficient of Agreement for Nominal Scales', *Educational and Psychological Measurement* 20(1): 37-46.

Colina, Sonia (2008) 'Translation Quality Evaluation: Empirical Evidence for a Functionalist Approach', *The Translator* 14(1): 97-134.

Conrad, Susan (2002) 'Corpus Linguistics Approaches for Discourse Analysis', *Annual Review of Applied Linguistics* 22: 75-95.

Coughlin, Deborah (2003) 'Correlating Automated and Human Assessments of Machine Translation Quality', in *Proceedings of the Machine Translation Summit IX*, New Orleans, 23-27 September, 63-70.

Craig, Hugh (1999) 'Authorial Attribution and Computational Stylistics: If You Can Tell Authors Apart, Have you Learned Anything About them?', *Literary and Linguistic Computing* 14(1): 103-113.

Creative Research Systems (Online). Available at http://www.surveysystem.com/ sscalc.htm, last accessed 3 February 2011.

Creswell, John W., Vicki L. Plano Clark, Michelle Gutmann and William Hanson (2003) 'Advanced Mixed Methods Research Designs', in Abbas Tashakkori and Charles Teddlie (eds) *Handbook of Mixed Methods in Social and Behavioral Research*, California & London: Sage, 209-240.

------ and Vicki L. Plano Clark (2007) *Designing and Conducting Mixed Methods Research*, California & London: Sage.

Crisafulli, Edoardo (2002) 'The Quest for an Eclectic Methodology of Translation Description', in Theo Hermans (ed.) *Crosscultural Transgressions: Research Models in Translation Studies II – Historical and Ideological Issues*, Manchester: St. Jerome, 26-43.

Danielsson, Pernilla (2003) 'Automatic Extraction of Meaningful Units from Corpora: A Corpus-Driven Approach Using the Word S*troke*', *International Journal of Corpus Linguistics* 8(1): 109-127.

Dayrell, Carmen (2007) 'A Quantitative Approach to Compare Collocational Patterns in Translated and Non-translated Texts', *International Journal of Corpus Linguistics* 12(3): 375-414.

de Beaugrande, Robert and Wolfgang Dressler (1981) *Introduction to Text Linguistics*, London & New York: Longman.

de Sutter, Gert, Isabelle Delaere and Koen Plevoets (2012) 'Lexical Lectometry in Corpus-Based Translation Studies – Combining Profile-Based Correspondence Analysis and Logistic Regression Modeling', in Michael O. Oakes and Meng Ji (eds) *Quantitative Methods in Corpus-Based Translation* Studies, Amsterdam & Philadelphia, John Benjamins, 325-345.

Deffner, Gerhard (1984) *Lautes Denken – Untersuchung zur Qualität eines Datener hebungsverfahrens*, Frankfurt: Lang.

Delizée, Anne (2012) 'A Global Rating Scale for the Summative Assessment of Pragmatic Translation at Master's Level: An Attempt to Combine Academic and Professional Criteria', in Ilse Depraetere (ed.) *Perspectives on Translation Quality*, Berlin & Boston: Walter de Gruyter, 9-24.

Depraetere, Ilse and Thomas Vackier (2011), 'Comparing Formal Translation Evaluation and Meaning-Oriented Translation Evaluation: Or How QA Tools Can(not) Help', in Ilse Depraetere (ed.) *Perspectives on Translation Quality*, Berlin and Boston: Walter de Gruyter, 25-50.

Désilets, Alain, Geneviève Patenaude and André Sirois (2009) 'Up Close and Personal with a Translator – How Translators Really Work', Tutorial presented at the Twelfth Machine Translation Summit, August 26, Ottawa, Ontario, Canada; 2pp. Available at http://www.mt-archive.info/MTS-2009-Desilets-3.pdf, last accessed 16 December 2012.

------, Louise Brunette, Christiane Melançon and Geneviève Patenaude (2008) 'Reliable innovation: A Techie's Travels in the Land of Translators', in *Proceedings of the Association for Machine Translation in the Americas (AMTA 2008)*, Waikiki, Hawaii, 21-25 October, 339-345.

Doherty, Sharon, Anna M. MacIntyre and Tara Wyne (2010) 'How Does It Feel for *You*? The Emotional Impact and Specific Challenges of Mental Health Interpreting', *Mental Health Review Journal* 15(3): 31-44.

Doherty, Stephen (2012) *Investigating the Effects of Controlled Language on the Reading and Comprehension of Machine Translated Texts: a Mixed-Methods*

Approach, Unpublished PhD thesis, Dublin City University.

------ and Sharon O'Brien (2012) 'A User-Based Usability Assessment of Raw Machine-Translated Technical Instructions', in *Proceedings of the Association of Machine Translation in the Americas (AMTA 2012)*, San Diego, California, unpaginated.

------, Sharon O'Brien and Michael Carl (2010) 'Eye Tracking as an MT Evaluation Technique', *Machine Translation* 24(1): 1-13.

Dörnyei, Zoltan (2007) *Research Methods in Applied Linguistics*, Oxford: Oxford University Press.

Dragsted, Barbara (2004) *Segmentation in Translation and Translation Memory Systems: An Empirical Investigation of Cognitive Segmentation and Effects of Integrating a TM System into the Translation Process*, Copenhagen Business School, Faculty of Language, Communication and Cultural Studies, Ph.D. Series 5.2004.

------ (2010) 'Coordination of Reading and Writing Processes: An Eye on Uncharted Territory', in Gregory Shreve and Erik Angelone (eds) *Translation and Cognition*, Amsterdam & Philadelphia: John Benjamins, 41-62.

------ and Inge Gorm Hansen (2008) 'Comprehension and Production in Translation: A Pilot Study on Segmentation and the Coordination of Reading and Writing Processes', in Susanne Göpferich, Arnt Lykke Jakobsen and Inger Mees (eds) *Looking at Eyes. Eye Tracking Studies of Reading and Translation Processing*, Copenhagen Studies in Language 36, Copenhagen: Samfundslitteratur, 9-30.

Dreyfus, Hubert and Stuart Dreyfus (2005) 'Peripheral Vision: Expertise in Real World Contexts', *Organization Studies* 26(5): 779-792.

Duchowski, Andrew (2003) *Eye Tracking Methodology: Theory and Practice*, New York: Springer.

Eckstein, Harry (1992/2000) 'Case Study and Theory in Political Science', in Harry Eckstein *Regarding Politics, Essays in Political Theory, Stability and Change*, Berkeley: University of California Pres, reprinted in Roger Gomm, Martyn Hammersley and Peter Foster (eds) *Case Study Method: Key Issues, Key Texts*, London, California & London: Sage, 119-164.

Edley, Nigel and Lia Litosseliti (2010) 'Contemplating Interviews and Focus Groups', in Lia Litosseliti (ed.) *Research Methods in Linguistics*, London & New York: Continuum: 155-179.

Englund-Dimitrova, Birgitta (2005) *Expertise and Explicitation in the Translation Process*, Amsterdam & Philadelphia: John Benjamins.

Ericsson, K. Anders (2002) 'Towards a Procedure for Eliciting Verbal Expression of Non-Verbal Experience Without Reactivity: Interpreting the Verbal Overshadowing Effect within the Theoretical Framework for Protocol Analysis', *Applied Cognitive Psychology* 16(8): 981-987.

------ (2010) 'Expertise in Interpreting', in Gregory Shreve and Erik Angelone (eds) *Translation and Cognition*, Amsterdam & Philadelphia: John Benjamins, 231-262.

------ and, Herbert A. Simon (1980) 'Verbal Reports as Data', *Psychological Review* 87: 215-251.

------ and Herbert A. Simon (1998) 'How to Study Thinking in Everyday Life: Contrasting Think-Aloud Protocols with Descriptions and Explanations of Thinking', *Mind, Culture and Activity* 5(3): 178-186.

------ and Herbert A. Simon (1999) *Protocol Analysis: Verbal Reports as Data*, Cambridge, MA: MIT Press, 3rd edition.

Ericsson, K. Anders, Ralf Krampe and Clemens Tesch-Romer (1993) 'The Role of Deliberate Practice in the Acquisition of Expert Performance', *Psychological Review* 100: 363-406.

ESOMAR (Online) *Guideline for Online Research*. Available at http://www.esomar.org/knowledge-and-standards/codes-and-guidelines/guideline-for-online-research.php, last accessed 16 December 2012.

Eynon, Rebecca, Jenny Fry and Ralph Schroeder (2009) 'The Ethics of Internet Research', in Nigel G. Fielding, Raymond M. Lee and Grant Blank (eds) *The Sage Handbook of Online Research Methods*, California & London: Sage, 23-41.

Fairclough, Norman (1992) *Discourse and Social Change*, Cambridge: Polity Press.

------ (2002) 'Critical Discourse Analysis as a Method in Social Scientific Research', in Ruth Wodak and Michael Meyer (eds) *Methods of Critical Discourse Analysis*, California & London: Sage, 121-136.

------ (2003) *Analyzing Discourse: Textual Analysis for Social Research*, London & New York: Routledge.

------ (2010) *Critical Discourse Analysis: The Critical Study of Language,* London: Longman, 2nd edition.

Fielding, Nigel G., Raymond M. Lee and Grant Blank (eds) (2008) *The Sage Handbook of Online Research Methods*, California & London: Sage.

Fink, Arlene (2005) *Conducting Research Literature Reviews*, California & London: Sage, 2nd edition.

Flanagan, Marian and Dorothy Kenny (2007) 'Investigating Repetition and Reusability of Translations in Subtitle Corpora for Use with Example-Based Machine Translation', in Matthew Davies, Paul Rayson, Susan Hunston and Pernilla Danielsson (eds) *Proceedings of the Corpus Linguistics Conference CL2007*, Birmingham: University of Birmingham. Available at http://ucrel.lancs.ac.uk/publications/CL2007/paper/129_Paper.pdf, last accessed 24 July 2012.

Fleiss, Joseph L. (1971) 'Measuring Nominal Scale Agreement Among Many Raters', *Psychological Bulletin* 76(5): 378-382.

Fleiss, Joseph L., Bruce Levin and Myunghee Cho Paik (2003) *Statisical Methods for Rates and Proportions*, Oxford: Wiley.

Fougner Rydning, Antin and Christian Michel Lachaud (2010) 'The Reformulation Challenge in Translation', in Gregory Shreve and Erik Angelone (eds) *Translation and Cognition*, Amsterdam & Philadelphia: John Benjamins, 85-108.

Frankenber-García and Diana Santos (2003) 'Introducing COMPARA: The Portuguese-English Parallel Corpus', in Federico Zanettin, Silvia Bernardini and Dominique Stewart (eds) *Corpora in Translator Education,* Manchester: St. Jerome: 71-87.

Fraser, Janet (1996a) 'The Translator Investigated: Learning from Translation Process Analysis', *The Translator* 2(1): 65-79.

------ (1996b) 'Mapping the Process of Translation', *Meta* 41(1): 84-96.

Frey, Lawrence R., Carl H. Botan, Gary L. Kreps (1991) *Investigating Communication – An Introduction to Research Methods*, Englewood Cliffs, N. J.: Prentice Hall.

Fulford, Heather and Joaquín Granell Zafra (2004) 'The Uptake of Online Tools and Web-Based Language Resources by Freelance Translators: Implications for Translator Training, Professional Development, and Research', in *Proceedings of the Second International Workshop on Language Resources for Translation Work, Research and Training*, Stroudsburg, PA: Association for Computational Linguistics, 50-57.

Geertz, Clifford (1973/2010) 'Thick Description: Toward an Interpretive Theory of Culture', in Geertz Clifford *The Interpretation of Cultures,* New York: Basic Books, reprinted in Erickson, Paul A. and Liam D. Murphy (eds) *Readings for a History of Anthropological Theory,* Ontario: University of Toronto Press, 3rd edition, 341-359.

Gerring, John (2007) *Case Study Research: Principles and Practices*, Cambridge: Cambridge University Press.

Gile, Daniel (1995) *Basic Concepts and Models for Interpreter and Translator Training*, Amsterdam & Philadelphia: John Benjamins.

------ (2004) 'Integrated Problem and Decision Reporting as a Translator Training Tool', *JoSTrans, Journal of Specialised Translation* 2: 2-20.

Gillham, Bill (2000) *Case Study Research Methods*, London & New York: Continuum.

Glaser, Barney G. and Anselm L. Strauss (2004) 'Theoretical Sampling', in Clive Seale (ed.) *Social Research Methods: A Reader*, London & New York: Routledge, 226-231.

Gomm, Roger, Martyn Hammersley and Peter Foster (eds) (2000) *Case Study Method: Key Issues, Key Texts*, California & London: Sage.

Goodwin, Phil (2010) 'Ethical Problems in Translation: Why We Might Need Steiner After All', *The Translator* 16(1): 19-42.

Göpferich, Susanne (2008) *Translationsprozessforschung. Stand – Methoden – Perspektiven*, Tübingen: Narr.

------ (2009), 'Comprehensibility Assessment Using the Karlsruhe Comprehensibility Concept', *JoSTrans, Journal of Specialised Translation* 11: 21-52.

------ (2010), 'Data Documentation and Data Accessibility in Translation Process Research', *The Translator* 16(1): 93-124.

------, Arnt Lykke Jakobsen and Inger Mees (eds) (2008) *Looking at Eyes. Eye Tracking Studies of Reading and Translation Processing*, Copenhagen: Samfundslitteratur.

------, Arnt Lykke Jakobsen and Inger M. Mees (eds) (2009) *Behind the Mind: Methods, Models and Results in Translation Process Research,* Copenhagen: Samfundslitteratur.

Gouadec, Daniel (1981) 'Paramètres de l'évaluation des traductions', *Meta* 26(2): 99-116.

------ (1989) 'Comprendre, évaluer, prévenir. Pratique, enseignement et recherche face à l'erreur et à la faute en traduction', TTR 2(2): 35-54.

------ (2010) 'Quality in Translation', in Yves Gambier and Luc Van Doorslaer (eds) *Handbook of Translation Studies, Vol. 1*, Amsterdam & Philadelphia: John Benjamins, 270-275.

Gries, Stefan Th. (2006) 'Some Proposals Towards More Rigorous Corpus Linguistics', *Zeitschrift für Anglistik und Amerikanistik* 54(2): 191-202.

Guba, Egon G. and Yvonna S. Lincoln (2005) 'Paradigmatic Controversies, Contradictions, and Emerging Influences', in Norman K. Denzin and Yvonna S. Lincoln (eds) *The Sage Handbook of Qualitative Research,* California & London: Sage, 3rd edition, 191-216.

Guerberof, Ana (2008) *Productivity and Quality in the Post-Editing of Outputs from Translation Memories and Machine Translation*, Unpublished Minor Dissertation, Universitat Rovira I Virgili, Spain.

Halverson, Sandra (2009) 'Elements of Doctoral Training: The Logic of the Research Process, Research Design, and the Evaluation of Research Quality', in Ian Mason (ed.) *Training for Doctoral Research,* Special Issue of *The Interpreter and Translator Trainer* 3(1): 79-106.

Hanna, Sameh Fekry (2006) *Towards a Sociology of Drama Translation: A Bourdieusian Perspective on Translations of Shakespeare's Great Tragedies in Egypt.* Unpublished PhD thesis, The University of Manchester, Centre for Translation and Intercultural Studies.

Hansen, Gyde (ed.) (1999) *Probing the Process in Translation – Methods and Results,* Copenhagen: Samfundslitteratur.

------ (ed.) (2002) *Empirical Translation Studies: Process and Product*, Copenhagen: Samfundslitteratur.

------ (2010a) 'Some Thoughts about the Evaluation of Translation Products in Empirical Translation Process Research', in Inger Mees, Fabio Alves and Susanne Göpferich (eds) *Methodology, Technology and Innovation in Translation Process Research*, Copenhagen: Samfundslitteratur, 389-402.

------ (2010b) 'Integrative Description in Translation Processes', in Gregory Shreve and Erik Angelone (eds) *Translation and Cognition*, Amsterdam & Philadelphia: John Benjamins, 189-211.

Hanson, Eamonn, W. Schaufeli, T. Vrijkotte, N. Plomp, G. Godaert (2000) 'The Validity and Reliability of the Dutch Effort-Reward Imbalance Questionnaire', *Journal of Occupational Health Psychology* 5(1): 142-155.

Hareide, Lidun and Knut Holfland (2012) 'Compiling a Norwegian-Spanish Parallel Corpus: Methods and Challenges', in Michael O. Oakes and Meng Ji (eds) *Quantitative Methods in Corpus-Based Translation* Studies, Amsterdam & Philadelphia, John Benjamins, 75-113.

Harvey, Keith (2003) *Intercultural Movements: 'American Gay' in French Translation,* Manchester: St Jerome.

Hatim, Basil (2007) 'Intervention at Text and Discourse Levels in the Translation of 'Orate' Languages', in Jeremy Munday (ed.) *Translation as Intervention*, London & New Yorkí Continuum, 84-96.

------ and Ian Mason (1990) *Discourse and the Translator,* London & New York: Longman.

------ and Ian Mason (1997) *The Translator as Communicator*, London & New York: Routledge.

Hayes, John R., Linda Flower, Karen Schriver, James Stratman and Linda Carey (1987) 'Cognitive Processes in Revision', in Sheldon Rosenberg (ed.) *Advances in Psycholinguistics, Vol. 2: Reading, Writing and Language Learning*, Cambridge: Cambridge University Press, 176-240.

Hess, Eckhard H. and James Polt (1964) 'Pupil Size in Relation to Mental Activity in Simple Problem Solving', *Science* 143: 1190-1192.

Hewson, Claire, Peter Yule, Dianna Laurent and Carl Vogel (2003) *Internet Research Methods: A Practical Guide for the Social and Behavioural Sciences,* California & London: Sage.

------ and Dianna Laurent (2008) 'Research Design and Tools for Internet Research', in Nigel G. Fielding, Raymond M. Lee and Grant Blank (eds) *The Sage Handbook of Online Research Methods*, London, Thousand Oaks & New Delhi: Sage, 58-78.

Hine, Christine (2000) *Virtual Ethnography*, California & London: Sage.

Hofstede, Geert, Gert Jan Hofstede and Michael Minkov (2010) *Cultures and Orga-nizations: Software for the Mind*, New York: McGraw-Hill, 3rd edition.

House, Juliane (1977) *A Model for Translation Quality Assessment,* Tübingen: Gunter Narr.

------ (1997) *Translation Quality Assessment: A Model Revisited*, Tübingen: Gunter Narr.

------ (2001) 'Translation Quality Assessment: Linguistic Description versus Social Evaluation', *Meta* 46(2): 243-257.

------ (2009) *Quality*, in Mona Baker and Gabriela Saldanha (eds) *Routledge Encyclope-dia of Translation Studies*, London & New York: Routledge, 2nd edition, 222-225.

Hubscher-Davidson, Severine (2009) 'Personal Diversity and Diverse Personalities in Translation: A Study of Individual Differences', *Perspectives: Studies in Translatol-ogy* 17(3): 175-192.

Inghilleri, Moira (2003) 'Habitus, Field and Discourse: Interpreting as a Socially Situ-ated Activity', *Target* 15(2): 243-268.

------ (ed.) (2005a) *Bourdieu and the Sociology of Translation and Interpreting*, Special Issue of *The Translator* 11(2).

------ (2005b) 'The Sociology of Bourdieu and the Construction of the 'Object' in Translation and Interpreting Studies', *The Translator* 11(2): 125-145.

------ (2009a) 'Ethics', in Mona Baker and Gabriela Saldanha (eds) *Routledge En-cyclopedia of Translation Studies*, London & New York: Routledge, 2nd edition, 100-104.

------ (2009b) 'Sociological Approaches', in Mona Baker and Gabriela Saldanha (eds) *Routledge Encyclopaedia of Translation Studies,* London & New York: Routledge, 2nd edition, 279-282.

Jääskeläinen, Riitta (1993) 'Investigating Translation Strategies', in Sonja Tirkkonen-Condit and John Laffling (eds), *Recent Trends in Empirical Translation Research*, Joensuu: University of Joensuu, 99-119.

------ (2002) 'Think-Aloud Protocol Studies into Translation: An Annotated Bibliogra-phy', *Target* 14(1): 107-136.

------ (2010a) 'Are All Professionals Experts? Definitions of Expertise and Reinter-pretation of Research Evidence in Process Studies', in Gregory Shreve and Erik Angelone (eds) *Translation and Cognition*, Amsterdam & Philadelphia: John Benjamins, 213-227.

------ (2010b) 'Looking for a Working Definition of 'Translation Strategies'', in Inger Mees, Fabio Alves and Susanne Göpferich (eds) *Methodology, Technology and Innovation in Translation Process Research*, Copenhagen: Samfundslitteratur, 375-387.

------ (2011) 'Back to Basics: Designing a Study to Determine the Validity and Reli-ability of Verbal Report Data on Translation Processes', in Sharon O'Brien (ed.) *Cognitive Explorations of Translation*, London: Continuum, 15-29.

------ and Sonja Tirkkonen-Condit (1988) 'Automatised Processes in Professional vs. Non-Professional Translation: A Think-Aloud Protocol Study', in Sonja Tirkkonen-Condit (ed.) *Empirical Research in Translation and Intercultural Studies*, Tübingen: Gunter Narr, 89-109.

Jakobsen, Arnt Lykke (1998) 'Logging Time Delay in Translation', in Gyde Hansen (ed.) *LSP Texts and the Process of Translation*, Copenhagen: Copenhagen Business School, 73-102.

------(2002) 'Orientation, Segmentation and Revision in Translation', in Gyde Hansen (ed.) *Empirical Translation Studies: Process and Product*, Copenhagen: Samfundslitteratur, 191-204.

------ (2003) 'Effects of Think Aloud on Translation Speed, Revision and Segmentation', in Fabio Alves (ed.) *Triangulating Translation*, Amsterdam & Philadelphia: John Benjamins, 69-95.

------ (2005) 'Instances of Peak Performance in Translation', *Lebende Sprachen* 50(3): 111-116.

------ and Kristian T.H. Jensen (2008) 'Eye Movement Behaviour Across Four Different Types of Reading Task', in Susanne Göpferich, Arnt Lykke Jakobsen and Inger Mees (eds) *Looking at Eyes. Eye Tracking Studies of Reading and Translation Processing*, Copenhagen: Samfundslitteratur, 103-124.

------ and Lasse Schou (1999) 'Translog Documentation', in Gyde Hansen (ed.) *Probing the Process in Translation – Methods and Results*, Copenhagen: Samfundslitteratur, 151-186.

James, Nalita and Hugh Busher (2009) *Online Interviewing*, California & London: Sage.

Jensen, Astrid (2000) *The Effect of Time on Cognitive Processes and Strategies in Translation*, Unpublished PhD thesis, Copenhagen: Copenhagen Business School.

Jensen, Kristian T.H. (2008) 'Assessing Eye-Tracking Accuracy in Translation Studies', in Susanne Göpferich, Arnt Lykke Jakobsen and Inger Mees (eds) *Looking at Eyes. Eye Tracking Studies of Reading and Translation Processing*, Copenhagen: Samfundslitteratur, 157-174.

------ (2009) 'Indicators of Text Complexity, in Susanne Göpferich, Arnt Lykke Jakobsen and Inger Mees (eds) *Behind the Mind: Methods, Models and Results in Translation Process Research*, Copenhagen: Samfundslitteratur, 61-80.

------ (2011a) 'Distribution of Attention Between Source Text and Target Text During Translation', in Sharon O'Brien (ed.) *Cognitive Explorations of Translation*, London: Continuum, 215-237.

------ (2011b) *Allocation of Cognitive Resources in Translation – An Eye-Tracking and Key-Logging Study*, PhD thesis, Copenhagen Business School, Denmark.

Ji, Meng (2012) 'Hypothesis Testing in Corpus-Based Literary Translation Studies', in Michael O. Oakes and Meng Ji (eds) *Quantitative Methods in Corpus-Based Translation Studies*, Amsterdam & Philadelphia, John Benjamins, 53-72.

------ and Michael P. Oakes (2012) 'A Corpus Study of Early English Translations of Cao Xueqin's *Hongloumeng*', in Michael P. Oakes and Meng Ji (eds) *Quantitative Methods in Corpus-Based Translation Studies,* Amsterdam & Philadelphia: John Benjamins, 177-208.

Johansson, Stig, Jarle Ebeling Signe Oksefjell (n.d.) *English Norwegian Parallel Corpus: Manual*. Available at http://www.hf.uio.no/ilos/english/services/omc/enpc/ENPCmanual.pdf, last accessed 9 June 2012.

Johnson, R. Burke and Anthony J. Onwuegbuzie (2004) 'Mixed Methods Research: A Research Paradigm Whose Time Has Come', *Educational Researcher* 33(7): 14-26.

Johnson, Timothy, Patrick Kulesa, Young Ik Cho and Sharon Shavitt (2005) 'The Relation Between Culture and Response Styles: Evidence from 19 Countries', *Journal of Cross Cultural Psychology* 36: 264-277.

Junker, Buford H. (2004) 'The Field Work Situation: Social Roles for Observation' in Clive Seale (ed.) *Social Research Methods: A Reader,* London & New York: Routledge, 221-225.

Just, Marcel A. and Patricia A. Carpenter (1980) 'A Theory of Reading: From Eye Fixations to Comprehension', *Psychological Review* 87: 329-354.

Kaakinen, Johanna and Jukka Hyönä (2005) 'Perspective Effects on Expository Text Comprehension: Evidence from Think-Aloud Protocols, Eye Tracking and Recall', *Discourse Processes* 40(3): 239-257.

Kang, Ji-Hae (2007) 'Recontextualization of News Discourse: A Case Study of Translation of News Discourse on North Korea', *The Translator* 13(2): 219-242.

Károly, Adrienn (2011) 'Translation Competence and Translation Performance – Lexical, Syntactic and Textual Patterns in Student Translations of a Specialized EU Genre', *English for Specific Purposes* 31(1): 36-46.

Ke, Shih-Wen (2012) 'Clustering a Translational Corpus', in Michael P. Oakes and Meng Ji (eds) *Quantitative Methods in Corpus-Based Translation Studies,* Amsterdam & Philadelphia: John Benjamins, 149-174.

Kennedy, Graeme (1998) *An Introduction to Corpus Linguistics*, London & New York: Longman.

Kenny, Dorothy (2001) *Lexis and Creativity in Translation: A Corpus-based Study,* Manchester, St. Jerome Publishing.

------ (2005) 'Parallel Corpora and Translation Studies: Old Questions, New Perspectives? Reporting *That* in GEPCOLT: a Case Study', in Geoff Barnbrook, Pernilla Danielsson and Michaela Mahlberg (eds) *Meaningful Texts: The Extraction of Semantic Information from Monolingual and Multilingual Corpora*, London & New York: Continuum, 154-165.

------ (2009) 'Unit of Translation', in Mona Baker and Gabriela Saldhana (eds) *Routledge Encyclopedia of Translation Studies*, London & New York: Routledge, 2nd edition, 96-99.

Kilgarriff, Adam (2005) 'Language is Never Ever Ever Random', *Corpus Linguistics and Linguistic Theory* 1(2): 263-276.

------ and Gregory Grefenstette (eds) (2003) *Web as Corpus*, Special Issue of *Computational Linguistics* 29(3).

Kim, Mira (2007) 'Translation Error Analysis: A Systemic Functional Grammar Approach', in Dorothy Kenny and Kyongjoo Ryou (eds) *Across Boundaries: International Perspectives on Translation Studies*, Newcastle upon Tyne: Cambridge Scholars Publishing, 161-175.

Koskinen, Kaisa (2008) *Translating Institutions: An Ethnographic Study of EU Translation*, Manchester: St Jerome Publishing.

------ (2010) 'Agency and Causality: Towards Explaining by Mechanisms in Translation Studies', in Tuija Kinnunen and Kaisa Koskinen (eds) *Translators' Agency*, Tampere: Tempere University Press, 165-187.

------ and Tuija Kinnunen (2010) 'Introduction', in Tuija Kinnunen and Kaisa Koskinen (eds) *Translators' Agency*, Tampere: Tempere University Press, 4-10.

Kress, Gunther and Theo van Leeuwen (1996) *Reading Images: The Grammar of Visual Design,* London & New York: Routledge.

Kress, Gunther and Theo van Leeuwen (2001) *Multimodal Discourse: The Modes and*

Media of Contemporary Communication, Arnold: London.

Krings, Hans P. (1986a) *Was in den Köpfen von Übersetzern vorgeht*, Tübingen: Gunter Narr Verlag.

------ (1986b) 'Translation Problems and Translation Strategies of Advanced German Learners of French (L2)', in Juliane House and Shoshana Blum-Kulka (eds) *Interlingual and Intercultural Communication*, Tübingen: Narr, 159-176.

------ (1988) 'Blick in die 'Black Box' – Eine Fallstudie zum Übersetzungsprozess bei Berufsübersetzern', in Rainer Arntz (ed.) *Textlinguistik und Frachsprache*, AILA-Symposium 1987, Hildesheim: Ohm, 393-411.

------ (2001) *Repairing Texts: Empirical Investigations of Machine Translation Post-Editing Processes*, Kent, Ohio: The Kent State University Press, edited/translated by G.S. Koby.

Kuo, Sai-Hua and Mari Nakamura (2005) 'Translation or Transformation? A Case Study of Language and Ideology in the Taiwanese Press', *Discourse & Society* 16(3): 393-417.

Kvale, Steinar (1996) *InterViews: An Introduction to Qualitative Research Interviewing*, California & London: Sage.

Lachaud, Christian M. (2011) 'EEG, EYE and Key: Three Simultaneous Streams of Data for Investigating the Cognitive Mechanisms of Translation', in Sharon O'Brien (ed.) *Cognitive Explorations of Translation*, London: Continuum: 131-153.

Lagoudaki, Elina (2008) *Expanding the Possibilities of Translation Memory Systems: From the Translator's Wishlist to the Developer's Design*, Unpublished PhD thesis, Imperial College London.

Langdridge, Darren and Gareth Hagger-Johnson (2009) *Introduction to Research Methods and Data Analysis in Psychology*, Edinburgh: Pearson Education, 2nd edition.

Lather, Patti (1986) 'Issues of Validity in Openly Ideological Research: Between a Rock and a Soft place', *Interchange* 17(4): 63-84.

Lauscher, Susanne (2000) 'Translation Quality Assessment: Where Can Theory and Practice Meet?', *The Translator* 6(2): 149-168.

Laviosa, Sara (1997) 'How Comparable can 'Comparable Corpora' Be?', *Target* 9(2): 282-319.

------ (1998a) 'The English Comparable Corpus: A Resource and a Methodology', in Lynne Bowker, Michael Cronin, Dorothy Kenny and Jennifer Pearson (eds) *Unity in Diversity? Current Trends in Translation Studies,* Manchester: St. Jerome, 101-112.

------ (1998b) 'Core Patterns of Lexical Use in a Comparative Corpus of English Narrative Prose', *Meta* 43(4): 557-570.

------ (2002) *Corpus-Based Translation Studies: Theory, Findings, Applications,* Amsterdam & New York: Rodopi.

------ (2011) 'Corpus-Based Translation Studies: Where Does It Come from? Where Is It Going?', in Alet Kruger, Kim Wallmach and Jeremy Munday (eds) *Corpus-based Translation Studies: Research and Applications,* London & New York: Continuum, 13-32.

Laviosa-Braithwaite, Sara (1997) 'Investigating Simplification in an English Comparable Corpus of Newspaper Articles', in Kinga Klaudy and János Kohn (eds) *Transferre Necesse Est*: Proceedings of the Second International Conference on Current Trends in Studies of Translation and Interpreting, 1996, Hungary, Budapest:

Scholastica, 531-540.

LDC (2002) Linguistics Data Consortium, *Linguistic data annotation specification: Assessment of fluency and adequacy in translations.* Revision 1.5. Available at http://www.ldc.upenn.edu/Catalog/docs/LDC2003T17/TransAssess02.pdf, last accessed 16 December 2012.

Le Grange, Lesley and Peter Beets (2005) '(Re)conceptualizing Validity in (Outcomes-Based) Assessment', *South African Journal of Education* 25(2): 115-119.

Leech, Geoffrey (2005) 'Adding Linguistic Annotation', in Martin Wynne (ed.) *Developing Linguistic Corpora: a Guide to Good Practice,* Oxford: Oxbow Books: 17-29. Available at http://ota.ahds.ac.uk/documents/creating/dlc/index.htm, last accessed 4 May 2012.

Leeson, Lorraine (2008) 'Quantum Leap: Leveraging the Signs of Ireland Digital Corpus in Irish Sign Language/English Interpreter Training', *The Sign Language Translator and Interpreter* 2(2): 149-176.

Lewis, Michael and Tanja Staehler (2010) *Phenomenology: An Introduction*, London: Continuum.

Lewins, Ann and Christina Silver (2007) *Using Software in Qualitative Research: A Step-by-Step Guide*. California & London: Sage.

Lincoln, Yvonna S. and Egon G. Guba (1979/2000) *The Only Generalization Is: There Is No Generalization,* in Yvonna S. Lincoln and Egon G. Guba (1979) *Naturalistic Enquiry,* Newbury Park, CA: Sage, reprinted in Roger Gomm, Martyn Hammersley and Peter Foster (eds) *Case Study Method: Key Issues, Key Texts*, California & London: Sage, 27-44.

Lofland, John (2004) 'Field Notes', in Clive Seale (ed.) *Social Research Methods: A Reader*, London & New York: Routledge, 232-235.

Lörscher, Wolfgang (1988) 'Thinking-Aloud as a Method for Collecting Data on Translation Processes', in Sonja Tirkkonen-Condit (ed.) *Empirical Research in Translation and Intercultural Studies*, Tübingen: Gunter Narr, 67-77.

------ (1991) *Translation Performance, Translation Process, and Translation Strategies: A Psycholinguistic Investigation*, Tübingen: Gunter Narr Verlag.

Louw, Bill (1993) 'Irony in the Text or Insincerity in the Writer: The Diagnostic Potential of Semantic Prosodies', in Mona Baker, Gill Francis and Elena Tognini-Bonelli (eds) *Text and Technology: In Honour of John Sinclair*, Amsterdam & Philadelphia: John Benjamins, 157-76.

Luz, Saturnino and Mona Baker (2000) 'TEC: A Toolkit and API for Distributed Corpus Processing', in Steven Bird and Gary Simmons (eds) *Proceedings of Exploration-2000: Workshop on Web-Based Language Documentation and Description*: Philadelphia: University of Pennsylvania, 108-112. Available at http://www.ldc.upenn.edu/exploration/expl2000/papers/luz/, last accessed 4 July 2012.

Madden, Raymond (2010) *Being Ethnographic: A Guide to the Theory and Practice of Ethnography*, California & London: Sage.

Maltby, Matthew (2010) 'Institutional Identities of Interpreters in the Asylum Application Context: A Critical Discourse Analysis of Interpreting Policies in the Voluntary Sector', in Mona Baker, Maeve Olohan, María Calzada Pérez (eds) *Text and Context: Essays on Translation & Interpreting in Honour of Ian Mason*, Manchester: St Jerome, 209-236.

Mann, Chris and Fiona Stewart (2005) *Internet Communication and Qualitative Re-*

search: A Handbook for Researching Online, California & London: Sage.

Marco, Josep (2009) 'Training Translation Researchers: An Approach Based on Models and Best Practice', in Ian Mason (ed.) *Training for Doctoral Research,* Special Issue of *The Interpreter and Translator Trainer* 3(1): 13-37.

Martínez Melis, Nicole and Amparo Hurtado Albir (2001), 'Assessment in Translation Studies: Research Needs', *Meta* 46(2): 272-287.

Mason, Ian (2000) 'Audience Design in Translating', *The Translator* 6(1): 1-22.

------ (2001) 'Translator Behaviour and Language Usage: Some Constraints on Contrastive Studies', *Hermes, Journal of Linguistics* 26: 65-89.

------ (2005) 'Projected and Perceived Identities in Dialogue Interpreting', in Juliane House, M. Rosario Martín Ruano and Nicole Baumgarten (eds) *Translation and the Construction of Identity,* International Association for Translation and Intercultural Studies, 30-52.

------ (2006) 'Ostension, Inference and Response: Analysing Participant Moves in Community Interpreting dialogues', *Linguistica Antverpiensia New Series* NS5 - *Taking Stock: Research and Methodology in Community Interpreting,* 103-120.

------ (2009a) 'Research Training in Translation Studies', in Ian Mason (ed). *Training for Doctoral Research,* Special Issue of *The Interpreter and Translator Trainer* 3(1): 1-12.

------ (2009b) 'Translator Moves and Reader Response: the Impact of Discoursal Shifts in Translation', in Barbara Ahrens, Lothar Cerny, Monika Krein-Kuhle and Michael Schreiber (eds) *Translationswissenschaftliches Kolloquium I. Beitrage zur Übersetzungs- und Dolmetschswissenschaft (Koln/Germersheim),* Frankfurt-am-Main: Peter Lang, 55-70.

------ (2009c) 'Role, Positioning and Discourse in Face-to-Face Interpreting', in Raquel de Pedro Ricoy, Isabelle Perez and Christine Wilson (eds) *Interpreting and Translating in Public Service Settings: Policy, Practice, Pedagogy,* Manchester: St Jerome, 52-73.

------ and Adriana Şerban (2003) 'Deixis as an Interactive Feature in Literary Translations from Romanian into English', *Target* 15(2): 269-294.

Matthews, Bob and Liz Ross (2010) *Research Methods: A Practical Guide for the Social Sciences,* Edinburgh: Pearson Education Ltd.

Matthews, Gerald, Ian Deary and Martha Whiteman (2003) *Personality Traits,* Cambridge: Cambridge University Press, 2nd edition.

Mauranen, Anna and Pekka Kujamäki (eds) (2004) *Translation Universals. Do They Exist?,* Amsterdam & Philadephia: John Benjamins.

Mautner, Gerlinde (2009) 'Corpora and Critical Discourse Analysis', in Paul Baker (ed.) *Contemporary Corpus Linguistics,* London & New York: Continuum, 32-46.

McEnery, Tony and Andrew Wilson (1996) *Corpus Linguistics,* Edinburgh: Edinburgh University Press.

------, Richard Xiao and Yulio Tono (2006) *Corpus-based Language Studies. An Advanced Resource Book,* London & New York: Routledge.

McLellan, Eleanor, Kathleen M. Macqueen and Judith I. Neidig (2003) 'Beyond the Qualitative Interview: Data Preparation and Transcription', *Field Methods* 15(1): 63–84.

Medawar, Peter (1996) 'Is the Scientific Paper a Fraud?', in Peter Medawar (ed.) *The Strange Case of the Spotted Mice and Other Classic Essays on Science,* Oxford:

Oxford University Press: 33-39.

Mees, Inger, Fabio Alves and Susanne Göpferich (eds) (2010) *Methodology, Technology and Innovation in Translation Process Research*, Copenhagen: Samfundslitteratur.

MeLLANGE (2007) *Multilingual eLearning in Language Engineering*. Available at http://corpus.leeds.ac.uk/mellange/about_mellange.html, last accessed 16 December 2012.

Meyer, Bernd (2001) 'How Untrained Interpreters Handle Medical Terms', in Ian Mason (ed.) *Triadic Exchanges. Studies in Dialogue Interpreting*, Manchester: St. Jerome, 87-106.

Meyer, Charles F. (2002) *English Corpus Linguistics: An Introduction*, Cambridge: Cambridge University Press.

Millán-Varela, Carmen (2004) 'Exploring Advertising in a Global Context: Food for Thought', *The Translator* 10(2): 245-267.

Mirlohi, Mehdi, Joy Egbert and Behzad Ghonsooli (2011) 'Flow in Translation: Exploring Optimal Experience for Translation Trainees', *Target* 23(2): 251-271.

Monacelli, Claudia (2000) 'Mediating Castles in the Air: Epistemological Issues in Interpreting Studies', in Maeve Olohan (ed.) *Intercultural Faultlines: Research Models in Translation Studies I – Textual and Cognitive Aspects*, Manchester: St. Jerome, 193-214.

Mouton, Johann and H.C. Marais (1996) *Basic Concepts in the Methodology of the Social Sciences*, South Africa: HSRC Series in Methodology; translated from *Methodologie van die Geesteswetenskappe: Basiese begrippe*, by K.F. Mauer.

Munday, Jeremy (2004) 'Advertising: Some Challenges to Translation Theory', *The Translator* 10(2): 199-219.

------ (2007) 'Translation and Ideology: A Textual Approach', *The Translator* 13(2): 195-217.

------ (2008) *Style and Ideology in Translation: Latin American Writing in English*, London & New York: Routledge.

------ (2009) 'The Concept of the Interpersonal in Translation', *Synaps 23*: 15-27. Available at http://www.nhh.no/en/research---faculty/department-of-professional-and-intercultural-communication/publications/synaps.aspx, last accessed 10 May 2012.

------ (2010) 'Evaluation and Intervention in Translation', in Mona Baker, Maeve Olohan and María Calzada Pérez (eds) *Text and Context: Essays on Translation & Interpreting in Honour of Ian Mason*, Manchester: St Jerome, 77-94.

------ (2011) 'Looming Large: A Cross-Linguistic Analysis of Semantic Prosodies in Comparable Reference Corpora', in Alet Kruger, Kim Wallmach and Jeremy Munday (eds) *Corpus-based Translation Studies: Research and Applications*. London & New York: Continuum, 169-186.

------ (2012) *Evaluation in Translation: Critical Points in Translator Decision Making*, London & New York: Routledge.

Muñoz Martín, Ricardo (2010) 'On Paradigms and Cognitive Translatology', in Gregory Shreve and Erik Angelone (eds) *Translation and Cognition*, Amsterdam & Philadelphia: John Benjamins, 169-187.

Napier, Jemina (2011) '"It's not what they say but the way they say it" A Content Analysis of Interpreter and Consumer Perceptions of Signed Language Interpreting in Australia', *International Journal of the Sociology of Language* 207: 59-87.

------, Della Goswell and Rachel Locker McKee (2006) *Sign Language Interpreting: Theory and Practice in Australia and New Zealand*, Sydney: The Federation Press.

Newmark, Peter (1988) *A Textbook of Translation*, London: Prentice Hall.

Nida, Eugene and Charles Taber (1969) *Theory and Practice of Translation*, London: United Bible Societies.

Nisbett, Richard, E. (2003) *The Geography of Thought: How Asians and Westerners Think Differently – and Why*, London: Brealy.

Nord, Christiane (1997) *Translating as a Purposeful Activity. Functionalist Approaches Explained*, Manchester: St. Jerome.

O'Brien, Sharon (2006) 'Eye Tracking and Translation Memory Matches', *Perspectives: Studies In Translatology* 14(3): 185-205.

------ (2007) 'Pauses as Indicators of Cognitive Effort in Post-Editing Machine Translation Output', *Across Languages and Cultures* 7(1): 1-21.

------ (2008) 'Processing Fuzzy Matches in Translation Memory Tools: an Eye-Tracking Analysis', in Susanne Göpferich, Arnt Lykke Jakobsen and Inger Mees (eds) *Looking at Eyes: Eye Tracking Studies of Reading and Translation Processing,* Copenhagen: Samfundslitteratur, 79-102.

------ (2010a) 'Controlled Language and Readability', in Gregory Shreve and Erik Angelone (eds) *Translation and Cognition*, Amsterdam & Philadelphia: John Benjamins, 143-168.

------ (2010b) 'Eye Tracking in Translation Process Research: Methodological Challenges and Solutions', in Inger Mees, Fabio Alves and Susanne Göpferich (eds) *Methodology, Technology and Innovation in Translation Process Research*, Copenhagen: Samfundslitteratur, 251-266.

------ (ed.) (2011a) *Cognitive Explorations of Translation*, London: Continuum.

------ (2011b) 'Towards Predicting Post-Editing Productivity', *Machine Translation* 25(3): 197-215.

------ (2012) 'Towards a Dynamic Quality Evaluation Model for Translation', *JosTrans: Journal of Specialised Translation* 17. Available at http://www.jostrans.org/issue17/art_obrien.pdf, last accessed 5 December 2012.

O'Leary, Zina (2010) *The Essential Guide to Doing Your Research Project*, California & London: Sage.

Oakes, Michael P. (1998) *Statistics for Corpus Linguistics,* Edinburgh: Edinburgh University Press.

------ (2012) 'Describing a Translation Corpus', in Michael P. Oakes and Meng Ji (eds) *Quantitative Methods in Corpus-Based Translation Studies,* Amsterdam & Philadelphia: John Benjamins, 115-148.

------ and Meng Ji (eds) (2012) *Quantitative Methods in Corpus-Based Translation Studies,* Amsterdam & Philadelphia: John Benjamins.

------ and Tony McEnery (2000) 'Bilingual Text Alignment – an Overview', in Simon Philip Botley, Anthony Mark McEenry and Andrew Wilson (eds) *Multilingual Corpora in Teaching and Research*, Amsterdam & Atlanta: Rodopi, 1-37.

Olohan, Maeve (2001) 'Spelling Out the Optionals in Translation: A Corpus Study', in Paul Rayson, Andrew Williams, Tony McEnery, Andrew Hardie and Shereen Khoja (eds) *UCREL Technical Papers 13,* Special Issue: *Proceedings of the 2001 Corpus Linguistics conference*, Lancaster University: 423-432. Available at http://ucrel.lancs.ac.uk/publications/CL2003/CL2001%20conference/papers/olohan.pdf, last accessed 20 May 2013.

------ (2002) 'Comparable Corpora in Translation Research: Overview of Recent Analyses Using the Translational English Corpus', in Yuste Rodrigo, Elia (ed.) *Proceedings of the First International Workshop on Language Resources for Translation Work, Reseach & Training*, Paris: ELRA (European Language Resources Association), 5-9. Available at http://www.lrec-conf.org/proceedings/lrec2002/pdf/ws8.pdf, last accessed 9 June 2012.

------ (2003) 'How Frequent are the Contractions? A Study of Contracted Forms in the Translational English Corpus', *Target* 15(1): 59-89.

------ (2004) *Introducing Corpora in Translation Studies*, London & New York: Routledge.

------ and Mona Baker (2000) 'Reporting *That* in Translated English: Evidence for Subconscious Processes of Explicitation?', *Across Languages and Cultures* 1(2): 141-158.

------ and Mona Baker (2009) 'Coherence and Clarity of Objectives in Doctoral Projects: A Research Design Workshop', in Ian Mason (ed.) *Training for Doctoral Research*, Special Issue of *The Interpreter and Translator Trainer* 3(1): 143-64.

Paloposki, Outi and Kaisa Koskinen (2004) 'Thousand and One Translations. Revisiting Retranslation', in Gyde Hansen and Kirsten Malmkjær (eds) *Claims, Changes and Challenges*, Amsterdam & Philadelphia: John Benjmins, 27–38.

Paltridge, Brian (2006) *Discourse Analysis: An Introduction*, London & New York: Continuum.

Papineni, Kishore, Salim Roukos, Todd Ward and Wei-Jing Zhu (2002) 'BLEU – A Method for Automatic Evaluation of Machine Translation', in *Proceedings of the 40th Annual Meeting of the Association for Computational Linguistics* (ACL), Philadelphia, July 2002, 311-318.

Partington, Alan (2004) 'Corpora and Discourse, a Most Congruous Beast', in Alan Partington, John Morley and Louann Haarman (eds) *Corpora and Discourse,* Bern: Peter Lang, 11-20.

Pavlovič, Nataša (2007) 'Directionality in Translation and Interpreting Practice: Preliminary Report on a Questionnaire Survey in Croatia', in Anthony Pym and Alexander Perekrestenko (eds) *Translation Research Projects I*, Tarragona: Inter-cultural Studies Group, 79-96.

------ (2009) 'Collaborative Translation Protocols', in Susanne Göpferich, Arnt Lykke Jakobsen and Inger Mees (eds) *Behind the Mind: Methods, Models and Results in Translation Process Research*, Copenhagen: Samfundslitteratur, 81-105.

Peirce, Charles S. (1878) 'Deduction, Induction, and Hypothesis', *Popular Science Monthly* 13: 470–82.

Pöllabauer, Sonja (2004) 'Interpreting in Asylum Hearings: Issues of Role, Responsibility and Power', *Interpreting* 6(2): 143-180.

Pym, Anthony (1998) *Method in Translation History*, Manchester: St. Jerome.

------ (2001) 'The Return to Ethics in Translation Studies', *The Translator* 7(2): 129-138.

------ (2012) *On Translator Ethics*, translated by Heike Walker, Amsterdam & Philadelphia: John Benjamins.

Rasinger, Sebastian (2008) *Quantitative Research in Linguistics: An Introduction*, London: Continuum.

Rayner, Keith (1998) 'Eye Movements in Reading and Information Processing: 20 Years of Research', *Psychological Bulletin* 124: 372-422.

------ and Sara C. Serono (1994) 'Eye Movements in Reading', in Morton A. Gernsbacher (ed.) *Handbook of Psycholinguistics*, San Diego: Academic Press, 57-81.

Reiss, Katharina and Hans J. Vermeer (1984) *Grundlegung einer allgemeinen Translationstheorie*, Tübingen: Niemeyer.

Riessman, Catherine Kohler (2005) 'Exporting Ethics – A Narrative about Narrative Research in South India', *Health – An Interdisciplinary Journal for the Social Study of Health, Illness and Medecine* 9(4): 473-490.

Risku, Hanna (2010) 'A Cognitive Scientific View on Technical Communication and Translation: Do Embodiment and Situatedness Really Make a Difference?', *Target* 22(1): 94-111.

Robinson, Douglas (1991) *The Translator's Turn*, Baltimore: Johns Hopkins University Press.

Rothe-Neves, Rui (2003) 'The Influence of Working Memory Features on some Formal Aspects of Translation Performance', in Fabio Alves (ed.) *Triangulating Translation*, Amsterdam & Philadelphia: John Benjamins, 97-119.

Rybicki, Jan (2006) 'Burrowing into Translation: Character Idiolects in Henryk Sienkiewicz's Trilogy and Its Two English Translations', *Literary and Linguistic Computing* 21(1): 91-103.

------ (2010) 'Translation and Delta Revisited: When We Read Translations, Is It the Author or the Translator that We Really Read?', paper presented at *Digital Humanities 2010*, London: Kings College London.

------ (2011) 'Alma Cardell Curtin and Jeremiah Curtin: The Translator's Wife's Stylistic Fingerprint', paper presented at *Digital Humanities 2011*, Standford: Stanford University Library. Available at http://dh2011abstracts.stanford.edu/xtf/view?docId=tei/ab-195.xml;query=;brand=default, last accessed 27 July 2012.

------ (2012) 'The Great Mystery of the (Almost) Invisible Translator: Stylometry in Translation', in Michael P. Oakes and Meng Ji (eds) *Quantitative Methods in Corpus-Based Translation Studies*, Amsterdam & Philadelphia: John Benjamins, 231-248.

Saldanha, Gabriela (2004) 'Accounting for the Exception to the Norm: A Study of Split Infinitives in Translated English', *Language Matters, Studies in the Languages of Africa* 35(1): 39-53.

------ (2005) *Style of Translation: An Exploration of Stylistic Patterns in the Translations of Margaret Jull Costa and Peter Bush,* Unpublished PhD thesis, Dublin City University.

------ (2009a) 'Linguistic Approaches', in Mona Baker and Gabriela Saldanha (eds) *Routledge Encyclopedia of Translation Studies*, London & New York: Routledge, 2nd edition, 148-152.

------ (2009b) 'Principles of Corpus Linguistics and their Application to Translation Studies Research', *Tradumàtica* 7. Available at http://webs2002.uab.es/tradumatica/revista/num7/articles/01/art.htm, last accessed 9 June 2012.

------ (2011a) 'Translator Style: Methodological Considerations', *The Translator* 17(1): 25-50.

------ (2011b) 'Emphatic Italics in English Translations: Stylistic Failure or Motivated Stylistic Resources?', *Meta* 56(2): 424-442.

------ (2011c) 'Style of Translation: the Use of Foreign Words in Translations by Margaret Jull Costa and Peter Bush', in Alet Kruger, Kim Wallmach and Jeremy Munday (eds) *Corpus-based Translation Studies: Research and Applications,* London &

New York: Continuum, 237-258.

Salmons, Janet (2010) *Online Interviews in Real Time*, California & London: Sage.

Saukko, Paula (2003) *Doing Research in Cultural Studies: An Introduction to Classical and New Methodological Approaches*, London, California & London: Sage.

Schäffner, Christina (ed.) (1998), *Translation and Quality*, Clevedon: Multilingual Matters.

Secară, Alina (2005) 'Translation Evaluation – A State of the Art Survey', in *Proceedings of the eCoLoRe-MeLLANGE Workshop*. Available at http://ecolore.leeds.ac.uk/downloads/workshop/, last accessed 16 December 2012.

Séguinot, Candace (1989) *The Translation Process: An Experimental Study in The Translation Process*, Toronto: H.G. Publications, School of Translation, York University, 21-53.

Sela-Sheffy, Rakefet (2005) 'How to Be a (Recognized) Translator: Rethinking Habitus, Norms, and the Field of Translation', *Target* 17(1): 1-26.

Selting, Margret, Peter Auer, Birgit Barden, Jörg Bergmann, Elizabeth Couper-Kuhlen, Susanne Günthner, Christoph Meier, Uta Quasthoff, Peter Schlobinski and Susanne Uhmann (1998) 'Gesprächsanalytisches Transkriptionssystem GAT', *Linguistische Berichte* 173: 91-122.

Semino, Elena and Mick Short (2004) *Corpus Stylistics: Speech, Writing, and Thought Presentation in a Corpus of English Writing,* London & New York: Routledge.

Setton, Robin (2011) 'Corpus-Based Interpreting Studies: Overview and Prospects', in Alet Kruger, Kim Wallmach and Jeremy Munday (eds) *Corpus-based Translation Studies: Research and Applications,* London & New York: Continuum, 33-75.

Shih , Claire Yi-yi (2006) 'Revision from Translators' Point of View: An Interview Study', *Target* 18(2): 295–312.

Shreve, Gregory (2006) 'The Deliberate Practice: Translation and Expertise', *Journal of Translation Studies* 9(1): 27-42.

------ and Erik Angelone (eds) (2010) *Translation and Cognition*, Amsterdam & Philadelphia: John Benjamins.

------, Isabel Lacruz and Erik Angelone (2010) 'Cognitive Effort, Syntactic Disruption, and Visual Interference in a Sight Translation Task', in Gregory Shreve and Erik Angelone (eds) *Translation and Cognition*, Amsterdam & Philadelphia: John Benjamins, 63-84.

Silverman, David (2006) *Interpreting Qualitative Data*, California & London: Sage, 3rd edition.

Simard, Michel, George Foster, Marie-Luise Hannan, Elliott Macklovitch and Pierre Plamondon (2000) 'Bilingual Text Alignment: Where Do We Draw the Line?', in Simon Philip Botley, Anthony Mark McEenry and Andrew Wilson (eds) *Multilingual Corpora in Teaching and Research*, Amsterdam & Atlanta: Rodopi, 39-64.

Sinclair, John (2003) *Reading Concordances: An Introduction,* London: Longman.

------ (2005) 'Corpus and Text – Basic Principles', in Martin Wynne (ed.) *Developing Linguistic Corpora: A Guide to Good Practice*, Oxford: Oxbow Books, 1-16. Available at http://ota.ahds.ac.uk/documents/creating/dlc/index.htm, last accessed 4 May 2012.

Sinclair, Stacey, Curtis Hardin and Brian Lowery (2006) 'Self-Stereotyping in the Context of Multiple Social Identities', *Journal of Personality and Social Psychology* 90(4): 529-542.

Sjørup, Annette C. (2011) 'Cognitive Effort in Metaphor Translation: An Eye-Tracking Study', in Sharon O'Brien (ed.) *Cognitive Explorations of Translation*, London: Continuum, 197-214.

Smith, Jacqui and K. Anders Ericsson (1991) *Towards a General Theory of Expertise: Prospects and Limits*, Cambridge & New York: Cambridge University Press.

Sperber, Ami D. (2004) 'Translation and Validation of Study Instruments for Cross-cultural Research', *Gastroenterology* 126(1): S124-S128.

Stake, Robert E. (1978/2000) 'The Case Study Method in Social Inquiry', *Educational Researcher* 7 (February): 5-8, reprinted in Roger Gomm, Martyn Hammersley and Peter Foster (eds) *Case Study Method: Key Issues, Key Texts*, California & London: Sage, 19-26.

------ (2005) 'Qualitative Case Studies', in Norman K. Denzin and Yvonna S. Lincoln (eds)*The Sage Handbook of Qualitative Research*, California & London: Sage, 3rd edition, 443-466.

Starfield Sue (2010) 'Ethnographies', in Brian Paltridge and Aek Phakiti (eds) *Continuum Companion to Research Methods in Applied Linguistics*, London & New York: Continuum, 50-65.

Stratman, James and Liz Hamp-Lyons (1994) 'Reactivity in Concurrent Think-Aloud Protocols. Issues for Research', in Peter Smagorinsky (ed.) *Speaking About Writing: Reflections on Research Methodology*, California & London: Sage, 89-112.

Stubbs, Michael (1986) 'Lexical Density: A Technique and Some Findings', in Michael Coulthard (ed.) *Talking about Text. Discourse Analysis,* Monograph No 13, English Language Research, Birmingham, University of Birmingham, 27-42.

------ (1995) 'Collocations and Semantic Profiles: On the Cause of the Trouble with Quantitative Studies', *Functions of Language* 2(1): 23-55.

------ (1996) *Text and Corpus Analysis: Computer-Assisted Studies of Language and Culture,* Oxford & Malden: Blackwell Publishers.

------ (2001) *Words and Phrases: Corpus Studies of Lexical Semantics*, Oxford and Malden: Blackwell.

------ (1997/2002) 'Whorf's Children: Critical Comments on Critical Discourse Analysis', in Ann Ryan and Alison Wray (eds) *Evolving Models of Language*, Clevedon: Multilingual Matters, 100-116, reprinted in Michael Toolan (ed.) *Critical Discourse Analysis; Critical Concepts in Linguistics, Vol. III*, London & New York: Routledge, 202-218.

Sturge, Kate (2004) *'The Alien Within', Translation into German during the Nazi Regime*, Munich: Iudicium.

Stymne, Sara and Lars Ahrenberg (2012) 'On the Practice of Error Analysis for Machine Translation Evaluation', in *Proceedings of the LREC 2012 Conference*, Paris: European Language Resources Association, 1785-1790. Available at http://www.lrec-conf.org/proceedings/lrec2012/index.html, last accessed 30 April 2013.

Sunderland, Jane (2009) 'Research Questions in Linguistics', in Lia Litosselti (ed.) *Research Methods in Linguistics*, London: Continuum, 9-28.

Susam-Sarajeva, Şebnem (2001) 'Is One Case Always Enough?', *Perspectives: Studies in Translatology* 9(3): 167-176.

------ (2002) 'A 'Multilingual' and 'International' Translation Studies?', in Theo Hermans (ed.) *Crosscultural Transgressions: Research Models in Translation Studies II, Historical and Ideological Issues,* Manchester: St. Jerome, 193-207.

------ (2006) *Theories on the Move: Translation's Role in the Travels of Literary Theories*, Amsterdam & New York: Rodopi.

------ (2009) 'The Case Study Research Method in Translation Studies', in Ian Mason (ed.) *Training for Doctoral Research: Special Issue of The Interpreter and Translator Trainer* 3(1): 37-56.

Taboada, Maite and William C. Mann (2006) 'Rhetorical Structure Theory: Looking Back and Moving Ahead', *Discourse Studies* 8(3): 423-459.

Taylor, Christopher (2003) 'Multimodal Transcription in the Analysis: Translation and Subtitling of Italian Films', *The Translator* 9(2): 191-205.

Teich, Elke (2003) *Cross-Linguistic Variation in System and Text: A Methodology for the Investigation of Translations and Comparable Texts*, Berlin & New York: Mouton de Gruyter.

Temple, Bogusia and Alys Young (2004) 'Qualitative Research and Translation Dilemmas', *Qualitative Research* 4(2): 161-178.

Tipton, Rebecca (2010) 'On Trust: Relationships of Trust in Interpreter-Mediated Social Work Encounters', in Mona Baker, Maeve Olohan and María Calzada-Pérez (eds) *Text and Context: Essays on Translation and Interpreting in Honour of Ian Mason*, Manchester: St Jerome Publishing, 188-208.

Tirkkonen-Condit, Sonja (ed.) (1988) *Empirical Research in Translation and Intercultural studies*, Tübingen: Gunter Narr.

------, Sonja and Riitta Jääskeläinen (eds) (2000) *Tapping and Mapping the Processes of Translation and Interpreting*, Amsterdam & Philadelphia: John Benjamins.

Titscher, Stefan, Michael Meyer, Ruth Wodak and Eva Vetter (2000) *Methods of Text and Discourse Analysis*, translated by Bryan Jenner, Los Angeles, California & London, etc.: Sage.

Tognini Bonelli, Elena and Elena Manca (2001) *Corpus Linguistics at Work,* Amsterdam & Philadelphia: John Benjamins.

------ (2002) 'Welcoming Children, Pets and Guests: A Problem of Non-Equivalence in the Language of "Agriturismo" and "Farmhouse Holidays"', *Textus, English Studies in Italy* 15(2): 317-334.

Tommola, Jorma (1986) 'Translation as a Psycholinguistic Process', in Lars Wollin and Hans Lindquist (eds) *Translation Studies in Scandinavia*, Lund: Gleerup, 140-149.

Torikai, Kumiko (2011) 'Conference Interpreters and their Perception of Culture: From the Narratives of Japanese Pioneers', *Translation and Interpreting Studies* 5(1): 75-93.

Toury, Gideon (1988) 'Experimentation in Translation Studies: Achievements, Prospects and Some Pitfalls', in Sonja Tirkkonen-Condit (ed.) *Empirical Research in Translation and Intercultural Studies*, Tübingen: Gunter Narr, 45-66.

------ (1995) *Descriptive Translation Studies and Beyond,* Amsterdam & Philadelphia: John Benjamins.

Turner, Graham H. and Frank Harrington (2000) 'Issues of Power and Method in Interpreting Research', in Maeve Olohan (ed.) *Intercultural Faultlines: Research Models in Translation Studies I – Textual and Cognitive Aspects*, Manchester: St. Jerome, 253-265.

Tymoczko, Maria (2002) 'Connecting the Two Infinite Orders: Research Methods in Translation Studies', in Theo Hermans (ed.) *Crosscultural Transgressions: Research*

Models in Translation Studies II: Historical and Ideological Issues, Manchester: St. Jerome, 9-25.

------ (2007) *Enlarging Translation, Empowering Translators*, Manchester: St. Jerome.

Valdeón, Roberto A. (2005) 'Asymmetric Representations of Languages in Contact: Uses and Translations of French and Spanish in *Frasier*', *Linguistica Antverpiensia New Series*: NS4 - *Fictional Representations of Multilingualism and Translation*: 279-294.

------ (2007) 'Ideological Independence or Negative Mediation: BBC Mundo and CNN en Español's (translated) Reporting of Madrid's Terrorist Attacks', in Myriam Salama-Carr (ed.) *Translating and Interpreting Conflict*, Amsterdam & New York: Rodopi, 99-118.

Valentini, Cristina, and Sabrina Linardi (2009) 'Forlixt 1: A Multimedia Database for AVT Research', in *The Translation of Dialects in Multimedia*, Special Issue of *inTRAlinea*. Available at http://www.intralinea.it/specials/dialectrans/ita_more.php?id=765_0_49_0_M, last accessed 4 July 2012.

van Dam, Helle and Karen Korning Zethsen (2008) 'Translator Status: Helpers and Opponents in the Ongoing Battle of an Emerging Profession', *Target* 22(2): 194-211.

------ and Karen Korning Zethsen (2010) 'Translator Status: A Study of Danish Company Translators', *The Translator* 14(1): 71-96.

van Leeuwen, Theo and Carey Jewitt (eds) (2001) *Handbook of Visual Analysis*, California & London: Sage.

Vehovar, Vasja and Katja Lozar Manfreda (2008) 'Overview: Online Surveys', in Nigel G. Fielding, Raymond M. Lee and Grant Blank (eds) *The Sage Handbook of Online Research Methods*, California & London: Sage, 177-194.

Waddington, Christopher (2001), 'Different Methods of Evaluating Student Translations: The Question of Validity', *Meta* 46(2): 311-325.

Wadensjö, Cecilia (1998) *Interpreting as Interaction,* London & New York: Longman.

------ (1999) 'Telephone Interpreting and the Synchronization of Talk in Social Interaction', *The Translator* 5(2): 247-64.

------ (2000) 'Co-Constructing Yeltsin – Explorations of an Interpreter-Mediated Political Interview', in Maeve Olohan (ed.) *Intercultural Faultines: Research Methods in Translation Studies I: Textual and Cognitive Aspects*, Manchester: St Jerome, 233-252.

Walther, Joseph B. (2012) 'Interaction Through Technological Lenses: Computer-Mediated Communication and Language', *Journal of Language and Social Psychology* XX(X): 1-18.

Weber, Orest, Pascal Singy and Patrice Guex (2005) 'Gender and Interpreting in the Medical Sphere: What is at Stake?', in José Santaemilia (ed.) *Gender, Sex and Translation: The Manipulation of Identities*, Manchester: St Jerome: 137-147.

Wengelin, Åsa (2006) 'Examining Pauses in Writing: Theory, Methods and Empirical Data', in Kirk P.H. Sullivan and Eva Lindgren (eds) *Computer Keystroke Logging and Writing: Methods and Applications*, Amsterdam: Elsevier, 107-130.

White, John, Theresa O'Cornell and Francis O'Mara (1994) 'The ARPA MT Evaluation Methodologies: Evolution, Lessons and Future Approaches', in *Proceedings of the First Conference of the Association for Machine Translation in the Americas* (AMTA 1994), 193-205.

White, Julie, Sarah Drew and Trevor Hay (2009) 'Ethnography Versus Case Study: Positioning Research and Researchers', *Qualitative Research Journal* 9(1): 18-27.

Widdowson, Henry G. (1998/2004) 'The Theory and Practice of Critical Discourse Analysis', *Applied Linguistics* 19(1): 136-151, reprinted in Clive Seale (ed.) *Social Reseach Methods: A Reader*, London & New York: Routledge, 366-370.

------ (2001) 'Coming to Terms With Reality: Applied Linguistics in Perspective', in David Graddol (ed.) *Applied Linguistics for the 21st century*, AILA review 14: 2-17. Available at http://www.aila.info/download/publications/review/AILA14.pdf, last accessed 6 October 2010.

------ (2004) *Text, Context, Pretext: Critical Issues in Discourse Analysis*, Malden, MA & Oxford: Blackwell.

Wiechmann, Daniel and Stefan Fuhs (2006) 'Corpus Linguistics Resources: Concordancing Software', *Corpus Linguistics and Linguistic Theory* 2(1): 109-130.

Williams, Jenny and Andrew Chesterman (2002) *The Map: A Beginner's Guide to Doing Research in Translation Studies*, Manchester: St. Jerome.

Winters, Marion (2007) 'F. Scott Fitzgerald's *Die Schönen und Verdammten* : A Corpus-based Study of Speech-act Report Verbs as a Feature of Translators' Style', *Meta* 52(3): 412-425.

------ (2009) 'Modal Particles Explained: How Modal Particles Creep into Translations and Reveal Translators' Styles', *Target* 21(1): 74-97.

Wodak, Ruth (2001) 'What CDA Is About – A Summary of Its History, Important Concepts and Its Developments', in Ruth Wodak and Michael Meyer (eds) *Methods of Critical Discourse Analysis,* California & London: Sage, 1-13.

------ and Michael Meyer (2009) 'Critical Discourse Analysis: History, Agenda, Theory, and Methodology', in Ruth Wodak and Michael Meyer (eds) *Methods of Critical Discourse Analysis,* California & London: Sage, 2nd edition, 1-33.

Wolf, Michaela (2005) 'The Creation of A "Room of One's Own": Feminist Translators as Mediators Between Cultures and Genders', in José Santaemilia (ed.) *Gender, Sex and Translation: The Manipulation of Identities*, Manchester: St Jerome: 15-25.

------ (2011) 'Mapping the Field: Sociological Perspectives on Translation', *International Journal of the Sociology of Language* 207: 1-28

------ and Alexandra Fukari (eds) (2007) *Constructing a Sociology of Translation*, Amsterdam & Philadelphia: John Benjamins.

Wood, Linda A. and Rolf O. Kroger (2000) *Doing Discourse Analysis: Methods for Studying Action in Talk and Text,* California & London: Sage Publications.

Woods, Anthony, Paul Fletcher and Arthur Hughes (1986*) Statistics in Language Studies,* Cambridge, New York & Melbourne: Cambridge University Press.

Wynne, Martin (ed.) (2005) *Developing Linguistic Corpora: a Guide to Good Practice*. Oxford: Oxbow Books. Available at http://ota.ahds.ac.uk/documents/creating/dlc/index.htm, last accessed 4 May 2012.

Yagi, Sane M. (1999) 'Computational Discourse Analysis for Interpretation', *Meta* 44(2): 268-279.

Yin, Robert K. (2009) *Case Study Research: Design and Methods*, Los Angeles, London, etc.: Sage, 4th edition.

Zagar Galvão, Elena and Isabel Galhano Rodrigues (2010) 'The Importance of Listening with One's Eyes: A Case Study of Multimodality in Simultaneous Interpreting', in Jorge Díaz Cintas, Anna Matamala and Josélia Neves (eds) *New Insights into*

Audiovisual Translation and Media Accessibility: Media for All 2, Amsterdam & New York: Rodopi, 241-253.

Zanettin, Federico (2012) *Translation-Driven Corpora,* Manchester: St Jerome Publishing.

------, Silvia Bernardini and Dominic Stewart (eds) (2003) *Corpora in Translator Education*, Manchester: St Jerome Publishing.

Index

A

abduction 15, 63, 86
acceptability (in quality assessment) 100
adequacy (in quality assessment) 104
action research 16, 174
agency (and agents) 150
Alves, Fabio 35, 50, 109, 111, 112, 116, 117, 118, 118, 120, 138, 161
Angelone, Erik 109, 117, 179, 120, 121, 124, 136, 138
anonymity 44, 47-48 161-162, 179-180, 187, 221, 225, 241
anova 122, 200
appendix 177, 238-239, 241
applied research 15-16, 56, 69, 150
archival research 219-220
area of interest 140
argument-centred approach 63-64
asset management 110
associative relationships (definition) 18
attention unit 120
average sentence length 87-88
automatic evaluation metrics (AEM) 104-105, 107
automaticity 123

B

Baker, Mona 1-2, 17, 18, 41, 42, 68, 75, 76
Baker, Paul 56, 59, 85, 86, 88, 90
basic research (definition) 15
Baxter, Judith 51, 53, 220
bell curve 196-197
Bernardini, Silvia 57, 60, 69, 70, 75, 89, 114, 116, 117, 120,125, 131, 151
between-subject design 114
bilingual protocol 127
boundaries (in case study research) 211, 215-217
Bourdieu, Pierre 38, 180, 181, 203, 206, 210, 216, 223
Bowker, Lynne 50, 55, 70, 71, 73
British National Corpus 67, 69, 77, 78

C

Calzada-Pérez, María 55, 69, 82
carry-over effect 114
case-study 207-233
    critical or crucial cases 213, 214
    deviant cases 213
    embedded case study 213
    extreme cases 201, 213
    cross-case analysis 212
    multiple case study 211-212
    revelatory cases 213
    single case study 211-215
    typical cases
causality 6-7, 18, 32, 36-37, 61, 89, 200, 209-210, 229
causal sequencing 235
central tendency 196, 198, 241
Chesterman, Andrew 1, 5, 6, 7, 12, 13, 15, 16, 17, 18, 19, 27, 40, 41, 64, 120, 150
Chi-squared test 199-200
circular argument 57-59
co-text 89-92
coding 130, 189-195, 228-229, 232, 239
    inter-coder agreement (or reliability) 106, 107, 131, 193
    intra-coder agreement (or reliability) 193
    qualitative coding 189-194
    quantitative coding 195
    reproducibility 193
    stability 193
cognitive approaches 6-7, 109-149
cognitive effort 102, 112, 120, 135-145
cognitive load 13, 103, 107
cognitive process 50, 109
cognitive rhythm 112
Cohen's kappa 106, 131
collection of data (definition) 9
colligation 89-91
collocation 89-91
collocate 89-91
COMPARA 68, 75

comparability, comparative data 66, 172
competence 69, 109, 112-117, 147,
comprehensive analysis (in CDA and CL) 93
confirmation bias 188
concept (definition) 12
conceptual research 4, 15, 19, 64, 150
concordance 89-92, 242
concordancer 86, 89, 92, 241
concurrent strategies (in mixed methods research) 201, 203
condition (in translation process research) 117
confidence intervals 60, 164, 198
confidence level 164, 198, 200
confidentiality 47, 134, 161-163, 179-180, 184, 222, 225-226 (see also anonymity and informed consent)
constructivism 10-12, 53, 150
content analysis 190
contextual inquiry 145
context of culture 81
context of situation 81
contextualization, requirement of (in CDA and CL) 94-95
control group 15, 66-67
control corpora 69
conversation protocol 125
correlation measures 107, 159
corpora, corpus
    alignment 79-80
    analysis 50-51, 55-83, 85-95, 111
    annotation 76-80
    bidirectional parallel corpora 68-69, 72
    building 60, 70-80, 238
    comparable corpora 61, 67-70, 72
    corpus-based approach 61-62
    corpus-driven approach 61-62
    header 76-77
    parallel-corpora 67-70
    reference corpora 69
    software 239 (see also concordancer)
    translation corpora (see parallel corpora)
copyright 75-76
coverage error 153

creativity 112
credibility 22, 28-29, 33, 35-36, 38, 40, 49, 237, 242
critical discourse analysis 50-68, 80-86, 92-95, 188
critical approaches 5, 11, 53-54
    critical realism 53
    critical-interpretive approaches 53
Cronbach alpha measure 159
cross-tabulation (see tabulation)
cued retrospection 122, 125
cultural approaches 7, 205
cumulative-frequency tables 197-198

D

data (definition and typology) 20-22
database 224-225, 227, 230
deception 45
deduction 14-15, 22, 61-63, 64
descriptive research 6, 50-51, 205
dialogue protocol 125
directionality 116
discourse
    definition 50-53
    key concepts 83-85
discourse analysis (see critical discourse analysis)
discourse level 83
dispersion 85, 88, 197

E

effect size 60
electroencephalography (EEG) 148
elicitation of data (definition) 9
elite bias 188
emergent design 130, 189, 211-212
empiricism 5, 11,
empirical research 4, 15, 19, 36, 38, 64, 96, 108, 110, 150, 191, 207, 234
EN15038 standard 99
English-Norwegian Parallel Corpus (ENPC) 68, 80
epistemology (definition and general discussion) 10-12
Ericsson, K. Anders 119, 123, 124, 126, 127, 130, 131
error typology and categorization 78, 96, 98, 101, 104, 105, 107

ethics 31, 41-49, 115, 118, 151, 154, 161-163, 171, 178, 179-180, 184-186, 240

ethnography 16, 208, 225-226, 233

European Comparable and Parallel Corpus (ECPC) 69

evaluative research16, 50, 95-96 (see also quality assessment)

experiential knowledge 233

experimental group 15

experimental research 15, 31, 96, 114, 122

expertise 109

explanatory research 5-6, 17-19, 50-51, 64, 84, 89, 118, 152, 192, 194, 205-206, 228-229

explorative research 16, 64, 95, 152

external relations (of texts) 83-84

eye mind hypothesis 136

eye tracking 103-104, 107, 113, 136-145, 239

F

factor (in multifactorial research design) 117

Fairclough, Norman 51, 53, 63, 64, 83-85, 94

falsifiablity 39, 62

features of translation 6, 56, 60, 62, 68, 69, 88

fittingness 37, 211

fixation 103, 107, 137

fixation count 140

fixation duration 140

focus groups 168-188, 220-221

Fleiss' kappa 106, 131

fluency (in quality assessment) 104

framework (definition) 12

functional magnetic resonance imaging (fMRI) 148

G

galvanic skin test 148

gaze data 139

gaze path 137

gaze replay 141

generalization, generalizability 33, 35,

36-38, 61, 152, 164-165, 167, 169, 181, 209-214.

genre 81, 83-84, 97

Gerring, John 36, 212, 213, 214

Gillham, Bill 4 170, 207, 210, 211, 222, 227, 228

going native 169, 188

Göpferich, Susanne 109, 117, 121, 129, 132, 148

grounded theory 146, 190-192, 194

Guba, Egon G. 2, 11, 12, 23, 28, 29, 37, 209, 211

H

Hansen, Gyde 101, 109, 111, 118

hapax legomena 87

Harvey, Keith 65, 94-95, 225

Hatim, Basil 55, 80, 81

Hawthorne effect 31, 153, 222

heatmap 141

hermeneutic circle 63

historical research 3, 207, 218, 233

holistic research 208

holistic quality assessment 98-99, 107

hotspot 141

House, Juliane 95, 99-100, 101, 108

hypothesis 6, 7, 14-19, 25-26, 39-40, 54, 64, 78, 88, 93, 123, 188, 194, 207, 230, 235-237

definition 18

hypothesis-testing research 4, 61-62, 64, 93, 123, 141

hypothesis-generating research 4, 36-37, 61-62, 85, 123, 126, 141, 165, 195, 202, 209-211

null-hypothesis (see separate entry)

I

IMRAD structure 234-243

impression management 153, 169, 184

induction 4, 14-15, 22, 37, 61-63, 70, 189, 228

informant (definition) 150

informed consent 42-45, 48, 118, 162-163, 167, 179, 184, 220, 225

Inghilleri, Moira 41, 150, 206

Inputlog 132

interdisciplinarity 1-3, 63, 236,

internal relations (of texts) 83-84
Internet-mediated research 46, 47-48, 162-163, 165, 166-168, 173, 179, 186-188
interpretivism 4, 10-12, 16, 22, 23, 27, 51, 56, 169, 178, 184
intertextuality 52, 65, 85, 94-95
interviews 168-188, 220-221
   face-to-face 186
   Internet-mediated interviews 186-188
   interview profiles 186, 235
   language of, 177-178
   life-story interviews 173
   schedules 169, 171, 238
   semi-structured interviews 170, 172-173
   structured interviews 169, 172-173
   telephone interviewing 186
   unstructured interviews 172-173
introspection 122-132

J

Jääskeläinen, Riitta 109, 115, 120, 123, 124
Jaksobsen, Arnt Lykke 112, 120, 121, 122, 124, 125, 132, 133, 135, 138, 161
Jensen, Kristian T. H. 115, 117, 120, 122, 130, 136, 138, 144, 145, 161

K

Karlsruhe comprehensibility concept 117
Kenny, Dorothy 56, 68, 69, 71, 73, 74, 75, 87, 88, 119
keystroke logging 113, 238-239
keywords (in corpora) 87
Koskinen, Kaisa 6, 7, 16, 25, 36, 205, 206, 208, 209, 210, 214, 215, 216, 217, 219, 220, 221, 223, 225, 226, 229-230, 235-236
Krings, Hans P. 13, 31, 109, 124, 125
Kroger, Rolf E. 28, 29, 38, 40, 51, 54, 56, 66, 86, 92, 93, 240

L

language competence 56
language performance 56

language user (dimension) 99
language use (dimension) 99
Laviosa, Sara 56, 60, 62, 68, 69, 87, 88
Learner Translation Corpus (LTC) 69-70, 78
lemmatization 87
lexical density 88
Likert scales 104, 155-158
Lincoln, Yvonna S. 2, 11, 12, 23, 28, 29, 37, 209, 211
linear mixed effects modelling 145
linguistic toolkit 80-85
literature review 19-20, 218, 236-237
LISA QA model 98-99, 101
longitudinal design 119
Lörscher, Wolfgang 13, 24, 116, 120, 121, 124

M

machine translation 31, 102-105, 109, 198
Mann-Whitney U-tests 200
Mason, Ian 1, 55, 57, 58, 59, 61, 63, 64, 65, 80, 83, 84, 85
Matthews, Bob, 10, 11, 12, 16, 18, 20, 23, 35, 42, 147, 151, 166, 190, 195, 196, 197, 200
measurement error 153
MeLLANGE 69, 101
memo, memoing 193, 231-232, 235
meta-cognition 111
meta-evaluation 98
method (definition) 13
methodology (definition) 13
mixed methods approach (definition) 23
models
   of translation studies 5-7
   definition 12
multi-factorial design 117
multimodal corpora 70
Munday, Jeremy 54, 55, 56, 57, 69, 81, 82, 91

N

naturally occurring language 170
netiquette 188
non-parametric data 122, 144, 160, 200

normal distribution 60, 122, 195-197, 200
noting the exception 188
null hypothesis 18, 19, 25, 60, 199-200

O

O'Brien, Sharon 98, 100, 103, 109, 112, 117, 122, 135, 137, 138
Oakes, Michael P. 56, 60, 69, 74, 79, 88, 90, 241
objectivism (definition) 10-12
observation 221-223
    detached observation 222
    observer effect (see Hawthorne effect)
    participant observation 221-22
observation length 140
Olohan, Maeve 17, 18, 56, 68, 69
online research (see Internet-mediated research)
ontology (definition) 10-12
operationalization 17, 23-25, 35, 71, 116, 120-121, 136, 143, 153-154, 171, 181, 194, 215-216,
order of discourse 53, 94

P

p-value 199-200
paired t-tests 200
parametric data 60, 159
parallel forms test 160-161
parallel processing 136
participant (definition) 150-152
pauses 112
Pearson's correlation co-efficient (Pearson's r) 122, 159, 200
personality profiling 146
phenomenology 16
physical artefacts 224
pilot study 22
    in surveys 158
    in interviews 178
plagiarism 48-49
population 32-36, 44, 46, 71-73, 152-154, 158, 162, 164-166, 187, 198, 208, 212, 214-216
positivism 10-12, 18, 22, 28-29, 53, 169, 177
postpositivism 11, 20, 28, 209

post-editing 109
poststructuralism 53, 205
power relations (between researcher and participant) 43, 45-46, 162, 163, 166, 173, 178, 179, 184
pragmatics 80, 82
privileged knowledge 57-59
problem indicator 120
problem-based approach 63-64
process indicator 131
process-oriented research 50, 109-148
product-oriented research 50-108
protection from harm 46-47
psychometric test 147
pupil diameter 136, 139, 142
Pym, Anthony 3, 41, 207

Q

qualitative analysis software 204, 225, 231-232, 239
qualitative approach (definition) 22-23
qualitizing 203-204
quality
    ensuring research quality 27-41
    in CL and CDA 92-95
quality assessment 95-108
quantitative approach (definition) 22-23
quantitizing 203-204
quasi-longitudinal design 119
questionnaire 21, 151-168, 195
    definition 151
questions
    catchall questions 156
    closed questions 104, 157, 162, 175
    double negatives 155, 174
    double-barrelled questions 156, 174
    filter questions 154
    hypothetical questions 156, 174
    leading questions 155, 174
    multiple-choice questions 156-157
    open questions 104, 157, 172, 175
    phrasing and language issues 154-156, 171, 174, 177-178
    sensitive questions 154-155, 174

R

randomization 118
ranking (in quality assessment) 102-104
readability 100, 109
   index 117
reading regressions 103, 107
realism 10-12, 51, 53
recruiting participants 34, 47, 106, 115, 135, 139, 169, 179, 180-183, 187, 238
reductionism 96
register 80-81, 85, 101
regular expressions 89
reliability
   definition 35
   in questionnaire research 159-161
replicability (see reliability)
representativeness 59-60, 71-76, 164, 167, 169
reproducibility (see reliability)
research diary 40, 163, 183, 189, 193, 225, 230-231
research question (definition and key issues) 16-19
research construct 27, 107, 130, 151, 153, 154, 158, 159-161, 171, 176, 181, 194, 196, 215
researcher bias effect 29-31, 153, 167, 169
researcher personal attribute effect 29-31, 184
researcher unintentional expectancy effect 29-31, 184, 222
respondent (definition) 150
response rate 151, 153, 165-167, 182, 196
rhetorical structure theory 116
Ross, Liz 10, 11, 12, 16, 18, 20, 23, 35, 42, 151, 166, 190, 195, 196, 197, 200
routine task 115

S

saccade 136
SAE J2450 99, 101
Saldanha, Gabriela 56, 59, 62, 65, 67, 69, 94, 168, 177, 180, 190, 191
sampling
   cluster sampling 34
   convenience sampling 34, 164, 181
   event sampling 222
   general discussion and typology 33-34,
   in corpora 71-73,
   in quality-assessment research 105,
   in questionnaire surveys 151-153, 164-165, 195
   in interviews and focus groups 163-165
   interval sampling 222
   non-probability sampling 164
   probability-based sampling 33, 164
   purposive sampling 72, 180-181
   random sampling 33, 72, 164, 180
   sampling error 153
   sampling frame 71
   snowball sampling 34
   stage sampling 34
   stratified sampling 34, 72
   systematic sampling 34
   theoretical sampling 83, 212
Saukko, Paula 13, 28, 30, 205
saturation 182, 192-193
screen recording 113
semantic preference 89-91
semantic prosody 89-91
semiotics 55, 65, 224
sensitization 31, 230
sequential approach (in mixed-methods research) 201-203
Shreve, Gregory 109, 112, 117, 120, 118, 121
Silverman, David 12, 18, 27, 35, 38, 39, 40, 42
significance tests (see statistical significance)
Sinclair, John 74, 92, 154
Sketch engine 91
Skopos theory (in quality assessment) 99
social constructivism (see constructivism)
social desirability 153, 169, 184
sociological approaches 140, 205-206
Spearman's rho 107, 160, 200
split-half method 159
Stake, Robert E, 37, 180, 209, 226, 233
standard deviation 144, 195, 197, 241

statistical tests (see statistical significance)
situatedness 110, 146
statistics 60, 74, 87-88, 122, 164, 107,
    195-199, 224, 232
    descriptive statistics, 144, 195, 224
    inferential statistics 195, 224
statistical significance 60, 121, 87, 90
strategy (definition) 120
Stubbs, Michael 55, 58, 59, 60, 66, 88, 91
Sturge, Kate 36, 206, 207, 213, 216, 218,
    220, 224, 229, 238
Susam-Sarajeva, Şebnem 3, 4, 8, 206, 207,
    208, 210, 211-212, 218, 219, 236
style (in CDA) 83-84
subject fraud 167
survey 21, 23, 28, 51, 52, 104, 115, 144,
    147, 151-168
    definition 151
systemic functional grammar 54-55,
    80-82, 101

T

tabulation 39, 197, 203, 230
tagging (see annotation)
task description 115
temporal unit 120
test-retest method 159
text (definition) 52
    text as a means to an end 51, 220
    text as an end in itself 51, 220
text encoding initiative (TEI) 132
text type (in participant-oriented re-
    search) 116
text profiling 117
thematic analysis 189-190
theory (definition) 12
think aloud protocol (TAP) 104, 113,
    122-132
Tipton, Rebecca 168, 170, 171, 176, 179
Tobii Studio 142
tools (definition) 13
Toury, Gideon 36, 68, 110, 124, 125, 229
transcription 128-130, 186, 238
transferability 37-38, 211
transformational strategies (in mixed
    methods research) 201, 203-204
translated questionnaires 152

translation brief 97, 115
translation memory 109, 134, 143, 198
translation process protocol 132
Translational English Corpus 67, 75,
Translog 132
triangulation 5, 38-39, 56, 60, 109, 118,
    127, 131, 201, 210, 217, 233
    definition 23,
Tymoczko, Maria 11, 12, 15, 20, 24, 28,
    41, 59, 66, 67, 93
type-token ratio 87
typicality 57, 65, 214
typology (definition) 12

U

unit of analysis 24, 119, 207, 211, 239
unit of data 23
unit of translation 112, 119
universals (see features of translation)
usability 100, 107, 141
validity
    general discussion 27-35
    in qualitative research 38-41
    in questionnaire research 159-161
    threats 29-33
variability 54, 71, 164, 241
variables (definition and typology)
    25-27
    intervening variable 18
variance 122, 200, 230, 241
verbal reports (in case study research)
    220-221
vignettes 186, 232
visual data displays 193, 231

W

warrantability 29, 38, 40, 59, 92
Wilcoxon signed-rank 200
Williams, Jenny 1, 15, 16, 17, 64
whitecoat effect 118
within-subject design 114
Wood, Linda A. 28, 29, 38, 40, 51, 54, 56,
    66, 86, 92, 93, 240
word frequencies 87, 117
word index 87
word sketches 91
working memory 112

written protocol 122
written sources (in case study research)
218-220

Y

Yin, Robert K. 38, 207, 230

Z

Zanettin, Federico 56, 67, 69, 70, 72-73,
75, 78, 79, 80, 87